THE GRAPHIC HISTORY OF THE
JEWISH HERITAGE

TORAH CROWN
by Ludwig Y. Wolpert

THE
GRAPHIC
HISTORY
OF THE
JEWISH
HERITAGE

An encyclopedic presentation
with illustrations, charts,
vignettes and tables

Edited by

PINCHAS WOLLMAN–TSAMIR

The Biblical Period

SHENGOLD PUBLISHERS, INC.
New York

English Translations: SIDNEY B. HOENIG, JACOB SLOAN AND DAVID SEGAL

Design: EMANUEL SCHARY AND JOSEPH TAUBMAN

Library of Congress Catalogue Card Number 63-13318

Published by Shengold Publishers, Inc., New York, with the cooperation of the Foundation for a Graphic History of Jewish Literature.

Printed in the United States of America.

*Recorded forever in the hearts and memories of all Mankind
is the epic struggle of the sainted martyrs
among whom were esteemed members of my family
who perished in the recent Nazi holocaust,
even as they imparted with expiring breath
the immortal Jewish heritage,
testament of our people and our faith,
to succeeding generations.*

PREFACE

Publication of the first volume of this encyclopedic work, impels me to tell how The Graphic History of the Jewish Heritage was conceived and the course of its progress over a period of many years. It is the story of an idea and its realization.

It was during my studies in Frankfurt a. Main, Germany, that I first began to ponder the problem of how to present effectively the vast panorama of our spiritual heritage and its impressive procession of personages in striking and schematic form.

Our generation seeks to obtain its knowledge as expeditiously as possible. The pressures of contemporary society leave us little time to read or absorb the limitless number of books that pour from prolific presses each year. How much less time do we have then, for exploration of the immense wealth of Jewish literature. Yet the ancient and classic writings are still regarded as among the most illustrious contributions to the world's civilization and culture. It is sad then that the Jewish heritage remains a "sealed fountain" to so many people.

A possible felicitous solution to this problem occurred to me at the University in Frankfurt. Why couldn't the graphic method and formula used to illustrate scientific data be adapted to the field of Jewish literature? I began to envisage an attractive, lucid format which would present essential information in a minimum of time and space. It would be ideal for use by students, scholars and the general public. And so I set about drafting a series of outlines of the first charts for the Bible, the Talmud and subsequent Jewish literature.

By means of visual techniques and graphic presentations, the reader would be introduced quickly and concisely to the world of patriarchs, prophets, kings and sages, to Jewish literary works of every period throughout the ages, and to the grandeur of this picturesque history. I hoped too that my work would serve both as a reference aid for scholars and an inspiration and stimulus to those possessing only limited knowledge of the Jewish heritage, to explore further the original source books.

The rise of Nazi persecution impelled me to leave Germany, and in 1936 I migrated to Palestine. There I became an instructor in Seminaries and in Secondary Schools, and I also continued to plan and draft the charts, tables and maps for my project. In 1941, I showed about twenty hand-drawn charts to a number of leading publishers in Jerusalem and Tel Aviv. They reacted enthusiastically. Heartened by their warm interest, I continued with my work during my subsequent years of study at the Hebrew University in Jerusalem where I did further research on the charts and tables. My services in the Israeli War of Independence (1947-48) interrupted my progress in what by this time had begun to occupy much of my endeavors.

The project reached a promising stage when in 1951 I was invited to England by my dear friend, Mr. Samuel Benster of Manchester. Various British educators and scholars who studied the charts encouraged me further.

Upon my return to Israel, I began to view and organize the project in broader and encyclopedic form. I consulted with graphic artists in Jerusalem. I outlined four volumes to encompass the Biblical period, the Talmudic period, the Middle Ages and the Modern times. I expanded the work further to include genealogical, chronological and synchronical tables which would telescope all personalities and events described in the text into a readily visual pattern that would serve as a bridge between the literary and historical purposes of the work. The important studies of Samuel Arrowsmith, Dr. Zunz and others were adapted to this new graphic formula.

Now the work, the meetings relating to it and the trips to and from Jerusalem consumed extended periods of my time. The project which was initially called "The Atlas of Hebrew Literature" and which was later given the title of "The Graphic History of the Jewish Heritage," grew. Hundreds of books were consulted; thousands of sources and dates were checked, in order to prepare factually accurate summaries of books, events and biographies of Biblical, Talmudic and Midrashic personalities. I soon realized that this was now a massive project which one person could not hope to complete. A group of research men was required and I therefore invited a group of scholars of the Hebrew University and other Institutions of Higher Learning to work with me. Then I brought the project to the attention of the Ministry of Education where it elicited deep interest and the promise of support.

Innumerable difficulties and delays occurred. Material had to be redrafted and sometimes discarded. Charts and tables had to be redesigned and redrawn. Eventually the charts and texts were ready. I returned to England with the first two volumes covering the Biblical and Talmudic periods, and part of the material for the third volume on the Middle Ages.

In January, 1954, an extensive portion of this work was exhibited in Woburn House, London, before leading representatives of British Jewry, under the sponsorship of the Central Council for Jewish Religious Education, and the patronage of the Hon. Eliahu Eilat, Israeli Ambassador to Great Britain. The impressive Master Chart which presented visually the historic panorama of Jewish creativity from ancient times to the present, was displayed there. At the exhibition, the Chairman, the late Dr. Abraham Cohen, Biblical scholar and then president of the Board of Deputies of British Jews, stated:

> "The Atlas is a revolutionary educational method to impart to students in training colleges, a comprehensive knowledge of Jewish history and Hebrew literature . . . In these charts we have a remarkable condensation of a huge mass of material. What would occupy perhaps one hundred pages in a text book is presented on a single chart . . . I am convinced that it will prove to be of tremendous value, not only to our students, but equally to our teachers and instructors."

Rabbi Israel Brodie, Chief Rabbi of Great Britain and the Commonwealth, who addressed the exhibition, said:

> "Visual aids in education have for some time been recognized as an exceedingly helpful medium, yet nothing in that line has hitherto been produced for teaching Jewish history and literature . . . The great virtue of the Atlas and charts of Jewish history and literature is that it helps students and teachers to appreciate the vast panorama of Jewish life and letters throughout the ages."

The Anglo-Jewish Press reported full and enthusiastic approval of the project. Profoundly encouraged, I returned to Israel determined to complete the work. Despite the support and counsel given me by so many scholars at the Hebrew University, this was more easily said than achieved. There were many budgetary problems. The Ministry of Education, the Ministry of Religions and the Jewish Agency all applauded the great educational and cultural value of the Atlas, and advanced some measure of financial aid to help in the preparation of the material. Obviously however, much greater funds were needed to cover the cost of printing dozens of exhaustive tables, preparing illustrations, editing text and translations and publishing the work in an attractive form.

Due to these extracurricular problems, progress on the work was again interrupted for several years. During that time, at the request of the Minister of Education, I directed the "Yad Vashem" project of registration of the victims of the Nazi holocaust. Upon completion of the registry in Israel (comprising 1,500,000 names), I came to the United States in the hope of publishing an English edition of The Graphic History of the Jewish Heritage.

Once in America, there ensued a period of activity. Scholars, educators and religious leaders saw the work and were enthused and committees were formed to aid the project. A well attended exhibit was held in the Jewish Theological Seminary, New York City. With the generous help of my dear friends Benjamin Harris, Max Bressler and Samson Krupnick, my work was exhibited in Chicago. In the meantime, a Foundation was established to aid in the English publication of the first volume of this work.

Among the many who helped advance the project I must make special mention of Herman Wouk, eminent author, who was one of the first to lend his support and encouragement to the publication of this work. He agreed to serve as Chairman of a national committee then in formation and contributed generously of his time, effort, counsel and means. It was through his endeavors too, that a patron was found for the project in the person of his friend, Mr. Joseph Schlang.

Mr. Schlang accepted the leadership of the Foundation for a Graphic History of Jewish Literature. This was the decisive turning-point in the realization of this project. Very substantial funds were advanced to the Foundation for a Graphic History of Jewish Literature by Mr. Schlang and the Broad St. Foundation Inc., of which Joseph Schlang and his family are the sole contributors. His generous aid enabled the work to progress and reach the stage where printing, publication and promotion became possible. It is difficult for me adequately to thank Mr. Joseph Schlang for the generous assistance he has given this project. Without his support, the difficulties of completing the English edition might well have proven insurmountable.

I wish to express my abiding gratitude to Dr. David S. Andron for his devoted cooperation in advancing the many phases and aspects of the work, and in the supervision, emendation and coordination of the texts, charts and details of this current English edition. Thanks to his thoughtful and excellent advice and aid, the printing and publishing of this work were successfully achieved.

May I finally convey my deep sense of indebtedness to Moshe Sheinbaum, president of Shengold Publishers, for his wise counsel and highly valued assistance since my arrival in the United States. He has been unstinting in his efforts to assure the publication of this volume in a most engaging and attractive format.

Pinchas Wollman–Tsamir

March 1963, New York City

Our abiding tribute and
appreciation to

JOSEPH SCHLANG

distinguished communal leader
and devoted patron
of Jewish scholarship
whose generous support of

THE GRAPHIC HISTORY
OF THE JEWISH HERITAGE

merits our deepest gratitude

ACKNOWLEDGMENTS

In the course of the years during which I compiled this work, I profited from the counsel and guidance of scholars and educators alike and I am pleased to express my sincere thanks and deep appreciation to them. I wish to voice particular gratitude to my friends and colleagues at the Hebrew University in Jerusalem and the Bar-Ilan University in Ramat Gan and other institutions of higher learning, who contributed to the first volume of this Graphic History of the Jewish Heritage.

I am indebted to my friend Dr. Judah Felix, Professor of Bar-Ilan University for his assistance in guiding and conferring with the artists who prepared the charts and tables and for his helpful contributions which include the text for "The Forty-Three Kings" as well as the translation and adaptation of the Chronological and Synchronical Tables according to Dr. Zunz and Samuel Arrowsmith. I extend my thanks too, to Dr. Asher Weiser, Professor at Bar-Ilan University, for providing the contents of the Books of the Bible and of the weekly portions; to Rabbi Shalom Meisel and the late Dr. Noah Braun of the Hebrew University, for their "Synopsis of the Pentateuch"; to Zeev Kaspi M.A. for "The Judges"; to Dr. J. M. Grintz of the editorial staff of the Hebrew Encyclopedia, for "The Forty-Eight Prophets"; to Dr. Baruch Kanel for "The High Priests"; and to my dear friend, the late Akiva Schlesinger M.A. for "The Genealogical Tables".

I express my thanks also to Dr. J. Wiesenberg of University College, London, for his assistance in the preparation of the English version of the Master Chart—the General Plan to this project. Contributors to the following volumes will be acknowledged in the subsequent books as they appear.

I wish to acknowledge my sincere appreciation to the staff of artists and draftsmen who prepared the Hebrew charts and the drawings: in Israel, to Z. Grundman, Lippman-Rothschild, E. Preiss, M. Gabrieli, I. Kristal and S. Almog; to Dr. J. Hertz of London for his hundreds of excellent vignettes and illustrations, and to J. Rothschild for drafting the "Key" to the Graphic History; and to Rev. J. Halpern and Rev. N. J. de Fries of London and to Dr. S. Halpern of Jerusalem for their suggestions for vignettes.

The preparation of the English edition of this book has left me indebted to Dr. Sidney Hoenig, Professor at Yeshiva University, New York, for his translation, and authentication of the sources and chronology of the tables; to Jacob Sloan, David Segal and Dr. Chaim Levin for participating in the translations; to Bernard I. Sandler for his preparation of the Index; to Mrs. Priscilla Fishman for her proofreading and apt suggestions; to the designers and artists, Emanuel Schary and Joseph Taubman, for their helpful advice and efforts, and the preparation of the English charts; to Samuel E. Bloch for his valuable assistance; and to Samuel Sloan for his active cooperation during the initial stages of the project.

I wish to convey my thanks to Ludwig Y. Wolpert for his gracious permission to use his portrayal of The Burning Bush on the jacket design and the reproduction of his Torah Crown in the pages of this book.

I am immensely grateful to the distinguished scholars, educators and leaders of the Jewish communities in Israel, Great Britain and the United States who examined the charts and manuscripts, offered their wise counsel, thoughtful suggestions, generous encouragement and in many instances, both written and oral approval of this project.

I thank them all, but I must take this occasion to extend my appreciation to some of them by name: In Israel, Professor Benjamin Mazar, former president, Hebrew University; Dr. Ephraim Auerbach, Chairman, Institute of Jewish Studies, Hebrew University; Professors Yehezkel Kaufman and Shimon Halkin, Hebrew University; Professor Isaiah Leibovitz, Editor, Hebrew Encyclopedia; the late Professor Pinchas Churgin, past president, Bar-Ilan University; the Chief Rabbis of Israel: the late Dr. Yitzhak Halevi Herzog and Rabbi Yitzhak Nissim; Rabbi Yehuda Unterman, Chief Rabbi of Tel Aviv—Jaffa; Yitzhak Ben Zvi, President of Israel; David Ben Gurion, Prime Minister of Israel; Professor B. Dinur, former Minister of Education; Justice M. Silberg, Chairman of the Supreme Court; Dr. Zerah Wahrhaftig, Minister of Religion; Z. Shazar, Chairman, Cultural Department, Jewish Agency.

In Great Britain: Rabbi I. Epstein, Principal, Jews College, London; Dayan Dr. I. Gruenfeld, London; Rabbi Dr. Elie Munk, London; Dr. A. Steinberg, Cultural Department, World Jewish Congress; Dr. Judah Slotki, Director, Jewish Education, Leeds; Dr. B. Weiss, Manchester University.

In the United States: Dr. Samuel Belkin, President, Yeshiva University; Dr. I. Lewin, Yeshiva University; Professor W. F. Albright, Johns Hopkins University; Professor Salo Baron, Columbia University; Dr. Abraham Heschel and Dr. Abraham Halkin, Jewish Theological Seminary of America; Dr. Nelson Glueck, President, Hebrew Union College–Jewish Institute of Religion; Dr. Arthur Hyman, Professor, New York University; Dr. Solomon Grayzel, Editor, Jewish Publication Society of America; Dr. Meyer Waxman; Rabbi Dr. Leo Jung; Rabbi Dr. Immanuel Jakobovits; Dr. Abraham Duker, former president, College of Jewish Studies, Chicago; and Rabbi Oscar Fassman, President, Hebrew Theological College, Chicago.

I am grateful too, to my friends in London, Dr. H. W. Kugelman, Dr. O. Rabinowitz and Mr. M. Adler, and especially to Mr. Samuel Benster of Manchester for their generous assistance and sincere encouragement throughout the years. I extend my thanks also to Rabbi Norman Lamm for his ever ready cooperation.

I am particularly indebted to Dr. Max Gruenewald and Rabbi Dr. Joseph Lookstein, co-directors of the Wurzweiler Foundation, who have been most generous in their assistance; to Messers Herman Wouk, Charles Gutwirth, Louis Ludwig, William Salzman, Hermann Merkin, Dr. William Roth, Henry Hirsch, Mortimer J. Propp, Charles C. Bloch, Saul Linzer, and to the Harry and Jane Fischel Foundation in New York; and to Messers Benjamin Harris, Samson Krupnick, Max Bressler, Ben Vollen, Paul Vishny, Samuel Katzin, Harry Director, Mrs. Maxwell Abbell, Philip D. Sang and David Borowitz, all of Chicago; to these many distinguished leaders I extend my grateful and personal appreciation for their earnest and generous cooperation in the advancement of this work.

I am pleased to acknowledge my thanks to the Jewish Publication Society of America for its kind permission to use its version of the Holy Scriptures in quotations, in our texts, charts and tables.

P. W.

CONTENTS

INTRODUCTION

The Graphic History of the Jewish Heritage is an encyclopedic survey of Jewish literature and its historical development, presented in a totally new format. The wealth of the Jewish heritage in all its ramifications, is set forth concisely by means of charts, tables and other visual techniques. These are accompanied by short summaries, biographical sketches, and by explanatory notes on the literary works, the authors, the history and thought of the general period.

The key to The Graphic History of the Jewish Heritage which will comprise four volumes, is a comprehensive Master Chart, a general plan for the whole project. This lists the main sections of the books and the names of the historical personalities mentioned in this work according to the subjects or the periods.

The headings in the Master Chart refer the reader to one of the more detailed charts. Each of these deals with an entire era, its important literary works, authors and other personalities. In general, the work follows a chronological-historical order, which is presented in the central column of the Master Chart.

This volume covers the Biblical period. It encompasses three groups of data:

1. It describes in charts and text, the literary masterpieces of the Jewish heritage beginning with the thirty-nine books of the Bible. The Pentateuch is divided into the fifty-four portions of the week, and these are summarized, as are the books of the Prophets and the Scriptures.

2. It presents the great Biblical figures: the early generations recorded in the Pentateuch, the Patriarchs, the leaders of the people, from Moses through the fifteen Judges, the forty-eight Prophets and the seven Prophetesses, the forty-three Kings of Judah and Israel, and the twenty-five High Priests who served in the First Temple era.

3. It includes a series of genealogical, chronological and synchronical tables. The genealogical tables cover the twenty-six generations from Adam to Moses. The chronological tables encompass the period from the creation of the world to the division of the Kingdoms of Judah and Israel. The synchronical tables include the Kings, Prophets and High Priests of Judah and Israel during the period of the First Temple as well as a brief description of the events that occurred during that era.

The brief summaries of the weekly portions of the Bible contain only primary and central ideas or events. Further details and information are to be found in the supplementary synopsis which contains additional data including many other laws and commandments mentioned in each of the fifty-four portions of the Pentateuch.

In summarizing the weekly portions of the Pentateuch and of the books of the Bible, the biographical sketches of the Judges, the Kings, the Prophets, the High Priests, etc., we intended to distill from the vast wealth of sources only those characteristics which reflect the timeless ethical, religious, and national ideas and values of vital interest and significance to mankind. For all other details the reader is naturally referred to the sources themselves.

Forthcoming volumes will cover the periods of the Second Temple, of the Mishnah and Talmud, the Middle Ages, and Modern Times. The graphic and textual material will include both: (1) complete enumeration and biographical sketches of the Kings, the rulers, the other High Priests, the Sages of the Great Assembly, the Tannaim, Amoraim, Saboraim, Exilarchs, Gaonim, etc.; as well as (2) the order and summaries of the Mishnah, Tosefta, Baraitoth, the Babylonian and the Palestinian Talmudim, the Midrashim, the Apocryphal literature (including the Dead Sea Scrolls), the Poskim (codifiers), the Rambam, the Tosafists, the Rabbinic and other literature, etc., as listed in the Master Chart, up to and until our own generation.

The following format is used throughout the work. Each section includes (1) a short introduction which explains the period and the background, (2) a general chart encompassing the entire subject, and (3) a short summarizing text corresponding to the numbers on the chart.

The sections and chapters are headed by symbolic drawings and vignettes illustrating their special characteristics or central themes.

It is easy to see the practical value of the graphic approach. From the ancient Chinese, who stated that "one picture is worth one thousand words", to contemporary psychologists and educators, the use of visual aids has been encouraged to facilitate the learning process. A graphic illustration—be it picture, table or chart—lends itself to a total perspective and hence to the rapid assimilation of many details related to a central theme. (For this reason, I employed a summarizing chart to display more effectively the problems of extension of the Hebrew language, morphology, grammar, etc., in my book published by Hermon-Verlag, Frankfurt a. Main 1935.)

Because The Graphic History provides a maximum of information in a minimum of time and space by its compact charts and summaries, it is of special value to High Schools, Colleges, Libraries and religious and other institutions where students may use it as a review of known material and as a guide for independent research work. In fact, everyone seeking knowledge of the Jewish heritage will find this volume particularly useful and valuable.

Finally, it is hoped that The Graphic History of the Jewish Heritage will open new horizons for those readers who are not familiar with the rich depths and broad sweep of the spiritual legacy bequeathed to them by the thousands of great men and books that compose the Jewish heritage.

The structural organization of The Graphic History of the Jewish Heritage and the formulation of its basic principles involved the consideration of a number of scholarly problems, as for example, Bible interpretation, different textual readings, various versions concerning chronology, and the authorship of various Biblical works. In order to ensure the scientific accuracy and pedagogic usefulness of The Graphic History, the charts and tables were submitted to various distinguished scholars for their opinion. Among those I consulted were several members of the faculty of the Hebrew University in Jerusalem, among them my teachers, Professors M. Cassuto, S. Assaf, H. Albeck, M. S. Segal, J. Klausner, N. Tur-Sinai and Yehezkel Kaufman, etc.

We strove always to maintain a scholarly and objective approach towards the number of questions which had to be resolved. In some of the charts and texts, dealing with matters of chronology, the number of Prophets, the order of their listing, etc., differing scholarly views have been noted, without statement of preference for the validity of one viewpoint over the other. It is not within the competence of this work to serve as a final arbiter in such matters.

For all English quotations as well as for the transliterations of Hebrew names, of weekly portions, books, persons, or places mentioned in the Bible, we employed the text of the Jewish Publication Society in its translation of the Bible, (1917). We extend our deep appreciation to the Society for permission to use its translation.

For purposes of identification, we included the Hebrew names only in the introductory charts and in the captions in the text of the Books of the Bible, the weekly portions, the Judges, the Kings, the Prophets and the High Priests.

In the interest of brevity we have, wherever feasible, condensed Talmudic and Midrashic material into a form which nevertheless communicates the central meaning of the passage involved.

A number of informative appendices illustrate the various and related aspects of the Jewish heritage incidental to the Biblical period. They serve to illumine certain features and facets of our work. These several appendices consist of direct excerpta from authoritative works and of adaptations and interpretive variations of original compositions. In this connection, we herewith express acknowledgement and appreciation to the publishers of The Popular Bible and Encyclopedia and Scriptural Dictionary, edited by Samuel Fallows, Barnes' Biblical Dictionary, and Ayre's Treasury of Bible Knowledge.*

It is virtually impossible to note the many sources, texts and works which have been consulted by my colleagues and me in the course of this work. Only a limited number of them are listed in the "Sources Quoted". We have sailed the vast seas of classic Jewish and cognate literature in our quest for information, authority and authenticity.

The reader's forgiveness and indulgence are asked for any errors of translation or printing which may have crept into this volume. If such are found and reported to us they will be gratefully acknowledged and corrected in the next edition.

THE EDITOR

* Refer to pages 168 and 210.

"And he wrote upon the tables the words of the covenant, the ten words"
(Exodus 34.28).

Moses on Mount Sinai, writing the Torah by divine instruction.

TORAH = Pentateuch, Prophets, Hagiographa
(Torah, Nebiim, Ketubim: Tanach).

TORAH = Commandments (Mitzvot, Testimonies,
Statutes, Laws, Teachings and Worship).

TORAH

1	2	
Genesis בראשית (Book of Jashar) (50)*	**Exodus** שמות (Book of Redemption) (40)	**Lev**... א... (Book of...

PROPHE...

Former Prophets נביאים ראשונים

Latte...

6	7	8	9	10	11	12
Joshua יהושע (24)	**Judges** שופטים (21)	**Samuel** שמואל א׳ (31) ב׳ (24)	**Kings** מלכים א׳ (22) ב׳ (25)	**Isaiah** ישעיהו (66)	**Jeremiah** ירמיהו (52)	**Ezekie**... חזקאל (48)
Conquest of Canaan under Joshua.	The history of the tribes in the period of the Judges.	Reigns of Saul and David.	The annals of the Kings of Judah and Israel.	The prophecies of Isaiah, son of Amoz.	The prophecies of Jeremiah.	The prophecie... Ezekiel.
Author: Begun by Joshua, completed by Phinehas, son of Eleazar the priest.	Author: Samuel.	Author: Begun by Samuel, completed by Gad and Nathan.	Author: Jeremiah.	Author: Hezekiah, king of Judah and his circle.	Author: Jeremiah.	Author: Men of Great Assemb...

HAGIOGRA...
(Scr...

Wisdom (Emet) Books,
ספרי א״מת
marked by a mnemonic derived from the initials
of the Hebrew Titles of Job, Proverbs and Psalms

Five Megillot (Scrolls) חמש מגילות

14	15	16	17	18	19	20
Psalms תהלים (150)	**Proverbs** משלי (31)	**Job** איוב (42)	**Song of Songs** שיר השירים (8)	**Ruth** רות (4)	**Lamentations** איכה (5)	**Ecclesiastes** קהלת (12)
The psalms of David.	Proverbs of Solomon, son of David.	The disputations between Job and his companions on providence and its mysterious ways.	Songs of love and friendship.	A pastoral idyll.	Elegies on the destruction of Jerusalem and the Temple.	Philosophic reflections.
Author: Attributed to David and ten elders (who preceded him): Adam, Melchizedek, Abraham, Moses, Heman, Jeduthun, Asaph and the 3 sons of Korah.	Author: Hezekiah and his circle.	Author: Moses. Interpreted by some sages as an allegory.	Author: Hezekiah and his circle.	Author: Hezekiah and his circle.	Author: Jeremiah.	Author: Hezekiah and his circle.

TORAH = 613 Commandments: 248 positive;
365 negative.

TORAH = Reading of the Law, Study of the
Mishna, Talmudic (Gemara) Analysis.

תורה

4	5
Numbers במדבר (Book of Census) (36)	**Deuteronomy** דברים (Repetition of the Law) (34)
ticus ויקרא (e Priests) ")	

נביאים ts

r Prophets   נביאים אחרונים

13 The Twelve Prophets   תרי עשר

Hosea הושע (14)	Joel יואל (4)	Amos עמוס (9)	Obadiah עובדיה (1)	Jonah יונה (4)	Micah מיכה (7)	Nahum נחום (3)	Habakkuk חבקוק (3)	Zephaniah צפניה (3)	Haggai חגי (2)	Zechariah זכריה (14)	Malachi מלאכי (3)

of | Includes all (12) of the Minor Books of the Prophets.

the | Authors: The Men of the Great Assembly. "Because their prophecies were brief, the early prophets did not edit their own books. However, Haggai, Zechariah and Malachi, the last of the prophets, realizing that the divine spirit was departing from Israel, wrote down their own prophecies, and, subjoining the works of the earlier prophets, put together a large volume less likely to be lost". (Rashi, Baba Bartha 15a)

PHA כתובים
(tures)

Other Writings   שאר הכתובים

חמ

21 **Esther** אסתר (10)	22 **Daniel** דניאל (12)	23 **Ezra-Nehemiah** נחמיה עזרא (10) (13)	24 **Chronicles** דברי הימים I (29) II (36)
The miracle of Purim in the days of Mordecai and Esther.	The esoteric prophecies of Daniel and his experiences in the period of the Exile.	Events in Judea during the days of Ezra the Scribe and Nehemiah, son of Hacaliah; the construction of the Second Temple.	A complete resume of early Jewish history from the creation of man to the Exile from Palestine.
Author: Men of the Great Assembly.	Author: Men of the Great Assembly.	**Author:** Ezra, The sages called both books by the title "Ezra".	Author: Begun by Ezra and completed by Nehemiah.

* Number of chapters.

TORAH

תורה

The Pentateuch is the unique and inspired Book of Books given by God to the Jews through Moses, the father of the prophets, first in the desert, and then again in the plains of Moab in Transjordan near Jericho. Principally, it teaches the commandments, statutes, and laws by which the Jews, God's chosen people, are to live in the chosen land which God has promised the patriarchs, Abraham, Isaac, and Jacob. But the Pentateuch also presents a brief account of Jewish history from its earliest beginnings. This includes the story of God's revelation to the patriarchs and His covenant with them; the descent to Egypt; the Exodus; the events in the desert during the first, part of the second, and the 40th year of the Exodus; the conquest of the Transjordan area; and, finally, the death of Moses. This historical narrative is told with reverence and religious awe. Israel is represented as the people of the covenant of God whose mission is to fulfill His Law in the world, to be His chosen people, the source of prophets and teachers whose moral preachments will lift mankind from the abyss of idolatry.

The Pentateuch consists of five books: Genesis, Exodus, Leviticus, Numbers, and Deuteronomy.

TORAH

(Pentat

The written law, transmitted by Moses from Sinai, as the basic wo

1. Genesis	2. Exodus	3. Le
בראשית	שמות	א
(Book of Jashar) [a]	(Book of Redemption) [b]	(Book of

Contents: Creation of the world. The Patriarchs. Jacob and his sons go down to Egypt. Jacob blesses his sons before his death.

Contents: Bondage of children of Israel in Egypt. Exodus. Revelation. The Tabernacle and its vessels.

Contents: Prie pertaining to s rality, the Land days.

Weekly Portions
Genesis

1.	Bereshit	1.1-6.8	בראשית
2.	Noah	6.9-11.32	נח
3.	Lekh Lekha	12.1-17.27	לך לך
4.	Vayera	18.1-22.24	וירא
5.	Haye Sarah	23-1-25.18	חיי שרה
6.	Toledot	25.19-28.9	תולדות
7.	Vayetze	28.10-32.3	ויצא
8.	Vayishlah	32.4-36.43	וישלח
9.	Vayeshev	37.1-40.23	וישב
10.	Miketz	41.1-44.17	מקץ
11.	Vayigash	44.18-47.27	ויגש
12.	Vayehi	47.28-50.26	ויחי

Weekly Portions
Exodus

1.	Shemot	1.1-6.1	שמות
2.	Vaera	6.2-9.35	וארא
3.	Bo	10.1-13.16	בא
4.	Beshalah	13.17-17.16	בשלח
5.	Yitro	18.1-20.23	יתרו
6.	Mishpatim	21.1-24.18	משפטים
7.	Terumah	25.1-27.19	תרומה
8.	Tetzaveh [c]	27.20-30.10	תצוה
9.	Ki Tissa	30.11-34.35	כי תשא
10.	Vayakhel	35.1-38.20	ויקהל
11.	Pekude [c]	38.21-40.38	פקודי

Weekly
Lev

1.	Vayikra	1
2	.Tzav	6
3.	Shemini	9.1
4.	Tazria	12.1
5.	Metzora [c]	14.1
6.	Ahare Mot	16.1
7.	Kedoshim [c]	19.1
8.	Emor	21.1
9.	Behar	25.
10.	Behukkotai [c]	26.3

[a] (Aboda Zara 25a)
[b] (Nahmanides)
[c] One portion read during leap year; two portions read in other years.

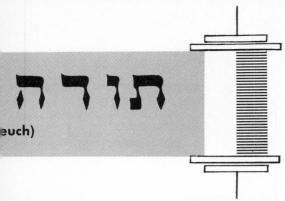

תורה
(...euch)

...k of Jewish legislation (2448-2488 AM) is divided into FIVE BOOKS:

...viticus	**4. Numbers**	**5. Deuteronomy**
...ויק	במדבר	דברים
...he Priests)	(Book of Census)	(Repetition of the Law)

...viticus

...stly code. Rules
...crifices, diet, mo-
...of Israel and holy

4. Numbers

Contents: Census. More statutes and laws. Adventures of the Hebrews on route to Canaan through the desert.

5. Deuteronomy

Contents: Recapitulation of laws with additions. Moses admonishes the children of Israel. His last testament.

...Portions
...iticus

...1-5.26	ויקרא
...1-8.36	צו
...-11.47	שמיני
...-13.59	תזריע
...-15.33	מצורע
...-18.30	אחרי מות
...-20.27	קדושים
...-24.23	אמור
...26.2	בהר
...7.34	בחקותי

Weekly Portions
Numbers

1.	Bamidbar	1.1-4.20	במדבר
2.	Naso	4.21-7.89	נשא
3.	Behaalotekha	8.1-12.16	בהעלותך
4.	Shelah	13.1-15.41	שלח
5.	Korah	16.1-18.32	קרח
6.	Hukkat	19.1-22.1	חוקת
7.	Balak	22.2-25.9	בלק
8.	Phinehas	25.10-30.1	פנחס
9.	Mattot	30.2-32.42	מטות
10.	Mase	33.1-36.13	מסעי

Weekly Portions
Deuteronomy

1.	Devarim	1.1-3.22	דברים
2.	Vaethanan	3.23-7.11	ואתחנן
3.	Ekev	7.12-11.25	עקב
4.	Re'eh	11.26-16.17	ראה
5.	Shofetim	16.18-21.9	שופטים
6.	Ki Tetze	21.10-25.19	תצא
7.	Ki Tavo	26.1-29.8	תבא
8.	Nitzavim	29.9-30.20	נצבים
9.	Vayelekh	31.1-30	וילך
10.	Haazinu	32.1-52	האזינו
11.	Vezot Haberakhah	33.1-34.12	וזאת הברכה

The patriarchs Abraham, Isaac, and Jacob, shepherds and farmers.

"And Isaac sowed in that land . . . And he had possessions of flocks, and posses-sions of herds" (Genesis 26.12-14).

GENESIS   בראשית

The first of the Five Books of Moses begins with the creation of the world out of void and darkness. God made light, life, and order. It tells how every species was created according to its kind in a definite time and order sequence. In six days the Lord made heaven and earth, and daily looked on his work and saw that it was good. On the sixth day he finished, and God saw everything that He had made, and behold it was good. On the seventh day God rested from all of His labors. So He blessed the sabbath day and sanctified it above all the days of the week.

But man, corrupting God's good world, brought on himself a Deluge and a Babel of tongues. Salvation first appeared in the person of Abraham, who elevated the human species through the recognition of the oneness of the Creator. God chose Abraham to be the teacher of true divinity to the world. Sending Abraham to the land of Canaan, God promised to make him into "a great nation and a blessing." In Canaan, God made a covenant with Abraham, to whose seed he offered the land of Canaan, which they should inherit after a 400-year period during which they should be strangers "in a land not theirs." Meanwhile, "the iniquity of the Amorite [the generic term for the original inhabitants of Canaan] is not yet full" (Genesis 15.16). During these 400 years, the goodly seed of Abra-ham would be preserved and would ripen, until they should be worthy of the lofty promise of God's covenant with Abraham. The book of Genesis goes on to chroni-cle the lives of the patriarchs Isaac and Jacob. Jacob goes down to Egypt "with seventy souls." Genesis concludes with Jacob's prophetic blessings to his sons; his death and burial in the land of Canaan; and an anticipation of the Exodus from Egypt—Joseph's last request that his bones be carried out of Egypt for burial in the homeland when the children of Israel return to the Promised Land.

BERESHIT בראשית

The primeval world, covered with water, swathed in darkness. And God said, "Let there be light."

"And God said: 'Let there be light'. . . and God divided the light from the darkness" (Gen. 1.3-4).

Bereshit — God created the world in six days. On the first day He created the light and called it "day"; the darkness He called "night". On the second day He created the expanse of the heavens. On the third day the waters were assembled into oceans and dry land was seen. This was called "earth". Next, vegetation flourished. On the fourth day the luminaries were fixed in the sky. On the fifth day, fish, reptiles, and fowl were created. On the sixth day, the beasts, animals, and man were created. On the seventh day, God rested from all His labors. Therefore he blessed the seventh day and sanctified it. Man was created alone; afterward, God took a rib from Adam's side and fashioned a wife for him; Adam called her Eve, meaning "the mother of all living things." At first Adam and Eve lived happily in the Garden of Eden; but they ate the fruit of the forbidden tree of knowledge and were driven out of Paradise. The sons of man multiplied and progressed. However, their ways were evil and God decided to erase all men from the face of the earth. Only Noah found favor in the eyes of God.

NOAH נח

Noah and his wife behold a rainbow in the sky: God's promise never to destroy mankind.

"Go forth from the ark, thou, and thy wife" (Gen. 8.16).

Noah — Noah was commanded to build an Ark for shelter from the Flood that would overwhelm the earth. In the Ark he placed his wife and three sons, Shem, Ham, and Japheth, together with their wives; also two of each species of creature on earth, one male and one female to perpetuate the species (seven were allowed for the species that were ritually clean). The Flood that covered the earth drowned all living things except those in the Ark with Noah. After a year, the waters receded and the earth dried. Noah let all the creatures out of the Ark, that they might be fruitful and multiply on earth. He sacrificed in thanksgiving to God. God, for His part, promised Noah that He would never again send a flood that would destroy the earth. The sign for this agreement, or covenant, is the rainbow.

Men increased and spread over the world; in the land of Shinar they sought to build a tower whose peak should reach to heaven. Here, they thought to concentrate all the earth's population. But God, irked at man's presumption, confused their speech. Previously all men had spoken one language. Now they spoke various languages; not being able to understand each other, they could not work together, and the building of the Tower of Babel ceased.

Terah, the father of Abram, came to Haran.

LEKH LEKHA לך לך

Abraham, in Transjordan with his flocks of sheep and camels, sees Palestine, the Promised Land, in the distance.

"Lift up now thine eyes, and look . . . for all the land which thou seest, to thee will I give it, and to thy seed for ever" (Gen. 13.14-15).

Lek Lekha — At the command of God, Abram left Haran and journeyed to Canaan. There God appeared to him and said: "Unto thy seed will I give this land" (Genesis 12.7). There was a famine in the land of Canaan, and Abram took his household to Egypt. On his return, he and his nephew Lot separated peaceably, Lot choosing to settle in the plain of Sodom. In the battles between the northern kings and those of the plain of Sodom, Lot was captured. Learning of his nephew's plight, Abram armed his followers and pursued Lot's captors. He defeated them and rescued his nephew and the other captives from Sodom. God made a covenant with Abram to give him and his seed after him the land of Canaan ("The Covenant between the Parts"). When Abram's wife Sarai saw that she was barren she gave Hagar, her handmaiden, to Abram as wife. Hagar bore Abram a son, who was called Ishmael. At God's command, Abram changed his name to Abraham, and his wife's name to Sarah. He was circumcised, together with all the males of his household.

VAYERA וירא

Abraham welcomes the three angels into his tent.

"As he sat in the tent door in the heat of the day; and he lifted up his eyes and looked, and, lo, three men stood over against him" (Gen.18.1-2).

Vayera — God appeared to Abraham as he sat at the door of his tent in the heat of the day. Lifting up his eyes, Abraham beheld three men (actually, angels in the form of men). Abraham ran toward them, took them into his tent, and treated them hospitably. One of the angels foretold that in a year Sarah would bear a son. The other angels went on to Sodom to destroy the city because of its wickedness; only Lot, Abraham's righteous nephew, was to be saved. God revealed this plan to Abraham, who pleaded that Sodom be saved for the sake of the righteous persons living in it. But it turned out that Sodom could not be saved—there were not 10 righteous persons in the whole city. Lot was saved, and lived in a cave. There his two daughters bore him two sons: Benammi, or Ammon, and Moab. In fulfillment of the angel's prophecy, Sarah bore a son, who was named Isaac. When the lad grew up, God tested Abraham's devotion by bidding him offer Isaac as a sacrifice. Abraham prepared to carry out God's bidding; at the last moment, an angel intervened, and Isaac was saved. Abraham had passed the hardest trial of all.

HAYE SARAH חיי שרה

The cave of Machpelah at Hebron. Eliezer leaves Hebron with camels on Abraham's instructions.

"And after this, Abraham buried Sarah his wife in the cave of the field of Machpelah before Mamre" (Gen. 23.19).

Haye Sarah — Sarah died at the age of 127 in Hebron, and was buried in the Cave of Machpelah, which Abraham purchased as a family grave yard. Anxious for Isaac to marry one of his kinfolk rather than an idolatrous Canaanite woman, Abraham sent his trusted servant Eliezer to his former home in Mesopotamia where his brother Nahor lived. Approaching the city, Eliezer prayed for the success of his mission. He determined on a procedure: He would ask each girl he met, "Give me your pitcher and let me drink"; the girl who would reply, "Drink, and I will give thy camels drink also" should be Isaac's destined bride (Genesis 24.14). Rebekah, daughter of Bethuel, the son of Abraham's brother Nahor, came to the well to draw water, and responded with the correct formula to Eliezer's request. Thanking God for His kindness, the old family retainer presented himself to Rebekah's family, explained his mission, and received permission for Rebekah to accompany him back to Canaan as Isaac's prospective wife. Isaac loved Rebekah, and was consoled in her after his mother's death. Abraham took another wife, Keturah, and she bore him sons whom he dispatched to the east. At the age of 175 Abraham died and was buried next to Sarah in the Cave of Machpelah.

TOLEDOT תולדות

Isaac blesses Jacob, whose arms are wrapped in the skins of young goats.

"And his father Isaac said unto him: 'Come near now, and kiss me, my son'. . . And he smelled the smell of his raiment, and blessed him" (Gen. 27.26-27).

Toledot — Like Sarah, Rebekah at first was barren. After Isaac prayed to God on her behalf, she bore twin boys—Esau and Jacob. Esau grew up a hunter, Jacob an upright dweller in tents. One day, Esau returned from the field very hungry, and disdainfully sold his "elder son" birthright to Jacob for a pot of lentil soup. Isaac was old and blind and likely to die soon. He called Esau and instructed him to prepare Isaac's favorite dishes, that he might bless him before his death. However, Rebekah, who favored Jacob for his superior merits, arranged for Jacob to secure his father's coveted blessing instead of his elder brother. Fearing Esau's revenge, and anxious lest Jacob marry a Canaanite woman, his mother sent him to her brother Laban, who lived in Paddan-Aram. Before leaving, Jacob received Isaac's blessing, the continuation of God's original blessing to Abraham: that he and his seed would inherit the land of Canaan. Isaac bade Jacob marry one of his uncle Laban's daughters.

VAYETZE ויצא

Jacob's dream.

"And he dreamed, and behold a ladder set up on the earth, and the top of it reached to heaven; and behold the angels of God ascending and descending on it" (Gen. 28. 12).

Vayetze — On his way to Haran, Jacob lay down to rest at a place where God appeared to him in a dream, promising to be with him and to give the land to him and his seed after him. Rising the next morning, Jacob lifted the stone on which he had slept, and set it up as a pillar. He called the place Beth-el, meaning "house of God", and vowed to serve God there when he returned to his father's house. The Lord would be his God.

In Haran Jacob worked twenty years as a shepherd for Laban—seven years for his first wife, Leah, seven years for his second wife, Rachel, and six years for the sheep. His wives gave him their maid servants Bilhah and Zilpah as wives. Jacob's four wives bore him 11 sons: Reuben, Simeon, Levi, Judah, Dan, Naphtali, Gad, Asher, Issachar, Zebulun, and Joseph; he also had one daughter named Dinah. At God's direction, Jacob returned home to his father's house. On the way he met the angels of God.

VAYISHLAH וישלח

Rachel's tomb.

"And Rachel died, and was buried in the way to Ephrath — the same is Bethlehem. And Jacob set up a pillar upon her grave" (Gen. 35.19-20).

Vayishlah — Approaching the boundary of the land of Seir where his brother Esau dwelt, Jacob prudently sent messengers ahead to inform Esau of his coming and of his wealth. The messengers returned with the news that Esau was advancing toward Jacob with 400 men. Terrified, Jacob divided his camp into two sections, so as not to lose all in the event of an attack. He sent gifts to Esau and prayed God to save him from his brother. Jacob crossed the stream of Jabbok with his camp. There, as he stood alone, an angel approached and wrestled with him. At the end of the struggle, the angel declared: "Thy name shall be called no more Jacob, but Israel; for thou hast striven with God and with men, and hast prevailed" (Genesis 32.29). Thus encouraged, Jacob met Esau, whom he treated with the utmost deference. Embracing, the two brothers kissed, wept, and were reconciled. Jacob journeyed on to Shechem. There the rape of Jacob's only daughter, Dinah, by the prince of that city, led to the vengeful destruction of Shechem by two of Dinah's brothers. Proceeding to Beth-el, Jacob kept the vow he had made to return thither. On the way, Rachel gave birth to Jacob's last and youngest son, Benjamin. But Rachel died in childbirth, and Jacob buried her on the way to Ephrath, which is Beth-lehem.

VAYESHEV וישב

The brothers strip Joseph and throw him into the pit. A caravan of Ishmaelites is seen in the background.

"And it came to pass, when Joseph was come unto his brethren, that they stripped Joseph of his coat" (Gen. 37.23).

Vayeshev — Jacob and his sons dwelt in the land of Canaan as shepherds. Of all his sons,

Jacob loved Joseph best. His obvious favoritism, and Joseph's account of his grandiose dreams, produced hatred and jealousy among the brothers. Joseph's brothers sold the hated favorite to some Ishmaelite merchants, who took Joseph to Egypt with them. There Potiphar, an officer of the Pharaoh and captain of his guard, bought Joseph as a slave. The Hebrew lad quickly rose to a position of responsibility in his master's household. However, Joseph rejected the advances of Potiphar's wife; she slandered him, and he was imprisoned. But in prison, too, God was with Joseph, and he won the confidence of the jailers. He became known as an interpreter of dreams by correctly reading the significance of the dreams of the Pharaoh's butler and baker when they were his prison-mates.

MIKETZ מקץ

His brothers bow before Joseph who is now the ruler of Egypt.

"And Joseph was the governor over the land . . . And Joseph's brethren came, and bowed down to him" (Gen. 42.6).

Miketz — Two years later, Pharaoh dreamt a dream in two slightly different versions. The dream terrified the king of Egypt; but none of his sages could explain it satisfactorily. Pharaoh's butler remembered Joseph's masterly interpretations of dreams, and informed Pharaoh. Joseph was brought before Pharaoh and explained the dream as forecasting seven years of plenty that were to come to the land of Egypt, only to be succeeded by seven years of famine. He advised Pharaoh to appoint a wise overseer to collect wheat during the years of plenty and distribute it during the years of famine. Pharaoh appointed Joseph himself to this post as his viceroy.

As Joseph had forecast, the Egyptian stores of wheat were in great demand during the seven years of famine. Among those who came to buy wheat in Egypt were Joseph's older brothers. Joseph recognized them, but they did not know him. Joseph so contrived that the brothers came to Egypt a second time, bringing Benjamin, Joseph's full brother with them. Joseph received them cordially; but then he made it seem as though Benjamin had stolen a goblet, and insisted that he stay behind as a servant. The brothers refused to abandon Benjamin, and all decided to return to Joseph's home.

VAYIGASH ויגש

Jacob and his family come down to Egypt in ox-drawn carts.

"And they took their cattle, and their goods, which they had gotten in the land of Canaan, and came into Egypt, Jacob, and all his seed with him" (Gen. 46.6).

Vayigash — Judah approached Joseph and offered himself as a servant in Benjamin's stead, as he was responsible for the youngest son to their father. Unable to contain himself any longer, Joseph revealed himself to his dumb-struck brothers. He bade them return to Canaan, gather together their families and possessions, and return to Egypt for the duration of the famine. At Beersheba God removed Jacob's doubts as to the wisdom of this course of action; He appeared to Jacob with the words: "Fear not to go down into Egypt; for I will there make of thee a great nation" (Genesis 46.3).

Jacob came to Egypt "with seventy souls." Joseph gave them the land of Goshen to settle in. There they flourished and multiplied.

VAYEHI ויחי

Jacob blesses Ephraim and Manasseh.

"And Israel stretched out his right hand, and laid it upon Ephraim's head, who was the younger, and his left hand upon Manasseh's head" (Gen. 48.14).

Vayehi — Jacob lived in Egypt 17 years. On his death bed, he blessed his sons, predicting the destiny of the tribes that were to descend from each of them. Ephraim and Manasseh, Joseph's two sons, were included in the roster of Jacob's sons, the heads of future tribes. Jacob died; the Egyptian physicians embalmed his body, after the custom of the country. Jacob was buried in the land of Canaan, in the Cave of Machpelah, together with his ancestors.

Joseph continued to provide for his brothers after their father's death. Before his own death, Joseph made his brothers swear that when they returned to Canaan they would take his bones with them to the Promised Land. Joseph died; meanwhile, his embalmed body was placed in a coffin, awaiting the return to Canaan.

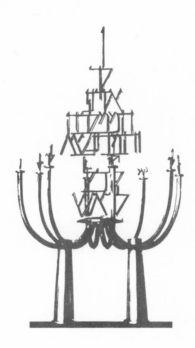

The Israelites leave Egypt, the land of bondage.
"For the children of Israel went out with a high hand" (Exodus 14.8).

EXODUS   שמות

The second book of the Pentateuch begins by naming the sons of Jacob who came to Egypt, seventy in all. In Egypt, "the childen of Israel were fruitful, and increased abundantly, and multiplied, and waxed exceedingly mighty; and the land was filled with them" (Exodus 1.7). This extraordinary increase terrifies the Egyptians, who react by persecuting the Hebrews, putting them to hard labor and drowning their male babies in the Nile River. But the Hebrews continue to grow strong. Moses, miraculously saved from drowning when he was an infant, grows up in Pharaoh's very household. As an adult, he is forced to flee Egypt, after slaying an Egyptian overseer who had been mistreating a Hebrew slave. One day, when Moses is tending the sheep of his father-in-law Jethro on mount Horeb, God appears to him in a burning bush. God has heard the cries of the children of Israel suffering at the hands of their Egyptian oppressors. Now he commands Moses to return to Egypt and deliver His people from bondage; the children of Israel are to journey to this very mountain, Horeb, to worship God.

With the aid of his brother Aaron, Moses succeeds in his mission of liberation. Subjected to ten plagues, the Egyptians finally consent to let the Hebrews leave in the spring. To commemorate the slaves' departure, the festival of Passover is ordained—so called because God has passed over the homes of the children of Israel when he smote the first-born of all men and beasts in the last and final plague. On Mount Sinai, the entire congregation of Israel receives the Torah, and a covenant is established between God and Israel. Moses then takes the blood shed for the covenant, and sprinkling it over the people, declares: "Behold the blood of the covenant, which the Lord hath made with you in agreement with all these words" (Exodus 24.8). The sacred celebration is marred, however, by the worship of the golden calf ; when Moses tarries before coming down the mount whither he has ascended to receive the tablets of the covenant, the people relapse into Egyptian idolatry. The calf-worshippers are severely punished, and God is placated by the intercession of Moses. As a result of the incident of the golden calf, God reveals to Moses the thirteen Divine attributes, and the loyal sons of Levi, who have refused to join in the idolatrous worship of the golden calf, are rewarded by being assigned to the Tabernacle and Temple service. Aaron and his sons are then chosen to head the tribe of Levi as priests. The book of Exodus closes with an account of the construction of the Tabernacle (also called the Tent of Meeting) and its vessels.

SHEMOT שמות

Moses trembles before the burning bush.

"And he looked, and, behold, the bush burned with fire, and the bush was not consumed" (Exod. 3.2).
"And Moses hid his face; for he was afraid to look upon God" (3.6).

Shemot — The children of Israel increased and multiplied and the land of Goshen was filled with them. But a new king arose in Egypt; one who had not known Joseph. He said to his people: "The children of Israel are too many and too mighty for us; come, let us deal wisely with them, lest they multiply, and it come to pass, that, when there befalleth us any war, they also join themselves unto our enemies, and fight against us, and get them up out of the land" (Exodus 1.9-10). The new Pharaoh made slaves of the Hebrews. He also commanded that every new-born male infant was to be cast into the river Nile. However, Moses was saved from this infanticide by the king's daughter and grew up in Pharaoh's court. He was forced to flee Egypt after slaying an Egyptian whom he found mistreating a Hebrew slave. Moses went to Midian, where he tended sheep for his father-in-law Jethro in the desert near mount Horeb. God appeared to Moses in a burning bush and told him to return to Egypt, for it was his mission to liberate the children of Israel and lead them to the land of Canaan. With the help of his brother Aaron, Moses united the Hebrew slaves into a people. Then he came before Pharaoh with God's demand that he "let My people go."

VAERA וארא

Moses and Aaron exhort Pharaoh to release the Israelites.

"And Moses and Aaron went in unto Pharaoh" (Exod. 7.10)
"The Lord, the God of the Hebrews, hath sent me unto thee, saying: Let My people go" (7.16).

Va-era — God told Moses that He had first appeared to Abraham, Isaac, and Jacob as *El Shaddai,* and had made a covenant with the patriarchs to give them the land of Canaan. Now, hearing the unhappy cry of the children of Israel, the Almighty was reminded of his covenant.

Pharaoh refused to let the children of Israel depart from the land of Egypt. God brought seven plagues on the Egyptians, in an attempt to force Pharaoh's hand: blood, frogs, gnats, flies, murrain, boils, and hail. At first Pharaoh conceded to Moses, "I and my people are wicked. Entreat the Lord, and let there be enough of these mighty thunderings and hail; and I will let you go" (Exodus 9.27-28). But, when the plagues stopped, Pharaoh's heart was hardened again, and he refused to let the Israelites go.

BO בא

Israelites hurriedly partake of paschal lamb. Egyptian first-born are slain by God.

"And ye shall eat it in haste — it is the Lord's passover" (Exod. 12.11).
"The Lord smote all the first-born in the land of Egypt" (12.29).

Bo — God sent Moses to Pharaoh once more with the following words: "Go in unto Pharaoh . . . and tell . . . him: '. . . If thou refuse to let My people go, behold, tomorrow will I bring locusts into thy border'" (Exodus 10.1-4). Pharaoh would not be moved. Then God punished Egypt with a thick darkness. Yet Pharaoh remained adamant. Finally, Moses warned the King of Egypt that God would send the most fearful plague of all, the death of all the first-born in the land, both of men and beasts. The Israelites were given the ordinance of the Passover, so named because God passed over the homes of the Israelites when he killed the first-born of the Egyptians, on midnight of the fifteenth day of the first month (Nissan). Pharaoh was shaken, at last. He sent the children of Israel from the land. They consisted of "about six hundred thousand men on foot, beside children". In their haste to leave Egypt, the Israelites baked *matzoth* from dough that was not leavened. Hence the prohibition against eating leavened bread on Passover.

BESHALAH   בשלח

The waters of the Red Sea divide to make a path for the Israelites.

"And the children of Israel went into the midst of the sea upon the dry ground; and the waters were a wall unto them on their right hand, and on their left" (Exod. 14. 22).

Beshalah — Fearful of the hostile tribes the Israelites might encounter on the direct route to Canaan through the land of the Philistines, God sent the newly-freed slaves by way of the desert near the Red Sea. As they journeyed, they were guided by a pillar of cloud by day and a pillar of fire by night. The Israelites had left Egypt presumably to worship their God in the desert. When Pharaoh learned that the children of Israel would not return to Egypt, he pursued them to the banks of the Red Sea at the head of an army of chosen troops. But a miracle occurred: the children of Israel were able to pass between the waves of the Red Sea that divided before them and stood upright like columns. The Egyptian hosts, plunging into the Red Sea after them, were all drowned. At this sight, the children of Israel sang a song of praise to God. On their journey through the desert, the children of Israel were sustained by manna from heaven; water issued from a rock for them at the bidding of God. The Amalekites did battle with the Israelites, but were defeated by Joshua, the son of Nun, and his men.

YITRO   יתרו

The revelation of the Law on Mount Sinai.

"And it came to pass on the third day, when it was morning, that there were thunders and lightnings and a thick cloud upon the mount, and the voice of a horn exceeding loud (Exod. 19.16).

Yitro — Word reached Jethro, Moses' father-in-law, and a priest of Midian, of what God had done for the Israelites. He went to meet Moses in the desert. Jethro advised Moses to appoint judges, in order to ease the burden of his sole leadership; Moses should confine himself to the most difficult questions.

In the third month, the children of Israel heard the Ten Commandments at Mount Sinai: God's voice declared: "I am the Lord thy God . . . Thou shalt have no other gods before Me. Thou shalt not make unto thee a graven image. . . . Thou shalt not take the name of the Lord thy God in vain. . . . Remember the sabbath day, to keep it holy. . . . Honor thy father and thy mother. . . . Thou shalt not murder. . . . Thou shalt not commit adultery. . . . Thou shalt not steal. . . . Thou shalt not bear false witness against thy neighbor. . . . Thou shalt not covet thy neighbor's house . . . wife . . . nor any thing that is thy neighbor's (Exodus 20.2-14).

MISHPATIM   משפטים

Moses instructs the Israelites in the divine Law.

"And he took the book of the covenant, and read in the hearing of the people; and they said: 'All that the Lord hath spoken will we do, and obey' " (Exod. 24.7).

Mishpatim — The laws that Moses submitted to the children of Israel after they had heard the Ten Commandments dealt with the following subjects:

The Hebrew servant; murder, filial aggression and blasphemy; kidnapping; criminal assault; maiming of a servant; the butting bull; accidents and damages; theft; property damage; watchmen; seduction; proselytes, the orphaned and the widowed; lending and borrowing; the sanctification of God and man; relations with the enemy; the Sabbatical year; the Sabbath; the three pilgrim festivals; idolatry.

This portion concludes with the renewal of the covenant with God. The children of Israel accepted the covenant with the words: "All that the Lord hath spoken will we do, and obey" (Exodus 24.7). Moses then ascended Mount Sinai to receive the tablets of the Law.

TERUMAH תרומה

The Tent of Meeting.

"Moreover thou shalt make the tabernacle with ten curtains"(Exod.26.1). "And thou shalt hang up the veil under the clasps, and shalt bring in thither within the veil the ark of the testimony" (26. 33).

Terumah — The children of Israel were asked for an offering toward the construction of the Tabernacle and its vessels: "Gold, and silver, and brass; and blue, and purple, and scarlet, and fine linen, and goats' hair; and rams' skins dyed red, and sealskins, and acacia-wood; oil for the light, spices for the anointing oil, and for the sweet incense; onyx stones, and stones to be set, for the ephod, and for the breastplate" (Exodus 25.3-7). The ark was to be made of acacia-wood, covered inside and out with gold. The table too was to be made of acacia-wood. There were to be a golden candelabra, a tent of curtains and boards, outer curtains and inner curtains, and an altar of acacia-wood, covered with copper. Finally, the construction of the court-yard of the Tabernacle was described.

TETZAVEH תצוה

Aaron in the robes of the High Priest, bearing incense. A menorah in the background.

"And thou shalt make holy garments for Aaron thy brother, for splendour and for beauty" (Exod. 28.2).

Tetzaveh — Moses was told: "Thou shalt command the children of Israel, that they bring unto thee pure olive oil beaten for the light, to cause a lamp to burn continually. In the tent of meeting, without the veil which is before the testimony, Aaron and his sons shall set it in order, to burn from evening to morning before the Lord." For Aaron and his sons were to serve as priests to God. The priestly garments are described in great detail, as well as the various offerings that the priests were to bring on the day of their anointment. This portion concludes with the laws relating to the offering of incense on the altar.

KI TISSA כי תשא

When Moses beholds the people worshipping the golden calf, he shatters the Tables of Law.

"As soon as . . . he saw the calf and the dancing . . . Moses' anger waxed hot, and he cast the tables out of his hands" (Exod. 32.19).

Ki Tissa — The children of Israel were counted and each man over 20 years of age contributed half a shekel as "ransom". Bezalel, son of Uri, and Oholiab, son of Ahisamach, were appointed to head the artisans who made the Tabernacle and its vessels. The Israelites were warned not to violate the Sabbath day.

God gave Moses two tablets of stone containing the Ten Commandments, written "with the finger of God." However, to the impatient Israelites, Moses seemed to be tarrying too long on the mountain. They made a golden calf, which Moses found them worshipping. In his fury, he broke the two tablets of the Law. The idolaters were killed by the members of the loyal tribe of Levi. Moses prayed successfully to God to spare the children of Israel despite their backsliding. He ascended mount Sinai again, and there received a new set of stone tablets. When he descended, "The skin of Moses' face sent forth beams; and Moses put the veil back upon his face, until he went in to speak with Him" (Exodus 34.35).

VAYAKHEL ויקהל

The people bring a profusion of gifts for the tabernacle—until they are told to cease.

"And they came, both men and women, as many as were willing-hearted, and brought . . . all jewels of gold" (Exod. 35.22).

Vayakhel — Moses gathered the people together and instructed them in the holiness of the Sabbath. He also instructed them in how to build the Tabernacle and its vessels. Bezalel and Oholiab headed the skilled craftsmen working on the Tabernacle. The people gave liberally toward the sanctuary—so liberally, in fact, that it was necessary to ask them to stop. Once again, the details of the Tabernacle and its vessels are given, at the end of this portion.

PEKUDE פקודי

The cloud covers the completed tabernacle as the Israelites stand in the distance.

"Then the cloud covered the tent of meeting, and the glory of the Lord filled the tabernacle" (Exod. 40.34).

Pekude — "These are the accounts of the Tabernacle, even the Tabernacle of the testimony, as they were rendered according to the commandment of Moses, through the service of the Levites, by the hand of Ithamar, the son of Aaron the priest" (Exodus 38.21). "All the gold that was used for the work . . . was twenty and nine talents, and seven hundred and thirty shekels, after the shekel of the sanctuary. And the silver of them that were numbered of the congregation was a hundred talents, and a thousand seven hundred and three-score and fifteen shekels" (Exodus 38. 24-25). "And of the blue, and of purple, and scarlet, they made plaited garments, for ministering in the holy place " (Exodus 39.1).

With the conclusion of the Tabernacle, Moses blessed the children of Israel.

On the first day of the first month in the second year since the departure of the children of Israel from Egypt the Tabernacle was set up. A cloud covered it and the glory of God filled the Tabernacle. When the cloud rose, the children of Israel continued on their journey through the desert toward the Promised Land.

Priests engaged in the service of the Sanctuary.

"And Moses brought Aaron's sons, and clothed them with tunics, and girded them with girdles, and bound head-tires upon them; as the Lord commanded Moses"
(Leviticus 8.13).

LEVITICUS   ויקרא

The third book of the Pentateuch opens with God's call to Moses from the Tent of Meeting to receive the laws relating to sacrifices. Essentially, this book contains the laws of holiness, i.e., those laws which prescribe how both God and Israel are to be sanctified. "Ye shall be holy; for I the Lord your God am holy" (Leviticus 19.2). Since the major part of the book is devoted to the priestly service, it is also known as the book of the Priestly Code. Besides describing the sacrificial laws, Leviticus also tells of the offerings Aaron and his sons made in their worship at the altar; explains which animals may be eaten and which not; how human beings become defiled and how they may be cleansed; and the nature of the festivals to be known as "convocations of holiness." This book describes the sanctified fallow and jubilee years, and notes the blessings which follow from the observance of the ways of God, and the curses that result from their non-observance. Leviticus sums up: "These are the commandments, which the Lord commanded Moses for the children of Israel in mount Sinai" (Leviticus 27.34).

VAYIKRA ויקרא

Two lambs offered as a sacrifice in atonement for a sin.

"And he shall bring forfeit unto the Lord for his sin which he hath sinned" (Lev. 5.6).

Vayikra — God called to Moses from the tent of meeting and revealed the sacrificial laws. The burnt-offering was to consist of a male animal without blemish; if it be a fowl, it was to be a turtle-dove or a young pigeon. The purpose of this offering, which was to be completely burned, was to make atonement for evil thoughts. The meal-offering was to consist of fine flour, raw, cooked, or stewed, generally intended as a free-will offering. The peace-offering, of cattle or sheep, either male or female, was another free-will offering, or vow, offered in the name of a family. The sin-offering was intended to make amends for sins committed by error. Different categories of individuals and groups were to sacrifice different animals for sin-offerings. The anointed priest and the congregation offered a young bullock, the prince a he-goat, a common person a she-goat. The person who touched an unclean object, or failed to keep a vow, must bring a female lamb or a female goat for a sin-offering; and if he could not afford either, he must bring two young pigeons or turtle-doves—the first as a burnt-offering, the second as a sin-offering. A ram served as a guilt-offering in the case of a violation of a negative ("Thou shalt not") commandment, or in cases of theft of articles set aside as holy.

TZAV צו

Moses anoints Aaron and his sons as priests.

"And he poured of the anointing oil upon Aaron's head, and anointed him, to sanctify him" (Lev. 8.12).

Tzav — An elaboration of the sacrificial laws: the burnt-offering, the meal offering, the sin-offering; guilt-offering and peace-offering. Moses consecrated Aaron and his sons for the priesthood: he made their offerings of consecration, sprinkled them with the oil of anointment, and taught them the order of sacrifice "And at the door of the tent of meeting shall ye abide day and night seven days, and keep the charge of the Lord, that ye die not; for so I am commanded" (Leviticus 8.35).

SHEMINI שמיני

Kosher and non-kosher animals arrayed opposite each other.

"These shall ye not eat of them . . . the camel . . . the rock-badger . . . the hare . . . the swine . . . they are unclean unto you" (Lev. 11.4-8).

Shemini — On the eighth day of their consecration, Aaron and his sons offered sacrifices for themselves and the people, at Moses' command. Then Moses and Aaron came out of the tent of meeting, blessing the people. The glory of God appeared; a fire from Heaven consumed the burnt-offering on the altar. At the sight, the people cried out and fell on their faces. Nadab and Abihu, Aaron's sons, offered "strange fire" on the altar; a fire issued forth and devoured them. Aaron held his peace.

The priests are commanded not to drink wine or strong drink when entering the tent of meeting "that ye may put difference between the holy and the common, and between the unclean and the clean" (Leviticus 10.10).

The portion details the laws describing cleanliness and uncleanliness in regard to the eating of animals, fowls, and fish.

TAZRIA תזריע

A woman with new-born child offers a sacrifice.

"And if her means suffice not for a lamb, then she shall take two turtle-doves, or two young pigeons" (Lev. 12.8).

Tazria — Cleanliness and uncleanliness are further defined, here in relation to childbirth and leprosy. "If a woman be delivered, and bear a man-child, then she shall be unclean seven days . . . And she shall continue in the blood of purification three and thirty days . . . But if she bear a maid-child, then she shall be unclean two weeks . . . and she shall continue in the blood of purification threescore and six days. And when the days of her purification are fulfilled . . . she shall bring a lamb of the first year for a burnt-offering, and a young pigeon, or a turtle-dove, for a sin-offering, unto the door of the tent of meeting, unto the priest" (Leviticus 12.2-6). Suspected lepers are to be brought to the priest, who quarantines the case for seven days. A careful description of the varieties of leprosy is followed by rules for the leper's identification and isolation. "And the leper in whom the plague is, his clothes shall be rent, and the hair of his head shall go loose, and he shall cover his upper lip, and shall cry: 'Unclean, unclean.' All the days wherein the plague is in him he shall be unclean; he is unclean; he shall dwell alone; without the camp shall his dwelling be" (Leviticus 13.45-46).

METZORA   מצורע

A leper is brought before the priest.

"And the priest shall look, and, behold, if the plague of leprosy be healed in the leper" (Lev. 13.3).

Metzora — This portion describes the laws for the purification of the leper after he is healed. "Then shall the priest command to take for him that is to be cleansed two living clean birds, and cedar-wood, and scarlet, and hyssop. And the priest shall command to kill one of the birds in an earthen vessel over running water. As for the living bird, he shall take it, and the cedar-wood, and the scarlet, and the hyssop, and shall dip them and the living bird in the blood of the bird that was killed over the running water. And he shall sprinkle upon him that is to be cleansed from the leprosy seven times, and shall pronounce him clean, and shall let go the living bird into the open field. And he that is to be cleansed shall wash his clothes, and shave off all his hair, and bathe himself in water, and he shall be clean; and after that he may come into the camp, but

shall dwell outside his tent seven days. And it shall be on the seventh day, that he shall shave all his hair off his head and his beard and his eyebrows . . . and he shall bathe his flesh in water, and he shall be clean" (Leviticus 14.4-9). Finally, after bringing an offering to the priest on the eighth day, the former leper shall be formally clean.

Leprosy was understood to affect objects as well as people. The portion describes the various cases of leprosy and prescribes their treatment: "This is the law for all manner of plague of leprosy, and for a scall; and for the leprosy of a garment, and for a house; and for a rising, and for a scab, and for a bright spot; to teach when it is unclean, and when it is clean; this is the law of leprosy" (Leviticus (14.54-57).

AHARE MOT   אחרי מות

The High Priest on the Day of Atonement chooses by lot a goat and scapegoat.

"And Aaron shall cast lots upon the two goats: one lot for the Lord, and the other lot for Azazel" (Lev. 16.8).

Ahare Mot — After the death of Aaron's two sons, God said to Moses: "Speak unto Aaron thy brother, that he come not at all times into the holy place within the veil, before the ark-cover which is upon the ark; that he die not; for I appear in the cloud upon the ark-cover" (Leviticus 16.2). Only on the Day of Atonement, "the tenth day of the seventh month" may Aaron enter the Holy of Holies, entirely alone, to "make atonement for the holy place, because of the uncleannesses of the children of Israel." Aaron was to bring a bullock as a sin-offering and a ram as a burnt-offering. He was to accept from the children of Israel two he-goats for a sin-offering and a ram for a burnt-offering. One of the goats was to be chosen by lot as a sin-offering to God; the other was to be dispatched to the desert, (to Azazel), a scapegoat carrying the sins of the children of Israel.

The portion enumerates the laws prohibiting the consuming of blood. It concludes with regulations pertaining to sexual morality.

KEDOSHIM קדושים

The Jew views the giving of alms as one aspect of social justice.

"Ye shall do no unright-eousness in judgment, in meteyard, in weight, or in measure. Just balances, just weights . . . shall ye have" (Lev. 19.35-36 .

Kedoshim — "Ye shall be holy; for I the Lord your God am holy. Ye shall fear every man his mother, and his father, and ye shall keep My sabbaths. . . . Turn ye not unto the idols . . . And when ye reap the harvest of your land, thou shalt not wholly reap the corner of thy field . . . neither shalt thou gather the fallen fruit of thy vineyard; thou shalt leave them for the poor and the stranger. . . . Ye shall not steal; neither shall ye deal falsely, nor lie one to another. And ye shall not swear by My name falsely. . . . Thou shalt not oppress thy neighbor, nor rob him; the wages of a hired servant shall not abide with thee all night until morning. Thou shalt not curse the deal, nor put a stumbling-block before the blind. . . . Ye shall do no unrighteousness in judgment. . . . Thou shalt not go up and down as a talebearer . . . neither shalt thou stand idly by the blood of thy neighbor. . . . Thou shalt love thy neighbor as thyself" (Leviticus 19.2-18). "Ye shall be holy unto Me; for I the Lord am holy, and have set you apart from the peoples, that ye should be Mine" (Leviticus 20.26).

EMOR אמור

Festival symbols: Matza, Lulav, Etrog, Shofar, Book of Remembrance.

"Seven days ye shall eat unleavened bread" (Lev. 23.6).
". . . a memorial . . . blast of horns . . ." (23.23). ". . . . the fruit of goodly trees" (23.40).

Emor — "And the Lord said unto Moses: Speak unto the priests the sons of Aaron, and say unto

them: There shall none defile himself for the dead among his people; except for his kin that is near unto him, for his mother, and for his father, and for his son, and for his daughter, and for his brother; and for his sister a virgin. . . . They shall not take a woman that is a harlot, or profaned; neither shall they take a woman put away from her husband" (Leviticus 21.1-7). The high priest "shall take a wife in her virginity. A widow, or one divorced, or a profaned woman, or a harlot, these shall he not take" (Leviticus 21.13-14). No priest with a blemish might approach the altar to offer a sacrifice—the impure priest might not even approach the holy food nor eat it. No animal with a blemish might be an offering.

The seasons of the holy convocations are then described: "The seventh day is a sabbath of solemn rest . . . ye shall do no manner of work . . . In the first month, on the fourteenth day . . . at dusk, is the Lord's passover. . . on the fifteenth day of the same month is the feast of unleavened bread . . . seven days ye shall eat unleavened bread" (Leviticus 23.3-6). The festival of the First Fruits (Shavuot) occurs on the fiftieth day after the first day of Passover. "In the seventh month, in the first day of the month, shall be a solemn rest unto you, a memorial proclaimed with the blast of horns, a holy convocation. Ye shall do no manner of servile work. . . . Howbeit on the tenth day of this seventh month is the day of atonement . . . and ye shall afflict your souls. . . . And ye shall do no manner of work in that same day; for it is a day of atonement, to make atonement for you before the Lord your God. . . . On the fifteenth day of this seventh month is the feast of tabernacles for seven days unto the Lord" (Leviticus 23.24-34).

"And ye shall take you on the first day the fruit of goodly trees, branches of palm-trees, and boughs of thick trees, and willows of the brook, and ye shall rejoice before the Lord your God . . . it is a statute for ever in your generations . . . And Moses declared unto the children of Israel the appointed seasons of the Lord" (Leviticus 23.40-41, 44).

BEHAR בהר

Fields lie fallow each seventh year. Shofar proclaims fiftieth year as Jubilee.

"The seventh year shall be a sabbath . . . neither sow thy field . . ." (Lev. 25.4). ". . . hallow the fiftieth year and proclaim liberty throughout the land (25.10).

Behar — "And the Lord spoke unto Moses in mount Sinai, saying. . . . When ye come into the land which I give you, then shall the land keep a sabbath unto the Lord. . . . in the seventh year shall be a sabbath of solemn rest for the land . . . thou shalt neither sow thy field, nor prune thy vineyard. . . . And the sabbath-produce of the land shall be for food for you: for thee, and for thy servant and for thy maid, and for thy hired servant and for the settler by thy side that sojourn with thee; and for thy cattle, and for the beasts that are in thy land: (Leviticus 25.1-7). Following seven sabbatical years, the 50th year is to be observed as a jubilee. "That which groweth of itself of thy harvest thou shalt not reap" (Leviticus 25.5). Scripture then states "And ye shall hallow the fiftieth year, and proclaim liberty throughout the land unto all the inhabitants thereof; it shall be a jubilee unto you. . . . Ye shall return every man unto his possession" (Leviticus 25.10-11).

The same laws pertaining to the sabbatical year hold true of the jubilee. In addition, all fields return to their original owners; every Hebrew slave is free to return to his home. A Hebrew slave can always be redeemed; if he is not redeemed, he goes free in the jubilee year.

"And if thy brother be waxen poor, and his means fail with thee; then thou shalt uphold him: as a stranger and a settler shall he live with thee. Take thou no interest of him or increase; but fear thy God; that thy brother may live with thee. Thou shalt not give him thy money upon interest, nor give him thy victuals for increase (Leviticus 25.35-37).

BEHUKKOTAI בחקותי

God's punishment: Jews leave flourishing fields and go into exile.

"But if ye will not hearken unto Me . . . I will bring the land into desolation . . . And you will I scatter among the nations" (Lev. 26.14, 32-33).

Behukkotai — "If ye walk in My statutes, and keep My commandments, and do them; then I will give you rains in their season, and the land shall yield her produce, and the trees of the field shall yield their fruit. . . . Ye shall eat your bread until ye have enough, and dwell in your land safely. . . . And I will have respect unto you, and make you fruitful, and multiply you; and will establish My covenant with you. . . . But if . . . ye shall reject My statutes, and if your soul abhor Mine ordinances, so that ye shall not do all My commandments, but break My covenant . . . I will chastise you seven times more for your sins. . . . And you will I scatter among the nations, and I will draw out the sword after you; and your land shall be a desolation. . . . When they are in the land of their enemies, I will not reject them . . . to break My covenant with them; for I am the Lord their God. . . . These are the statutes and ordinances and laws, which the Lord made between Him and the children of Israel in mount Sinai by the hand of Moses" (Leviticus 26.3-46).

The Israelites encamped under their standards in the wilderness.

"And the children of Israel shall pitch their tents, every man with his own camp, and every man with his own standard, according to their hosts" (Numbers 1.52).

NUMBERS

במדבר

The fourth book opens with God speaking to Moses "in the wilderness of Sinai in the tent of meeting, on the first day of the second month, in the second year after they were come out of the land of Egypt." God directs Moses to carry out a census, and to align the tribes in four large encampments under special standards during the journey to Canaan. Hence, this book's title, Numbers. Numbers also includes a detailed account of the functions of the Levites who bore the Tabernacle through the wilderness. In great detail, the dedication of the Tabernacle, the sacrifices made by the tribal heads, and Aaron's lighting of the lamps of the menorah are related.

Three weeks later, the Israelites continue on their journey, leaving the wilderness of Sinai behind them. At the threshold of the Promised Land the camp is disturbed by the exaggeratedly fearful reports of scouts sent ahead to spy out the land. As a result of the people's lack of faith in God at this time, they are doomed to continual wandering through the desert for another 38 years, until the entire generation "of little faith" shall have died out. Of this period nothing is related, for God does not reveal Himself again until the fixed years of wandering are over and the journey to the land of Canaan is resumed.

This time the Hebrews, instead of entering Canaan directly from the west, through Kadesh-barnea, circle to the east of Canaan. In Transjordan they conquer the lands of Sihon, the king of the Amorites, and Og, the king of Bashan. Then they camp "in the plains of Moab beyond the Jordan at Jericho" (Numbers 22.1). During their wanderings they receive new laws, which deal with a delayed Passover, vows and pledges, fringes on their garments, heave-offerings and tithes, the red heifer purification, the division of the land, holy day offerings, the abrogation of vows, the division of Transjordanian territory, the boundaries of the land, the men chosen to divide the land, and the cities of refuge. The book ends with the usual summary formula: "These are the commandments and the ordinances, which the Lord commanded by the hand of Moses unto the children of Israel in the plains of Moab by the Jordan at Jericho" (Numbers 36.13).

BAMIDBAR במדבר

Israelites encamp under standards bearing symbols of the ox, eagle, lion and man.

"A good way off shall they pitch round about the tent of meeting" (Num. 2.2).

Bamidbar — "And the Lord spoke unto Moses in the wilderness of Sinai, in the tent of meeting, on the first day of the second month, in the second year after they were come out of the land of Egypt, saying: 'Take ye the sum of all the congregation of the children of Israel, by their families, by their fathers' houses, according to the number of names, every male, by their polls; from twenty years old and upward, all that are able to go forth to war in Israel: ye shall number them by their hosts, even thou and Aaron'" (Numbers 1.1-3). Exclusive of the Levites, who were not numbered, the total sum of men of military age was 603,555. There follows a description of the Israelites' encampments during their journeys through the desert: there were four major camps, each of three tribes; one under the flag of Judah, one under the flag of Reuben, one under the flag of Ephraim, and one under the flag of Dan. The Levites camped separately near the sanctuary; among the Levites, each clan had a particular service to render in regard to the sanctuary.

NASO נשא

The priest blesses the people in accordance with divine instruction.

"Ye shall bless the children of Israel, ye shall say unto them: The Lord bless thee, and keep thee" (Num. 6.23-24).

Naso — The number of Levites between 30 and 50 years of age eligible to worship and minister in the tent of meeting was 8,580. All those per-

sons considered unclean—either because they were lepers, or had a discharge, or had touched a corpse—were expelled from the camp. Thereafter, follow the regulations affecting adultery and the Nazirites; and the account of the various offerings made by the princes of the tribes after the tabernacle was finally constructed.

BEHAALOTEKHA בהעלותך

The Menorah with its seven flames converging toward the center.

"When thou lightest the lamps, the seven lamps shall give light in front of the candlestick" (Num. 8.2).

Behaalotekha — "And the Lord spoke unto Moses, saying: 'Speak unto Aaron, and say unto him: When thou lightest the lamps, the seven lamps shall give light in front of the candlestick.' . . . And this was the work of the candlestick, beaten work of gold; unto the base thereof, and unto the flowers thereof, it was beaten work; according unto the pattern which the Lord had shown Moses, so he made the candlestick" (Numbers 8.1-4). After the Levites had been purified, they who were between their twenty-fifth (Numbers 8.24) and their fiftieth years, came to the tent of meeting to take the place of the firstborn in the holy service. In the second year after the Israelites had departed from Egypt, they observed the Passover festival on the 14th day of the first month, Nissan. Those who having touched a corpse were deemed impure, were required to wait a month to observe the festival. On the 20th day of the second month, the cloud rose from the tabernacle, and the children of Israel journeyed from mount Sinai, each tribe grouped around its standard, three days' distance behind the Ark. At this time, the Israelites began burdening Moses with their complaints. To ease the burden, 70 elders, on whom Moses' spirit rested, were delegated to serve under him.

SHELAH שלח

The spies return from Canaan bearing a cluster of grapes.

"And they came unto the valley of Eshcol, and cut down . . . one cluster of grapes, and they bore it upon a pole" (Num. 13.23).

Shelah — At Kadesh, in the wilderness of Paran, the children of Israel asked Moses to send forth scouts to reconnoiter the land of Canaan. When God consented, twelve spies were dispatched, one from each tribe, with specific instructions. Forty days later, the spies returned bearing the fruit of the land, as evidence of its fertility. But most of them came back with a pessimistic report: the natives of Canaan were mighty men, the cities strongly fortified. It was a land that "eateth up the inhabitants thereof" (Numbers 13.32). Of all the spies, only Joshua, the son of Nun, of the tribe of Ephraim, and Caleb, the son of Jephunneh, of the tribe of Judah, declared there was nothing to fear from the natives of Canaan. The Israelites, frightened by the fearful majority report, cried tearfully: "Were it not better for us to return into Egypt?" (Numbers 14.3). God grew wrathful at this lack of confidence in Him, and would have destroyed the entire congregation, were it not for Moses' intercession. However, He vowed that before the Israelites might enter the Promised Land they would wander in the desert for 40 years, until the entire rebellious generation — those above 20 years of age — should perish.

KORAH קרח

The earth cleaves asunder and swallows up Korah and his assembly.

"And the earth opened her mouth, and swallowed them up . . . and all the men that appertained unto Korah" (Num. 16.32).

Korah — Korah, son of Izhar, and Dathan and Abiram, sons of Eliab, led a rebellion of 250 men who refused to accept the leadership of Moses and Aaron. Moses tried in vain to persuade them that all was being done according to God's will. Finally, God Himself acted. "And it came to pass . . . that the ground did cleave asunder that was under them. And the earth opened her mouth, and swallowed them up, and their households, and all the men that appertained unto Korah, and all their goods. So they . . . went down alive into the pit; and the earth closed upon them, and they perished from among the assembly . . . And fire came forth from the Lord, and devoured the two hundred and fifty men" (Numbers 16.31-35). To prove that Aaron had indeed been chosen by God for his priestly function, Moses instructed every tribe to place its rod near the Ark of the Covenant; miraculously, Aaron's rod sprouted. Thus ended the controversy over the priesthood. The portion proceeds to describe the various emoluments that the priests and Levites received.

HUKKAT חקת

Moses strikes the rock with his staff and water gushes forth.

"And Moses . . . smote the rock with his rod twice; and water came forth abundantly" (Num. 20.11).

Hukkat — The portion begins with "the statute of the law" of the red heifer, whose ashes "shall be kept for the congregation of Israel as a water of sprinkling . . . a purification from sin" (Numbers 19.9). At the outset of their fortieth year in the wilderness, the children of Israel reached the desert of Zin and halted at Kadesh. There Miriam died. When the water gave out, God instructed Moses and Aaron to gather the Israelites before a rock; Moses was to speak to the rock, and it would gush water. But Moses, irritated at the people's complaints, struck the rock with his rod. For this lack of faith in the divine power, Moses and Aaron were punished with never being able to enter the Promised Land. From Kadesh the children of Israel moved on to mount Hor, where Aaron died. Thence they circled the land of Edom, and arrived at Transjordan from the east, defeating the forces of Sihon, king of the Amorites, and Og, king of Bashan.

BALAK בלק

Balaam views the tents of Israel and predicts a blessed future.

"And Balaam . . . saw Israel . . . and said: . . . How goodly are thy tents, O Jacob, thy dwellings, O Israel" (Num. 24.2-5).

Balak — Hearing of the Israelites' victory over the Amorites, Balak, king of Moab, became frightened. Jointly with the elders of Midian, he sent messengers to Balaam, the son of Beor, urging him to curse Israel. Balaam was both a soothsayer and a prophet, and it was believed that his curse would lead to the defeat of the Israelites. But Balaam, hearkening to the voice of God, twice refused to accompany Balak's messengers on the hostile mission. Finally God said to Balaam: "Go with the men; but only the word that I shall speak unto thee, that thou shalt speak" (Numbers 22.35). En route to Balak, an angel warned Balaam. When he arrived, he had Balak build seven altars and make appropriate sacrificial offerings preliminary to Balaam's cursing Israel. But when the time came, Balaam gave the Israelites his blessing instead of his curse. This reversal was repeated three times.

Moabite and Midianite women seduced some of the Israelites, persuading them to worship the idol Baal of Peor. As a result, a plague broke out in the Israelite camp. The plague ceased only when Phinehas stabbed an Israelite man to death for consorting with a Midianite woman.

PHINEHAS פנחס

Moses chooses Joshua as his successor in the presence of the army.

"And he took Joshua . . . before Eleazar . . . and . . . the congregation. And he laid his hands upon him" (Num. 27.22-23).

Phinehas — "And the Lord spoke unto Moses,

saying: 'Phinehas, the son of Eleazar, the son of Aaron the priest, hath turned My wrath away from the children of Israel, in that he was very jealous for My sake among them, so that I consumed not the children of Israel in My jealousy. Wherefore say: Behold, I give unto him My covenant of peace; and it shall be unto him, and to his seed after him, the covenant of an everlasting priesthood' " (Numbers 25.10-13). The children of Israel were commanded to do battle with the Midianites. Moses was instructed to give the daughters of Zelophehad the inheritance of their father, who had died without sons. Moses ordained Joshua as his successor. The portion concludes with a description of the observance of the various holy days.

MATTOT מטות

Map of the tribes of Gad, Reuben and the half-tribe of Manasseh in Transjordan.

"And Moses gave unto . . . Gad . . . Reuben and unto the half-tribe of Manasseh . . . the kingdom of Sihon" (Num. 32.33).

Mattot — Moses informed the tribal heads regarding the laws concerning vows. He sent 12,000 armed men (1,000 from each tribe) to war with the Midianites. The expedition was successful. Among those killed was Balaam. The tribes of Reuben and Gad, who had large herds of cattle, asked to be allowed to settle on grazing land in Transjordan. Moses agreed, on condition that these tribes lead the other tribes across the Jordan, and not return to Transjordan until all their brother tribes had been provided for. Part of the tribe of Manasseh conquered half of Gilead, and were granted it for their territory.

MASE מסעי

A man flees to one of the six cities of refuge to escape an avenging slayer. (Map)

"Three cities beyond the Jordan, and three cities . . . in . . . Canaan; they shall be cities of refuge" (Num. 35.14).

Mase — The portion begins with a detailed account of the various way stations on the Israelites' route to the Promised Land, from the time they left Egypt until they reached the plains of Moab, by the Jordan at Jericho. Instructions concerning the apportionment of the land followed. "And ye shall inherit the land by lot according to your families—to the more ye shall give the more inheritance, and to the fewer thou shalt give the less inheritance; wheresoever the lot falleth to any man, that shall be his" (Numbers 33.54). It was necessary that all the Canaanites be expelled. "But if ye will not drive out the inhabitants of the land from before you, then shall those that ye let remain of them be as thorns in your eyes, and as pricks in your sides, and they shall harass you in the land wherein ye dwell" (Numbers 33.55).

The portion gives specific instructions concerning the boundary lines and lists the names of the persons who should divide the land. The Israelites are commanded to set aside 48 cities and surrounding lands for the Levites, who have not been given territory as the other tribes were. Reference is made to the cities of refuge where the accidental murderer might flee for safety. The portion, and book of Numbers, ends with an injunction prohibiting the transfer of inherited land from one tribe to another through inter-tribal marriage.

Moses transmits to Joshua the sacred Scroll in the presence of the children of Israel.

"And Moses called unto Joshua, and said unto him in the sight of all Israel: 'Be strong and of good courage; for thou shalt go with this people into the land which the Lord hath sworn unto their fathers to give them'" (Deuteronomy 31.7).

DEUTERONOMY   דברים

The fifth, and last, book of the Pentateuch opens with Moses addressing the children of Israel in Transjordan in the 40th year of the 11th month since their departure from Egypt. The purpose of his address is twofold: first, to review, clarify, and complete the law; and second, to encourage the Israelites to achieve their great goal—the conquest of the Land of Canaan on the other side of the Jordan. Hence, this book is also called *Mishneh Torah,* or Repetition of the Law.

In solemn accents Moses first reviews the history of the wanderings through the desert and then recapitulates and fills in gaps in the legislation previously transmitted. Warning the children of Israel to shun apostasy, Moses renews the covenant between God and man: "that thou shouldest enter into the covenant of the Lord thy God—and into His oath—which the Lord thy God maketh with thee this day; that He may establish thee this day unto Himself for a people, and that He may be unto thee a God, as He spoke unto thee" (Deuteronomy 29.11-12). Moses writes down the Law, and entrusts it for safekeeping to the priests, Levites, and elders of Israel.

Deuteronomy concludes with the song of Moses beginning with the words "Give ear, ye heavens, and I will speak". Here Moses prophetically describes the future relationship between God and Israel. Then he blesses the tribes of Israel and dies. Deuteronomy closes with the brief but moving characterization of Moses: "There hath not arisen a prophet since in Israel like unto Moses, whom the Lord knew face to face" (Deuteronomy 34.10).

DEVARIM דברים

Moses explains and interprets the Law to the people.

"Beyond the Jordan, in the land of Moab, took Moses upon him to expound this law" (Deut. 1.5).

Devarim — The first few verses introduce the entire book of Deuteronomy, which contains Moses' address to the Israelites in Transjordan after the defeat of the Amorites and Bashan. In this speech Moses summarizes the Torah as a whole. He reviews the causes that had led him to appoint judges and officials: "How can I myself alone bear your cumbrance, and your burden, and your strife? . . . And I charged your judges at that time, saying: 'Hear the causes between your brethren, and judge righteously between a man and his brother, and the stranger that is with him. Ye shall not respect persons in judgment; ye shall hear the small and the great alike'" (Deuteronomy 1.12-17).

Moses goes on to review the incident of the scouts sent to spy on Canaan, and the consequences of their pessimistic report. He reminds the Israelites how they had skirted Edom, Ammon, and Moab; and mentions the peoples who had formerly inhabited those regions. Finally, he recounts the story of the conquest of Transjordan, and the partition of the area between the tribes of Reuben, Gad, and half of the tribe of Manasseh.

Land, and God's refusal. The law-giver warns the children of Israel against practising idolatry in Canaan, calling their attention to their special history and mission. "Did ever a people hear the voice of God speaking out of the midst of the fire, as thou hast heard, and live? Or hath God assayed to go and take Him a nation from the midst of another nation, by trials, by signs, and by wonders, and by war, and by a mighty hand, and by an outstretched arm, and by great terrors, according to all that the Lord your God did for you in Egypt before thine eyes?" (Deuteronomy 4.33-34). Moses sets aside three cities of refuge on the east side of the Jordan. He repeats the Ten Commandments, with slight variations for the purpose of clarity. The first section of the Shema beginning "Thou shalt love the Lord thy God with all thy heart" and ending "And thou shalt write them upon the door-posts of thy house, and upon thy gates" is in this portion (Deuteronomy 6.4-9). Moses urges the Israelites to show no mercy to the seven Canaanite nations. "And when the Lord thy God shall deliver them up before thee, and thou shalt smite them; then thou shalt utterly destroy them; thou shalt make no covenant with them, nor show mercy unto them; neither shalt thou make marriages with them: thy daughter thou shalt not give unto his son, nor his daughter shalt thou take unto thy son . . . For thou art a holy people unto the Lord thy God: the Lord thy God hath chosen thee to be His own treasure, out of all peoples that are upon the face of the earth" (Deuteronomy 7.2-6). Finally, Moses stresses the need for strict observance of the various ritual commandments.

VAETHANAN ואתחנן

A Jew recites the Shema.

"Hear, O Israel: the Lord our God, the Lord is One" (Deut. 6.4).

Vaethanan — The portion begins with Moses' plea to God for permission to enter the Promised

EKEV עקב

The seven fruits of Israel: wheat, barley, grapes, figs, pomegranates, olives, dates.

"For the Lord thy God bringeth thee unto a good land . . . a land of wheat and barley . . . a land of olive-trees and honey" (Deut. 8.7-8).

Ekev — Moses declares: "And it shall come to pass, because ye hearken to these ordinances, and keep, and do them, that the Lord thy God shall keep with thee the covenant and the mercy which He swore unto thy fathers, and He will love thee, and bless thee, and multiply thee" (Deuteronomy 7.12-13). The Israelites are not to fear the Canaanite nations: witness the providence and supervision of God over His people in the desert, though they sinned. In passing, Moses makes a general reference to the incident of the Golden Calf. The Israelites were not to inherit the land of Canaan because of their own virtues: "Not for thy righteousness, or for the uprightness of thy heart, dost thou go in to possess their land; but for the wickedness of these nations the Lord thy God doth drive them out from before thee, and that He may establish the word which the Lord swore unto thy fathers" (Deuteronomy 9.5). After mentioning God's powerful miracles in Egypt and the desert (particularly in reference to Dathan and Abiram), Moses dwells on the importance of the Promised Land. The portion continues with the second part of the Shema, beginning "And it shall come to pass, if ye shall harken diligently unto My commandments" and ending "that your days may be multiplied, and the days of your children, upon the land which the Lord swore unto your fathers to give them, as the days of the heavens above the earth"(Deuteronomy 11.13-21). And the portion concludes with the promise: "There shall no man be able to stand against you: the Lord your God shall lay the fear of you and the dread of you upon all the land that ye shall tread upon, as He hath spoken unto you" (Deuteronomy 11.25).

RE'EH ‏ראה‏

Six tribes each, atop mount Ebal and mount Gerizim, with the Ark in the valley between.

"Thou shalt set the blessing upon mount Gerizim, and the curse upon mount Ebal" (Deut. 11.29).

Re'eh — "Behold, I set before you this day a blessing and a curse: the blessing, if ye shall hearken unto the commandments of the Lord your God, which I command you this day; and the curse, if ye shall not hearken" (Deuteronomy 11.26). When the Israelites enter Canaan, six tribes are to stand upon Mount Gerizim and bless all those who will keep God's commandments,

and six tribes are to stand on Mount Ebal and curse all those who will disobey God's commandments.

Sacrifices are to be offffered only in the place that God shall choose. He who wishes to offer a meat sacrifice which he may eat, and lives too far from the proper place of offering, may slaughter the offering in his own house, but it will not be considered a sacrifice. He must be careful not to consume any of the blood.

Those who incite others to idolatrous acts are to be exterminated. The portion goes on to state the rules defining purity and impurity in regard to animals, fish and fowl—the basic ritual dietary laws. The portion also contains the rules regarding tithes, money moratoria, a prohibition on interest, and regulations regarding the Hebrew slave, the first-born of animals, and the three pilgrim festivals.

SHOFETIM ‏שופטים‏

A prophet anoints a king from among his brethren.

"Thou shalt . . . set him king over thee, whom the Lord thy God shall choose; one from among thy brethren" (Deut. 17. 15).

Shofetim — "Judges and officers shalt thou make thee in all thy gates, which the Lord thy God giveth thee, tribe by tribe; and they shall judge the people with righteous judgment. . . . Thou shalt not plant thee an Asherah of any kind of tree beside the altar of the Lord thy God, which thou shalt make thee. Neither shalt thou set thee up a pillar, which the Lord thy God hateth" (Deuteronomy 16.18-22)."At the mouth of two witnesses, or three witnesses, shall he that is to die be put to death; at the mouth of one witness he shall not be put to death" (Deuteronomy 17.6). "If there arise a matter too hard for thee in judgment . . . thou shalt arise, and get thee up unto the place which the Lord thy God shall choose. . . . And thou shalt do according to the tenor of the sentence, which they shall declare unto thee from that place which the Lord shall choose" (Deuteronomy 17.8-9).

If, like the other nations, the children of Israel in Canaan should desire a king, "Thou shalt in any wise set him king over thee, whom the Lord thy God shall choose; one from among thy brethren shalt thou set king over thee; thou mayest not put a foreigner over thee, who is not thy brother. Only he shall not multiply horses to himself. . . . Neither shall he multiply wives to himself. . . . Neither shall he greatly multiply to himself silver and gold. . . . He shall write a copy of this law in a book, out of that which is before the priests the Levites. And it shall be with him, and he shall read therein all the days of his life; that he may learn to fear the Lord his God" (Deuteronomy 17.15-19). The children of Israel may expect prophets to rise in the Promised Land, men of God like Moses himself. "And it shall come to pass, that whosoever will not hearken unto My words which he shall speak in My name, I will require it of him" (Deuteronomy 18.19). How may the Israelites distinguish a true prophet from a false one? "When a prophet speaketh in the name of the Lord, if the thing follow not, nor come to pass, that is the thing which the Lord hath not spoken; the prophet hath spoken it presumptuously, thou shalt not be afraid of him" (Deuteronomy 18.22).

The portion also treats of the cities of refuge. It cites the speech that the priest and officers are to make to troops before battle, and states the laws of warfare that apply to any city not of the seven Canaanite nations. The portion ends with the regulations dealing with the heifer offered as atonement when a slain person is found in the field and the identity of the murderer is not known.

KI TETZE תצא

A conquering soldier takes a woman captive from among the enemy.

"When thou goest forth to battle . . . and seest among the captives a woman of goodly form . . . and wouldest take her to thee to wife" (Deut. 21. 10-11).

Ki Tetze — "When thou goest forth to battle against thine enemies, and the Lord thy God de-

livereth them into thy hands, and thou carriest them away captive, and seest among the captives a woman of goodly form, and thou . . . wouldest take her to thee to wife; then thou shalt bring her home to thy house. . . . And it shall be, if thou have no delight in her, then thou shalt let her go whither she will; but thou shalt not sell her at all for money" (Deuteronomy 21.10-14). "If a man have a stubborn and rebellious son . . . all the men of his city shall stone him with stones, that he die" (Deuteronomy 21.18-21). The body of a hanged man "shall not remain all night upon the tree, but thou shalt surely bury him the same day; for he that is hanged is a reproach unto God; that thou defile not thy land" (Deuteronomy 21.23). "Thou shalt not see thy brother's ox or his sheep driven away, and hide thyself from them; thou shalt surely bring them back unto thy brother" (Deuteronomy 22.1). "Thou shalt not take the dam with the young; thou shalt in any wise let the dam go, but the young thou mayest take unto thyself" (Deuteronomy 22.6-7).

"When thou buildest a new house, then thou shalt make a parapet for thy roof, that thou bring not blood upon thy house, if any man fall from thence" (Deuteronomy 22.8). "Thou shalt not plough with an ox and an ass together. Thou shalt not wear a mingled stuff, wool and linen together" (Deuteronomy 22.10-11). The man who "lays wanton charges" against his wife shall be chastised by the elders of the city. "A bastard shall not enter into the assembly of the Lord" (Deuteronomy 23.3). "If brethren dwell together, and one of them die, and have no child, the wife of the dead shall not be married abroad unto one not of his kin; her husband's brother shall go in unto her, and take her to him to wife, and perform the duty of a husband's brother unto her. And it shall be, that the first-born that she beareth shall succeed in the name of his brother that is dead" (Deuteronomy 25.5-6). "An Ammonite or a Moabite shall not enter into the assembly of the Lord; . . . because they met you not with bread and with water in the way, when ye came forth out of Egypt; and because they hired against thee Balaam the son of Beor from Pethor of Aram-na haraim, to curse thee. . . . Thou shalt not seek their peace nor their prosperity all thy days forever. Thou shalt not abhor an Edomite, for he is thy brother; thou shalt not abhor an Egyptian, because thou wast a stranger in his land. The children of the third generation that are born unto them may enter into the assembly of the Lord" (Deuteronomy 23.4-9). Finally, the portion ends with a reminder of eternal enmity against a dread foe: "Remember what Amalek did unto thee by the way as ye came forth out of Egypt" (Deuteronomy 25.17).

KI TAVO   תבא

A Jew offers first-fruits before the priest and makes his declaration.

"And now, behold, I have brought the first of the fruit of the land, which Thou, O Lord, hast given me" (Deut. 26.10).

Ki Tavo—"And it shall be, when thou art come in unto the land which the Lord thy God giveth thee for an inheritance . . . thou shalt take of the first of all the fruit of the ground . . . and shalt go unto the place which the Lord thy God shall choose to cause His name to dwell there. And the priest shall take the basket out of thy hand, and set it down before the altar of the Lord thy God . . . and thou shalt set it down before the Lord thy God, and worship before the Lord thy God. . . . When thou hast made an end of tithing all the tithe of thine increase in the third year . . . thou shalt say before the Lord thy God: 'I have put away the hallowed things out of my house, and also have given them unto the Levite, and unto the stranger, to the fatherless, and to the widow. . . . I have not transgressed any of Thy commandments, neither have I forgotten them' " (Deuteronomy 26.1-13). "And it shall be when ye are passed over the Jordan, that ye shall set up these stones, which I command you this day, in mount Ebal, and thou shalt plaster them with plaster. . . . And thou shalt write upon the stones all the words of this law very plainly" (Deuteronomy 27.4-8).

The portion goes on to treat of the blessings and curses with which Moses charged the children of Israel; for further emphasis, the covenant made in mount Horeb is reaffirmed in Moab.

NITZAVIM   נצבים

Moses speaks to all Israel, men and women, from the woodman to the drawer of water.

"Ye are standing this day all of you before the Lord your God: your heads, your tribes, your elders, and your officers" (Deut. 29.9).

Nitzavim — "Ye are standing this day all of you before the Lord your God . . . that thou shouldest enter into the covenant of the Lord thy God —and into His oath—which the Lord thy God maketh with thee this day; that He may establish thee this day unto Himself for a people, and that He may be unto thee a God, as He spoke unto thee, and as He swore unto thy fathers, to Abraham, to Isaac, and to Jacob. Neither with you only do I make this covenant and this oath; but with him that standeth here with us this day before the Lord our God, and also with him that is not here with us this day. . . . The secret things belong unto the Lord our God; but the things that are revealed belong unto us and to our children for ever, that we may do all the words of this law" (Deuteronomy 29.9-28). "I call heaven and earth to witness against you this day, that I have set before thee life and death, the blessing and the curse; therefore choose life, that thou mayest live, thou and thy seed" (Deuteronomy 30.19).

VAYELEKH   וילך

Moses writes the sacred Torah.

"And Moses wrote this law, and delivered it unto the priests . . . and unto all the elders of Israel" (Deut. 31.9).

Vayelekh — "And Moses went and spoke these words unto all Israel. And he said unto them: 'I am a hundred and twenty years old this day; I can no more go out and come in; and the Lord hath said unto me: Thou shalt not go over this Jordan. . . .' And Moses called unto Joshua, and said unto him in the sight of all Israel: 'Be strong and of good courage; for thou shalt go with this people into the land which the Lord hath sworn unto their fathers to give them; and thou shalt cause them to inherit it. . . .' And Moses wrote this law, and delivered it unto the priests the sons of Levi, that bore the ark of the covenant of the Lord, and unto all the elders of Israel. . . . Now therefore write ye this song for you, and teach thou it the children of Israel; put it in their mouths, that this song may be a witness for Me against the children of Israel" (Deuteronomy 31.1-19).

HAAZINU האזינו

Moses addresses all the assembled Israelites.

"Give ear, ye heavens, and I will speak: And let the earth hear the words of my mouth" *(Deut. 32.1).*

Haazinu — Moses' song beginning "Give ear, ye heavens, and I will speak" contains the principal elements in the unique relationship between God and his people Israel. Moses opens with a call to heaven and earth to witness his declaration. From the beginning of time, Moses asserts, the Lord had chosen Israel for a special place among the nations of the world. He had first singled out Israel in the desert, whence he lovingly led them into the land of Canaan. But Israel, Moses prophesies, would abandon their God for foreign idols. Then God would send a cruel nation to enslave and torment the children of Israel. Eventually however, God would have compassion on His beloved people and wreak vengeance on Israel's tormentors. All the nations would then behold how the Lord had avenged the blood of His servants and had made expiation for the land of His people.

At God's command, Moses prepares to ascend mount Nebo, in the land of Moab. From there at a distance he is to glimpse the Promised Land and die; as Aaron had died at mount Hor. "Because ye trespassed against Me in the midst of the children of Israel at the waters of Meribath-kadesh, in the wilderness of Zin; because ye sanctified Me not in the midst of the children of Israel" (Deuteronomy 32.51).

VEZOT HABERAKHAH וזאת הברכה

Moses ascends mount Nebo and proceeds to his destined burial-place.

"And Moses went up . . . unto mount Nebo . . . And the Lord showed him all the land . . . And Moses the servant of the Lord died there" *(Deut. 34.1-5).*

Vezot Haberakhah—"This is the blessing, wherewith Moses the man of God blessed the children of Israel before his death" (Deuteronomy 33.1). Beginning with a restatement of the revelation of God to Israel at mount Sinai, Moses proceeds to stress the mutual love between God and the congregation of Israel, as evidenced in the giving of the Torah. Then Moses blesses each tribe individually (except for Simeon), and remarks on Israel's strength and good fortune when the people rely on the Almighty.

Moses ascends mount Nebo, where God shows him all of the Promised Land in the distance. And there Moses died, at the age of 120. "And he was buried in the valley in the land of Moab over against Beth-peor; and no man knoweth of his sepulchre unto this day. . . . His eye was not dim, nor his natural force abated. And the children of Israel wept for Moses in the plains of Moab thirty days; so the days of weeping in the mourning for Moses were ended. And Joshua the son of Nun was full of the spirit of wisdom; for Moses had laid his hands upon him; and the children of Israel hearkened unto him, and did as the Lord commanded Moses. And there hath not arisen a prophet since in Israel like unto Moses" (Deuteronomy 34.6-10).

The prophet reproaches his people and urges them to turn from their evil ways, but they turn their backs upon him.

"Hear O heavens, and give ear, O earth,
For the Lord hath spoken:
Children I have reared, and brought up,
And they have rebelled against Me" (Isaiah 1.2).

PROPHETS (BOOKS)   נביאים

The Biblical books known as the Prophets contain both the divinely inspired utterances of those exceptional men and women and the narrative accounts of the events that influenced, and were influenced by, them. This literature extends from the death of Moses, father of the prophets, through Haggai, Zechariah, and Malachi, with whose deaths "the spirit of prophecy departed from Israel" (Yoma 9b). Periods varied as to the extent and quality of prophecy; there were times when prophecy was a rare phenomenon (1 Samuel 3.1.); at other periods, such as those when Isaiah and Jeremiah were active, a number of great prophets arose simultaneously. In general, prophets sprang up in time of cultural and political upheaval, as in that of Assyrian expansion and the one preceding the destruction of the Temple. The prophetic aim was defensive: to warn the people against abandoning the ways of God under pressure from alien influences that often threatened Israel's spiritual as well as political existence. Ezekiel portrays the prophet as a "watchman of the city" in time of danger. According to the Pentateuch, the prophet is privileged to hear "the word of God" and to see "the vision of God". " 'Hath the Lord indeed spoken only with Moses? hath He not spoken also with us?' . . . And the Lord . . . said: '. . . If there be a prophet among you, I the Lord do make Myself known unto him in a vision, I do speak with him in a dream. My servant Moses is not so; he is trusted in all My house; with him do I speak mouth to mouth . . . and not in dark speeches' " (Numbers 12.2-8). The implication is of gradations in prophecy. The sages said: "No two prophets prophesy in the same style" (Sanhedrin 89).

The books of the Prophets may be classified as follows:

  1. *Former Prophets:* Joshua, Judges, Samuel (I and II), and Kings (I and II).

  2. *Latter Prophets:* Isaiah, Jeremiah, Ezekiel, and "The Twelve." "The Twelve" consists of prophetic utterances from different periods that were collected under one rubric because their brevity might have caused them to be over looked.

A judge, a priest and a king administer the life of the community.

"Then came near the heads of fathers' houses of the Levites unto Eleazar, the priest, and unto Joshua the son of Nun" (Joshua 21.1).

FORMER PROPHETS נביאים ראשונים

The Former Prophets — Joshua, Judges, Samuel I and II, and Kings I and II — relate the history of the Israelites from the conquest of Canaan to the Babylonian exile in 586 B.C.E. These works describe the transformation of the people from nomadic tribes to a powerful and united monarchy under David and Solomon, and then trace the decline of the two kingdoms, the domination of the people by Egypt and Babylon, and the destruction of the Temple and national sovereignty.

PROPHETS

The Pentateuch is followed by a section known as PROPHETS, cont
of Israel, whose vicissitudes they relate from the time of Joshua
a period of almost one thousand years. These books are subdivide
The order of the books and their authors accords with Baba Bathr

THE FORMER PROPHETS ם

Begins with the conquest of the land of Canaan under Joshua, and ends with

6. Joshua יהושע

Contents: Conquest of Canaan under Joshua, and its division among the twelve tribes of Israel.

Author: Begun by Joshua. Completed by Phinehas, son of Eleazar.

7. Judges שופטים

Contents: The history of the tribes during the period when "Judges ruled." There were 15 judges:

1. Othniel
2. Ehud
3. Shamgar
4. Barak and Deborah
5. Gideon
6. Abimelech
7. Tola
8. Jair
9. Jephthah
10. Ibzan
11. Elon
12. Abdon
13. Samson
14. Eli
15. Samuel

Author: Samuel

8. I Samuel שמואל א׳

Contents: The priestly rule of the house of Eli. Samuel: his origin, activity, and influence. Samuel anoints Saul as the first king of Israel. Saul's experiences and battles. Saul is removed by Samuel. Samuel secretly anoints David as King.
The curse and death in battle of Saul.

Author: Begun by Samuel. Completed by Gad and Nathan.

THE LATTER PROPHETS ם

These include the books of the three major prophets,

10. Isaiah ישעיה

Contents: Prophecies of Isaiah, the son of Amoz. The divine ethics. Political counsel. Moral preachments. Injunctions, threats, consolations. Israel's mission. Prophecies concerning the fate of nations beside Israel.

Author: Hezekiah and his circle.

11. Jeremiah

Contents: Prophecies of
The divine ethics. Morali
addressed to the leaders
prophets. Lamentations ov
tion of the Temple and o
of encouragement and ce
Prophecies concerning the
side Israel. Chronicle of t
exile and of the period
Gedaliah, son of Hilkiah,
Author: Jeremiah

13. THE TWELVE PROP

Hosea, Joel, Amos, Obadiah, Jonah, Micah, Nahum,

נחום מיכה יונה עובדיה עמוס יואל הושע

Contents: Twelve books containing prophecies, injunctions, etc., o (Hosea and Amos) through Haggai, Zechariah, and Malachi, who p Second Temple era.

Authors: The Men of the Great Assembly. "Because their prophecie Haggai, Zechariah, and Malachi, the last of the prophets, realizin prophecies, and, subjoining the works of the earlier prophets, put

נביאים

...ining 19 Books. These embrace the entire history of the ancient people ...(2489 A.M.) through the days of Ezra and Nehemiah (3448 A.M.) — ...into: Former Prophets, Latter Prophets and Twelve (Minor) Prophets.
...14-15.

נביאים ראשונ...

...the destruction of the Holy Temple in Jerusalem (3339 A.M.). **Books included are:**

II Samuel שמואל ב׳

Contents: David assumes the kingdom at Hebron. His preparation for rule over all Israel. David's rule; his wars, victories, conquests; his private life; the rebellions against him. Nathan and Gad.

Author: Begun by Samuel. Completed by Gad and Nathan.

9. I Kings מלכים א׳

Contents: Annals of the kings of Judah and Israel. David's last testament. The anointing of Solomon. The building of the Temple. Solomon's wisdom and strength. The division of the Kingdom of Israel after Solomon's death. Ahijah, the Shilonite. The kingdoms of Ephraim and Judah: their individual histories, kings and mutual relations. Elijah: his appearance and activity.

Author: Jeremiah.

II Kings מלכים ב׳

Contents: Period of the two kingdoms continued: internal and external relations. Elisha: his religious and political activity. The exile of Ephraim. First exile of Judah under King Jehoiachin. Final exile under King Zedekiah, and the destruction of the Temple.

Author: Jeremiah.

נביאים אחרונ...

...saiah, Jeremiah, Ezekiel and the Twelve Minor Prophets.

ירמיה

...Jeremiah, son of Hilkiah. ...y and prayer. Injunctions ...f the people, priests, false ...er the calamitous destruc- ...the land of Israel. Words ...nsolation. Israel's mission. ...fate of other nations be- ...e events leading up to the ...immediately afterwards. ...and departure for Egypt.

12. Ezekiel יחזקאל

Contents: Prophecies of Ezekiel, son of Buzi. Visions of God. Prophecies uttered in Babylon; the sins of Jerusalem and its ultimate destruction. Laws, injunctions, and consolations for the future. Importance of sacrificial worship; unity of priesthood and prophecy. Diagram of the future Temple and the order of sacrifice.

Authors: Men of the Great Assembly.

...HETS תרי עשר

Habakkuk, Zephaniah, Haggai, Zechariah, Malachi.
מלאכי זכריה חגי צפניה חבקוק

...f the minor prophets, from the first prophets whose works are recorded ...rophesied at the close of the First Temple and the beginning of the

...s were brief, the early prophets did not edit their own books. However, ...g that the divine spirit was departing from Israel, wrote down their own ...together a large volume less likely to be lost" (Rashi, Baba Bathra 15a).

FORMER PROPHETS

JOSHUA יהושע

Joshua bids the sun and moon stand still while he and his army pursue the enemy.

"And he said in the sight of Israel: 'Sun, stand thou still upon Gibeon; And thou, Moon, in the valley of Aijalon'" *(Josh. 10.12).*

The Book of Joshua — The book of Joshua is an historic continuation of the book of Deuteronomy, with which it shares a common tone and style. Joshua is commanded to conquer the land of Canaan at the head of the Israelites, there to establish a community based on observance of the laws of the Torah. "Now it came to pass after the death of Moses, the servant of the Lord, that the Lord spoke unto Joshua the son of Nun, Moses' minister, saying: 'Moses My servant is dead; now therefore arise, go over this Jordan, thou, and all this people, unto the land which I do give to them, even to the children of Israel . . . This book of the law shall not depart out of thy mouth, but thou shalt meditate therein day and night, that thou mayest observe to do according to all that is written therein; for then thou shalt make thy ways prosperous, and then thou shalt have good success'" (Joshua 1.1-8).

Joshua contains 24 chapters, which may be divided as follows so far as contents are concerned:

1. The story of the conquest of Canaan—Chapters 1-12.
2. The division of the land among the tribes—Chapters 13-21.
3. Joshua's final acts—Chapters 22-24.

The most important events in the book of Joshua are: The crossing of the Jordan; the capture of Jericho and Ai; the battles at Gibeon and the waters of Merom; the division of the land; the building of an altar by the eastern, Transjordanian tribes near the Jordan boundary as a witness of their rights to the land for purposes of worship as part of God's holy people. Finally, the book ends with Joshua's last words and the covenant in Shechem.

JUDGES שופטים

A judge leads his people with spear and Scroll of the Law.

"And the Lord raised up judges, who saved them out of the hand of those that spoiled them" *(Judg. 2.16).*

The Book of Judges — The book of Judges covers the period between the death of Joshua and the birth of Samuel, founder of the kingdom —a period that may be characterized as one of consolidation. The purpose of Judges is to teach the relationship between a people's political situation and its spiritual life. When they are faithful to God, all goes well with the tribes. But when they forsake His ways, there are severe economic and political difficulties. The men and women who arise during this period to lead the tribes against their enemies are called judges.

The book begins with the continued account of the conquest of Canaan by the tribes after the death of Joshua. Various pagan nations have been permitted to remain in the land during this time of consolidation to test Israel and reveal "whether they will keep the way of the Lord to walk therein, as their fathers did keep it, or not" (Judges 2.22). National decline begins with the death of "the elders that outlived Joshua, who had seen all the great work of the Lord, that He had wrought for Israel" (Judges 2.7). The book of Judges gives relatively lengthy accounts of the heroes and leaders who played a large role in the history of the nation — Ehud, Deborah and Barak, Gideon, Jephthah, and Samson.

Toward the end of Judges appears an account of the apportionment of territory in the north to the tribe of Dan, and their setting up of the idol of Micah. The incident of the concubine of Gibeah almost results in the total extermination of the tribe of Benjamin. These two events indicate the anarchic situation that seemed to call for the tribes' unification under a monarchy.

THE BOOKS OF SAMUEL

The book of Samuel covers the period from the decline of the judges to the end of King David's active reign; i.e., the beginning of monarchy. Evident throughout is recognition of a Divine Providence deeply concerned over the fate of Israel (I Samuel 15.29); even though Saul, Israel's first king, proves unworthy of his position, Israel will still prosper under God. The book of Samuel is divided into two parts, known as I Samuel and II Samuel respectively.

I. SAMUEL   שמואל א׳

Hannah offers the child Samuel to serve with Eli the High Priest, in the House of God.

"And (Hannah) brought him unto the house of the Lord in Shiloh" (I. Sam. 1.24).

"And Hannah prayed, and said: My heart exulteth in the Lord" (2.1).

I Samuel—opens with the birth of Samuel at a time when the priesthood had lost its authority due to the abuses of the two sons of Eli. There is a hiatus of prophetic guidance: "There was no frequent vision" (I Samuel 3.1); but the hiatus is soon filled by Samuel. "And all Israel from Dan even to Beer-sheba knew that Samuel was established to be a prophet of the Lord" (I Samuel 3.20). After the calamitous destruction of Shiloh by the Philistines, Samuel places himself at the head of the people as an organizing and stabilizing spiritual force. Under Samuel, the tribes lose their fear of the Philistines. "So the Philistines were subdued, and they came no more within the border of Israel; and the hand of the Lord was against the Philistines all the days of Samuel. . . . And there was peace between Israel and the Amorites" (I Samuel 6.13-14).

In his latter days, Samuel, at God's advice, yields to the popular demand for a king and anoints Saul, of the tribe of Benjamin, "young and goodly, and there was not among the children of Israel a goodlier person than he: from his shoulders and upward he was higher than any of the people" (I Samuel 9.2). Saul defeats the Ammonites and Philistines in battle. But he soon reveals an impatient independence that brings him into conflict with Samuel on two occasions: first, when he sacrifices at Gilgal without waiting for Samuel to arrive; and then when he seizes the forbidden booty (anathema) of the Amalekites and fails to take the life of Agag, king of the Amalekites. After the latter incident, Samuel secretly anoints David, the son of Jesse, from Bethlehem in Judah, at God's command.

This point marks the beginning of Saul's decline. "Now the spirit of the Lord had departed from Saul, and an evil spirit from the Lord terrified him" (I Samuel 16.14). When David defeats Goliath, the Philistine giant, in personal combat, Saul's melancholy assumes violent proportions and he bends every effort to persecute David. The book of I Samuel ends with the disastrous defeat of mount Gilboa where Saul and his three sons perish in battle; the Philistines recapture a number of cities (I Samuel 31.1-7).

II. SAMUEL   שמואל ב׳

David brings the Ark to Jerusalem to the accompaniment of joyous music.

"And David arose . . . and . . . all the people . . . to bring up . . . the ark of God . . . And David and all . . . Israel played before the Lord with all manner of instruments" (II. Sam. 6.2-5).

II Samuel—is entirely devoted to the account of the establishment and strengthening of David's kingdom. It opens with the news of the defeat of mount Gilboa reaching David and his moving eulogy over Saul and Jonathan, his eldest son and David's close friend. In general, this book renders most episodes briefly, but gives fuller treatment to matters of great political or ethical import —such as the brutal murder of Abner, Saul's general; the capture of Jerusalem and the transfer of the Ark to that city, the new capital of Judah; and David's wish to build a house of God in Jerusalem, as a reward for which God promises David that his posterity will rule forever.

II Samuel also contains accounts of David's wars; the incident of Bath-sheba; the incest of Amnon and Tamar; Absalom's rebellion; the revenge of the Gibeonites; and David's song of thanksgiving for the success of his kingdom (II

Samuel 22). The book concludes with the popular census and its consequence in a plague; and finally, with David's purchase of a threshing floor from Araunah that he might build an altar there.

The whole book is written throughout in a fluent and lively style. David is described in every mood—weak as well as strong, contrite as well as victorious. He emerges as a great man moved by very human passions.

THE BOOKS OF KINGS

Written in a concise but lucid style, I and II Kings demonstrate the disastrous effects of apostasy from God's ways.

Highly impressive and inspiring episodes—particularly dealing with the prophets Elijah and Elisha — illumine the books of Kings. It is a fascinating and absorbing source for a chronicle of the monarchic period — and particularly important as an historical document with significant moral and ethical implications.

The historic years covered are from approximately 960 B.C.E. till 586 B.C.E. Tradition notes Jeremiah as the author, though he may only be the final editor, for the book reveals the compilation of many early texts and sources. Though essentially a chronicle of the past, its purpose is to prepare for true monotheism, since the many historic facts used contain a definitely religious note. Often it is difficult to differentiate between history and commentary. What emerges particularly is the thesis that ethics and a philosophy of religion cannot be separated from the history of national life.

I. KINGS   מלכים א׳

Solomon directs the building of the Temple.

"I purpose to build a house for the name of the Lord my God, as the Lord spoke unto David my father" (I. Kings 5.19).

I Kings—The first book of Kings deals with the period of the early monarchy, opening with a description of David's last days and concluding with the reign of Jehoshaphat. It dwells on the most important events: the kingdom of Solomon; the building of the Temple in Jerusalem; and the division of the kingdom after Solomon's death after the insurrection led by Jeroboam, the son of Nebat. Then, it proceeds to chronicle the activity of the great prophet Elijah and the iniquities of the Northern king Ahab.

II. KINGS   מלכים ב׳

Hezekiah shatters the idols while the Levites instruct children in the Torah.

"He removed the high places, and broke the pillars, and cut down the Asherah" (II. Kings 18. 4).

II Kings—The second book starts with the visit of Elijah to the messengers of the king of Samaria (Ahaziah, son of Ahab) and concludes with the death of Gedaliah, the son of Ahikam, the Judean governor after the destruction of Jerusalem, and with the liberation of Jehoiachin, king of Judah, in the 37th year of his exile in Babylon. In it there is a portrayal of Elijah's political actions, and Elisha's miracles. A description is given of Jehu and his dynasty; the Assyrian wars that culminate with the destruction of the northern kingdom whose capital was Samaria, and the last-minute rescue of Jerusalem due to the intervention of the prophet Isaiah and the righteous king Hezekiah. II Kings also includes illustrations of the pagan practices of King Manasseh which fatally breached the foundations of the kingdom of Judah. On the other hand, the righteousness of the good King Josiah is held up as an example of possibilities for good in the Judean monarchy. II. Kings ends with the tyrannical domination of the Kingdom of Judah by Babylon and the destruction of the country.

A prophet reproves a king.

"Then said Isaiah to Hezekiah: 'Hear the word of the Lord of hosts: Behold, the days come, that all that is in thy house, and that which thy fathers have laid up in store until this day, shall be carried to Babylon; nothing shall be left, saith the Lord' " (Isaiah 39.5-6).

LATTER PROPHETS   נביאים אחרונים

These books contain the great utterances and teachings of Isaiah, Jeremiah and Ezekiel.

The prophets, as spokesmen of God, were not idle dreamers divorced from the realities of life. Possessing profound insight, they expressed universal ideals in immortal words that have remained relevant to this very day.

ISAIAH　ישעיה

Isaiah exhorts the judge to deal justly with the widow and orphan, but the judge turns a deaf ear.

"Woe unto them that decree unrighteous decrees . . . To turn aside the needy from judgment... That widows may be their spoil" (Isa. 10.1-2).

The Book of Isaiah — Isaiah, the son of Amoz, was consecrated as a prophet in the year of King Uzziah's death, at a time when Assyria was threatening the kingdoms of both Judah and Israel. After Jeroboam II and Uzziah had won a good number of military victories, adding to the country's wealth and territory, a period of severe social decay began to set in. Widespread idolatry was undermining the land's moral fibre. Isaiah declared: "And He said: 'Go, and tell this people: Hear ye indeed, but understand not; And see ye indeed, but perceive not. Make the heart of this people fat, And make their ears heavy And shut their eyes" (Isaiah 6.9-10). When the prophet asks: "Lord, how long?" God replies, "Until cities be waste without inhabitant, And houses without man, And the land become utterly waste, And the Lord have removed men far away, And the forsaken places be many in the midst of the land" (Isaiah 6.11-12). The people will not be aroused from their lethargy of indifference until the land of Judah will be devastated and they themselves exiled. Yet Isaiah also foresees the possibility of a national and religious revival such as that experienced during the days of King Hezekiah. "Behold, a king shall reign in righteousness, And as for princes, they shall rule in justice. And a man shall be as in a hiding-place from the wind . . . As in the shadow of a great rock in a weary land. And the eyes of them that see shall not be closed, And the ears of them that hear shall attend" (Isaiah 32.1-3).

The book of Isaiah is divided into two parts: part I, consisting of chapters 1-39; and part II, chapters 40-61. Part I deals with the Assyrian period. The prophet argues against submission to foreign domination, or the extending of an invitation to foreign forces to enter and defend the country. In Isaiah's view, the only hope for Judah's salvation lies in its acceptance of tran-

scendent religious and moral values. Ultimately, Isaiah's policy triumphed; Judah was saved when the enemy was miraculously stricken while on the verge of conquering Jerusalem. Parenthetically, Isaiah prophesied the coming of a messianic era when the word of God would go forth out of Zion, and peace and faith reign in the world.

Part II of the book of Isaiah deals with the period of the return to Zion. Chiefly, it offers consolatory hopes to the exiles—hence its title of "The Book of Consolations." This book is further subdivided into:

a) Chapters 40-47, in which the prophet foresees the return of Zion's children to their homeland, bitterly attacks pagan practices, and prophesies the destruction of Babylon;

b) Chapters 48-55, wherein Isaiah stresses the mission of the "servant of the Lord," who, by spreading the word of the God of Israel will bring salvation to the world; and

c) Chapters 55-66, describing the difficulties experienced by the returning exiles, and their struggles with their sinful brethren and external enemies, both of whom will suffer downfall.

JEREMIAH　ירמיהו

The Temple aflame, Rachel weeps for her children who are seen going, in chains, into exile.

"A voice is heard in Ramah, Lamentation, and bitter weeping, Rachel weeping for her children" (Jer. 31.15).

The Book of Jeremiah — Jeremiah was one of the priests from Anathoth, in the territory of Benjamin (now the Arab village of Anata, some 6 km. northeast of Jerusalem). Jeremiah began to prophesy as a young man in the 13th year of the reign of Josiah (ca. 627 B.C.E.). After the destruction of the Temple, he continued to prophesy in Egypt whither he was taken by the political refugees who fled when Gedaliah, son of Ahikam, was murdered. Throughout his life, Jeremiah struggled against the political and moral factors that contributed to the downfall of Judah, but the situation was already so acute that his prophecies were of no avail.

Until the year of the battle of Carchemish (605 B.C.E.) when Babylon defeated Judah, Jeremiah's prophecies fell on deaf ears. But after that disastrous event, he was recognized as a true prophet. Yet, despite this public recognition, the government policy did not change, the monarchy hastening the national catastrophe with its impenitent actions.

Despite the violence he suffered at the hands of his adversaries, Jeremiah never ceased preaching repentance and peace with Babylon—for he foresaw no possibility for genuine political independence. The style of his prophecies is graceful, notable for analogies from nature, with which the prophet was intimately familiar from his early years in Anathoth. In days of blackest despair he uttered prophecies of consolation and predicted the return of the exiles. With great descriptive power, he portrays God's reconciliation with His people of Judah and Israel returning from exile in a spirit of unity and repentence. (Jeremiah 2.1-3; 3.11-25; 30.1-3; 50.4-8; 51.50-51).

EZEKIEL יחזקאל

Ezekiel presages the restoration of life into the dry bones that fill the valley.

" 'Son of man, can these bones live?' . . . So I prophesied . . . and the breath came into 'them, and they lived" (Ezek. 37.3,10).

The Book of Ezekiel — Ezekiel began to prophesy in the 5th year of the exile of Jehoiachin (592 B.C.E.), while living in Babylon, whither he had apparently been taken in 604 B.C.E. after the battle of Carchemish. Hence, Ezekiel appeared as a stranger among the exiles living near the river Chebar who had been exiled with Jehoiachin. His main aim was to prevent Judah from allying herself with Egypt and rebelling against Babylon. But it was not until the news of the destruction of the Temple reached Babylon that Ezekiel was accepted as a true prophet: "And

lo, thou art unto them as a love song of one that hath a pleasant voice, and can play well on an instrument; so they hear thy words, but they do them not—when this cometh to pass—behold, it cometh—then shall they know that a prophet hath been among them" (Ezekiel 33.32-33). Ezekiel further inveighed against the desecration of Jerusalem, to which he had sent his prophecies from Babylon.

The book of Ezekiel consists of two parts:
1. Prophecies of reproof (Chapters 1-24).
2. Consolations (Chapters 25-48).
This division is not however absolute: in the prophecies of reproof he introduces brief consolatory passages, and chapter 33 rightly belongs with the reproving chapters.

Ezekiel's style is distinguished by its high literary accomplishment. His prophecies are everywhere notable for remarkable flights of language. One need but read his prophecies on Tyre and Egypt, or any of his many parables, to perceive his great artistic distinction and power.

Ezekiel's prophecies constantly assert that all that befalls Israel is purposeful. Exile, he maintains, has been thrust on Israel in order to bring the people to a realization of the need for repentance—once that is realized, and put into practice, Israel will be freed from exile. Ezekiel is also a valuable source for information concerning the historic past of Israel unknown from other sources and analyzed in an almost scientific manner. The prophet is famous for his large and detailed plan of the structure of the future Temple, and for his plan of a new division of the land of Israel, to be put into effect at the time of the return to Zion. Ezekiel stresses the fact of Divine reward and punishment, and compares himself to a watchman of a city: even as the watchman must warn the city of approaching danger, so the prophet must warn the evil-doer of the consequences of his acts.

Twelve prophetic scrolls bound together.

"Write the vision,
And make it plain upon tables,
That a man may read it swiftly" (Habakkuk 2.2).

THE TWELVE PROPHETS   תרי עשר

The small size of these prophetic works led to their being gathered into one volume. The arrangement seems to be according to size, on the one hand, and to chronological considerations, on the other. Hosea, being the largest book, begins the collection, which ends with the last prophets of the post-exilic period. The Septuagint arranges the works solely according to size, beginning with the largest.

HOSEA הושע

The tefillin thong is wound about the left hand so that it forms the letter "Shin".

"And I will betroth thee unto Me forever . . . in righteousness, and in justice" (Hosea 2.21).

The Book of Hosea — Hosea prophesied in Ephraim at the beginning of the appearance of Assyria over the horizon of that kingdom. The moral decline in Ephraim at the end of the days of Jeroboam II had weakened the country politically. There were two distinct political lines in Ephraim: one to seek aid from Egypt, the other to come to terms with Assyria, supposedly still an ally. But Hosea was opposed to alliance with either of these two formidable powers, seeking instead a religious and social revival that would inevitably strengthen Ephraim's political force. Hosea was also concerned with the similar problems of the sister kingdom of Judah.

The book of Hosea consists of 14 chapters. The first three chapters describe how the word of God came to Hosea. They are distinctive for the symbolism taken from the prophet's own troubled personal life. The remaining chapters contain "words of reproof," alternately with expressions of God's tremendous love for His people. Thus Hosea frequently reminisces about the very beginning of Israel's existence as a distinct people: "When Israel was a child, then I loved him,/ And out of Egypt I called My son" (Hosea 11.1). "And she shall respond there, as in the days of her youth,/ And as in the day when she came up out of the land of Egypt" (Hosea 2.17).

JOEL יואל

Four species of locust swarm in from the North to consume the land.

"That which the palmer-worm hath left hath the locust eaten; And that which the locust hath left hath the canker-worm eaten" (Joel 1.4).

The Book of Joel — Joel contains four chapters, and may be divided into two parts.

Chapters 1 and 2 deal with the coming of the "day of the Lord" characterized by a plague of locusts and famine.

The second part, chapters 3 and 4, describes the day of the Lord as one when those nations that fought against Judah shall be judged in the valley of Jehoshaphat.

Joel does not reprove the people for any particular transgression. Rather, he urges them to repent, visualizing a happy future. For repentance is efficacious; God will withdraw his terrible judgment, and the people will be saved: "So shall ye know that I am the Lord your God/ Dwelling in Zion My holy mountain;/ Then shall Jerusalem be holy./ And there shall no strangers pass through her any more . . ./ Judah shall be inhabited for ever,/ And Jerusalem from generation to generation./ And I will hold as innocent their blood that I have not held as innocent;/ And the Lord dwelleth in Zion" (Joel 4.17-21).

It appears from the arangement of the chapters and the subjects mentioned that Joel was a contemporary of Isaiah and Amos. The famine he describes is also mentioned in Amos. Likewise, the enemies mentioned, and the miraculous rescue of Jerusalem, are reminiscent of the prophecies of Amos and Isaiah.

AMOS עמום

Inside Jerusalem's walls are seen the harvesting of fruits and the ploughing of the soil.

"And I will turn the captivity of My people Israel, and they shall build the waste cities, and inhabit them" (Amos 9.14).

The Book of Amos — Amos' background may be discerned from his reply to Amaziah, the priest of Beth-el: "I was no prophet, neither was I a prophet's son; but I was a herdman, and a dresser of sycamore-trees; and the Lord took me from following the flock, and the Lord said unto me: Go, prophesy unto My people Israel" (Amos 7.14-15). Born in the city of Tekoa, Amos prophesied during the reign of Uzziah in Judah and Jeroboam II in Ephraim—most probably at the end of their reigns, when the terror of Assyria was an immediate threat (the prophet speaks about the exile beyond Damascus). Amos fought social corruption which he regarded as a consequence of religions corruption.

Thus, Amos began to prophesy in a very tense atmosphere. The country had been subjected to the devastation of famine; Amos saw the "day of the Lord" on the horizon. "The Lord roareth from Zion,/ And uttereth his voice from Jerusalem;/ And the pastures of the shepherds shall mourn,/ And the top of Carmel shall wither" (Amos 1.2). He continually emphasizes his people's uniqueness; consequently more is to be expected from them: "You only have I known of all the families of the earth;/ Therefore I will visit upon you all your iniquities" (Amos 3.2).

Amos' style is bold and direct; the verses flow with descriptive power. In literary cadences, he describes the "day of the Lord" when God will wreak retribution on Israel's wicked neighbors— Aram, Philistia, Tyre, Edom, Ammon, and Moab. But Israel (and Judah too) will suffer on that fearful day—they too had deserted the ways of God. Yet there is hope for repentance after that day. God will show mercy on His people: "And I will plant them upon their land,/ And they shall no more be plucked up/ Out of their land which I have given them,/ Saith the Lord thy God" (Amos 9.15).

OBADIAH עובדיה

Judah revives the Land even unto the Negev (port of Elath).

"And the house of Jacob shall be a fire, And the house of Joseph a flame . . . And they shall kindle . . . and . . . possess the mount of Esau" (Obadiah 1.18-19).

The Book of Obadiah — Only one chapter has come down to us from the prophet Obadiah; it is devoted completely to an account of the destruction of Edom. In the pride of its heart, Edom had entrusted its defense to its mountainous and rocky topography. "The pride of thy heart hath beguiled thee,/ O thou that dwellest in the clefts of the rock,/ Thy habitation on high;/ That sayest in thy heart:/ 'Who shall bring me down to the ground?' " (Obadiah 1.3). But Edom had

allowed its allies to persuade it to leave the mountain fastnesses to battle on the frontier. This foolish action proved Edom's downfall, which the prophet sees as an act of retribution for the violence Esau had done to Jacob when Jacob was in straits. Obadiah stresses the fact that Zion shall be saved from its predicament; its savior will bring punishment down upon Edom. In its contents, Obadiah's prophecy is simiar to those of the other prophets who treated of the Assyrian war, namely Amos and Isaiah. Hence, Obadiah follows immediately after Amos in the order of the twelve prophets.

JONAH יונה

Jonah sits beneath a gourd tree outside the city of Nineveh.

"God prepared a gourd . . . to come up over Jonah, that it might be a shadow over his head" (Jonah 4.6).

The Book of Jonah — Jonah consists of four chapters. It tells the story of the prophet Jonah, the son of Amittai who flees toward Tarshish in disobedience to God's will—the Lord had sent him to Nineveh to urge the people of that corrupt city to repent: "Their wickedness is come up before Me" (Jonah 1.2). Unless they mend their ways, the city will be destroyed. A storm arises which threatens the ship in which Jonah is sailing. To the consternation of the sailors, Jonah confesses his responsibility for the disaster, and himself suggests that he be cast into the ocean to relieve the storm. Miraculously, he is saved from death by drowning—a big fish swallows Jonah, and later spews him forth on to dry land. Recognizing that no flight from God is possible, Jonah proceeds to Nineveh and, as God has commanded him, urges the people of that great city to repent. His words are heeded, much to his dismay, for Nineveh was Israel's mortal enemy. Vexed, Jonah goes outside the city to see what will become of it. God raises up a gourd to shield the prophet from the sun, but makes it whither overnight. Jonah, suffering, prays for death, and God reprimands him: "Thou hast had pity on the gourd, for which thou hast not labored, neither madest it grow, which came up in a night, and perished in a night; and should not I have pity on Nineveh, that great city, wherein are more than sixscore thousand persons that cannot discern between their right hand and their left hand, and also much cattle?" (Jonah 4.10-11).

The book of Jonah is a classic statement of the practical value of repentance, of God's compassion for all His creatures—and that there is no flight from His presence.

MICAH מיכה

The vision of universal peace wherein swords shall be beaten into plowshares and spears into pruning-hooks.

"Nation shall not lift up sword against nation, Neither shall they learn war any more (Micah 4.3).

The Book of Micah — The prophet Micah came from the city of Moresheth in Judah, near Gath. His prophecies, dealing with the capitals of Judah and Ephraim, Jerusalem and Samaria, were delivered in the days of Jotham, Ahaz, and Hezekiah, kings of Judah—i.e., he was a younger contemporary of Isaiah. Mention is made of Micah as a prophet from the days of Hezekiah in the book of Jeremiah (26.18); there, too, one of his prophecies is recorded: "Zion shall be plowed as a field,/ And Jerusalem shall become heaps,/ And the mountain of the house as the high places of a forest" (cf. Micah 3.12).

Seven chapters of the book of Micah have survived in which the prophet concentrates on three principal points:

1. the moral decline that resulted in the national catastrophe at the time of Assyria's rise;

2. the last-minute rescue of Jerusalem; and

3. the saving remnant of Judah.

Micah formulates three religious dicta: "It hath been told thee, O man, what is good,/ And what the Lord doth require of thee:/ Only to do justly, and to love mercy, and to walk humbly with thy God" (Micah 6.8). The book of Micah also contains a prophecy concerning "the end of days" similar to that of Isaiah, with a slight expansion. Micah's style is polished and fluent.

NAHUM נחום

The dams are opened, water floods the palace, Nineveh is laid waste.

"The gates of the rivers are opened, And the palace is dissolved" (Nahum 2.7).

The Book of Nahum — Three chapters have survived from the book of the prophet Nahum, all of which are devoted to a description of the destruction of the city of Nineveh, the capital of Assyria, and Judah's destined liberation from Assyrian domination. Throughout these chapters Nineveh is presented as still rich and powerful militarily. Since the destruction of Nineveh may have occurred in 612 B.C.E., many scholars regard Nahum as having lived at that time. However, at the time of its destruction, Nineveh was already impoverished and Judah had for some time been completely independent—a situation that does not accord with Nahum's description. We must conclude that Nahum flourished in the period toward the end of the reign of Manasseh —i.e., the beginning of the second half of the 6th century B.C.E.

The prophet declares that Nineveh's coming doom is an act of divine retribution. God is all-compassionate; but he is also the God of vengeance. The divine judgment had already been decreed—but its execution was delayed until 612 B.C.E. because, in prophetic terms, the iniquity of Nineveh was not yet complete, and the Lord was giving the people of Assyria a last opportunity to repent.

HABAKKUK חבקוק

Human beings caught as in a net symbolizing the triumph of evil over virtue.

"And makest men as the fishes of the sea...They catch them in their net . . . Therefore they rejoice and exult" (Habakkuk 1.14-15).

The Book of Habakkuk — Habakkuk begins his prophecy with a protest against the success of the imperialistic Chaldeans. Since Judah appears in his prophecies as an independent and prosperous nation, we may place Habakkuk at the beginning of the reign of Josiah, when the Chaldeans were just beginning to expand.

The book of Habakkuk contains three chapters. In the first chapter the prophet raises the eternal question: How can unrighteousness exist in the world side by side with Divine Providence? "Thou that are of eyes too pure to behold evil,/ And that canst not look on mischief,/ Wherefore lookest Thou, when they deal treacherously,/ And holdest Thy peace, when the wicked swalloweth up/ The man that is more righteous than he?" (Habakkuk 1.13). The answer is given in the second chapter: "For the vision is yet for the appointed time,/ And it declareth of the end, and doth not lie;/ Though it tarry, wait for it;/ Because it will surely come, it will not delay" (Habakkuk 2.3). In the third chapter, a prayer similar to those of the book of Psalms, the prophet describes the salvation of God, answering those who seek Him in time of distress: "O Lord, I have heard the report of Thee, and am afraid;/ In the midst of the years make it known;/ In wrath remember compassion" (Habakkuk 3.2).

ZEPHANIAH צפניה

A flashing torch reveals evil-doers in the black of night.

"I will search Jerusalem with lamps; And I will punish the men that are settled on their lees" (Zephaniah 1.12).

The Book of Zephaniah — Zephaniah, who prophesied during the reign of Josiah in Judah, speaks of "the day of the Lord" when the evil-doers of Judah shall be destroyed, together with the evil-doers of Ethiopia, Assyria, Ammon and Moab. After that dread day, His name will be broadcast throughout the world; even distant nations shall serve Him. An idyllic age will begin for Israel: "The remnant of Israel shall not do iniquity,/ Nor speak lies,/ Neither shall a deceitful tongue be found in their mouth;/ For they shall feed and lie down,/ And none shall make them afraid" (Zephaniah 3.13) Zephaniah feels hatred only for those neighbors of Judah that had oppressed his country: Philistia, Am-

mon, Moab. He is not particularly concerned over the fall of Assyria, or the Ethiopian victims.

The time of Zephaniah's prophecy is apparently the period of Assyrian decline—ca. 612 B.C.E., when Nineveh fell. Babylon was becoming a great power, capable of defeating even Egypt, Assyria's ally. The atmosphere was electric with currents of political and cultural disturbance; men sought desperately to read the future. In this age of uncertainty, Zephaniah insists that there is no recourse save in the perfection of the world through the kingdom of God. Under that holy kingdom, Israel, first nation of all to repent, will enlighten the world through living by God's Torah.

HAGGAI חגי

A modest house of worship with the prophet's vision of the glorious temple of the future, in background.

"The glory of this latter house shall be greater than that of the former . . . and in this place will I give peace" (Haggai 2.9).

The Book of Haggai — The book of Haggai consists of four prophecies delivered in a period of as many months during the second year of the reign of Darius, king of Persia (520 B.C.E.). In the first prophecy, dated the first of Elul, Haggai turns to Zerubbabel, governor of Judah, and Joshua, the High Priest, with a reproof directed at those men of little faith who were saying: "The time is not come, the time that the Lord's house should be built" (Haggai 1.2). Fifteen years earlier, the building of the Second Temple, a project authorized by Cyrus, had been interrupted and had never been completed. To Haggai, the failure of the community of Jerusalem to prosper was directly due to the lack of a Temple. Haggai's words made a strong impression, and the Judeans returned to complete the Temple.

In his second prophecy, dated the 21st of Tishri, Haggai encourages the builders. In his third prophecy, dated the 24th of Kislev, he remonstrates at the persistence of impure worship for lack of a Temple. His fourth prophecy, uttered the same day, encourages Zerubbabel: "I . . . will make thee as a signet; for I have chosen thee" (Haggai 2.23). Haggai's greatness lay in his ability to reprove the heads of the Judean government and to choose the proper time for exhorting the people as well as their leaders to rebuild the Temple.

ZECHARIAH· זכריה

Old men in repose observe children at play in the streets of Jerusalem.

"There shall yet old men and old women sit in the broad places of Jerusalem . . . And . . . boys and girls playing" (Zech. 8.4-5).

The Book of Zechariah — There are 14 chapters in the book of Zechariah. These are divided into two parts: 1. chapters 1-8; and 2. chapters 9-14. These chapters vary greatly as to content, form, style, and time.

The first part is mainly a sequel to Haggai's call for the rebuilding of the Temple. It consists of remonstrances to the Judeans to forsake the wicked ways of their ancestors. Zechariah envisages the building of a wall around Jerusalem, and describes the scorn of God directed against the wicked nations. In addition, he serves as a mediator in the controversy between Zerubbabel, the governor of Judea, and Joshua, the High Priest. The first part of Zechariah also contains answers to those who question the observance of the fast days after the destruction of the First Temple. Zechariah employs illustrative metaphors full of elaborate detail.

The second part of the book of Zechariah is further subdivided into two sections: 1. chapters 9-11; and 2. chapters 12-14. Each section begins with the heading, "The burden of the word of the Lord"; the language in these chapters is almost mystically allusive.

The motive for Zechariah's prophecies was apparently the difficulties attendant on the reconstruction of the walls around Jerusalem; this work was accompanied by many internal and external problems. The Judean settlement contended with a host of personal controversies, based on ambition and faction, in addition to the larger political questions. The prophet concludes by reporting a great miracle: Jerusalem had been taken by the enemy, half of its population exiled, when suddenly a great plague broke out and decimated the armies of the enemy. The result, in Zechariah's view, was the sanctification of God's name, and the sanctification of Jerusalem above all cities. "And it shall come to pass, that every one that is left of all the nations that came against Jerusalem shall go up from year to year to worship the King, the Lord of hosts, and to keep the feast of tabernacles" (Zechariah 14.16).

MALACHI מלאכי

The nations of the world cast away their weapons and turn to Zion.

"I will send you Elijah the prophet Before the coming Of the . . . day of the Lord" (Malachi 3.23).

The Book of Malachi — Malachi is the last of the prophets. The sages asserted: "With the death of the last of the prophets, Haggai, Zechariah, and Malachi, the Holy Spirit departed from Israel" (Yoma 9b). Malachi prophesied at a time when the Second Temple had long been established. The Judeans had left behind them the enthusiasm engendered by the reconstruction of the Temple in the days of Haggai and Zechariah, and developed an attitude of apathy toward the Temple service. This indifference was the cause of enormous difficulty, social as well as religious and communal.

The book of Malachi contains three chapters, all admonitory. The prophet opens with an outburst at the Judeans for having failed to appreciate God's singular relationship with them: they honor Him neither as Father nor as Master. Malachi then reproves the priests—their conduct had lowered the Temple's prestige to the point where it might perhaps be best to close the sanctuary's doors. He also admonishes the Judeans for misalliances with foreign women, a practice calculated to undermine the purity of family life and of the holy seed. "And I will come near to you to judgment;/ And I will be a swift witness/ Against the sorcerers, and against the adulterers,/ And against false swearers;/ And against those that oppress the hireling in his wages,/ The widow, and the fatherless,/ And that turn aside the stranger from his right,/ And fear not Me" (Malachi 3.5). Finally, Malachi calls for repentence, for a return to God "Before the coming/ Of the great and terrible day of the Lord" (Malachi 3.23).

A sage writing a small scroll.

"Are they not written in the book of the chronicles of the kings of Judah?"
(II. Kings 20.20).

HAGIOGRAPHA
(Scriptures)

כתובים

The third main division of the Bible is called Scriptures. The title, meaning writings, refers to the tradition that the books included in this section are of human authorship, written directly by saintly individuals. Thus, Scriptures are to be distinguished from the Pentateuch, the Torah which is the word of God as spoken to Moses, and from the books of the Prophets, which are the divinely inspired speech of the prophets.

The traditional order of the books of Scriptures is: Psalms, Proverbs, Job, the Song of Songs, Ruth, Lamentations, Ecclesiastes, Esther, Daniel, Ezra, Nehemiah, I and II Chronicles. The Talmudic masters have preserved a different order (Baba Bathra 14b): Ruth, Psalms, Job, Proverbs, Ecclesiastes, the Song of Songs, Lamentations, Daniel, Esther, Ezra-Nehemiah (as one book), I and II Chronicles. The differences in order are probably due to diverse preferences for the various books and to dissimilar estimates of the time when they were composed.

HAGIOGRAPHA

The Hagiographa include maxims, proverbs, ethical preachment, and
Proverbs, Job, Song of Songs, Ruth, Lamentations, Ecclesiastes, Esther,
two books of Ezra and Nehemiah as one book; the two books of
Books, marked by a mnemonic derived from the initials of the He

WISDOM BOOKS [EM

14. Psalms תהלים

Contents: Songs of praise to God,
attributed to the "Sweet singer of
Israel", and others.

Author: Attributed to David (and 10
Elders: Adam, Melchizedek, Abraham,
Moses, Heman, Jeduthun, Asaph and
3 sons of Korah).

15. Prover

Contents: Aphoris
wisdom attributed
of all men," and
e.g., the sages in

Author: Hezekiah

THE FIVE SCROLLS

17. Song of Songs
שיר השירים

Contents: Songs of love and friend-
ship ascribed to King Solomon. Interpreted as an allegory for the love
between God and the community of
Israel.

Author: Hezekiah and his circle.

18. Ruth רות

Contents: A pastoral idyll of life in
Palestine during the days of the
judges. Concludes by tracing the
genealogy of David to Ruth and
Boaz.

Author: Hezekiah and his circle.

19. Lament
כה

Contents: Scroll of
moaning the destru
and the Temple ar
people from the H

Author: Jeremiah

THE OTHER WRITINGS

22. Daniel דניאל

Contents: The esoteric prophecies of
Daniel. His miraculous feats during
the Babylonian Exile. His historical
predictions and Messianic visions.

Author: Men of the Great Assembly

23. Ezra עזרא

Contents: The history of Judea in the
days of Ezra. The building of the
Second Temple and the return to
Zion from Babylonian exile. Ezra
renews the Covenant between God
and Israel. His ordinances for the
propagation of the faith, with emphasis on study of the Torah.

Author: Ezra

Nehemiah

Contents: Events i
of Nehemiah, Pe
in Judah: His poli
the return from e
the enemies of Ju
He rebuilds the
His national ordi
organization of t

Author: Ezra

כתובים

poetry imbued with divine spirit. They comprise eleven books: Psalms,
Daniel, Ezra-Nehemiah and Chronicles 1 & 2. (The sages viewed the
Chronicles were considered parts of a single book.) *Wisdom (Emet)*
brew titles of Job, Proverbs and Psalms.

ספרי אמ״ת [E

bs משלי

ms and words of
o Solomon, "wisest
o other aphorists,
Hezekiah's circle.

and his circle.

16. Job איוב

Contents: The story of Job. His disputations with his friends on Providence and its mysterious ways.

Author: Moses. Some interpreted
the book of Job as an allegory (Baba
Bathra 15a).

חמש מגילור

ations
א

Lamentations be-
ction of Jerusalem
d the exile of the
ly Land.

20. Ecclesiastes
קהלת

Contents: Philosophic reflections on
the life of man and his lot, ascribed
to King Solomon.

Author: Hezekiah and his circle.

21. Esther אסתר

Contents: The miracle of Purim.
Mordecai and Esther rescue the Jews
of Persia and Media from Haman's
machinations in the days of Aha-
suerus.

Author: Men of the Great Assembly.

שאר הכתובים

נחמיה

n Judea in the time
sian representative
tical influence after
xile. Relations with
dah and Benjamin.
walls of Jerusalem.
ances and the re-
e priestly watches.

24. Chronicles I & II דברי הימים א׳וב׳

Contents: A complete resume of early Jewish history, beginning
with the creation of man and ending with the proclamation of
Cyrus, King of Persia, permitting his Jewish subjects to rebuild
the Second Temple and return to Zion.

Author: Begun by Ezra. Completed by Nehemiah.

WISDOM BOOKS ספרי אמ"ת

Psalms, Proverbs and Job — Moral philosophy, problems of theology, didactic aphorisms, and hymns of praise to God and His justice are contained in these works. They are acknowledged literary masterpieces and exhibit a synthesizing of a realistic outlook on life with elevated principles and a firm faith in God.

PSALMS תהלים

King David plays his harp and gazes heavenward for inspiration.

"When I behold Thy heavens . . . What is man, that Thou art mindful of him?" (Ps. 8.4-5).

Psalms — The book of Psalms is a collection of 150 religious songs. In the psalms individual men pray to God in time of trouble, or thank and praise Him for granting succor, or express their personal need to come closer to Him, or urge those who have strayed from the path of righteousness to return. Its intense spirituality and simple beauty of expression have caused the book of Psalms to be accepted as folk literature by Jews and non-Jews alike—indeed, by all those who seek to pour out their hearts to their Creator. Since the psalms are written in the first person— even when the speaker identifies himself with the people at large—the sympathetic reader is able to feel as though he too is expressing his deepest and most sacred emotions; it is as though he is speaking directly to his Creator.

Of the composition of Psalms, the sages asserted: "David wrote the book of Psalms, including in it the works of the [ten] elders" (Baba Bathra 14b). Their names are at the head of many of the psalms. The preceding quotation is the source for the tradition that King David himself composed the book of Psalms.

The 150 psalms are divided into five sections: 1-41; 42-72; 73-89; 90-106; 107-150. Some consecutive psalms are related in content. In general, however, there is no systematic connection. Apparently, the book of Psalms consists of several separate compilations. Thus, the second section concludes with the formula: "The prayers of

David the son of Jesse are ended" (Psalms 72.20). Undoubtedly, this marks the conclusion of one collection of psalms; later, another collection of psalms was discovered and added to the first one.

PROVERBS משלי

Wisdom in the guise of a beautiful woman, gives Solomon a scroll.

"Say unto wisdom: 'Thou art my sister', And call understanding thy kinswoman" (Prov. 7.4).

Proverbs — The book of Proverbs is divided into eight sections, each with a different heading:

1. Proverbs 1-9: "The proverbs of Solomon the son of David, king of Israel."
2. Proverbs 10-22.16: "The proverbs of Solomon."
3. Proverbs 22.17-24.22: "Incline thine ear, and hear the words of the wise,/ And apply thy heart unto my knowledge."
4. Proverbs 24.23-34: "These also are sayings of the wise."
5. Proverbs 25-29: "These also are proverbs of Solomon, which the men of Hezekiah king of Judah copied."
6. Proverbs 30: "The words of Agur the son of Jakeh; the burden. The man saith unto Ithiel, unto Ithiel and Ucal."
7. Proverbs 31.1-9: "The words of King Lemuel; the burden wherewith his mother corrected him."
8. Proverbs 31.10-31: A song of praise to the "woman of valor" in acrostic form.

Each of these sections is a collection of proverbs in a distinctly different form. The book of

Proverbs as a whole primarily aims to teach the one way of life capable of bringing happiness to those who practice it. The basis of this way of life is the fear of God, derived from a strong faith in the rule of reward and punishment. The mentor is a wise and experienced man. The Torah is identified with wisdom—that which develops man's capacity to comprehend the essential meaning of existence.

The age mirrored in the book of Proverbs is a placid one, free of any upheaval, religious, cultural or political. The nation is represented as under a monarchical government. In houses where wisdom is taught, sages guide youths, whom they address with affection as their sons.

The final verses of the book of Proverbs describing the "woman of valor" (Proverbs 31.10-31) have been accepted as a hymn of praise lauding the diligence and wisdom of the Jewish woman; it is recited at home on the Sabbath eve before the Kiddush ceremony.

JOB   איוב

Job, a leper, in sackcloth and ashes, is comforted by his three friends.

"Job's three friends . . . made an appointment together to come to bemoan him and to comfort him" (*Job 2.11*).

Job — The book of Job is a large, philosophic treatment of the classic problem of reward and punishment. The proverbial Job—righteous, wise,

God-fearing, wealthy—is put to the most difficult of tests at the behest of Satan, to determine whether his fear of heaven is genuine—a consequence of his recognition of the one God—or whether it is based on Job's experience of its practical value in leading to good fortune. The query is posed: When fortune no longer smiles on Job, will he curse God and turn to other deities, after the pagan fashion? Suffering, Job does indeed argue that there is no justice in the world; nevertheless, he cleaves to God from whom he seeks justification of His ways. Job engages in lengthy philosophic disputations with four friends: Eliphaz the Temanite, Bildad the Shuhite, Zophar the Naamathite, and Elihu, the son of Barachel the Buzite, of the family of Ram. Elihu, a younger man, leads the discussion from the question of the justification of God's ways to a consideration of God's wondrous works. At the end of these deliberations, God answers Job out of a whirlwind and overwhelms him with evidence of the incomprehensibility of divine providence. Job is forced to concede man's pettiness in relation to the power of God. In his words: "I had heard of Thee by the hearing of the ear;/ But now mine eye seeth Thee;/ Wherefore I abhor my words, and repent,/ Seeing I am dust and ashes" (Job 42.5-6). After this submission, Job is permitted to regain his former happy state.

The moral of the book of Job is: Mortal man cannot judge the ways of God in the world. Suffering at times is inflicted on men to test their devotion to God. He who truly recognizes his creator will never forsake Him. The book is rich in depth of thought and power of metaphor.

5 MEGILLOT חמש מגלות

The Five Scrolls — The Song of Songs, Lamentations, Ecclesiastes, Esther and Ruth are known as the Five Scrolls (*Megillot*), as each of them is read in the synagogue from a scroll on a specific holiday or festival: the Song of Songs on Passover, Ruth on Shavuoth, Lamentations on Tisha B'ab, Ecclesiastes on Sukkoth, and Esther on Purim.

SONG OF SONGS שיר השירים

A young shepherd and shepherdess meet with their flocks.

"O thou fairest among women, Go thy way forth ... And feed thy kids, beside the shepherds' tents" (Song of Songs 1.8).

Song of Songs — The Song of Songs means "the most excellent song of all." This scroll is one large love poem. It expresses the tender feelings of a shepherdess and her beloved in all their nuances: their longing for one another, their joy at meeting, their sorrow at absence. The lovers describe each others physical charms against the background of the beauties of the countryside where they spend delightful hours.

The scroll is suffused with a spirit of purity and the sanctification of the senses. Rabbi Akiba regarded the Song of Songs as representing the acme of holiness: "All the scriptures are holy, but the Song of Songs is the Holy of Holies" (Yadaim, 3.5). The sages considered the scroll to be allegory for a dialogue between God and His people. Rabbi Akiba also declared: "He who chants the Song of Songs in a tavern, treating it as a mere song, has no portion in the world-to-come" (Tosefta Sanhedrin 12,10). The Talmudic masters asserted that Solomon wrote the Song of Songs as a young man (Midrash Shir Hashirim 1,1).

The literary excellence of the Song of Songs is universally acknowledged. It is chanted on the eve of Sabbath when the Sabbath Queen is ushered in, that love and holiness might reign in Jewish homes. Many celebrants also recite this scroll at the Passover Seder after the reading of the Hag-gadah, as a fitting celebration of God's love for Israel in the season of spring and youth.

RUTH רות

Ruth follows behind the reapers who intentionally drop gleanings for her.

"And she went, and came and gleaned in the field after the reapers" (Ruth 2.3).

Ruth — The scroll of Ruth is an idyllic tale describing peaceful rural life in Judah during the time of the Judges. It tells the story of a family from Bethlehem. In a time of famine, the father, Elimelech, takes his wife Naomi and two sons Mahlon and Chilion to the land of Moab. There they remain ten years. After Elimelech's death, his sons marry Moabite women, Orpah and Ruth. The sons die childless, and Naomi decides to return home to Judah. She tells her daughters-in-law to return to their parents' homes, but Ruth prefers to accompany Naomi to Judah. In their poverty, Ruth becomes a gleaner after the reapers in the field of Boaz, of the family of Elimelech, her father-in-law; in time, Boaz takes Ruth to wife. By this marriage, according to the Biblical injunction, the name of the dead is perpetuated, "that the name of the dead be not cut off from among his brethren" (Ruth 4.10). Ruth becomes the ancestress of King David, founder of the Davidic dynasty.

Ruth is portrayed everywhere in the scroll with an aura of piety and devotion, as one who understands her duties at all times: when she cleaves to her mother-in-law; when she gleans in the fields; and even when humbling herself, she visits Boaz at night in the granary to ask him to marry her, that the name of the dead might be perpetuated. It is no wonder that she is chosen to be David's ancestress. The scroll of Ruth is suffused with the calm, steady light of virtue, loyalty, faith, and a deserved reward.

LAMENTATIONS איכה

A woman mourns as Jerusalem burns and the Jews go into exile.

"She weepeth sore in the night, And her tears are on her cheeks; She hath none to comfort her" (Lam. 1.2).

Lamentations — The scroll of Lamentations contains five chapters of elegy over the destruction of the First Temple—hence the title. Chapters 1, 2, and 4 are written in alphabetical acrostic form, chapter 3 in a triple acrostic. Chapter 5 consists of 22 verses, corresponding to the number of letters in the Hebrew alphabet. The sentiment running through all of Lamentations is one of deep anguish.

The sages attributed the composition of Lamentations to the prophet Jeremiah. The author, who personally suffered from the destruction of Jerusalem and the ruin of the Temple, links his individual tragedy with that of the nation. "I am the man that hath seen affliction/By the rod of His wrath" (Lamentations 3.1). The elegy is chanted in the synagogue on Tisha B'Ab; this has influenced the recital of other liturgical compositions (*Kinnot*) after services on that day.

ECCLESIASTES קהלת

The aged King Solomon points to the palace and exclaims "All is vanity!"

"Vanity of vanities, saith Koheleth; Vanity of vanities, all is vanity" (Eccl. 1.2).

Ecclesiastes — The scroll of Ecclesiastes is attributed to Solomon in the text itself: "The words of Koheleth the son of David, king in Jerusalem" (Ecclesiastes 1.1). Koheleth is Solomon, who "amassed" wisdom. An examination of the contents of the book leads one to the conclusion that it was composed in Solomon's later years, for much of Ecclesiastes is based on wisdom gained through a variety of experiences. The sages put it thus: "When a person is young, he recites songs; in his maturity he utters proverbs; when he grows old he declares 'Vanity of vanities, all is vanity' [the second verse of Ecclesiastes]".

Basically, Ecclesiastes teaches the foolishness of involvement in affairs that are irrelevant to the reality of life. There is no point struggling to change the course of the world. "One generation passeth away, and another generation cometh;/ And the earth abideth for ever" (Ecclesiastes 1.4). The wise man recognizes the world's frustrations: "For much wisdom is much vexation;/ And he that increaseth knowledge increaseth sorrow" (Ecclesiastes 1.18); yet, "The wise man, his eyes are in his head;/ But the fool walketh in darkness" (Ecclesiastes 2.14). In addition to folly, Ecclesiastes despises miserliness and greed. Instead, he tells men to enjoy life while they can, stressing, however, that they will have to account for their deeds. "Rejoice, O young man, in thy youth;/ And let thy heart cheer thee in the days of thy youth,/ And walk in the ways of thy heart,/ And in the sight of thine eyes;/ But know thou, that for all these things/ God will bring thee into judgment" (Ecclesiastes 11.9). Every extreme is a "vanity of vanities"—i.e., the worst of vanities.

Besides its hortatory passages, the scroll of Ecclesiastes contains many profound maxims and sophisticated wisdom. The last chapter describes in a remarkable image the decline of old age, ending with memorable verses: "Before the silver cord is snapped asunder,/ And the golden bowl is shattered,/ And the pitcher is broken at the fountain,/ And the wheel falleth shattered into the pit;/ And the dust returneth to the earth as it was,/ And the spirit returneth unto God who gave it" (Ecclesiastes 12.6-7).

The scroll of Ecclesiastes is read in the synagogue on the festival of Sukkoth—the festival symbolizing the end of the year, as the book of Ecclesiastes concerns man's end in life.

ESTHER אסתר

Mordecai counsels Esther at the gates of the palace.

"Mordecai . . . told it unto Esther the queen; and Esther told the king thereof in Mordecai's name" (Esther 2.22).

Esther — The scroll of Esther is named after the heroine of the miracle commemorated by the Purim holiday.

The scroll is remarkable for the conciseness of its narrative. Only the bare essentials appear in the pages of this work. Indeed, many questions that might arise in a reader's mind remain unanswered, such as: What is the reason for the king's having arranged this great banquet? Why does Queen Vashti refuse to obey her master? What is Mordecai doing in Shushan? Why does Mordecai command his niece Esther not to divulge her people and origin? Why does Mordecai refuse to bow down to Haman, even for the sake of conformity? What is the source of Haman's hatred of Mordecai's people? What is the background of the strange practices in the royal court of Persia and Medea? Finally, what is the reason for the sudden reversal in the fortune of the Jews of Persia after Esther has placed her life in jeopardy to intercede on their behalf and after the traditional three days of fasting and prayer in time of distress?

An entire tractate in the Talmud is devoted to the scroll of Esther, and Jewish law prescribes that men, women and children alike must listen to the reading of the scroll in the synagogue and take part in the joyous and unique Purim celebration.

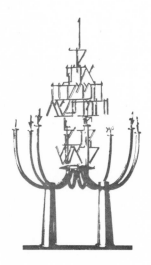

OTHER WRITINGS שאר הכתובים

Daniel, Ezra, Nehemiah and Chronicles—For the most part these four books belong to the Persian era and deal with the return to Zion. They record the beginnings of the scribal period, and in their descriptions of the widespread study and observance of the laws of the Torah, bear witness to the triumph of the Mosaic faith and the continuity of Jewish tradition.

DANIEL דניאל

Daniel unharmed in the lions' den.

"Then the king commanded, and they brought Daniel, and cast him into the den of lions" (Dan. 6.17).

Daniel — The book of Daniel contains twelve chapters, some in Hebrew, others in Aramaic. It tells the story of Daniel and his companions, Hananiah, Mishael, and Azariah, who when still young, were brought to the royal court of Nebuchadnezzar, king of Babylon, to be trained for the king's service. Among the noblemen exiled from Judah with King Jehoiachin, they were both exceedingly devout and wise. Many miracles are performed for their benefit. Hananiah, Mishael, and Azariah are saved from a fiery furnace into which they have been cast for refusing to bow down to an image set up by Nebuchadnezzar. Daniel escapes unscathed from a lion's den into which he has been flung in the days of King Darius, the Mede, because he had been discovered praying to God and facing toward Jerusalem.

According to the Talmudic masters, Daniel was a great sage, one who could both reveal and interpret the meaning of dreams. Of particular significance are his apocalyptic references to the coming of the Messiah. But Daniel is not to be confused with the Daniel (spelled in Hebrew without י) mentioned in Ezekiel together with Job and Noah as one of the sages who were unable to save their generation despite their own virtue. Such identification is impossible, since Daniel was still a young man in Ezekiel's life time; he could not have been held up as a paragon of wisdom to the prince of Tyre (as Ezekiel does in 28.3), or as a righteous man capable of defending his generation from destruction. Undoubtedly the wise and righteous man Ezekiel refers to was a non-Jew in an evil generation, like Noah and Job. The fact that Daniel's name is listed between those of Noah and Job (Ezekiel 14.14-29) would indicate that Daniel lived before Job and was considered an exemplary figure in the time of Ezekiel.

EZRA עזרא

Ezra, with priests and Levites at his side, reads the Torah to his people.

"For Ezra had set his heart to seek the law of the Lord ... and to teach in Israel statutes and ordinances" (Ezra 7.10).

Ezra — The book of Ezra recounts the return of Babylonian captives to Zion from the time of the Cyrus proclamation through the rebuilding of the Temple in the days of Darius (chapters 1-6), as well as Ezra's actions on his arrival in Judea during the reign of Artaxerxes, king of Persia (chapters 7-10). The book contains authoritative documents shedding important light on many significant events during these two periods. Ezra is partly in Hebrew, partly in Aramaic. Cyrus' proclamation addressed to the Jews, is in simple Hebrew, while the antipathy of the Samaritans to the Judeans and their expressions of hatred are in Aramaic (Ezra 4.5-6.18). Also in Aramaic is the text of the official document by King Artaxerxes appointing Ezra (Ezra 7.11-26).

Of Ezra himself, the book notes: "This Ezra went up from Babylon; and he was a ready scribe in the Law of Moses, which the Lord, the God of Israel, had given; and the king granted him all his request, according to the hand of the Lord his God upon him. . . . For Ezra had set his heart to seek the law of the Lord, and to do it, and to teach in Israel statutes and ordinances" (Ezra 7.6,10). Ezra's mission was that of a spiritual guide. Having delivered to the Judeans funds with which he had been entrusted by the Jews of Babylon, Ezra recited a dramatic prayer; then he bent his efforts to combatting intermarriage and assimilation.

NEHEMIAH נחמיה

Rebuilding Jerusalem's walls with trowel and sword, as guard readies to sound the shofar.

"Everyone with one of his hands wrought in the work, and with the other held his weapon" (Nehemiah 4.11).

Nehemiah — The book of Nehemiah is a natural continuation of Ezra. Nehemiah went up to Jerusalem thirteen years after Ezra, in the twentieth year of the reign of Artaxerxes (about 444 B.C.E.). Since the two men cooperated in their spiritual mission, the two books bearing their names are sometimes regarded as one. They are thus recorded by the Talmudic masters (Baba Bathra 14b); the traditional Masoretic enumeration of the total number of verses for each book of the Bible records the total for both books at the end of Nehemiah. The book, written completely in Hebrew, tells how Nehemiah organized the religious life of those Jews who returned to Judea, and describes the measures he took to provide for their safety.

Nehemiah was cup-bearer to Artaxerxes in Shushan, the capital of Persia, and a favorite of the king. On learning from his brother Hanani that the walls of Jerusalem were breached, and that the new colony was in extreme peril, Nehemiah sought the king's permission to go up to Jerusalem with royal authority to organize the defense and welfare of the city. Artxerxes granted Nehemiah's request, and gave Nehemiah letters to the governors of the neighboring states urging them to aid the king's representative. Undoubtedly, the Persian king reasoned that the success of the new Judean settlement would redound to the safety of the Persian kingdom.

By a series of brilliant moves, Nehemiah quickly rebuilt the walls of Jerusalem. He augmented the settlement in Jerusalem proper to give it internal strength, and relieved some of the economic pressure within the community by releasing the poor from the payment of their debts. Together with Ezra, he reorganized the study of the Torah, the order of Sabbath and holy day worship, and everything concerned with the Temple service. He ordered the Judeans to divorce their foreign wives, in order to close ranks within the Judean community.

THE BOOKS OF CHRONICLES

Chronicles I and II sum up the story of Israel set forth in the Pentateuch and the Former Prophets, and parallel, for the most part, the geneological lists and historical accounts contained in those portions of the Bible. While Chronicles is divided into two sections, it is in effect one work, stressing God's kingship over His chosen land. Throughout, God is portrayed as controlling history, with kings and conquerors being but agents of His will.

The Temple worship of God is of central importance in Chronicles: the building of the Temple and the activities of the Levites are given a place of prominence in the narration. Judah is described as a holy community, while the Northern Kingdom is often condemned for its apostasy.

In tracing the origins of the sacred institutions of Judaism, Chronicles demonstrates their antiquity.

I Chronicles contains 29 chapters and II Chronicles, 36.

I. CHRONICLES דברי הימים א'

Ezra's vision of the generations of men passing before him.

"So all Israel were reckoned . . . they are written in the book of the kings of Israel (I. Chron. 9.1).

I Chronicles — 1 Chronicles begins by tracing Jewish genealogy from Adam to the partriarchs. It notes briefly the heredity line of the sons of Ishmael and Keturah (Abraham's concubine), that of the sons of Esau and of the kings who ruled in Edom before Israel became a monarchy, as well as the genealogical chain of the tribes of Israel. Despite these important though brief references, I Chronicles makes no mention either of Exodus or of the division of Canaan, or of the period of the Judges, or of the beginnings of the Judean monarchy.

Beginning with chapter 10, the book becomes more detailed, the death of Saul serving to introduce the narrative. It concentrates on a fairly full account of the reign of King David—his wars, the order of the Temple service, and preparations for building the Temple in Jerusalem. Of the 29 chapters in I Chronicles, 19 are devoted to David alone.

II. CHRONICLES

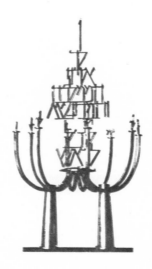

דברי הימים ב׳

A herald announces Cyrus' proclamation that the Temple be rebuilt.

"Thus saith Cyrus king of Persia . . . 'the Lord . . . hath charged me to build Him a house in Jerusalem'" (II. Chron. 36. 23).

II Chronicles — II Chronicles opens with the reign of Solomon, to which nine chapters are devoted. From this point on, the narrative treats of the reigns of the kings of Judah—the northern kingdom of Ephraim is mentioned only parenthetically, insofar as it touches on events in the southern kingdom of Judah. II Chronicles deals at length with the reign of the important monarchs, Hezekiah and Josiah. Mention is made of the impressive event of the renewal of the passover holiday during Josiah's reign. "And there was no Passover like to that kept in Israel from the days of Samuel the prophet; neither did any of the kings of Israel keep such a passover as Josiah kept . . . In the eighteenth year of the reign of Josiah was this passover kept" (II. Chronicles 35.18-19). It concludes with Cyrus' proclamation to the Babylonian exiles: "All the kingdoms of the earth hath the Lord, the God of heaven, given me; and He hath charged me to build Him a house in Jerusalem, which is in Judah. Whosoever there is among you of all His people—the Lord his God be with him—let him go up" (II Chronicles 36.23).

II Chronicles contains many historical details not recorded in the book of Kings—apparently its function was to supplement the latter book. On the other hand, there are many details found in the books of Kings and Samuel which are not recorded in II. Chronicles.

SYNOPSIS OF THE PENTATEUCH

GENESIS

BERESHIT (CHAPTERS 1-6)

1. The creation of the universe; the Sabbath.
2. The creation of man.
3. The Garden of Eden and its trees.
4. The river flowing out of Eden and its four tributaries.
5. The placing of Adam in Eden; his tasks.
6. Eating from the tree of knowledge prohibited.
7. The creation of woman.
8. The serpent; the sin and its punishment.
9. The expulsion of Adam and Eve from Eden; the role of the cherubim and the revolving flaming sword.
10. Cain and Abel: their occupations; their offerings; Cain's jealousy; the murder of Abel; Cain's punishment.
11. Cain's family.
12. The founding of a city in the name of Enoch.
13. Lamech, his wives and children.
14. The Lament of Lamech.
15. Seth; Enoch and his generation.
16. The generations from Adam to Noah.
17. The righteousness of Enoch, son of Jared.
18. Noah and his sons.
19. The sons of God wed the daughters of men; God's decision; the *Nephilim*.
20. Mankind grows increasingly evil; God regrets the creation of man; His decision; Noah finds favor in the eyes of God.

NOAH (CHAPTERS 6-11)

1. The righteousness of Noah.
2. The sons of Noah.
3. The wickedness of Noah's generation and the decree of the Deluge.
4. The construction of the ark; its purpose: the saving of Noah, his family, and male and female animals of every species of living creature.
5. Noah, his family and the animals enter the ark.
6. The Deluge: the rain; the rising of the waters; the subsiding of the waters; the resting of the ark on the mountains of Ararat; the reappearance of the mountain tops; the raven and the dove sent forth; the absorption of the waters.
7. The drying of the earth.
8. Departure from the ark; Noah offers sacrifices to God.
9. God vows that He will never again flood the earth or disrupt the regularity of the cycle of the seasons and the cycle of day and night.
10. God blesses Noah and his sons.
11. The eating of meat permitted.
12. The eating of a limb from a live animal prohibited.
13. The prohibition of murder and the punishment for that crime.
14. The covenant and the rainbow.
15. Noah's labor in the vineyard.
16. Noah's drunkenness; the deed of Ham; the filial respect shown by Shem and Japheth.
17. Noah curses Ham and blesses Shem and Japheth.
18. The genealogical tables of the 70 nations.
19. Nimrod.
20. Shem and Eber.
21. The erection of the tower of Babel; the confusion of tongues.
22. The ten generations from Noah to Abraham.
23. The family of Terah.
24. The departure of Terah, Abram, Sarai and Lot from Ur of the Chaldees; their arrival in Haran; the death of Terah.

LEKH LEKHA (CHAPTERS 12-17)

1. God commands Abram to leave his birthplace; God's promises to Abram.
2. Abram's departure from Haran and his arrival in Canaan. God appears to him at Shechem and promises to give the land to his descendants; Abram builds an altar in Shechem and Beth-el and calls on the name of the Lord.
3. The famine in Canaan; Abram, Sarai and Lot go down to Egypt.
4. Sarai is taken into the house of Pharaoh and is restored to Abram; Abram, Sarai and Lot return to the altar at Beth-el.
5. The quarrel between the shepherds of Abram and the shepherds of Lot; Abram's suggestion; the separation of the two men.
6. God's promise to Abram. Abram settles by the terebinths of Mamre.
7. The wars of Chedorlaomer and his allies against the kings of Sodom and the surrounding area; the victory of Chedorlaomer; Lot is taken into captivity.
8. Abram's war with the four kings; his victory; the rescue of Lot.
9. Melchizedek greets Abram with bread and wine and blesses him.
10. Abram rejects the goods of the king of Sodom, whom he has rescued from the four kings.
11. God reassures Abram, promising him a great reward, a vast progeny, and the land of Canaan as his inheritance.

12. God's covenant with Abram ("The Covenant between the Parts"): God tells Abram that his descendants will go into exile, and then be redeemed and return to the land. God gives the boundaries of the Promised Land and names the peoples inhabiting it.
13. Hagar; the birth of Ishmael.
14. God urges Abram to walk in His ways and be whole-hearted. The changing of the name Abram to Abraham; God's promises.
15. The covenant of circumcision.
16. The changing of the name Sarai to Sarah; God's promises to Abraham and His blessing of Sarah.
17. The blessing of the twelves princes of Ishmael.
18. The circumcision of Abraham and Ishmael and all the men of Abraham's household.

VAYERA (Chapters 18-22)

1. God appears to Abraham.
2. The arrival of three men.
3. Abraham runs to meet his guests and receives them very hospitably.
4. One of the guests foretells the birth of a son to Sarah.
5. Sarah laughs and then denies having done so.
6. God informs Abraham of the fate awaiting Sodom.
7. Abraham's intercession for the inhabitants of Sodom.
8. Two angels come to Sodom and are received in the house of Lot.
9. The people of Sodom surround Lot's house and demand that the guests be sent out to them.
10. Lot's rescue and his arrival in Zoar.
11. The destruction of Sodom.
12. Lot's wife, on looking back, turns into a pillar of salt.
13. Lot dwells in a cave; the deed of his daughters.
14. The progenitors of Moab and Ammon.
15. Abraham migrates to Gerar.
16. Sarah is taken by Abimelech and is then restored to Abraham.
17. Isaac: his birth; the circumcision; the banquet on the day of his weaning.
18. The expulsion of Hagar and Ishmael; their experience in the desert.
19. The covenant between Abraham and Abimelech.
20. The binding of Isaac.
21. The children of Nahor by Milcah and Reumah.
22. Rebekah, daughter of Bethuel.

HAYE SARAH (Chapters 23-25)

1. Sarah's age; her death; the mourning of Abraham.
2. The dealings between Abraham and Ephron and the children of Heth; the purchase of the cave of Machpelah as a burial plot; the burial of Sarah.
3. Eliezer's mission to Aram-naharaim (Mesopotamia); his experiences there; his success and his return with Rebekah.
4. The meeting of Isaac and Rebekah; their marriage.
5. The sons of Keturah, concubine of Abraham.
6. Abraham divides his property among his children.
7. Abraham's age; his death; his burial in the cave of Machpelah.

8. God blesses Isaac.
9. The sons of Ishmael: twelve princes according to their nations.
10. Ishmael's age; his death; the territory of the descendants of Ishmael.

TOLEDOT (Chapters 25-28)

1. The account of Isaac and Rebekah.
2. Jacob and Esau.
3. Esau sells his birthright to Jacob.
4. The famine in Canaan and Isaac's journey to Gerar.
5. God's revelation to Isaac; Isaac prolongs his stay in Gerar.
6. Rebekah is taken to Abimelech and is restored to Isaac.
7. Isaac's hundredfold harvest.
8. Isaac's prosperity and the jealousy of the Philistines.
9. At Abimelech's request, Isaac moves away to the valley of Gerar.
10. The wells.
11. Isaac moves to Beer-sheba where God assures him that He is with him.
12. The covenant between Isaac and Abimelech. Isaac's servants dig a well and find water.
13. Esau's marriages with the daughters of Heth.
14. Isaac's blessings and the rivalry of Jacob and Esau.
15. Esau's hatred of Jacob; Esau's plan.
16. Rebekah orders Jacob to flee to her brother-in-law in Haran; her conversation with Isaac.
17. Isaac calls Jacob, blesses him and commands him to go to Paddan-aram to take a wife from Rebekah's family.
18. Jacob goes to Paddan-aram.
19. Esau goes to Ishmael and marries the latter's daughter.

VAYETZE (Chapters 28-32)

1. Events involving Jacob on his way to Haran: he sleeps on a rock; the dream of the ladder and the angels of God; God's promise to him; Jacob's awe; the erection of a pillar to God; Jacob's vow.
2. Jacob's encounters near Haran; his arrival at the house of Laban; Jacob shepherds his uncle's flocks; the determination of Jacob's wages; his marriages.
3. Jacob's wives and sons.
4. The flocks given to Jacob for his additional labors.
5. Jacob's return to Canaan.
6. Laban's pursuit of Jacob; the argument between them.
7. Jacob and Laban make a covenant.
8. Jacob meets the angels of God in Mahanaim.

VAYISHLAH (Chapters 32-36)

1. Jacob sends messengers to Esau.
2. Esau sets out to meet his brother with 400 men.
3. Jacob's fear; his prayer and his gifts to his brother.
4. Jacob wrestles with the angel and is victorious.
5. The dislocation of the hollow of Jacob's thigh; eating the sinew of the thigh-vein in the hollow of the thigh prohibited.

6. The meeting of Esau and Jacob and their peaceful **separation.**

7. Jacob encamps in Succoth and then in Shechem; his activities there.

8. The violation of Dinah and the revenge of Simeon and Levi.

9. Jacob prepares to go up to Beth-el.

10. Jacob's arrival at Beth-el and his activities and experiences there; the altar; the death of Deborah, Rebekah's nurse; the revelation of God to Jacob; the Divine blessing; Jacob is renamed Israel; the libation and the pouring of oil on the pillar.

11. Events on the way to Bethlehem: the birth of Benjamin; the death and burial of Rachel; the pillar by the wayside.

12. The deed of Reuben on the way to Hebron.

13. The enumeration of Jacob's sons according to their mothers.

14. Jacob comes to his father Isaac in Hebron.

15. Isaac's age; his death and burial.

16. The wives of Esau; his descendants and their dwelling places.

17. The sons of Seir the Horite; the discovery of the hot springs in the wilderness.

18. The kings and chiefs of Edom.

VAYESHEV (Chapters 37-40)

1. The events preceding Joseph's sale into Egypt: his dreams; his brothers plot to kill him; he is sold to the Ishmaelites; the brothers deceive Jacob.

2. Jacob sees the coat of many colors dipped in blood and concludes that Joseph has been devoured by a wild beast; his great pain and mourning; his refusal to be comforted.

3. Episodes involving Judah: his friend, the Adullamite; his wife, the daughter of Shua; the death of his sons Er and Onan; the deed of Tamar; Perez and Zerah, sons of Judah by Tamar.

4. Joseph in Egypt: his labors and success in the house of Potiphar; his trial and imprisonment; the interpretation of the dreams of the chief butler and the chief baker; his request of the butler.

MIKETZ (Chapters 41-44)

1. The dreams of Pharaoh.

2. Joseph's interpretation and counsel.

3. The ascendancy of Joseph; his rule over Egypt.

4. The abundance in Egypt; the deeds of Joseph.

5. The birth of Joseph's sons, Manasseh and Ephraim, to his wife Asenath.

6. The famine in all the lands and in Egypt.

7. Joseph provides food for all peoples.

8. The descent of the brothers to Egypt and their experiences there: they come before Joseph and are accused of spying; their imprisonment and release; Simeon is kept as a hostage to ensure the coming of Benjamin; the brothers are given grain and provisions for the road.

9. The return of the brothers to Jacob and their experiences: their fear upon discovering their money in their sacks of corn; Jacob despairs and refuses to send Benjamin with them; Reuben's offer of surety refused; the exhaustion of the food supply; more argumentation concerning Benjamin; Judah assumes complete responsibility; Jacob acquiesces; his counsel and blessing.

10. The brothers' descent to Egypt, together with Benjamin, and their experiences there: their reception in the house of Joseph; they inform Joseph's steward of the return of their money; the steward's reply; they prepare a gift for Joseph; their meeting with Joseph; they dine with him and are sent away with a great deal of grain; the planting of the cup in Benjamin's sack; Joseph asserts he will take Benjamin as his slave.

VAYIGASH (Chapters 44-47)

1. Judah's speech before Joseph; he pleads to remain as Joseph's slave in Benjamin's stead.

2. Joseph makes himself known to his brothers; their fear; he calms them and asks that they inform Jacob of his position, and calls his father to come to him with all speed.

3. Pharaoh and his servants are pleased to learn of the arrival of Joseph's brothers.

4. Pharaoh gives wagons to Jacob's sons to convey their father and his household to Egypt, and promises that the good things of all the land of Egypt will be Jacob's.

5. Joseph's gifts to his father and brothers; the food for the journey.

6. The brothers return to Jacob and tell him what has befallen them; Jacob's spirit revives; his joy and decision to go to Joseph.

7. Jacob travels to Beer-sheba with his family and there offers sacrifices to the God of his fathers.

8. God's promise to Jacob in a vision at night.

9. The journey from Beer-sheba to Egypt.

10. The 70 persons who went down to Egypt.

11. The meeting of Jacob and Joseph.

12. Joseph counsels his brothers.

13. Joseph presents some of his brothers to Pharaoh.

14. Pharaoh agrees that Jacob and his sons may dwell in the land of Goshen.

15. Jacob appears before Pharaoh; their conversation.

16. Joseph settles his father and brothers in the land of Rameses and supplies them with all their needs.

17. Joseph's administration during the years of famine.

18. The Egyptians and their land become the property of the Pharaoh.

19. The immunity retained by the priestly estates in Egypt.

20. The children of Israel settle in the land of Egypt; they are fruitful and multiply.

VAYEHI (Chapters 47-50)

1. The length of Jacob's stay in Egypt.

2. Jacob's age.

3. Jacob charges Joseph to bury him in the cave of Machpelah.

4. Jacob's illness; the visit of Joseph, together with Manasseh and Ephraim.

5. Jacob tells Joseph of God's blessing him (Jacob)

in Luz, adopts Manasseh and Ephraim as his own children and explains why Rachel was buried on the way to Ephrath.

6. Jacob blesses Ephraim and Manasseh; the intentional switching of his hands, and placing Ephraim before Manasseh; Joseph's remark and Jacob's reply.

7. Jacob informs Joseph that the children of Israel will return to the Promised Land and that he has given him (Joseph) one portion more of Canaan than his brothers were given.

8. Jacob summons his sons.

9. Jacob blesses his sons and charges them to bury him in the cave of Machpelah.

10. The death and embalmment of Jacob; the Egyptians mourn him; the burial of Jacob.

11. The brothers' fear of Joseph.

12. Joseph comforts and reassures his brothers.

13. Joseph's age.

14. His progeny.

15. His final charge.

16. His death and embalmment; he is placed in a coffin in Egypt.

EXODUS

SHEMOT (CHAPTERS 1-6)

1. The names of the sons of Israel who went down to Egypt; the passing of that generation.

2. The great natural increase of the children of Israel.

3. The fear of the Egyptians and their designs against the Israelites.

4. The enslavement of the children of Israel and the hard labor forced upon them.

5. Pharaoh's decree ordering the murder of all newborn male Hebrew children.

6. The birth of Moses; his youth; his flight from Egypt.

7. Moses' experiences in Midian.

8. The children of Israel groan and cry out to God; God remembers His covenant with the patriarchs.

9. Moses at Mount Horeb: the revelation of God in the burning bush; Moses' mission; his reluctance; God's response; the Divine signs; Aaron is to help in the mission.

10. Moses leaves Jethro and returns to Egypt; God's directives.

11. Moses' experience at the inn on his way to Egypt.

12. The meeting of Moses and Aaron at the mountain of God.

13. The arrival of Moses and Aaron in Egypt; the gathering of the elders; the performance of the wondrous signs; the faith of the people.

14. Moses and Aaron present God's demand to Pharaoh; Pharaoh's refusal; the harsh decree calling for the withholding of straw from the Israelites.

15. The Israelite officers complain to Pharaoh and are rebuked by him; the officers complain to Moses and Aaron.

16. Moses' complaint to God; God's reply.

VAERA (CHAPTERS 6-9)

1. The continuation of God's reply to Moses' complaint; Moses is charged with telling the children of Israel that God will carry out His promises made to the patriarchs; the people do not listen to Moses.

2. Moses' mission to Pharaoh; his reluctance to go; the inclusion of Aaron in the mission.

3. The families of the tribes of Reuben, Simeon and Levi.

4. God informs Moses and Aaron of their tasks in their mission to Pharaoh and in the redemption of the children of Israel through signs, wonders and great judgments.

5. Moses' and Aaron's ages respectively at the time of their appearance before Pharaoh.

6. The sign of Moses' staff before Pharaoh.

7. The first plagues: blood, frogs, gnats, wild animals, pestilence, boils and hail.

BO (CHAPTERS 10-13)

1. God commands Moses to come before Pharaoh and tells him the reason for Pharaoh's stubbornness.

2. The last plagues: locusts, darkness and the slaying of the first-born.

3. The children of Israel are commanded to borrow jewels and garments of their Egyptian neighbors.

4. The Israelites find favor in the eyes of the Egyptains; Moses' great stature in Egypt.

5. The commandment to sanctify the new moon; the order of the calendar.

6. The paschal sacrifice and the feast of unleavened bread.

7. The answer to be given the wicked son.

8. The slaying of the first-born and its results.

9. The plundering of the Egyptians.

10. The exodus of the children of Israel from Egypt.

11. The duration of the Israelites' stay in Egypt.

12. The ordinance of the paschal sacrifice.

13. The law concerning the observance of Passover by a stranger.

14. The commandment to sanctify the first-born of men and animals to God.

15. The injunction to remember the exodus.

16. The prohibition against eating or owning leavened bread; the observance of the Passover; the commandment to eat unleavened bread.

17. The commandment to tell the story of the exodus on the first evening of Passover; the commandment

to explain the festival to the son who does not know how to ask.

18. The inclusion of this portion of Scripture (*Kadesh,* meaning "sanctification") in the tefillin.
19. The injunction to sanctify the first-born after the people shall have entered the land of Canaan.
20. The first-born of a donkey must be redeemed or be killed by having its neck broken.
21. The reply to the question of the simple son.
22. The inclusion of this portion of Scripture (Exodus 13:11-16: "And it shall be when the Lord shall bring thee, etc.") in the tefillin.

BESHALAH (CHAPTERS 13-17)

1. The circuitous route of the people through the wilderness near the Red Sea; the manner of the Israelites' departure from Egypt.
2. Joseph's remains are taken with the people.
3. The pillar of cloud and the pillar of fire.
4. The people return and encamp before Pi-hahiroth along the sea.
5. The Egyptians' pursuit of the Israelites.
6. The Israelites cry out to God; their complaint to Moses; Moses encourages the people.
7. God tells Moses to split the sea that the Israelites might be saved.
8. The darkness separating the Egyptians from the Israelites.
9. The splitting of the sea, the rescue of the Israelites and the drowning of the Egyptians.
10. The song of Moses and the children of Israel.
11. Miriam and the women dance with timbrels in hand; their song.
12. The children of Israel travel three days in the desert without finding water.
13. The bitter waters of Marah are made sweet; the establishment of statutes and ordinances there. God's declaration that the physical well-being of the Israelites depends upon their obedience to the Divine commandments.
14. The springs and palm trees of Elim.
15. The quail and the manna.
16. The lack of water in Rephidim; water is obtained from the rock; the naming of the place Massah ("Trying") and Meribah ("Strife").
17. The war with Amalek; God commands Moses to memorialize the victory in writing, and orally through Joshua, so that the remembrance of Amalek may be eternally obliterated.
18. Moses erects an altar and calls it Adonai-nissi ("The Lord is my banner"), declaring: "The Lord will have war with Amalek from generation to generation" (Exodus 17.16).

YITRO (CHAPTERS 18-20)

1. Jethro's visit to Moses in the desert; his amazement at the wonders wrought by God for the Israelites.
2. Moses appoints judges over the people in accordance with the counsel of Jethro.

3. The setting of bounds around Mount Sinai.
4. The giving of the Torah.
5. The admonition not to make idols of silver or gold.
6. The commandment to build an altar; laws concerning the altar.

MISHPATIM (CHAPTERS 21-24)

1. Laws concerning a Hebrew manservant.
2. Laws concerning a Hebrew maidservant.
3. Laws concerning the premeditated or unpremeditated killing of a human being.
4. Laws concerning the striking of one's parents.
5. Laws concerning the person who kidnaps and sells a human being.
6. Laws concerning the person who curses his parents.
7. Laws concerning bodily injuries done to one's neighbor.
8. Laws concerning the murder of a Canaanite slave.
9. Laws concerning the man who strikes a woman and causes her to miscarry.
10. Laws concerning the murder of a man other than the intended victim.
11. More laws concerning physical injury done to a person.
12. Laws concerning injuries made upon a major limb of a Canaanite slave.
13. Laws concerning an ox that gores a person to death.
14. Laws concerning injuries brought about by the digging of a pit.
15. Laws concerning damages done to an ox.
16. Laws concerning theft.
17. Laws concerning injuries caused by the tooth or foot of an animal.
18. Laws concerning injuries committed upon a person.
19. Laws concerning the four types of safekeeping of property.
20. Laws concerning seduction.
21. The law concerning a sorceress.
22. The law concerning bestiality.
23. The law concerning idolatrous sacrifices.
24. An admonition not to wrong or oppress the stranger.
25. An admonition not to afflict the widow or orphan; the punishment to be meted out to all who fail to heed the admonition.
26. Laws concerning loans and security.
27. An admonition not to curse God (the judges) or a ruler of the people.
28. An admonition not to delay in the giving of tithes, nor to change their proper order.
29. Laws concerning the first-born of men and animals.
30. The eating of a diseased animal or meat torn by an animal prohibited; other uses of such meat permitted.
31. An admonition not to utter a false report.
32. Laws concerning witnesses and judges; an admonition not to side with a majority who would pervert justice.
33. The commandment to restore lost possessions.
34. The commandment to unburden an animal that has fallen under its load.
35. Laws concerning judges.
36. A second admonition not to oppress the stranger.

37. The commandment to let the land lie fallow during the seventh year.
38. The commandment to rest on the Sabbath.
39. An injunction to observe all of God's commandments.
40. An admonition not to mention the names of other gods.
41. The commandment to observe the three festivals; the obligation of making three pilgrimages yearly and bringing offerings to God.
42. The sacrifice of the paschal lamb and the sprinkling of its blood prohibited prior to the removal of all leaven from the house.
43. The prohibition of leaving overnight the portions of the paschal lamb sacrificed away from the altar.
44. The commandment concerning the first fruits.
45. The cooking of meat in milk prohibited.
46. God declares that He is sending an angel (messenger) before the children of Israel to protect them and bring them into the land of Canaan, and that they must obey Him and not rebel against Him.
47. God promises the children of Israel manifold blessings if they will reject pagan rites, destroy all idolatry in the land, and worship God alone.
48. God's plan for the gradual conquest of the land.
49. The boundaries of the land.
50. An admonition not to make any covenant with the nations of Canaan or with their deities.
51. God commands Moses: Aaron and the heads of the people (Nadab, Abihu and the 70 elders) are to bow and worship the Lord from afar; Moses alone is to approach God.
52. The covenant between God and Israel; the sprinkling of the blood of the burnt-offerings and the peace-offerings, which the young men of Israel had sacrificed upon the altar built by Moses.
53. The ascent of Moses, Aaron and the leaders of the people to the mountain; the vision seen by them; the nobles of Israel are untouched by God; their consequent joy.
54. Moses tells the elders to remain with Aaron and Hur to judge the people.
55. Moses ascends the mountain at God's command to receive the tablets of the Law; Joshua accompanies Moses to the boundary of the mountain.
56. The glory of the Lord on the peak of the mountain, having the appearance of a consuming fire; the call to Moses on the seventh day; Moses remains on the mountain for 40 days and 40 nights.

TERUMAH (Chapters 25-27)
1. The offerings for the Tabernacle.
2. The ephod and the breastplate.
3. The ark, the ark-cover, and the two cherubim.
4. The table and its implements.
5. The seven-branched candelabrum and its ornaments and implements.
6. The construction of the Tabernacle; the measurements of the Tabernacle.
7. The curtain separating the holy place from the Holy of Holies.

8. The brass altar and its implements.
9. The courtyard of the Tabernacle and its measurements.

TETZAVEH (Chapters 27-30)
1. The kindling of the eternal light of the menorah.
2. The consecration of Aaron and his sons as priests.
3. The priestly garments: a tunic of checker-work, a mitre, a girdle, and linen breeches.
4. The four additional implements worn by the High Priest: the breastplate, the ephod, a robe and the golden diadem.
5. The names of the twelve tribes of Israel are inscribed on the twelve precious stones of the breastplate and on the two onyx stones on the shoulder pieces of the ephod.
6. The setting of the Urim and Thummim in the breastplate of judgment.
7. The daily offerings.
8. The altar for incense.

KI TISSA (Chapters 30-34)
1. The half shekel required of all who are twenty years of age and over.
2. The laver of brass and its base.
3. The anointing oil.
4. The preparation of incense from spices for holy use.
5. The wisdom of Bezalel and Oholiab in the construction of the Tabernacle and its implements.
6. The observance of the Sabbath; the prohibition of all forms of labor.
7. The Israelites worship the golden calf; Moses breaks the stone tablets upon coming down from the mountain.
8. At Moses' call "Whoso is on the Lord's side, let him come unto me" all the Levites assemble and kill about 3,000 men.
9. Moses beseeches God to forgive the people; his request is granted.
10. Moses admonishes the people.
11. God speaks to Moses face to face while a pillar of cloud covers the entrance to the Tent.
12. The revelation of the thirteen attributes of God's mercy.
13. God renews His covenant with the people.
14. Moses warns the Israelites not to mingle with the inhabitants of Canaan or imitate their idolatrous practices.
15. The commandment to eat unleavened bread for seven days.
16. The law concerning the first-born of animals and men.
17. The commandment to appear before the Lord three times every year.
18. The commandment to bring the first fruits to the house of God.
19. The cooking of meat in milk prohibited.
20. The writing of the second "tablets of testimony".
21. The skin of Moses' face sends forth beams of light.

VAYAKHEL (CHAPTERS 35-38)

1. Moses assembles the people in order to tell them the word of God.
2. The Sabbath of solemn rest; the kindling of fire prohibited.
3. The freewill-offerings to God and the people's donations to the Tabernacle.
4. The craftsmanship of Bezalel and Oholiab.
5. The construction of the Tabernacle and its implements; the ark, the table and the candelabrum.
6. The altar of incense and the altar of burnt-offerings.
7. The laver; the courtyard of the Tabernacle.

PEKUDE (CHAPTERS 38-40)

1. The accounts of the Tabernacle; the amount of silver, gold and brass donated by the people for its construction.
2. Description of the priestly garments and the implements of the Tabernacle.
3. The erection of the Tabernacle of the tent of meeting in the second year after the exodus from Egypt.
4. The designation of the location of the altars, the ark, the table, the candelabrum, and their implements.
5. The consecration of the Tabernacle after its completion; "The cloud covered the tent of meeting, and the glory of the Lord filled the Tabernacle".

LEVITICUS

VAYIKRA (CHAPTERS 1-5)

1. Laws of the burnt-offerings. } Voluntary offerings
2. Laws of the meal-offerings. }
3. Laws of the peace-offerings: sacrifices that are holy in a minor degree.
4. Laws of the sin-offerings. } Obligatory offerings
5. Laws of the guilt-offerings. }

TZAV (CHAPTERS 6-8)

1. Additional laws concerning the burnt-offerings, the daily meal-offerings of the High Priest and the dedicatory meal-offerings of the common priests.
2. Laws of the sin-offerings; they are obligatory and "most holy."
3. Laws of the guilt-offerings; they are obligatory and "most holy."
4. Laws of the peace-offering and the thanksgiving offering; sacrifices that are holy in a minor degree.
5. The eating of fat and blood prohibited.
6. The concluding section on the laws of sacrifice.*
7. Moses assembles all the congregation of Israel at the entrance of the tent of meeting; he washes Aaron and his sons, and dresses them in their priestly garments.

* Many statutes related to those included in chapters 1-7 are mentioned in different sections of the Torah:
  1) laws of the paschal lamb (Exodus 12; Deuteronomy 16);
  2) laws concerning the first-born, heave-offerings and tithes (Leviticus 27; Numbers 18; Deuteronomy 14-15);
  3) offerings of unclean persons (Leviticus 12.14-15);
  4) guilt-offerings for the betrothed bondswoman (Leviticus 19);
  5) offerings on the Sabbath, new moon and festivals (Leviticus 23; Numbers 28-29);
  6) the second Passover (Numbers 9);
  7) additional guilt-offerings (Numbers 5);
  8) the offering of the woman suspected of adultery and the offerings of the Nazirites (Numbers 5-6);
  9) meal-offerings, libations and other sacrifices (Numbers 15);
  10) the red heifer (Numbers 19);
  11) the heifer whose neck is broken (Deuteronomy 21);
  12) the first fruits (Deuteronomy 26).

8. The anointing of the Tabernacle and the altar, together with all of its implements, with sanctified oil.
9. The slaughter of the bullock of the sin-offering; the cleansing and sanctification of the altar by means of the blood of the bullock; the burning upon the altar of the fat upon the inwards, the lobe of the liver, and the two kidneys and their fat.
10. The burning of the bullock outside the camp; the sacrifice of a ram as a burnt-offering upon the altar, as commanded by Moses.
11. The sacrifice of the second ram (the ram of consecration); the sprinkling of its blood on the lobe of the right ear, the thumb of the right hand, and the large toe of the right foot of Aaron and each of his sons.
12. Aaron and his sons are presented to God by Moses as a symbolic wave-offering.
13. The waving of the breast of the ram of consecration; the sprinkling of the oil of anointment and the blood of the altar upon the garments of Aaron and his sons.
14. Other instructions concerning the seven days of consecration of Aaron and his sons.

SHEMINI (CHAPTERS 9-11)

1. Moses summons Aaron and his sons and the elders of Israel and orders them and the children of Israel to offer sacrifices before the revelation of the glory of God. The order of the sacrifices; Aaron blesses the people after offering up the sacrifices; the appearance of the glory of God and the joyous shouting of the people.
2. The death of Nadab and Abihu, sons of Aaron, by Divine fire upon their offering up a strange fire on the altar, an act not commanded by God.
3. The silent mourning of Aaron; the bearing of the corpses in their tunics to the outskirts of the camp

by Mishael and Elzaphan, sons of Uzziel, the uncle of Aaron, as God commanded Moses. The priests are forbidden to dishevel their hair, rend their garments, or go beyond the entrance of the tent of meeting as a sign of mourning for Nadab and Abihu.

4. The priests are forbidden, through all generations, to imbibe wine or strong drink before entering the tent of meeting. The priests are given the task of teaching the Israelites to differentiate between the holy and the common and the clean and the unclean.

5. Moses' instructions concerning the eating of the remainder of the meal-offering by the priests; Moses' orders concerning the breast of waving, the thigh of heaving and the goat of the sin-offering. Aaron's apology and his explanation to Moses.

6. Statutes concerning those living creatures forbidden as food; their impurity; God commands the children of Israel to sanctify themselves and to be holy. Final laws concerning the edibility of four-footed animals, fowl and all living creatures.

TAZRIA (CHAPTERS 12-13)

1. Laws concerning a woman who has given birth; her impure state and her means of becoming purified.

2. Laws concerning the impurity brought about by the plague of leprosy upon the body or upon clothing.

METZORA (CHAPTERS 14-15)

1. Laws concerning the leper and his purification. Plagues of houses and their purification.

2. Laws concerning a man or woman with a running issue.

AHARE MOT (CHAPTERS 16-18)

1. The laws of the Day of Atonement.

2. More laws concerning the priests and the Levites; laws concerning the sacrificial service; the consumption of blood prohibited.

3. Laws prohibiting incestuous relationships.

KEDOSHIM (CHAPTERS 19-20)

1. Holiness—the highest goal: "Ye shall be holy; for I the Lord your God am holy"; the fear of one's parents; the elimination of all idolatry in speech, thought and action.

2. Laws concerning the peace-offering and its consumption.

3. Laws obliging the Israelites to leave the gleanings of their fields untouched and to leave the corners of their fields unharvested; the law prohibiting the owner of a vineyard from gathering up fallen grapes or imperfect clusters.

4. Theft, deception or lying to one's neighbor prohibited; swearing falsely prohibited; defrauding or robbing one's neighbor prohibited; the withholding of a worker's wages overnight prohibited.

5. Cursing the deaf or putting a stumbling block before the blind prohibited; "Thou shalt fear thy God: I am the Lord."

6. The miscarriage of justice prohibited; favoring either the poor or the rich prohibited; the demand for righteous judgment; the prohibition of tale-bearing or standing by idly while the life of one's neighbor is threatened; the bearing of grudges prohibited; the commandment to rebuke one's neighbor rather than harbor hatred inwardly.

7. Vengeance-taking forbidden; the bearing of a grudge against one's fellow Israelite prohibited; "Thou shalt love thy neighbor as thyself: I am the Lord thy God."

8. Coupling between different kinds of animals prohibited; sowing a field with two kinds of seed, or wearing a garment made of wool and linen prohibited.

9. The law concerning a betrothed bondmaid; the atonement by sacrificing a ram as a guilt-offering.

10. Laws concerning forbidden fruit (fruit of a tree less than four years old).

11. Eating of the sacrifice before the blood is sprinkled, prohibited; soothsaying and divination prohibited; rounding the corners of one's hair or marring the corners of one's beard prohibited.

12. The cutting or tattooing of one's flesh prohibited; making one's daughter a prostitute prohibited.

13. The observance of the Sabbath and the reverence due the sanctuary.

14. Necromancy prohibited.

15. "Thou shalt rise up before the hoary head, and honor the face of the old man, and thou shalt fear thy God: I am the Lord."

16. The wronging of a stranger prohibited; the duty of loving and aiding the stranger, "for ye were strangers in the land of Egypt: I am the Lord your God."

17. "Ye shall do no unrighteousness in judgment, in meteyard, in weight, or in measure. Just balances, just weights, a just ephah, and a just hin shall ye have: I am the Lord your God, who brought you out of the land of Egypt. And ye shall observe all My statutes, and all Mine ordinances, and do them: I am the Lord."

18. The sacrificing of one's children to Molech prohibited; the punishment for that crime; "Be ye holy; for I am the Lord your God."

19. Cursing one's parents prohibited; the punishment for that crime; the punishment of the adulterer and the adulteress; the punishment of those who engage in various forbidden unions; the punishment for sodomy; the death penalty for any man or woman guilty of bestiality.

20. The observance of God's statutes and laws "that the land, whither I bring you to dwell therein, vomit you not out. And ye shall not walk in the customs of the nation, which I am casting out before you; for they did all these things, and therefore I abhorred them. But I have said unto you: 'Ye shall inherit their land, and I will give it unto you to possess it, a land flowing with milk

and honey.' I am the Lord your God, who have set you apart from the peoples."

21. The commandment to differentiate between clean and unclean animals and fowl; "And ye shall be holy unto Me; for I the Lord am holy and have set you apart from the peoples, that ye should be Mine." The punishment for necromancers.

EMOR (CHAPTERS 21-24)

1. Priests are forbidden to defile themselves for any dead person outside of their closest kin (father, mother, son, daughter, brother and virgin sister), and are forbidden to shave their beards or cut themselves (in token of mourning). Special laws of holiness for the priests. Laws concerning the daughter of a priest who defiles herself through prostitution.
2. Laws concerning the High Priest.
3. Blemishes of the priests which prevent them from offering the sacrifices.
4. Uncleanness of the priests which prevents them from eating the holy food.
5. Laws concerning the stranger, the tenant or hired servant of a priest, and any person born into a priestly household, in regard to the eating of holy food. The law concerning the eating of holy food by a priest's daughter who is a widow, the wife of a common man or a divorcee.
6. The law concerning a person who eats holy food unwittingly.
7. Laws concerning blemishes which disqualify an animal from being offered up as a sacrifice.
8. More laws concerning burnt-offerings and the sacrifice of thanksgiving.
9. The Sabbath, festivals and holy days.
10. Laws concerning the pure olive oil for the light.

The ordering of the lamps upon the candelabrum before God continually.
11. The arranging of two rows of shewbread and related laws.
12. The blaspheming of God's name and the penalty of death by stoning for that crime.
13. Laws concerning a person who inflicts mortal injury upon an animal or human being, or maims his fellow.

BEHAR (CHAPTER 25)

1. Laws of the sabbatical year.
2. Laws of the jubilee year.
3. Laws concerning Levitical dwellings and cities.
4. The prohibition of usury.
5. Laws concerning bondservants and hired servants.
6. Laws concerning idols, graven images, pillars and figured stones. The observance of the Sabbath and reverence for the sanctuary.

BEHUKKOTAI (CHAPTERS 26-27)

1. God declares that He will bless the people and the land if the children of Israel will observe His statutes and commandments.
2. The threat of what will befall the Israelites if they disobey God and His commandments.
3. God promises that He will not let His people perish in the lands of their enemies, but will remember His covenant with the patriarchs.
4. Laws concerning the valuation of a person's possessions in order to determine the proper payment of vows made to the Lord.
5. The redemption of a field. Laws concerning things devoted to God. The tithing of cattle and sheep.
6. The conclusion of the book of Leviticus.

NUMBERS

BAMIDBAR (CHAPTERS 1-4)

1. The census of the children of Israel.
2. The Levites are put in charge of the Tabernacle.
3. The banners and the order of the march.
4. The sons of Aaron and what happened to them.
5. Aaron and his sons are put in charge of the Levites.
6. The numbering of all Levites more than one month old. The ordering of the Levitical encampment. Duties of the Levites.
7. The numbering of the Israelites' first-born male children who are more than one month old.
8. The redeeming of the first-born.
9. God orders that a count be taken of the Kohathites who are 30 to 50 years of age. Their duties.
10. The duties of Aaron and his sons while the camp is on the march.

11. The Kohathites are warned not to touch or look at the holy objects.

NASO (CHAPTERS 4-7)

1. God orders that a census be taken of the Gershonites who are 30 to 50 years of age. Their duties.
2. The Kohathites, Gershonites, and Merarites: the number of men in each group and the total number.
3. Unclean persons are to be put out of the camp.
4. Stealing from a stranger and its penalties.
5. Offerings due the priests.
6. Laws concerning a woman suspected of adultery.
7. Laws of the Nazirite.
8. The commandment regarding the priestly blessing; the wording of the blessing.

9. The gifts given by the tribal princes to the Levites to help the latter in their work.
10. The offerings of the princes on the occasion of the dedication of the altar.
11. The manner of God's speaking with Moses.

BEHAALOTEKHA (CHAPTERS 8-12)

1. The arrangement of the lamps and the construction of the candelabrum.
2. The purification of the Levites. They begin to perform their duties in the Tabernacle service.
3. Levites between the ages of 25 and 50 are to take part in the service of the Tabernacle.
4. The observance of the Passover at the appointed time in the Sinai desert.
5. The delayed Passover: laws concerning its observance by Israelites and strangers (proselytes).
6. The cloud over the Tabernacle serves as a sign to the children of Israel, indicating to them when to camp and when to journey on.
7. Commandments concerning the trumpets and their functions.
8. The journey from the Sinai desert; the order of the march; the banners.
9. Moses requests his father-in-law Hobab to accompany the children of Israel through the desert; Hobab's refusal. The journey away from Mount Sinai with the ark carried ahead of the people.
10. Moses' prayer upon the setting forward of the ark and upon its resting.
11. The murmuring against God. The fire of the Lord in the camp. The people lust for meat. The remarkable qualities of the manna.
12. Moses complains to God about the difficulties of leading the people and satisfying their demands; God's reply.
13. The appointment of 70 elders; some of the Divine Spirit is transmitted to them.
14. Eldad and Medad prophesy in the camp. Joshua's jealousy for the honor of Moses. Moses' reply.
15. The quail; the death of those who lusted.
16. Aaron and Miriam speak out against Moses. Moses' humility.
17. God's zealousness for Moses. God declares what distinguishes Moses from all other prophets.
18. Miriam's leprosy; Aaron turns to Moses for help; Moses' prayer.
19. God's reply; the confinement of Miriam; the journey of the children of Israel delayed.
20. The people journey to the wilderness of Paran.

SHELAH (CHAPTERS 13-15)

1. The mission of the spies; their return and their negative report. The people weep and complain, and ask to return to Egypt. Moses and Aaron fall on their faces and Joshua and Caleb rend their garments.
2. The counsel of Joshua and Caleb and the reaction of the people.
3. God tells Moses of His intention of annihilating the people; Moses' reply and his prayer.
4. God's anger; Moses' prayer; God pardons the peo-

ple, but declares that they will not see the Promised Land. God's promise to Caleb.
5. God's decree concerning the Israelites in the desert. The death of the spies in a plague. The people mourn, and presumptuously try to enter the land without Moses or the ark. The crushing defeat of the Israelites at Hormah.
6. Laws concerning the meal-offerings, drink-offerings, burnt-offerings and peace-offerings.
7. The same law is to apply to the stranger as to the Israelite.
8. The commandment to set apart a portion of the dough and give it to the Lord.
9. Sacrifices to be offered by the community or private persons for sins committed through error. The punishment of the presumptuous sinner.
10. A man is discovered gathering wood on the Sabbath; his punishment.
11. The commandment to wear fringes on one's garments; the purpose of the fringes.

KORAH (CHAPTERS 16-18)

1. The dispute of Korah and his supporters, with Moses and Aaron.
2. Moses' reply and his defense of Aaron. The suggestion of a test by offering incense to the Lord.
3. Moses summons Dathan and Abiram; their impudent reply.
4. Moses beseeches God not to accept the gift of the rebels; Moses' self-vindication.
5. Korah and his supporters, and Moses and Aaron appear before God with their fire-pans.
6. Korah gathers together the entire congregation of Israel.
7. God tells Moses and Aaron of his intention of annihilating the children of Israel.
8. The prayer of Moses and Aaron.
9. God's reply.
10. Moses approaches Dathan and Abiram.
11. The separation of the congregation from Korah, Dathan and Abiram.
12. Moses describes the miracle that will prove that he is the emissary of God.
13. The opening of the earth, the swallowing up of the rebels and the closing of the earth.
14. The death by fire of the men who offered up incense.
15. The covering of the altar with the fire-pans as a memorial.
16. The children of Israel murmur against Moses and Aaron.
17. The plague; the termination of the plague upon Aaron's offering up incense to God.
18. The sign of the staffs. The blossoming of Aaron's staff. Aaron's staff is placed before the tent of testimony as a memorial before God.
19. The fear of the children of Israel for the holiness of the Tabernacle.
20. The priests and Levites are entrusted with all that pertains to worship in the Tabernacle, and with the safeguarding of the Tabernacle from trespass by common men.

21. The emoluments of the priests.
22. The first tithe.
23. The tithe of the tithe.

HUKKAT (Chapters 19-22)

1. The red heifer.
2. Defilement brought about by direct or indirect contact with a corpse; the purification for such defilement.
3. The death of Miriam.
4. The waters of Meribah ("Strife").
5. Negotiations between Israel and Edom; Israel is refused right of passage through the land of Edom.
6. The death of Aaron.
7. The battle with Arad and the victory of Israel.
8. The Israelites bypass the land of Edom. The complaints of the Israelites; the fiery poisonous serpents and the serpent of brass made by Moses.
9. The valley of Arnon.
10. The song of the well.
11. The battle with Sihon and the conquest of his land.
12. The song in parable form concerning Sihon's war with Moab.
13. The battle with Og and the conquest of his land.
14. The children of Israel in the plains of Moab.

BALAK (Chapters 22-25)

1. Moab's fear of the children of Israel.
2. The design of Balak, king of Moab. He calls upon the prophet Balaam to curse the children of Israel.
3. Balaam replies that God permits him to utter only that which He puts into his mouth.
4. Balaam goes to the king after receiving a second invitation.
5. An angel of God places himself before Balaam on the road.
6. The ass bearing Balaam turns off the path and is beaten by the prophet.
7. God opens the mouth of the ass and it reproves Balaam for the beating.
8. The angel's admonition to Balaam and the latter's reply.
9. The angel warns Balaam to speak only that which God will put in his mouth.
10. Balak receives Balaam in Ir-moab. The conversation between the two men.
11. The three attempts of Balak and Balaam to curse the children of Israel from the heights of Bamoth-baal, the field of Zophim, and the peak of Peor. On each occasion, God places a blessing in the mouth of Balaam instead of the intended curse.
12. Balak reproves Balaam; the prophet's reply.
13. Balaam prophesies of the greatness of Israel in the end of days.
14. Balak and Balaam return to their homes.
15. The deeds of the Israelites in Shittim. The promiscuous behaviour with the daughters of Moab and the worshipping of the Baal of Peor.
16. The outbreak of a plague. God commands the execution of the idolaters.
17. The deed of Zimri.
18. Phinehas, the son of Eleazar, kills Zimri and

the Midianite woman and the plague ceases.
19. The number of the plague's victims.

PHINEHAS (Chapters 25-30)

1. God bestows upon Phinehas, as a reward for his zeal, a "covenant of peace" and "the covenant of an everlasting priesthood."
2. The names of the man and woman slain by Phinehas, and their high rank.
3. God commands Moses to harass the Midianites for having beguiled the children of Israel.
4. The numbering of the children of Israel by families. The sin of Dathan and Abiram and the supporters of Korah, and their punishment; the special merit of the sons of Korah.
5. The law of the partition of the land.
6. The numbering of the Levites and their families. A detailed account of the family of Amram.
7. The suit of the daughters of Zelophehad.
8. The law of inheritance.
9. God informs Moses that he is to die on Mount Abarim.
10. Moses asks God to appoint his successor.
11. The appointment of Joshua.
12. The daily sacrifices; their offerings; laws concerning sacrifices to be offered up on the festivals.

MATTOT (Chapters 30-32)

1. Laws concerning vows.
2. God orders Moses to have the children of Israel execute vengeance upon the Midianites before Moses' death.
3. Phinehas and 12,000 armed men together with the holy vessels, go out in battle against Midian.
4. The victory of the children of Israel; the killing of all the conquered men; the burning of all the cities; the women and children of Midian together with much booty, are taken by the Israelites.
5. The laws concerning the purification of persons or vessels that have been contaminated by a corpse.
6. The ritual purification of implements.
7. The distribution of the booty and the captives of war.
8. The officers of the army present an offering of gold to the Lord as a memorial, after having counted their troops and found that not one man was missing.
9. The allocation of the territory on the east side of of the Jordan to the tribes of Reuben and Gad on condition that they first go armed before their brothers in the conquest of Canaan.
10. The territories conquered by Jair, Nobah and the sons of Machir.

MASE (Chapters 33-36)

1. A list of the journeys of the children of Israel in the desert.
2. The date of Aaron's death upon Mount Hor, and his age at his death.
3. God's commandments concerning the expulsion of the inhabitants of Canaan from the land, and the

destruction of their idols. The designation of the boundaries of the land; the partition of the land by lot. The names of the men appoined to divide the land among the children of Israel.

4. The commandment to set aside cities and adjacent areas for the Levites.
5. The commandment to set aside cities of refuge.
6. Laws concerning murderers.

7. The daughters of Zelophehad as well as all other daughters who become the heiresses of their fathers, are forbidden to marry outside of their own tribe so that property shall not pass from one tribe to another.

8. The daughters of Zelophehad marry their cousins of the tribe of Manasseh.

DEUTERONOMY

DEVARIM (CHAPTERS 1-2)

1. The location and date of Moses' recitation of the Mishneh Torah ("Repetition of the Torah")* to the children of Israel.
2. Some of the incidents at Horeb: God's commandment to inherit the land; the organization of courts; laws concerning judges.
3. The journey from Horeb to Kadesh-barnea.
4. Some of the happenings at Kadesh-barnea: Moses urges the people to take possession of the land; the people ask that spies be sent in advance; the return of the spies and their report; the people refuse to enter Canaan; the complaints and fears of the Israelites; Moses encourages and admonishes them; God's decree against the "evil generation"; Caleb is promised an inheritance in the land of Canaan; Moses is punished because of the sins of the people; God promises that Joshua will win Canaan for the Israelites; Canaan is promised to the children of the Israelites who left Egypt; the unsuccessful attack upon the Amorites; the length of the Israelites' stay in Kadesh.
5. The circuitous route of the Israelites in their journeys through the desert from Kadesh-barnea to the crossing of the brook Zered. The might of the countries of Edom, Moab and Ammon; the history of their settlements.
6. The crossing of the valley of Arnon; the peaceful overtures to Sihon; Sihon refuses to give the Israelites right of transit through his country; the battle against Sihon.
7. The conquest of the lands of Sihon and Og; the allocation of their territory to Reuben, Gad and half of Manasseh, on condition that those tribes go armed before the rest of the Israelites in the conquest of Canaan.
8. The designation of Joshua as leader of the people; victory is assured him in the conquest of Canaan.

i.e., the book of Deuteronomy, which summarizes and repeats the history and laws found in the rest of the Pentateuch, particularly in the books of Exodus, Leviticus and Numbers.

VAETHANAN (CHAPTERS 3-7)

1. Moses' plea that God let him enter the land; God's refusal.
2. Moses urges the people to uphold the laws and commandments of the Torah without adding to them or subtracting from them.
3. Israel's special status among the nations; the preeminence of the laws given Israel.
4. An admonition not to forget the revelation at Mount Sinai and the covenant with God, and not to make a likeness of God or worship any heavenly bodies; the commandment to tell one's children of the day of the revelation of God at Sinai.
5. The choosing of Israel to possess the land of Canaan; the Divine decree that Moses cannot enter the land.
6. God's wrath toward idol makers.
7. The designation of heaven and earth as witnesses of God's warning that He will exile the people if they anger him; the promise that when Israel will call upon God for help in time of trouble, He will recall His covenant with the patriarchs and come to His people's aid.
8. The unity and greatness of God; His special relationship with the people of Israel, and the implications of that relationship.
9. The setting aside of three cities of refuge by Moses.
10. The date and location of Moses' repetition of the laws given at Mount Sinai.
11. Moses calls all Israel together and urges them to study and observe God's commandments. God's covenant at Horeb is with all the descendants of the Israelites; the manner in which God addressed the people during the revelation.
12. The decalogue.
13. The Israelites' fear of the voice of God and the great fire; their request that Moses act as their intermediary; God's approval. The urging of the people to observe all God's commandments and be duly rewarded.
14. The declaration of God's unity.
15. The commandment to love God.
16. The commandment to study the Torah.

17. The commandment to recite the Shema (Deuteronomy 6.4-9).
18. The commandment to wear tefillin.
19. The commandment to affix a mezuzah on the doorposts of one's house.
20. The admonition not to forget the Lord as a result of the prosperity to be enjoyed in the land; the commandment to fear God, worship Him and swear by His name.
21. God's vengeance upon idolaters.
22. The admonition not to prove or test the Lord.
23. The urging of the Israelites to observe the commandments and do "that which is right and good in the sight of the Lord"; the reward for such behaviour.
24. The commandment to relate the story of the exodus to one's children; the benefits of observing God's commandments.
25. The commandment to annihilate the seven Canaanite nations and destroy their pillars, altars and graven images.
26. The admonition not to make any pact with the Canaanites or intermarry with them.
27. Israel: a people holy unto God, chosen because of His love of them and the merits of the patriarchs.
28. God's faithfulness in showing mercy to those who love Him and in punishing those who hate Him; the lesson to be derived therefrom.

EKEV (Chapters 7-11)

1. The reward for the fulfillment of the commandments.
2. The treatment of the nations of Canaan.
3. God's promise of victory to Israel in the conquest of Canaan, even as He did during the exodus from Egypt.
4. The ban against the use of anything connected with idol worship; the commandment to destroy all idolatrous articles and implements.
5. The way in which God led the people in the desert and the lesson to be derived therefrom; the purpose of the forty years' wandering in the desert.
6. The Land of Canaan and its resources are extolled.
7. The commandment to recite grace after meals.
8. The admonition not to forget the Lord and His kindness in time of plenty; the necessity of remembering that it is God who gives man the power to amass wealth.
9. The threat of punishment for forgetting the Lord, turning to idolatry and disobeying the Divine commandments.
10. The conquest of Canaan through natural means an impossibility; only God, in remembering His promise, can and will destroy the nations of the land.
11. Israel's right to Canaan: the promise made to the patriarchs.
12. Israel's rebellious behaviour in the desert. The activities and achievements of Moses; the tablets of the Law. The journeys in the wilderness. The death and burial of Aaron; the succession of Eleazar, his

son, to the High Priesthood; the consecration of the tribe of Levi to minister to God.
13. What God requires of Israel; the end result of observing the Divine commandments.
14. God's greatness; His choice of Israel and the lesson to be derived therefrom.
15. God's majesty and His ways.
16. The commandment to love the stranger.
17. The commandment to fear God, worship Him, cleave to Him and swear by His name.
18. The wonders of God; His great deeds on behalf of those who love Him and His punishment of those who hate Him; the lesson to be derived therefrom.
19. Differences between the land of Egypt and the land of Canaan.
20. Retribution for obeying or disobeying God's commandments; the calling of attention to this portion of the Torah by means of the tefillin, studying the portion, reciting it every morning and night and placing it in the mezuzah.
21. Canaan promised to the children of Israel for eternity.
22. Observance of the commandments, love of the Lord and walking in His ways as prerequisites to the inheriting of Canaan.
23. The promise that every place the Israelites conquer will be theirs.
24. The designation of the boundaries of the land; the promise that these boundaries will be attained.
25. The promise that the Israelites will be feared wherever they go.

RE'EH (Chapters 11-16)

1. The setting of a blessing and a curse before the children of Israel; the means of attaining the one or the other.
2. The commandment to recite the blessing and the curse on Mount Gerizim and Mount Ebal respectively; the location of the two mountains. The promise that the Israelites will inherit the land; the urging of the people to observe the commandments.
3. The commandment to destroy the sanctuaries and idols of the nations of Canaan.
4. The commandment to offer up sacrifices in the place chosen by God; the prohibition against sacrificing on the high places after the conquest of Canaan shall have been completed.
5. The commandment to eat of the offerings and rejoice in the chosen place; eating of the offerings outside its boundaries prohibited.
6. The admonition not to forsake the Levite.
7. Non-sacrificial slaughtering of animals permitted anywhere; the eating of blood prohibited—it may be spilled out on the earth like water.
8. The eating of meat not associated with any sacrifice permitted; the reason for this; the commandment concerning the slaughtering of an animal for non-sacrificial purposes; repeated admonitions against the consumption of blood.
9. Laws concerning burnt-offerings and sacrifices; an

admonition to obey these commandments and the reward thereof.

10. Worshipping other gods and worshipping God in the manner of the other nations prohibited.
11. Adding to or detracting from the commandments of the Torah prohibited.
12. The law concerning the prophet who would lead people to believe in false gods.
13. The law concerning incitement to idol worship.
14. The law concerning a city that has strayed from the Lord and the promise of mercy to those who execute His judgment.
15. The commandment to investigate and examine closely all the witnesses and evidence in capital cases.
16. Cutting one's flesh or tearing out one's hair in mourning for the dead prohibited; the reason for this prohibition.
17. Eating any abominable thing prohibited.
18. The animals, birds and fish that may or may not be eaten; touching the carcass of an unclean animal prohibited.
19. Eating a carcass prohibited; deriving other benefits from a carcass permitted; the advantage of the resident stranger over the foreigner.
20. The cooking of meat in milk prohibited.
21. The commandment of the second tithe and its purpose.
22. The commandment to give the tithe of the poor and to clear the house of tithes of previous years; the reward for observing this commandment.
23. The commandment to cancel all debts every seventh year; the reward for observing this commandment.
24. The commandment to give charity and loans; the reward for observing this commandment.
25. The years of service of the Hebrew bondman and bondwoman; the commandment to grant gifts liberally to the freed bondservant.
26. Laws concerning the first-born of a clean animal.
27. The observance of the month of Aviv ("spring"; that is, Passover should be in the spring season); the regulation of the calendar (leap years).
28. The paschal lamb and the Feast of Unleavened Bread.
29. The counting of seven weeks; the Feast of Weeks.
30. The Feast of Tabernacles.
31. The commandment to appear before the Lord on the three festivals and offer up the requisite sacrifices.

SHOFETIM (Chapters 16-21)

1. The commandment to appoint judges in every city.
2. Laws concerning judges.
3. The planting of a tree for idolatrous purposes prohibited.
4. The planting of a tree on the Temple Mount prohibited.
5. The setting up of a pillar for idolatrous purposes prohibited.
6. The sacrifice of an animal with a blemish prohibited.
7. Eating of sacrifices made abhorrent because they were intended to be eaten beyond the appointed time, prohibited.

8. The punishment of the idolater.
9. Laws concerning witnesses in capital cases.
10. Laws concerning the high court.
11. The law concerning the elder who refuses to obey the high court.
12. The law of choosing a king.
13. Laws concerning the king.
14. The return of the people to Egypt prohibited.
15. The inheritance of the tribe of Levi.
16. The emoluments of the priests.
17. The apportionment of the duties and emoluments of the priests.
18. The worship of Molech prohibited.
19. All types of witchcraft and necromancy prohibited.
20. The commandment to give heed to the words of a prophet; the punishment for those who transgress the words of the prophet.
21. The law concerning a false prophet or a prophet who speaks in the name of other gods.
22. The commandment to set up cities of refuge for murderers.
23. Laws concerning unpremeditated murder.
24. Laws concerning premeditated murder.
25. An admonition not to remove the landmarks of one's neighbor.
26. Laws concerning witnesses.
27. The law concerning false witnesses.
28. The section concerning the officers of the people and the anointed priest who were to address the people prior to their going out to battle.
29. The commandment to give an enemy the opportunity of surrendering peaceably before engaging in warfare.
30. The law concerning the treatment of persons conquered in a war with a city far removed from the territory of the Israelites.
31. The law concerning the treatment of members of the seven Canaanite nations who are defeated by the Israelites.
32. The destruction of trees prohibited.
33. The law concerning the breaking of a heifer's neck.

KI TETZE (Chapters 21-25)

1. Laws concerning a captive woman.
2. Laws concerning the birthright.
3. The law concerning a rebellious son.
4. The law concerning judicial hangings.
5. Laws concerning the return of lost property.
6. The commandment to help one's neighbor lift up and load any animal of his that has fallen down.
7. The wearing of men's clothing by women, or the reverse, prohibited.
8. The commandment to take only fledglings or eggs from the nest, and not the mother; the reward for the fulfillment of this commandment.
9. The commandment to build a parapet on one's roof and remove all obstacles and dangers from one's property.
10. The prohibition of sowing a vineyard with two kinds of seeds, plowing with an ox and ass to-

gether, and wearing a garment made of wool and linen.

11. The commandment to wear fringes on one's garments.
12. Laws concerning slander and calumny.
13. Laws concerning a woman proven guilty of the charge of unchastity leveled against her by her husband.
14. The punishment of a man and married woman who have committed adultery.
15. The punishment of a man who lies with a betrothed woman.
16. The punishment of a man who violates a betrothed woman.
17. The punishment of a man who violates a virgin who is not betrothed.
18. Having relations with the wife of one's father prohibited.
19. Persons who may never enter the assembly of the Lord.
20. Persons of the third generation who may enter the congregation of the Lord.
21. An admonition never to seek the welfare of Ammon and Moab.
22. Rules concerning conduct in a military camp.
23. Defiled persons forbidden to enter the camp.
24. Laws concerning a non-Jewish bondman who flees from his master
25. The prohibition against male or female engaging in acts of immorality.
26. The prohibition against bringing to God, in fulfillment of a vow, a sacrifice consisting of a harlot's hire or the hire of a dog.
27. The prohibition of usury.
28. Vows of sacred offerings.
29. Laws concerning one who works in the vineyard or field of his neighbor.
30. Laws of divorce; the prohibition against a man's remarriage to a woman he has divorced and who has been married to another.
31. Laws concerning the first year of marriage.
32. Laws concerning security for a debt.
33. The law concerning a man who kidnaps and sells a human being.
34. The admonition to obey the commands of the priests in regard to leprosy.
35. The commandment to remember what God did to Miriam.
36. Laws concerning the hired worker.
37. The testimony of relatives.
38. A man will be put to death for his own sin only.
39. Gifts due the poor.
40. The admonition not to pervert justice in the case of the stranger and the orphan.
41. Laws of flogging.
42. The admonition not to injure one's fellow.
43. The commandment not to muzzle an ox while the animal is treading grain.
44. Laws of the levirate marriage and the release by the ceremony of *halizah*.
45. The law concerning the shaming of a man. The law concerning one who pursues another.
46. Laws of weights and measures.
47. The commandment to remember what Amalek did to Israel and to blot out the remembrance of Amalek.

KI TAVO (Chapters 26-29)

1. The commandment to bring the first fruits of one's harvest to God; the commandment to make a declaration concerning the first fruits; the text of the declaration.
2. The commandment to make a declaration after the giving of the tithe; the text of the declaration; laws concerning the second tithe.
3. An admonition to heed the commandments and observe them wholeheartedly.
4. The reciprocal relationship between God and Israel.
5. The commandment to set up a pillar of stones on the east side of the Jordan, build an altar on Mount Ebal and offer up sacrifices to God to commemorate the inscribing of the Torah on stones.
6. The reminding of the Israelites that they have just become God's people and are now obligated to observe His commandments.
7. The commandment to bless and curse the people on Mount Gerizim and Mount Ebal respectively.
8. The words of the covenant in the plains of Moab.
9. The commandment to walk in God's ways.
10. The punishment that will befall those who will not serve God joyously. Returning to Egypt prohibited.
11. A strong admonition to observe all aspects of the covenant.

NITZAVIM (Chapters 29-30)

1. The making of the covenant; its participants.
2. The reason for the renewal of the covenant and the oath.
3. The confirmed evil-doer and the results of his sins: the destruction of the land and the dispersal of the people among the nations.
4. The things that are secret and the things that are revealed.
5. The commandment to repent; God's assurance of forgiveness and redemption to all who do repent.
6. The way to repent.
7. Free will and the admonition to choose the good.

VAYELEKH (Chapter 31)

1. Moses declares to Israel that (a) his life is drawing to a close and he cannot lead them in the conquest of the land; (b) God will go before them and fight for them as He did in the battle with Sihon and Og; (c) in accordance with God's word, Joshua will lead the people; (d) they shall not fear.
2. In the presence of all Israel, Moses declares to Joshua that (a) he (Joshua) will acquire Canaan for the people; (b) God will be with him and pass before him; (c) the people ought not to fear.
3. Moses writes down the Law and gives it to "the priests the sons of Levi" and to all the elders of Israel.
4. The commandment to assemble the people every seventh year.

5. God calls Moses and Joshua to the tent of meeting. He informs Moses of what will befall the children of Israel after his death, then tells the prophet to write down the song and teach it to the Israelites, so that it might be God's perennial witness; God promises Moses that the song will not be forgotten by the Israelites' descendants. God charges Joshua to be strong and of good courage in bringing the Israelites into the land.

6. Moses writes down the Law and teaches it to the children of Israel.

7. The commandment to write a Torah scroll (included in the commandment "Write ye this song for you").

8. Moses, upon his completion of the writing of the book of the Law, commands the Levites to place it in the side of the ark of the covenant; he rebukes the people for the sins they will commit after his death.

9. Moses orders that all the officers and all the elders of the tribes assemble to listen to the song and hear heaven and earth called as witnesses,

10. Moses recites the song before the entire people.

HAAZINU (Chapter 32)

1. The words of the song.
2. The recitation of the song to the people by Moses and Joshua.
3. An admonition to observe the Torah.
4. God commands Moses to ascend Mount Nebo, view the Promised Land and there die because of his sin at the waters of Meribah.

VEZOT HABERAKHAH (Chapters 33-34)

1. Moses blesses the tribes of Israel.
2. Moses ascends Mount Nebo and looks upon the Promised Land; the death of Moses; his burial in an unknown place.
3. Moses' age at his death; his exceptional vigor.
4. The period of mourning for Moses.
5. The wisdom of Joshua and the obedience of the people.
6. Moses' preeminence above all the prophets.

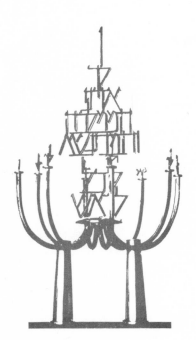

An old man gives a scroll to a young warrior who will lead his people.

"Moses received the Torah on Sinai, and handed it down to Joshua; Joshua to the elders" (Aboth 1.1).

"And when the Lord raised them up judges, then the Lord was with the judge, and saved them out of the hand of their enemies all the days of the judge"

(Judges 2.18).

THE JUDGES

The period of the judges, or civic leaders, who led the people in battle and took charge of one or more tribes in peacetime, begins with the death of Joshua and ends during the lifetime of Samuel. The judges were fifteen in number and their exploits were many and varied. During the period in which they lived, idolatry was rife in the land: "Every man did that which was right in his own eyes." Repeatedly God punished the sinful Israelites and then saved them by raising up another judge. Generally speaking, the author describes Israel's transition from a tribal grouping to a united kingdom and records the colorful deeds of the tribal leaders, or judges.

According to Rabbi Don Isaac Abarbanel in the preface to his work: "Nahalath Aboth", commentary on the Talmudic tractate Aboth (Ethics of the Fathers), it is to be inferred that the Judges who served Israel after the death of Joshua and during the period of approximately 400 years, are to be regarded as the *Elders* mentioned in Aboth I., in the phrase "And Joshua to the Elders" . . . and that they and their rabbinic courts were the principal recipients of the Tradition in their generation. The Elders therefore, are to be identified with the 15 Judges who appear in the pages that follow.

THE JUDGE	EVENTS	T O
1. Othniel, son of Kenaz	The first judge to rule in the period of Israelite subjection to Aram. This was the period of the incidents of the graven image of Micah, the Gibeah concubine and the subsequent vengeance on the Benjaminite tribe. Othniel relieved Israel from vassalage to Cushanrishathaim, king of Aram, and the land was tranquil.	
2. Ehud, son of Gera	He relieved Israel from vassalage to Eglon, king of Moab; the land was tranquil for four score years. According to the sages, this is also the period of the events recorded in the Book of Ruth.	
3. Shamgar, son of Anath	He relieved Israel from vassalage to the Philistines for the brief period of a year.	
4. Barak, son of Abinoam, & Deborah, the prophetess	They delivered Israel from vassalage to Jabin, king of Canaan, through the defeat of his general Sisera's army.	
5. Gideon, son of Joash	Also called Jerubbaal (1 Samuel 12.11). Jerubbesheth (2 Samuel 11.21) With 300 men he smote the Midianites. Refusing a crown, he returned to his home in Ophrah.	
6. Abimelech, son of Gideon	Internal struggles. He killed his seventy brothers but was slain by a woman when he laid siege to the city of Thebez.	
7. Tola, son of Puah	According to the sages, he was a very wise man. "Tola excelled all the members of the court (Sanhedrin) in dialectics and wisdom" (Midrash Yelamdenu).	
8. Jair, the Gileadite	"He was called Jair (Light) because he enlightened the wise with . . . his knowledge of Torah" (Midrash Yelamdenu). He passed down rule over the cities of Gilead to his stalwart sons.	
9. Jephthah, the Gileadite	Jephthah relieved Israel from vassalage to the Ammonites. Keeping his rash vow, he sacrificed his young daughter as a victory offering to God. But his victory resulted in strife between the men of Gilead and the tribe of Ephraim.	
10. Ibzan of Beth-lehem	Identified by some of the sages with Boaz, ancestor of David (Baba Bathra 91a).	
11. Elon, the Zebulunite	No record. Apparently a tranquil period.	
12. Abdon, the son of Hillel the Pirathonite	Tranquility continues. He is only recorded as having been happy in his children (Josephus, Antiquities of the Jews, V, Chap. 7, p. 15).	
13. Samson, son of Manoah	A Nazirite and warrior who delivered Israel from the Philistines by his strength. He fell into the clutches of the Philistines as a result of Delilah's treachery. Taunted, at the moment of his death he slew thousands of his tormentors.	
14. Eli, the priest	The priest who ruled over Israel in Shiloh. He died at the news that the Ark of the Lord had been captured by the Philistines.	
15. Samuel, the prophet	The last of the judges and the first of the prophets. With him ended the era of the Judges. The beginning of monarchical rule.	

NOTE:
A consistent system of chronology, covering the period from the Exodus and Conquest until the first Kings, has engaged the study of scholars for many years; it has never been successfully formulated. Estimates of the actual period of the Judges have been variously fixed at approximately 400 years (see F. Hastings, "Dictionary of the Bible," p. 399); 356 years according to A.A. Akavia in his "Sidre Zemanim," Tel Aviv, 1943; 334 years (1394 - 1060 B.C.E.) according to Samuel Arrowsmith in his "Bible Atlas," Lon-

don; and more recently, at approximately 200 years (1225-1020 B.C.E.). All of these dates, as conceded by scholars, are conjectural, irreconcilable and abounding in discrepancies in both the A.M.* and B.C.E. calculations.
The confusion is attributable to a number of uncertainties: e.g., the overlapping years of judges who ruled simultaneously; periods that were without a judge at all; the reckoning of successive periods as synchronical years; and variations in chronological calculations, using for instance, "roundness" in numbers.

TRIBAL ORIGIN	APPROX. YEARS OF RULE	APPROX. DATES A.M.	APPROX. DATES B.C.E.	RECENT VERSION	SOURCES	השופט
Judah	40	2516-2556	1394	Period of Judges ca. 1225-1020 B.C.E.	Judges 3.8-11, also chap. 19, 20	א. עתניאל בן קנז
Benjamin	80	2556-2636	1336		Judges 3.15-30	ב. אהוד בן גרא
	1	2636	1296		Judges 3.31	ג. שמגר בן ענת
Naphtali	40	2636-2676	1296	ca. 1100	Judges chap. 4	ד. ברק בן אבינועם ודבורה הנביאה
Manasseh	40	2683-2723	1249		Judges 6-8	ה. גדעון בן יואש ירובעל (שמא יב,יא),ירובשת (שב יא,כא)
Manasseh	3	2723-2726	1209		Judges 9.1-56	ו. אבימלך בן גדעון
Issachar	23	2726-2749	1206		Judges 10.1-2	ז. תולע בן פואה
Manasseh	22	2748-2770	1183-1161		Judges 10.3-5	ח. יאיר הגלעדי
Manasseh	6	2782-2788 (2786)*	1143-1137		Judges 11.1-12.7	ט. יפתח הגלעדי
Judah	7	2788-2795	1137-1130		Judges 12.8-10	י. אבצן מבית לחם
Zebulun	10	2795-2805 (2798-2807)*	1130-1120		Judges 12.11-12	יא. אילון הזבולוני
Ephraim	8	2805-2812 (2807-2815)*	1120-1112		Judges 12.13-15	יב. עבדון בן הלל הפרעתוני
Dan	20	2812-2832	1120		Judges 13-16	יג. שמשון בן מנוח
Levi	40	2832-2872	(1181) —1141	death of Eli ca. 1050	1 Samuel 1-4	יד. עלי הכהן
Levi	11	2872-2882	—1060**	ca. 1020 initial year of Saul's reign	1 Samuel 1-17	טו. שמואל הנביא

Note in RECENT VERSION column: Recent scholarship is inclined to fix the period of the Judges between the approximate years of 1225 B.C.E. and 1020 B.C.E. The dates appear in italics.

This Chart of Judges (see also p. 178, ff) offers information to guide the reader in the comparison of various versions of chronology, such as the masoretic A.M. system* largely based on the calculations of biblical and talmudic sources by A.A. Akavia and others, and the B.C.E. system of Samuel Arrowsmith which reflects the thought of the last century. All the dates, and the periods between them, as presented by the various versions are approximate. Contemporary research further illumines the events.

*The dates in parenthesis accord with Elijah Gaon's commentary on Seder Olam.
**Refer to Footnote on page 189.

*A.M. refers to the 'Anno Mundi' chronology originating with the beginnings of recorded time.

THE JUDGES

1. OTHNIEL, SON OF KENAZ

עתניאל
בן קנז

Othniel captures a hill-city.

"And Caleb said: 'He that smiteth Kiriath-sepher . . . to him will I give Achsah my daughter to wife.' And Othniel, the son of Kenaz . . . took it" (Judg. 1.12-13).

Othniel was the first judge in Israel and judged the people for 40 years. He was a member of the tribe of Judah and the younger brother of Caleb, son of Jephunneh. As a reward for capturing Kiriath-sepher, Othniel was given Achsah, Caleb's daughter, as his wife (Joshua 15.16-17; Judges 1.12-13).

The spirit of God came upon Othniel and he saved Israel from Cushan-rishathaim, king of Aram, who had oppressed the Israelites for eight years as a punishment for their having done evil in the sight of the Lord. After Othniel's victory the land was at peace for 40 years (Judges 3.7-11).

"Before the sun of Joshua had set, the sun of Othniel ben Kenaz arose, as it is written: 'And Othniel, son of Kenaz, the younger brother of Caleb, captured it' " (Yalkut Shimoni II.4)

"Seventeen hundred conclusions a minori ad majus, analogies and fine legal points not explicitly stated in the text of the Torah were forgotten during the period of mourning for Moses. Rabbi Abahu declared: 'Nevertheless, Othniel, son of Kenaz, restored them through his reasoning, as it is written: "Othniel, son of Kenaz, the younger brother of Caleb, captured it" ' " (Temurah 16a).

"He was named Othniel because God answered him [Sheanao-El]" (*ibid.;* and see 1 Chronicles 4.13).

"Othniel, son of Kenaz, pleaded before God that He fulfill his promise to Moses that Israel would be liberated whether they did His will or not; and God agreed" (Exodus Rabbah 3.1).

" 'And they said unto the olive tree, Reign thou over us' (Judges 9.8) This refers to Othniel, son of Kenaz, of the tribe of Judah, as it is written: 'The Lord called thy name. A leafy olive tree, fair with goodly fruit' " (Jeremiah 11.16; Yalkut Shimoni 65).

2. EHUD, SON OF GERA

אהוד בן גרא

Ehud slays King Eglon of Moab with a dagger thrust.

"And Ehud put forth his left hand, and took the sword from his right thigh, and thrust it into his (Eglon's) belly" (Judg. 3.21).

The second judge of Israel, Ehud judged the people for 80 years. His sons were chieftains of the inhabitants of Geba (1 Chronicles 8.6).

Ehud saved Israel from Eglon king of Moab who, together with Amalek and Ammon, had oppressed Israel for eighteen years because they had continued to do evil in the sight of the Lord. Since Ehud was left handed—although the text might mean that he was ambidextrous, like the 700 warriors of Benjamin (Judges 20.16)— he girded his sword upon his right thigh, under his garment. He gained entry to the king, under the guise of bringing him a gift from the people; thrust his sword into the monarch's belly, and fled. Returning to Mount Ephraim he gathered the people together and led them to a decisive victory over the Moabite army. Moab was subdued and the land was at peace for 80 years (Judges 3.12-30).

"Benjamin is a wolf that raveneth" (Genesis 49.27). Just as a wolf ravens [*hotef*], so did Ehud deceive [*hataf*] the heart of Eglon" (Genesis Rabbah 99).

3. SHAMGAR, SON OF ANATH

שמגר בן ענת

Philistines smitten by the ox-goad in Shamgar's hand.

"And after him was Shamgar the son of Anath, who smote of the Philistines six hundred men with an ox-goad" (Judg. 3.31).

Shamgar, son of Anath, who was judge after Ehud, slew 600 Philistines with an ox-goad and delivered Israel (Judges 3.31).

"In the days of Shamgar, son of Anath,/In the days of Jael, the highways ceased,/And the travellers walked through byways" (The Song of Deborah: Judges 5,6).

"The Holy One blessed be He said: 'In this world you [Israelites] have been saved by human beings: in Egypt, by Moses and Aaron; in the days of Sisera, by Barak and Deborah; and in the wars of Midian, by Shamgar, son of Anath, as it is written: "And he also saved Israel" ' " (Tanhuma, end of Ahare Mot).

4. BARAK AND DEBORAH

ברק בן אבינועם ודבורה הנביאה

Deborah sits in judgment beneath a palm tree. Barak pursues Sisera.

"Now Deborah, a prophetess . . . judged Israel at that time" (Judg. 4.4).
"Barak pursued . . . and all the host of Sisera fell by . . . the sword" (4. 16).

A general of the Israelites and a member of the tribe of Naphtali, Barak dwelt in Kedesh in Galilee (Joshua 21.32). Barak was commanded by God, through Deborah the prophetess, who judged Israel in those days, to battle Sisera, the general of the army of Jabin, king of Canaan, who had oppressed the children of Israel mightily for twenty years.

Barak agreed to answer Deborah's call on condition that she take part in the battle. The prophetess complied, but only after warning Barak that the glory of the victory would then be hers. The Israelite general gathered 10,000 men of the tribes of Naphtali and Zebulun and in a battle at the river Kishon, at the foot of Mount Tabor, crushed the army of Sisera with its 900 iron chariots. Sisera met his death at the hand of Jael, wife of Heber the Kenite (Judges 4.1-24). Deborah and Barak then celebrated their glorious victory in a moving song of thanksgiving (Judges 5).

"What right had Barak to be in the company of Deborah? The sages explained: 'Barak served the elders during the days of Joshua, and continued to do so even after the latter's death. Therefore he was brought to Deborah and placed at her side' " (Yalkut Shimoni § 42).

"Because Barak had faith in the God of Israel and believed the prophecy of Deborah, she gave him a portion of the song of victory, as it is written: 'Then sang Deborah and Barak' " (*ibid.*).

5. GIDEON, SON OF JOASH

גדעון בן יואש

Gideon routs the Midianite camp at night.

"And the three companies blew the horns, and broke the pitchers, and held the torches . . . and they cried: 'The sword for the Lord and for Gideon' " (Judg. 7.20).

A member of the tribe of Manasseh and the fifth judge of Israel, Gideon judged the people for 40 years. He was also called Jerubbaal, meaning "Let Baal contend against him (because he hath broken down his altar)" (Judges 6.32), and Jerubbesheth (2 Samuel 11.21). Gideon lived in Ophrah. He had 70 sons and the son of his concubine was Abimelech.

The angel of God who revealed himself to Gideon found the latter threshing wheat by the winepress in order to hide it from the Midianites (Judges 6.11). When the angel declared: "Go in this thy might and save Israel from the hand of Midian", Gideon humbly replied: "Behold, my family is poorest in Manasseh and I am the least in my father's house" (6.14-15).

After the angel showed him a sign, the spirit of the Lord came upon Gideon. He assembled his family and the tribes of Asher, Zebulun and Naphtali to wage war against Midian (6.34-35). At Gideon's request, God demonstrated his intention of saving Israel by performing the miracle of the dew and the woolen fleece (6.36-40).

The forces of Gideon encamped beside the well of Harod and "the camp of Midian was on the north side of them, by Gibeath-moreh, in the valley (Judges 7.1). With the 300 men who had lapped the waters of En-harod by bringing their hands to their mouths, rather than falling on their knees, Gideon broke into the enemy's camp and, with the help of the rest of Israel, crushed Midian, killing all their officers (7.9-25). Gideon then punished the inhabitants of Succoth and Pennuel, who had refused provisions and food to his men (8.16-17).

Towards the end of his life Gideon turned to idolatry, using for this purpose the ephod which he had made from the earrings given him by the men of his army (Judges 8.25; Bereshit Rabbah 44). Although he had made the ephod in order to serve God, it nevertheless became a stumbling block to all Israel (Yalkut Shimoni § 64).

"God said to Gideon: 'Since you are able to plead for Israel, they will be redeemed for your sake', as it is written: 'And thou shalt save Israel'" (Yalkut Shimoni § 62).

6. ABIMELECH, SON OF GIDEON

אבימלך בן גדעון

Jotham's parable of the trees that surround a thorn-bush and crown it king.

"The trees went forth ... to anoint a king over them ... Then said all the trees unto the bramble: Come thou, and reign over us" (Judg. 9. 8.14).

A Manassite and the sixth judge of Israel, Abimelech judged the people for three years. He was the son of the concubine, or maid-servant, of Gideon (Judges 9.18). He killed his 70 brothers "upon one stone"; only Jotham, the youngest of Gideon's sons, remained alive because he hid himself (Judges 9.5).

Jotham, by means of his parable of the trees and the bramble bush, reproached the people of Shechem for showing ingratitude to Gideon by crowning the murderer of his children. Jotham ended his parable by invoking a curse upon the Shechemites (9.56-57).

The curse of Jotham bore fruit. The men of Shechem rebelled against Abimelech and pledged their allegiance to Gaal, son of Ebed. In the ensuing battle Abimelech smote the forces of Gaal, captured Shechem and destroyed it, along with the "hold of the house of El-berith" and the multitude who had fled to the tower of Shechem. Abimelech was killed by his armour-bearer after his skull was split by a piece of a millstone cast down upon him by a woman during his attack upon the tower of Thebez (Judges 9.23-57; see 2 Samuel 11.21).

"Abimelech was not killed until he became haughty and murdered his brothers" (Yalkut Shimoni § 63).

"Then said all the trees unto the bramble: Come thou, and reign over us" (Judges 9.14). This refers to Abimelech. Just as the bramble bears no fruit and is full of thorns, so Abimelech possessed no good deeds (Yalkut Shimoni § 65).

7. TOLA, SON OF PUAH

תולע בן פואה

Tola sits as head of the Sanhedrin.

"There arose to save Israel Tola the son of Puah ... And he judged Israel twenty and three years" (Judg. 10.1-2).

A member of the tribe of Issachar and the seventh judge of Israel, Tola judged the people for 23 years.

He dwelt in Shamir in Mount Ephraim, where he was later buried (Judges 10.1-2).

8. JAIR
THE GILEADITE

יאיר
הגלעדי

Jair and his thirty sons.

"Jair, the Gileadite . . . judged Israel twenty and two years. And he had thirty sons . . . and they had thirty cities" (Judg. 10.3-4).

A Manassite and the eighth judge of Israel, Jair judged the people for 22 years.

"And he had thirty sons that rode on thirty ass colts, and they had thirty cities, which are called Havvoth-jair unto this day, which are in the land of Gilead. And Jair died, and was buried in Kamon" (Judges 10.3-5).

9. JEPHTHAH
THE GILEADITE

יפתח
הגלעדי

Jephthah's daughter greets her father upon his victorious return.

"And Jephthah came to Mizpah . . . and, behold, his daughter came out to meet him with timbrels and with dances" (Judg. 11.34).

The son of a harlot, Jephthah was the ninth of the judges and judged for six years. He dwelt in Mizpah until his father's sons, with the approval of the elders of Gilead, drove him away. He then went to live in the land of Tob. Approximately one year later the elders of Gilead asked Jephthah to be their captain and lead them in battle against the Ammonites, who had oppressed them for eighteen years. Jephthah agreed on condition that he become chief of the inhabitants of Gilead if he obtained victory over Ammon (Judges 11.1-11).

As commanded in the Torah (Deuteronomy 20.10) Jephthah first called upon the enemy to surrender peaceably. He refused the contention of the King of Ammon that Israel, on their way from Egypt to Canaan, had taken Ammonite territory, from the Arnon to the Jabbok and the Jordan;

Jephthah pointed out that Israel had requested of the kings of Edom, Moab and Ammon the right of transit through their respective lands, and had fought the Ammonites only after having been attacked.

The king of Ammon refused to heed the words of Jephthah and was sorely defeated by the latter. Jephthah then sacrificed his daughter in fulfillment of his vow, made before his victory, that whatsoever came forth from his house to greet him upon his safe return from battle would be offered up to God (Judges 11.28-40). Jephthah smote the tribe of Ephraim, who had gathered together and threatened to burn down his house for his not having called upon them to join him in battle against the Ammonites and thus have a share in the victory (12.1-17).

"Jephthah in his generation was like Samuel in his generation" (Rosh Hashanah 25b). Because he was not a student of the Torah, he lost his daughter" (Yalkut Shimoni § 67; Ecclesiastes Rabbah on Ecclesiastes 4.17).

"Jephthah had vowed improperly to offer up his daughter upon the altar. His pride prevented him from seeking an abrogation of his vow from Phinehas, the High Priest" (Yalkut Shimoni § 68).

10. IBZAN
OF BETH-LEHEM

אבצן
מבית לחם

The old judge stands at the well near the gate of Bethlehem. In the distance Jerusalem.

"Ibzan of Beth-lehem... had thirty sons, and thirty daughters ... And he judged Israel seven years" (Judg. 12.8-9).

The tenth judge in Israel, Ibzan judged the people for seven years. He dwelt in Bethlehem, apparently the Bethlehem that was located in Judah (Baba Bathra 91a; Josephus, Antiquities V, 7.13).

"He had thirty sons, and thirty daughters he sent abroad, and thirty daughters he brought in from abroad for his sons. . . . And Ibzan died, and was buried in Bethlehem" (Judges 12.9-10).

"Ibzan is Boaz" (Baba Bathra 91a). The Midrash, however, does not agree with this opinion (Ruth Rabbah 6) and Rashi questions it (Rashi, on 1 Chronicles 2.11).

11. ELON THE ZEBULUNITE

אילון הזבולוני

Elon views the ships in the bay of Haifa.

"And after him Elon the Zebulunite judged Israel . . . ten years" (Judg. 12. 11).

A Zebulunite and the eleventh of Israel's judges, Elon judged Israel for ten years. He was buried in Aijalon in the land of Zebulun (Judges 12.11-12).

12. ABDON THE PIRATHONITE

עבדון בן הלל הפרעתוני

Jews plant trees on the hills of Ephraim during a period of peace.

"Abdon the son of Hillel the Pirathonite . . . had forty sons and thirty sons' sons . . . and he judged Israel eight years" (Judg. 12.13-14).

An Ephraimite, Abdon was the twelfth judge of Israel and judged for eight years. "He had forty sons and thirty sons' sons, that rode on threescore and ten ass colts". Abdon was buried in Pirathon in the land of Ephraim, in the hill-country of the Amalekites (Judges 12.13-15).

13. SAMSON, SON OF MANOAH

שמשון בן מנוח

Blind Samson pulls down the pillars of the Philistine temple.

"And Samson said: 'Let me die with the Philistines.' And he bent with all his might; and the house fell . . . upon all the people that were therein" (Judg. 16.30).

A member of a Danite family from Zorah, Samson was the thirteenth of the judges and judged

Israel for twenty years. An angel of God informed the wife of Manoah that she would conceive and bear a son. "No razor shall come upon his head; for the child shall be a Nazirite unto God from the womb; and he shall begin to save Israel out of the hand of the Philistines" (Judges 13.5). Samson was born and grew with God's blessings, "and the spirit of the Lord began to move him at times in Mahaneh-Dan between Zorah and Eshtaol" (13.25).

His affairs with Philistine women prompted conflicts with the Philistines and the performance of his mighty deeds of valour. He was first attracted to a woman in Timnah and this led, directly or indirectly, to many exploits: the rending of a lion like a kid (14.5-6); the killing of 30 men of Ashkelon and the transferral of their garments to the 30 men who had answered his riddle correctly (14.11-20); the burning of the Philistines' fields of standing wheat (15.1-5); the taking of revenge upon those who had burnt his wife and her father (15.6-8); and the slaying of a thousand Philistine captors with the jawbone of an ass (15.9-17). His coming to a harlot in Gaza brought about another display of his strength: he removed the doors of the gates of the city, placed them on his shoulders, and carried them to the top of a mountain near Hebron (16.1-3). Finally, Samson's love for Delilah brought about the execution of his mightiest feat, as well as his death. Delilah, through persistent nagging, prevailed upon Samson to tell her the secret source of his power and then arranged for his capture by the Philistines, who put out his eyes and cast him into prison. The spirit of the Lord came upon Samson once more, in the Temple of Dagon, when by crushing the pillars of the temple he brought down the structure upon himself and the 3,000 Philistines who had come to see him in his disgrace (Judges 16.23-30).

"Samson was swayed by the lust of his eyes, therefore the Philistines put out his eyes" (Sotah 9b).

" 'And the spirit of the Lord began to move him in Mahaneh-dan.' Said Rabbi Issac of the school of Rabbi Ami: 'This teaches us that the Divine Presence tinkled before him like a bell' " (*ibid.*).

"Rabbi Isaac said: 'Zorah and Eshtaol were two high hills. Samson uprooted them and ground one against the other like millstones' " (*ibid.*).

" 'And Samson called unto the Lord, and said: "O Lord God, remember me, I pray Thee, and strengthen me, I pray Thee, only this once' " (Judges 16.28). Samson said: 'O Master of the World, remember how for twenty years I judged Israel and never told one of them to even move a stick for me from one place to another'."

"Rabbi Johanan said: 'Samson judged Israel as their Father in Heaven, as it is written: "Dan shall judge his people as *One*" ' " (Yalkut Shimoni § 69; Genesis 49.16).

"Rabbi Johanan also said: 'He was called Samson after the name of God, as it is written: "for the Lord God is a sun (*shemesh*) and a shield" ' (Psalm 84.12). The Philistines feared Samson even twenty years after his death" (Yalkut Shimoni § 71).

14. ELI THE PRIEST עלי הכהן

Eli, the High Priest, reproves his two sons, but they turn a deaf ear.

"And he said unto them: 'Why do ye such things? for ·I hear evil reports concerning you' . . . But they hearkened not unto . . . their father" (I. Sam. 2.23,25).

Eli, the fourteenth judge in Israel, apparently was chief among the High Priests of the sons of Ithamar, to whom the priesthood passed from the family of Phinehas, son of Eleazar, son of Aaron (Judges 20.28). He judged Israel for 40 years and dwelt in Shiloh.

Eli promised Hannah, the barren wife of Elkanah, that God would answer her prayer for a son (1 Samuel 1.17). Eli trained the boy, Samuel, in the service of the Lord in Shiloh (2.18-21). preparing him for his future role as judge and prophet. Samuel took on this role after the death of the two sons of Eli, who were "base men" and "they knew not the Lord" (2.12). They died in the war against the Philistines (4.11) and their father died thereafter as a punishment for his never having restrained them or admonished them (3.11-14; 4.16-18).

" 'Eli the priest sat upon his seat by the doorpost of the temple of the Lord' (1 Samuel 1.9).

Eli the priest—he was High Priest; *sat upon his seat*—for he was a king; *by the doorpost of the temple of the Lord*—he was head of a court" (Tanhuma, Shemini, 2).

"When Eli died, Shiloh was destroyed and the priests went to Nob. When Samuel died, Nob was destroyed and they came to Gibeon" (Zebahim 118b).

15. SAMUEL OF RAMAH שמואל הנביא

Saul, head and shoulders above the rest, is anointed by Samuel.

'Samuel took . . . oil, and poured it upon his (Saul's) head . . . and said . . . 'The Lord hath anointed thee' " (I. Sam. 10.1).

The fifteenth and last judge of Israel, Samuel lived in Ramah. He was a Levite of the family of Kohath (1 Chronicles 6.18-23) and served Israel for eleven years.

Samuel was the child for whom Hannah had prayed to God in Eli's presence and was consecrated to the service of God in accordance with his mother's vow (1 Samuel 1.11,27-28).

"And the child Samuel grew on, and increased in favor both with the Lord, and also with men" (2.26). God revealed Himself to ·Samuel and disclosed to him the future of the house of Eli (3.1-14). "And all Israel from Dan even to Beersheba knew that Samuel was established to be a prophet of God" (3.20).

Samuel urged the Israelites who had gathered at Mizpah to abandon all idol worship. They did so and consequently gained victory over the Philistines. Samuel bowed to the will of the people, who refused to have his sons serve as judges, and gave them a king as they demanded. However, he first forewarned them of the "manner of the king" and declared that God looked upon their request as a sign that they despised Him (10.17-19). Samuel believed that with the anointing of a ruler he had fulfilled his mission. In his last address to the people he reviewed his relationship with them and warned them to remain loyal to God, for any defection on their part would bring upon them and their king catastrophes from which their ancestors had been saved by judges who had been raised up by God (chapter 12).

Samuel began to contend with Saul, whom he had anointed, because the king did not obey the directives given him by the prophet in God's name 13.5-15; chapter 15). In accordance with the command of God, Samuel chose a successor to Saul—David, son of Jesse—and anointed him with oil (16.3).

"And Samuel died; and all Israel gathered themselves together, and lamented him, and buried him in his house at Ramah" (25.1).

"Rabbi Jeremiah, in the name of Rabbi Samuel, son of Rabbi Isaac, declared: 'A righteous person shall arise and his name shall be Samuel'" (Yalkut Shimoni § 78).

"Rabbi Eliezer said: 'The repetition "Samuel, Samuel" (1 Samuel 3.10) teaches us that the first call was directed to him and the second to his generation. For there is no generation that does not have one man like Moses and one man like Samuel'" (Yalkut Shimoni § 97).

"Rabbi Eliezer also said: 'The Divine Spirit revealed itself in three places: in the court of Shem, in the court of Samuel and in the court of Solomon'" (Makkoth 23).

Hearken unto their voice, and make them a king.

"Then Samuel told the people the manner of the kingdom, and wrote it in a book, and laid it up before the Lord" (I. Samuel 10.25).

THE MONARCHY

The history of the monarchy in Israel exhibits, at once, both moral progress and moral retrogression. The people's request for a king is at first spurned by the prophet Samuel, who feels that evil is the usual concomitant of kingship. Saul, the first king, is not entirely responsible; Samuel anoints a successor, David, who is extremely successful in uniting the various tribes under a centralized government. Under David's son Solomon, the kingdom attains a high degree of peacetime prosperity; and Solomon continues the Davidic dynasty which, according to tradition, is the precursor of the future Messiah.

After Solomon's death, however, unresolved domestic problems result in the division of the kingdom. Political unity at this point yields to prolonged rivalry between the northern kingdom of Israel, or Ephraim, and the southern kingdom of Judah. The Davidic dynasty retains the throne in Judah until the downfall of that kingdom; but in the north, there ensue numerous palace intrigues and frequent changes of dynasty.

Pagan rites present a problem in both kingdoms, but more particularly in Ephraim. Prophets and kings are almost in constant conflict; the former assail royally favored paganism with all its attendant immorality, and further insist that the king and the people practice morality and serve God in accordance with His commandments. Rare indeed are the "righteous" kings — men like Hezekiah and Josiah — who seek to purge the worship of God of all pagan elements.

The international political scene profoundly affects the two tiny kingdoms, for they are in virtually constant peril from the powerful surrounding nations which at times defeat them in battle and bear away much spoil. The northern kingdom is finally engulfed by the Assyrians in 722 B.C.E.; the Judean kingdom persists in its struggle until 586 B.C.E., when it is overthrown by Babylonia.

Many inscriptions, such as the Moabite Stone and the Black Obelisk, corroborate the Biblical account of the monarchic period, as do excavations of various sites such as Ezion-geber.

The 43 Kings of Judah and Israel

מ״ג מלכי יהודה וישראל

The Regnal Years, The Contemporary Prophets and High Priests

THE BEGINNING OF THE KINGDOM ראשית המלוכה

NAME OF KING	REGNAL YEARS	CHRONOLOGY APPROXIMATE DATES A.M.	B.C.E.	RECENT VERSION B.C.E.	CONTEMPORARY PROPHETS	HIGH PRIESTS
1. Saul, son of Kish שאול בן קיש	2-(20)	2883-2884	1095	1020-1004	Samuel	Phinehas Ahitub Ahijah Ahimelech
2. Ish-bosheth איש – בשת	2	2890-2891	1053			
3. David, son of Jesse דוד בן ישי	40	2884-2924 (2892)	1055-1015	1004-965	Samuel Gad the seer Nathan Asaph, Heman, Jeduthun (2 Chronicles 25)	Abiathar
4. Solomon, son of David שלמה בן דוד	40	2924-2964	1015-975	965-926*	Nathan Ahijah the Shilonite Iddo the seer	Zadok

NOTE: The chronology of the kings is subject to divergent versions. For example, according to I. Samuel 13.1, Saul ruled for two years; yet many historians fix his regnal term between twelve and twenty years and even more. The chronology of the first four kings is presented herein in the pattern of the three comparative systems referred to above.* *

Beginning with Rehoboam and Jeroboam respectively, the regnal chronology, in addition to following the masoretic system, based largely on calculations of A. A. Akavia and others, conforms to modern research. For parallel versions, see the works of F. Ruehl, F. X. Kugler, S. Mowinckel, E. R. Thiele, M. Vogelstein, W. F. Albright, H. Tadmor, as well as the "Interpreter's Dictionary of the Bible," 1961, and the "New Bible Dictionary", 1962.

*There is a margin of approximately five years between the terminal year of Solomon's reign (926 B.C.E.) and the initial year of Rehoboam's reign (931 B.C.E.).
**Cf. Note, Chart of Judges, p. 92; and Note, Chronological Tables, p. 178.

KINGS OF JUDAH   מלכי יהודה

	NAME OF KING	REGNAL YEARS	CHRONOLOGY APPROXIMATE DATES		CONTEMPORARY PROPHETS *	HIGH PRIESTS
			A.M.	B.C.E.		
1.	Rehoboam רחבעם בן שלמה	17	2965-2982	931-914	Shemaiah Iddo	Ahimaaz
2.	Abijah אביה	3	2982-2985	914-911	Iddo	Azariah*
3.	Asa אסא	41	2985-3024	911-870	Azariah, son of Oded, Hanani, Jehu	Azariah
4.	Jehoshaphat יהושפט	25	3025-3050	871-846	Obadiah, Elijah Eliezer, son of Dodavahu Jahaziel, son of Zechariah Jehu, son of Hanani	Amariah Johanan*
5.	Jehoram יהורם	8	3050-3058	851-843		
6.	Ahaziah אחזיה	1	3055	843-842		
7.	Athaliah עתליה	6	3056-3061	842-836		Jehoiada
8.	Joash יהואש (Jehoash)	40	3061-3101	836-796	Zechariah, son of Jehoiada	Zechariah, son of Jehoiada
9.	Amaziah אמציה	29	3101-3130	796-767	Amoz	
10.	Uzziah עוזיהו (Azariah)	52	3116-3168	791-740	Joel, Hosea, Amos, Micah Isaiah	Azariah II(III)
11.	Jotham יותם	16	3168-3184	751-735	Isaiah, Hosea, Amos Micah of Moreshet	
12.	Ahaz אחז	16	3184-3200	742-726	Isaiah, Oded, Hosea, Amos Micah	Uriah
13.	Hezekiah חזקיה	29	3200-3229	726-697	Isaiah, Hosea, Amos Micah Nahum	Azariah III
14.	Manasseh מנשה	55	3229-3284	697-642	Isaiah, Joel, Nahum, Habakkuk	
15.	Amon אמון	2	3284-3285	642-640		Shallum*
16.	Josiah יאשיהו	31	3285-3316	640-609	Zephaniah Huldah Habakkuk Jeremiah	Hilkiah
17.	Jehoahaz יהואחז	3 months	3316	609	Jeremiah	
18.	Jehoiakim יהויקים	11	3317-3327	608-597	Jeremiah, Uriah Daniel	Azariah IV*
19.	Jehoiachin יהויכין	3 months	3327	597	Jeremiah Daniel	
20.	Zedekiah צדקיהו	11	3327-3338	597-586	Jeremiah Daniel Ezekiel Obadiah	Seraiah Jehozadak

* **NOTE:** The exact dating of each prophet and the kings junder whom the prophecies were spoken are subject to varying opinions of scholars.

*According to Seder Olam Zuta.

KINGS OF ISRAEL מלכי ישראל

	NAME OF KING	REGNAL YEARS	CHRONOLOGY APPROXIMATE DATES		CONTEMPORARY PROPHETS	DYNASTY
			A.M.	B.C.E.		
1.	Jeroboam, son of Nebat ירבעם בן נבט	22	2965-2987	931-909	Ahijah the Shilonite Iddo	1. Jeroboam
2.	Nadab נדב	2	2986-2987	909-908		"
3.	Baasa, son of Ahijah בעשא בן אחיה	24	2987-3010	908-885	Jehu	2. Baasa
4.	Elah אלה	2	3010-3011	885-884		"
5.	Zimri זמרי	1 week	3011	884		3. Zimri
6.	Omri עמרי	12	3011-3022	884-873		4. Omri
7.	Ahab, son of Omri אחאב בן עמרי	22	3022-3044	875-853	Elijah, Eliezer, Jahaziel, Elisha, son of Shaphat, Micaiah, Obadiah*	"
8.	Ahaziah, son of Ahab אחזיה בן אחאב	2	3044	853-852	Elijah, Elisha	"
9.	Jehoram, son of Ahab יהורם בן אחאב	12	3045	852-841	Jona, Elisha, Joel*	"
10.	Jehu, son of Nimshi יהוא בן נמשי	28	3056-3084	841-814	Elisha, Jonah	5. Jehu
11.	Jehoahaz יהואחז	17	3084-3101	814-798	Elisha, Jonah	"
12.	Jehoash (Joash) יהואש	16	3101-3117	798-782	Elisha, Jonah	"
13.	Jeroboam II, son of Jehoash ירבעם בן יהואש	41	3114-3154	786-746	Jonah, Hosea, Amos	"
	(Interregnum)	11				
14.	Zechariah זכריה	6 months	3154	746-745	Hosea, Amos	"
15.	Shallum שלום	1 month	3155	745	Hosea, Amos	6. Shallum
16.	Menahem מנחם	10	3155-3165	745-736	Hosea, Amos	7. Menahem
17.	Pekahiah פקחיה	2	3165-3166	736-735	Hosea, Amos	"
18.	Pekah, son of Remaliah פקח בן רמליה	20(2)	3167-3187	751-731 (736-734)**	Hosea Oded*	8. Pekah
	Interregnum	9			Hosea	"
19.	Hoshea, son of Elah הושע בן אלה	9	3187-3195	731-722	Hosea	9. Hoshea

** Because of the disturbing interregnum there is a variance in reckoning. Tradition (II Kings 16.27) records 20 years inclusive for Pekah. The modern reckoning limits the reign to approximately 2 years.

* See biographies of the Prophets (beginning p. 134).

THE KINGS PRIOR TO THE
DIVISION OF THE KINGDOM

1. SAUL, SON OF KISH

שאול בן קיש

1 Samuel 9-31
1 Chronicles 9.39-10.14

The prophet Samuel and the people acclaim Saul king over Israel.

"And Samuel said . . . 'See ye him whom the Lord hath chosen' . . . And all the people shouted, and said: 'Long live the king'" (I. Sam. 10. 24).

Saul, the first king of Israel, was an imposing and tragic figure. The son of a farmer from the tribe of Benjamin, he was anointed king over Israel by the prophet Samuel, but not until after his victory over the Philistines in Michmas was he accepted as such by all the tribes. Two serious mistakes on his part antagonized his mentor Samuel: he himself offered up a sacrifice to God without waiting for the prophet, and he spared the life of Agag, king of the Amalekites. These instances of Saul's disobedience led Samuel to utter an ominous prophecy: "The Lord hath rent the kingdom of Israel from thee" (1 Samuel 15.28).

Suffering from melancholy, Saul summoned David to soothe his troubled spirit with music. Later, however, after David defeated Goliath in personal combat and became the object of popular adulation, Saul enviously suspected the young hero of aspiring to the throne. The king tried to kill the son of Jesse, but through the intervention of Jonathan, Saul's son, David was saved.

Before his last armed encounter with the Philistines, Saul had the spirit of Samuel raised up, only to receive the prophecy of his own imminent death. On the next day both Saul and Jonathan fell in battle on Mount Gilboa.

Despite the flaws that marred Saul's character, the sages regarded him as a great man and the victim of a tragic fate. One school of thought even viewed Saul as superior to David. "Saul was like the shoot of a sycamore tree, and David, like the shoot of an olive tree." Commenting on the statement: "Were you Saul and he David, I would have destroyed many a David out of regard for him", Rashi wrote: "For he was more righteous than thee" (Moed Katan 16b).

Saul's modesty, too, was highly praised. "Why did Saul merit kingship? Because he was modest" (Tosefta Berachoth).

The sages respected Saul's goodheartedness. "When God said: 'Now go and smite Amalek [and utterly destroy all that they have]', Saul said: 'The people may have sinned, but wherein have the animals sinned?'" (1 Samuel 15.3; Tanna d'bei Eliahu Rabbah 1).

The sages offered various explanations for Saul's unhappy end. One was that he lacked the sense of the dignity of his office. "Why was Saul punished? Because he did not defend his honor, as it is written: '[But certain base fellows said: "How shall this man save us?" And they despised him, and brought him no present.] But he was as one that held his peace'" (1 Samuel 10.27).

Others attributed Saul's downfall to his goodheartedness, out of place in a ruler. "Why did Saul's kingdom not survive? Because it was untarnished" [Monarchic rule must be maintained through suppression.] (Yoma 22b).

According to some of the sages, God was angry at David because he did not honor Saul sufficiently, allowing him to be buried in Jabesh-gilead rather than within the borders of Israel. "'There was a famine in the days of David. . . . And the Lord said: "It is for Saul."' God said: 'He was not treated properly. In Saul's day there was no idolatry, and yet he is [buried] outside the Holy land'" (Yalkut Shimeoni on 2 Samuel 21.1).

2. ISH-BOSHETH (ISH-BAAL), SON OF SAUL

איש-בשת

2 Samuel 2.8-4.12

The young king is led by Abner to Mahanaim in Transjordan.

"Now Abner the son of Ner . . . had taken Ish-bosheth the son of Saul . . . and he made him king over Gilead . . . and over all Israel" (II. Sam. 2.8-9).

The crippled Ish-bosheth was the second king of Israel and the first and last of Saul's descendants to wear a royal crown. After the death of his father on Mount Gilboa, Ish-bosheth was proclaimed king of Israel (the ten northern tribes) by Abner, Saul's general, and he reigned for two years. At the same time David began a reign in Hebron over Judah that lasted seven and one-half years. It follows that there was no king in Israel during the five and one-half year interval between Ish-bosheth's death and David's assumption of the latter's crown.

Ish-bosheth proved ungrateful to Abner, by whose grace he ruled. Consequently, Abner decided to transfer the kingship to David. However, Joab, David's general, intervened and killed Abner, and subsequently two servants of the Israelite royal household slew Ish-bosheth. Vexed at these incidents, David ordered that Rechab and Baanah, Ish-bosheth's murderers, be put to death.

3. DAVID, SON OF JESSE

דוד בן ישי

1 Samuel 16.11 - 1 Kings 2.11
1 Chronicles 3.9-29.30

David slays Goliath before the armies of Israel and Philistia.

"And David ran, and stood over the Philistine, and took his sword . . . and slew him, and cut off his head therewith. And . . . the Philistines . . . fled" (I. Sam. 17.51).

A colorful and many-sided figure, David came to symbolize both the past and the future of the people Israel. He was a warrior, a righteous king and "the sweet singer of Israel" (2 Samuel 23.1). In his youth "he was ruddy, and withal of beautiful eyes" and "smote both the lion and the bear" (1 Samuel 16.12; 17.36).

After Saul's death, David reigned over Judah in Hebron; and after the death of Ish-bosheth, Saul's crippled son, he reigned over all Israel from his capital of Jerusalem. He made a treaty with Hiram, king of Tyre, and defeated Moab, Ammon, Edom and the Arameans.

Determined to possess the beautiful Bath-sheba, David had her husband Uriah the Hittite killed, and incurred the curse of the prophet Nathan: "The sword shall never depart from thy house" (2 Samuel 12.10). David's subsequent reign was marred by a series of calamities: the rape of Tamar by Amnon; the murder of Amnon by Absalom; the rebellion and death of Absalom; the revolt of Sheba, son of Bichri; and the revolt of Adonijah.

While not all of David's actions were praiseworthy, his greatness evidenced itself in a number of ways: in his respectful behavior toward Saul, even when the latter was persecuting him; in his devotion to Jonathan; in his wholehearted joy at the return of the ark of the covenant; and in his love of Absalom, who was both his son and his enemy. His talents as a poet are revealed in his prayers, eulogies, and songs in the Psalms.

The sages saw in David:

A leader of men: "The Holy One blessed be He said: 'He who knows how to tend sheep shall tend My sheep'" (Exodus Rabbah 2).

A humble and devout man: "'Lord, my heart is not haughty'—when Samuel anointed me king; 'Nor mine eyes lofty'—when I slew Goliath; 'I did not walk with arrogance'—when I was returned to the throne; and I was not ashamed to be scorned before Thee that you might be honored" (Psalms 131; Genesis Rabbah 4).

A penitent sinner: One tradition declares that for 22 years David wept over his sins and ate his bread in the ashes. Some of the sages did not regard David as a sinner at all. "He who says that David sinned, errs." Bath-sheba, they held, had previously obtained a divorce from Uriah the Hittite. Some of David's advocates went so far as to insist that Uriah was a rebel and hence deserved to die. (Shabbath 56a).

A loving father: " 'A Psalm of David, when he fled from Absalom his son' (Psalms 3.1). A *Psalm* of David? Should it not read: 'A *Lamentation* of David'? When God said to him: 'Behold, I will raise up evil against thee out of thine own house' (2 Samuel 12.11) David was sad, but when he saw that it was Absalom who had rebelled, David was happy, saying: 'It is in the nature of things for a son to take pity on his father' " (Genesis Rabbah 7).

4. SOLOMON, SON OF DAVID   שלמה בן דוד

1 Kings 1.10 - 11.42
1 Chronicles 28.5 - 2 Chronicles 9.31

The Queen of Sheba and her retinue visit King Solomon.

"And when the queen of Sheba heard of the fame of Solomon . . . she came to prove him with hard questions. And she came to Jerusalem with a very great train . . ." (I. Kings 10.1-2).

Monarch during the golden age of Israel and builder of the Temple, Solomon was known as the wisest of all men. After the revolt of Adonijah, David had Solomon crowned. In a dream at Gibeon, Solomon prayed for wisdom and was granted it. Upon acceding to the throne, he prudently punished Adonijah, Joab, and Shimei, son of Gera.

By pursuing a policy of peace, Solomon made his nation secure. "And Judah and Israel dwelt safely, every man under his vine and under his fig-tree" (1 Kings 5.5). While his marriages with foreign princesses did help to ensure peaceful relations with other states, his wives introduced idolatrous cults into the land of Israel. In addition, the splendid buildings that Solomon erected proved economically burdensome to the people. Widespread discontent with excessive taxation was a factor in the division of Solomon's kingdom after his death.

Some of the sages denounced Solomon for his marriages with foreign women. "When Solomon married Pharaoh's daughter, the angel Gabriel came down to earth and planted a rod in the sea. Around it there gathered a sandbank, upon which a great city (Rome) was built" (Shabbath 56b).

Other sages, however, defended Solomon. "Anyone who says that Solomon himself sinned, is wrong." They insisted that his only fault lay in his failure to interfere with the sins of his foreign wives.

The rabbis held Solomon's wisdom in high esteem. "God said 'Ask what I shall give thee.' . . . 'Give Thy servant therefore an understanding heart' (1 Kings 3.5-9). God said to Solomon: 'You have asked for wisdom, not for wealth or goods or the lives of your enemies. I swear by your life that wisdom and understanding are given to you, and that through these you shall acquire wealth and goods as well' " (Song of Songs Rabbah 1).

Concerning Solomon's decline, "Rabbi Simeon, son of Lakish, said: 'At the outset Solomon ruled over the celestial hosts . . . and then he ruled only over all who lived on the earth. At first he ruled over all the world, later only over Israel . . . still later only over Jerusalem . . . still later only over his bed . . . and finally Solomon ruled over his staff alone, as it is written: "This is my portion of all my labor" ' " (Ecclesiastes Rabbah 81).

Royal Insignia of the House of David

"Judah is a lion's whelp . . .
The sceptre shall not depart from Judah,
Nor the ruler's staff from between his feet,
As long as men come to Shiloh;
And unto him shall the obedience of the peoples be"
(Genesis 49.9-10).

THE KINGS OF JUDAH

THE KINGS OF JUDAH

1. REHOBOAM, SON OF SOLOMON

רחבעם
בן שלמה

1 Kings 12.1-14.31
2 Chronicles 9.31-12.16

Rehoboam consults only with his young advisers.

"But he forsook the counsel of the old men . . . and took counsel with the young men that were grown up with him" (I. Kings 12.8).

Rehoboam was the first Judean monarch after the division of Solomon's kingdom into Israel (Ephraim) in the north and Judah in the south. The heavy load of taxation, the foreign cults introduced by Solomon's wives, the historical antagonism between Judah and the northern tribes, and Rehoboam's harsh reply to the people's emissaries, who requested that taxes be decreased—all led to the division of the kingdom.

In Rehoboam's day idolatry, with all its abominable practices, spread throughout Judah; therefore some of the prophets at first supported his rival Jeroboam and his competing new kingdom. The political and moral decline during that period led to a foreign incursion: Shishak, ruler of Egypt, invaded Judah, laid siege to Jerusalem, captured the city and pillaged it. Also, Rehoboam attempted to bring the northern tribes back under his rule, but the division of the kingdom had become an established reality.

The sages differed in regard to who or what was responsible for the secession of the Northern Kingdom. Some held that Rehoboam was culpable in that he heeded the counsel of his rash and immature advisors, rather than the wisdom of the elders, and replied harshly to the representatives of the people, who sought a reduction in taxes. "Rabbi Simeon, son of Elazar, said: 'If children tell you to build the Temple, do not listen to them; but if elders tell you to tear down the Temple, listen to them, for the construction of the young is destruction and the destruction of the old is construction' " (Tosefta Abodah Zarah 1; Nedarim 40a).

Other sages attributed the secession to the malign influence of Shechem, the city wherein Rehoboam was crowned. " 'And Rehoboam went to Shechem' [(1 Kings 12.1)]. We are taught in the name of Rabbi Jose: 'Shechem was a place destined for evil. There Dinah was violated, there Joseph was sold, there the kingdom of the house of David was divided' " (Sanhedrin 102).

Still another rabbinic opinion laid the blame for the division on David: "Rabbi Judah said in the name of Rab: 'When David said to Mephibosheth: "Thou and Ziba divide the land" [thus implying that the king believed the report slandering Mephibosheth], a voice issued forth from heaven and said to David: "Rehoboam and Jeroboam will divide the kingdom" ' " (Shabbath 56b).

2. ABIJAH (ABIJAM, ABIHU), SON OF REHOBOAM

אביה
(אבים, אביהו)
בן רחבעם

1 Kings 15.1-9
2 Chronicles 12.16-13.23

The Israelite army under banner depicting a calf, flees from the Judean army whose standard bears a lion.

"Israel fled before Judah . . . And Abijah . . . slew . . . of Israel five hundred thousand chosen men" (II. Chron. 13.16-17).

Both Biblical authors and the sages differed among themselves as to the merits of Abijah, who ruled over Judah for three eventful, turbulent years. The author of Kings regarded Abijah as continuing in his father's wicked ways, whereas the author of Chronicles described Abijah's war against Jeroboam as that of a righteous man against an evil-doer. Abijah's small force proved victorious and he captured a number of cities in Ephraim. In this war, he killed some 500,000 Israelites, for which he was condemned by the sages. They remarked that he mutilated the slain by cutting off their noses (Genesis Rabbah 65).

Nevertheless, the sages acknowledged Abijah's greatness and courage, interpreting a verse in the Song of Songs (2.12) as referring to him. " 'The flowers appear on the earth'—for in his day the kingdom of Judah flourished" (Exodus Rabbah 11).

3. ASA, SON OF ABIJAH
אסא בן אביה

1 Kings 15.8-24
2 Chronicles 13.23-16.14

In a Negev battle, Asa's troops defeat the huge Egyptian army of Zerah the Ethiopian.

"So the Lord smote the Ethiopians before Asa, and before Judah . . . And Asa and the people . . . pursued them unto Gerar" (II. Chron. 14. 11-12).

The righteous son of Abijah, Asa restored to Judah the undefiled worship of one God. He fortified the country; and, as a result of his victory over Zerah the Cushite, king of Egypt, many pilgrims from Ephraim were drawn to Jerusalem to worship in the Temple. Baasa, king of Israel, fearful of the political repercussions of these pilgrimages, built the strong fort of Ramah on the border between the two kingdoms. Asa turned to Hadad, king of Aram, for assistance, and the latter attacked and defeated the Ephraimite army. Asa then took the fort of Ramah, a deed for which he was reprimanded by Hanani the seer. Asa retaliated by having the prophet imprisoned. The king died during the forty-first year of his reign, after having suffered from a serious leg disease.

The sages lauded the military prowess of Asa. They recounted with approval that when Asa defeated Zerah the Cushite, he restored the booty which Shishak had removed from Jerusalem — the very same hoard of gold and silver which

Joseph had amassed and which the children of Israel had taken with them when leaving Egypt (Pesahim 119b).

The sages also commended Asa for placing himself completely in God's hands. "Asa said: 'I do not have the power to kill the enemy; I will but pursue them, and do Thou act.' The Holy One, blessed be He, said to him: 'I will do so.' As it is written: 'Asa and the people that were with him pursued them . . . for they were shattered before the Lord' [(2 Chronicles 14.12)]. The text does not read 'before Asa,' but 'before the Lord.' Israel's only true weapon is prayer, as it is said: 'And Asa cried unto the Lord his God . . . "Help us, O Lord our God, for we rely on Thee" [(14.10)]' " (Yalkut Shimoni, 2 Samuel, §22).

4. JEHOSHAPHAT, SON OF ASA
יהושפט בן אסא

1 Kings 15.24-22.51
2 Chronicles 17.1-21.1

Moabites, Philistines, and Arabs render tribute to the King. The Levites teach Torah to children.

"And some of the Philistines brought Jehoshaphat presents" (II. Chron. 17. 11).
"And . . . they went about . . . all the cities of Judah, and taught among the people" (17.9).

A righteous king, Jehoshaphat worked to eradicate idolatry from the land, as did his father before him. Under his rule Judah prospered. With an army of more than a million men he defeated the Edomites and forced the Moabites, Philistines and Arabians to pay him tribute.

Jehoshaphat appointed judges over all the cities of Judah. He also sent priests and Levites through the country to instruct the people in God's laws and commandments. After the long period of division between Judah and its neighbor to the north, the kingdom of Ephraim, Jehoshaphat felt that there was a great need for closer and friendlier relations between the two kingdoms. Hence, when Ahab, king of Ephraim, sought Jehoshaphat's aid in war, the latter replied: "I am as thou art, [and] my people as thy people" (1 Kings 22.4).

Unfortunately, Jehoshaphat's attempt to cement the alliance with Ephraim by marriage proved disastrous. Athaliah, daughter of Ahab, the wife of Jehoshaphat's son Jehoram, was responsible for the spread of idolatry throughout the land, and Judah was nearly absorbed by Ephraim.

The sages esteemed Jehoshaphat highly. "Whenever Jehoshaphat, king of Judah, saw a scholar, he would rise from his throne, embrace the man, and kiss him, crying: 'My master, my master! My teacher, my teacher!' " (Ketuboth 103). The food with which the ravens fed Elijah, they declared, came from the table of Jehoshaphat (Genesis Rabbah 31). Of Jehoshaphat's reliance on God, they remarked: "Jehoshaphat arose and said: 'I have no power to kill or pursue the enemy; I will but sing to Thee, and do Thou act.' The Holy One, Blessed Be He, replied: 'I will do so.' As it is written: 'And when they began to sing and to praise, the Lord set liers-in-wait against the children of Ammon, Moab, and Mount Seir, that were come against Judah; and they were smitten' [(2 Chronicles 20.22)]" (Yalkut Shimeoni, 2 Samuel, §22, Introduction).

The sages included Jehoshaphat among the ten great poets who uttered songs of praise to God. "Ten songs were recited: the song of David, the song of Moses. . . . The ninth song was recited by Jehoshaphat, as it is written: 'And when he had taken counsel with the people, he appointed them that should sing unto the Lord, and praise in the beauty of holiness as they went out before the army, and say: "Give thanks unto the Lord, for His mercy endureth for ever" ' [(2 Chronicles 20.21)]. The tenth song will be sung during the messianic era" (Yalkut Shimoni, Exodus 15 [The Song of the Sea]).

5. JEHORAM, SON OF JEHOSHAPHAT   יהורם בן יהושפט
1 Kings 22.51
2 Kings 8.16-9.24
2 Chronicles 21.1-22.1

Athaliah introduces Baal-worship in Judah.

"For he had the daughter of Ahab to wife; and he did that which was evil . . . Behold, the Lord will smite with a great plague thy people" (II. Chron. 21.6,14).

Jehoram ascended the throne while his father Jehoshaphat was still alive. Influenced by his

wife Athaliah, daughter of Ahab, king of Ephraim, he sinned and caused others to sin. He worshipped Baal and murdered all of his brothers. During his reign Judah experienced a period of decline, and Edom and Libnah rebelled. Elijah warned Jehoram of the punishment he would incur for his sinful behaviour. The dire prophecy, unheeded, came to pass: a plague broke out, and Jehoram, afflicted, died in agony. He was not buried in the tomb of his ancestors, nor was he cremated, as many kings were.

6. AHAZIAH (JEHOAHAZ, AZARIAH), SON OF JEHORAM   אחזיה (יהואחז, עזריה) בן יהורם
2 Kings 1.18; 8.24-9.28
2 Chronicles 22.1-9

An arrow pierces Ahaziah's body as he rides in a war-chariot to Megiddo.

"But when Ahaziah the king of Judah saw this, he fled . . . And Jehu . . . said: 'Smite him also in the chariot'. . . . And he (Ahaziah) . . . . died" (II. Kings 9.27).

The youngest son of Jehoram and Athaliah, Ahaziah succeeded his father to the throne of Judah and followed in the latter's wicked ways. Joining forces with his uncle, Joram, king of Israel, he battled against Aram. When the Judean monarch went to visit his wounded uncle in Jezreel, he fell into the hands of Jehu's men, who were rebelling against Joram, and both the King of Israel and Ahaziah were killed. Ahaziah's servants brought their master's body back to Jerusalem for burial.

The sages accused Ahaziah of grave misdeeds. " 'And he sought Ahaziah, and they caught him —now he was hiding in Samaria' [(2 Chronicles 22.9)]. Rabbi Levi commented: 'He was in the process of erasing the Divine Names from the Torah and replacing them with the names of pagan deities' " (Sanhedrin 102b).

7. ATHALIAH, DAUGHTER OF AHAB

עתליה
בת אחאב

2 Kings 11
2 Chronicles 22.2-23.21

Athaliah and her idolatrous priests slay the children of the Royal House of David.

"Now when Athaliah the mother of Ahaziah saw that her son was dead, she arose and destroyed all the seed royal" (II. Kings 11.1).

After the death of her son Ahaziah, Athaliah ascended the throne and ruled Judah for six years. Even prior to that, however, she had exerted her malign influence on Jehoram and Ahaziah, causing the widespread growth of the Baal-cult throughout the land; she even utilized the Temple vessels for idolatrous Baal worship. After her son's death, Athaliah wiped out the entire royal family except for Joash, who was secretly saved. In the sixth year of her reign, the priest Jehoiada incited the people to rebel against her; Athaliah was killed and Joash was crowned king. Athaliah, murderess of her own grandchildren, has ever remained a symbol of wickedness in Jewish tradition.

8. JOASH, SON OF AHAZIAH

יואש
בן אחזיה

2 Kings 11.2-12.22
2 Chronicles 22.11-24.27

Jehoiada the High Priest crowns seven year old Jehoash. The prophet Zechariah is stoned in the Temple.

"Then they brought out the king's son . . . and Jehoiada . . . anointed him; and they said: 'Long live the king'" (II. Chron. 23.11).

The sole survivor of Athaliah's slaughter of the royal family, Joash was seven years old when Jehoiada the priest crowned him king and had Athaliah executed. Jerome* was of the opinion

*A Christian translator of the Bible into Latin (the Vulgate) in the 4th century.

that the "insignia" placed upon Joash when he was crowned were tefillin.

During the lifetime of Jehoiada, Joash walked in the ways of the Lord. He did away with the worship of Baal and renovated the Temple. However, after the priest's death Joash turned aside from the righteous path; he had the prophet Zechariah, son of Jehoiada, murdered for admonishing him. During the reign of Joash, Hazael, king of Aram, attacked Jerusalem, and the people blamed their ruler for their troubles. There was a conspiracy against the king and he was killed. According to the author of Chronicles, the plotters were Ammonites and Moabites.

The rabbis believed that it was only after the priest Jehoiada's death that Joash abandoned his righteous ways(Numbers Rabbah 23).

9. AMAZIAH, SON OF JOASH

אמציה
בן יואש

2 Kings 14.1-20
2 Chronicles 24.27-25.28

Jehoash refuses Amaziah, comparing their kingdoms to a thorn-bush and a cedar-of-Lebanon.

'And Jehoash the king of Israel sent to Amaziah king of Judah, saying: 'The thistle . . . sent to the cedar . . . saying: Give thy daughter to my son to wife'" (II. Kings 14.9).

Amaziah "did that which was right in the eyes of the Lord," but not whole-heartedly.

After he consolidated his power, Amaziah executed the rebels who had murdered his father, but in accordance with the Biblical injunction, he did not kill the conspirators' children. When Edom attacked Judah, Amaziah hired Israelite mercenaries to fight for him, but at the advice of a prophet he sent them back to Ephraim. In anger, the mercenaries roamed throughout Judah, pillaging as they went. After his victory over Edom, Amaziah sought to take revenge upon Ephraim, but he was defeated by Joash, who took him captive and pillaged Jerusalem. The people of Judah, embittered with their king, rebelled against him and killed him.

The sages castigated Amaziah for turning to idolatry after his victory over Edom. "The Holy One, blessed be He, said: 'I smiled on Amaziah and gave the kingdom of Edom into his hand, but he brought their gods to Judah and bowed down to them'. . . . Rabbi Papa commented: 'Woe to him who could not distinguish between good and evil' " (Sanhedrin 23a).

10. UZZIAH (AZARIAH), SON OF AMAZIAH

עֻזִּיָּהוּ
(עֲזַרְיָה)
בֶּן אֲמַצְיָה

2 Kings 14.21-15.23
2 Chronicles 26.1-23

Because of his sacrilege, Uzziah is afflicted with leprosy. Farmers harvest bountiful crops.

"He built Elath, and restored it to Judah" (II. Kings 14.22).
"And they (the priests) . . . said . . . 'go out of the sanctuary; for thou hast trespassed' " (II. Chron. 26.18-19).

Uzziah "did that which was right in the eyes of the Lord." He expanded the boundaries of Judah, captured Elath, fought the Philistines and the Arabs, and exacted tribute from the Ammonites. He was a lover of the land: vineyards were planted and irrigation ditches were dug at his command. During Uzziah's reign a violent earthquake occurred, so memorable that it served to date the utterances of the prophet Amos. "The words of Amos . . . two years before the earthquake" (Amos 1.1).

Because he officiated at a sacrifice, although he was not a priest, Uzziah was afflicted with leprosy of the forehead; he remained in isolation for the rest of his life, his son Jotham reigning in his stead. The sages noted the disastrous consequences of Uzziah's attempt to emulate David. "Uzziah and others like him who set their eyes on that which was not fitting for them, were not given that which they sought; and that which they possessed, they lost" (Sotah 9b).

Of his love for the soil, the rabbis remarked: "There were three who had a passion for husbandry, yet no good came from it: Cain, the tiller of the soil; Noah, the man of the soil; and Uzziah, the lover of the soil" (Genesis Rabbah 22).

11. JOTHAM, SON OF UZZIAH

יוֹתָם
בֶּן עֻזִּיָּהוּ

2 Kings 15.32-38
2 Chronicles 27.1-9

The walls of Jerusalem are strengthened by Jotham who will not wear the crown in deference to his leprous father Uzziah.

"He built the upper gate of the house of the Lord, and . . . cities in the hill-country of Judah" (II. Chron. 27.3).

Beginning his reign during the illness of his father Uzziah, Jotham "did that which was right in the eyes of the Lord," but he failed to remove the "high places" from the land. Under his rule the nation prospered politically and economically. He was victorious in his wars with his neighbors, and Ammon was forced to pay a large tribute to Judah. Jotham was noted for erecting and repairing towers, large buildings and city walls.

The sages lauded Jotham for his righteousness. "Rabbi Simeon, son of Yohai, said: 'I can release the whole world from the final judgment . . . Had Jotham, son of Uzziah, been with us, (we could release it) from the day the world was created until its ultimate end' " (Sukkah 45b). Rashi commented on the above statement: Jotham was a righteous man, one who honored his father. All the while his father was a leper and Jotham served as judge, he never wore the crown and all the judgments he rendered were in his father's name.

12. AHAZ, SON OF JOTHAM

אָחָז
בֶּן יוֹתָם

2 Kings 16.1-18.1
2 Chronicles 27.9-28.27

Ahaz, rejecting the Temple altar, worships idols. Enemies besiege Jerusalem.

"For he sacrificed unto the gods of Damascus" (II. Chron. 28.23).
"The Lord . . . delivered him . . . into the hand of the king of Aram . . . And . . . of the king of Israel" (28.5).

The economic prosperity and political success of Judah at the outset of Ahaz' reign led to ethical and religious delinquency on the part of the people. Ahaz himself passed his son through fire as a sacrificial offering, and closed the synagogues and schools. Subsequently, Judah suffered a series of setbacks. The Edomites and the Philistines freed themselves from the Judean yoke, and Rezin, king of Aram, together with Pekah, son of Ramaliah, attacked Judah. Despite the warnings of Isaiah, Ahaz called for the help of the Assyrian king, who seized many of the Temple treasures.

According to the sages, Ahaz was among the wicked kings who have no portion in the world to come; even at his death, no eulogy was recited over him. The sages taught that when Ahaz died, the natural course of the day was changed so that there was no time in which to eulogize the king (Sanhedrin 96).

The rabbis declared that Ahaz sought to banish the Torah from Zion and that he shut the schools, saying: "If there are no kids, there will be no goats . . . If there are no children, there will be no pupils; if there are no pupils, there will be no scholars; if there are no scholars there will be no Torah . . . no synagogues . . . no houses of study . . . and . . . the Holy One, blessed be He, will not cause His Divine Spirit to rest upon the world (Leviticus Rabbah 11).

13. HEZEKIAH, SON OF AHAZ   חזקיה בן אחז

2 Kings 18.1-20.21
2 Chronicles 28.27-32.33

Hezekiah raises a Torah before the Sanhedrin. Sennacherib's army is smitten by a plague.

"And . . . in the service of . . . God, and in the Law . . . he . . . prospered" (II. Chron. 31. 21).
"These also are proverbs of Solomon, which the men of Hezekiah . . . copied out" (Prov. 25.1).

Hezekiah began to reign at the age of 25, during his father's lifetime. He "did that which was right in the eyes of the Lord," purifying the sacrificial worship. He defeated the Philistines, but during his reign the Assyrian army invaded Judah three times. Sargon captured Samaria and exiled the ten tribes of the kingdom of Ephraim. His son, Sennacherib, attacked and overran Judah, but when the Assyrian reached the gates of Jerusalem, Hezekiah, heeding the words of the prophet Isaiah, acted with courage and resolve, and prevented the enemy from entering Jerusalem. Then a miracle occurred; an angel of the Lord smote Sennacherib's army and the enemy was forced to retreat from Jerusalem.

Although Hezekiah was a righteous person, at times he came into conflict with the prophet Isaiah. Thus, Isaiah opposed Hezekiah's contacts with the ambassadors from Babylon.

Hezekiah was versed in the Torah and was a great poet. His prayer of thanksgiving after being cured of his illness (Isaiah 38) is one of the most beautiful prayers in the Bible.

The sages praised Hezekiah warmly. They interpreted his name to mean either "The Lord has strengthened him" or "He has strengthened Israel's faith in their Father in heaven" (Sanhedrin 24).

During Hezekiah's day the Torah was widely studied. Commenting on the verse: "And the yoke shall be destroyed by reason of fatness" (Isaiah 10.27), the sages declared: "God destroyed the yoke of Sennacherib because of the oil of Hezekiah, who visited the synagogues and schools . . . A search was made from Dan to Beer-sheba and not one person unlearned in the Torah could be found" (Sanhedrin 94).

The sages attributed some books of the Bible to Hezekiah and his circle.

Some of the sages looked upon the era of Hezekiah as the fulfillment of the messianic visions of the prophets. "Rabbi Hillel said: 'There will be no Messiah for Israel in the future, for they have already consumed him in the days of Hezekiah'" (Sanhedrin 99a). Some of the sages held that Hezekiah himself deserved to be the Messiah. "The Holy One, blessed be He, wished to make Hezekiah the Messiah" (Sanhedrin 94a).

14. MANASSEH, SON OF HEZEKIAH

מנשה בן חזקיהו

2 Kings 21.1-18
2 Chronicles 32.33-33.20

In retribution for his transgressions, Manasseh is led into captivity.

"And he made his son to pass through the fire" (II. Kings 21.6).
"Wherefore the Lord brought . . . captains . . . of Assyria, who took Manasseh . . . to Babylon" (II. Chron. 33.11).

At the age of twelve, Manasseh ascended the throne of his righteous father. Unlike his father, however, "he did that which was evil in the sight of the Lord." He restored the cult of Baal and Asherah and passed his son through idolatrous sacrificial fire. He was also responsible for much bloodshed in Jerusalem. God punished Manasseh by delivering him into the hands of his enemy, the king of Assyria, who exiled him to his land. After Manasseh was restored to his throne, however, he reverted to the worship of God and shattered all idols. Manasseh reigned for 55 years, longer than any other monarch, and was succeeded by his son Amon.

The sages disparaged Manasseh, accusing him of the murder of Isaiah, son of Amoz, who had prophesied against him. "Rabbi Simeon, son of Azzai, said: 'I found a genealogical scroll in Jerusalem, in which the following was written: "Manasseh murdered Isaiah" . . . When Manasseh introduced an idol into the Temple, Isaiah began to prophesy to Israel . . . Manasseh grew angry and said: "Arrest him!" . . . Isaiah fled to the forest and hid in a cedar tree . . . Manasseh then brought woodcutters, who sawed through the tree' " (Yebamoth 49b).

Some sages, however, defended Manasseh on the grounds that idolatry had great force of attraction during his lifetime. "Manasseh appeared to Rabbi Ashi in a dream and Rabbi Ashi said to him: 'Why did you pursue idolatry?' Manasseh answered: 'Had you been there, you would have pursued it yourself' " (Sanhedrin 102b). Some sages, taking Manasseh's penitence into account, said he has a portion in the world to come. "Rabbi Johanan said: 'He who declares that Manasseh has no portion in the world to come weakens the resolve of all penitents' " (Sanhedrin 102b).

15. AMON, SON OF MANASSEH

אמון בן מנשה

2 Kings 21.18-26
2 Chronicles 33.20-25

Amon interrupts the Temple service and burns a Torah scroll.

"And he forsook the Lord, the God of his fathers" (II. Kings 21.22).
"But this same Amon became guilty more and more" (II. Chron. 33.23).

Amon, who became king at the age of 22, reverted to the idolatrous practices of Manasseh. After two years' time he was murdered by the palace courtiers, who were opposed to his pro-Assyrian policies. However, the insurrectionists were killed by "landed gentry," who apparently were pro-Assyrian, and they crowned Josiah as his father's successor.

The Talmudic sages castigated Amon for having burnt the Torah and having brought the Divine service in the Temple to a halt. "Amon burnt the Torah scroll and brought desolation upon the altar" (Sanhedrin 103b).

Nevertheless, the sages did not include Amon among those who have no share in the world to come, out of respect for Josiah; "The son brings merit to the father" (Sanhedrin 104a). Yet he was called wicked. "Rabbi Levi said: 'The Holy One, blessed be He, declared: "With the destruction of the Temple, righteous persons arose, and with its rebuilding, wicked persons arose, like Amon and his associates" ' " (Song of Songs Rabbah 4).

16. JOSIAH, SON OF AMON

יאשיהו בן אמון

2 Kings 21.26-23.30
2 Chronicles 33.25-35.27

Josiah reads to the people the Torah scroll, found by Hilkiah the High Priest.

"And the king went up to the house of the Lord . . . and he read in their ears all the words of the book of the covenant" (II. Chron. 34.30).

At the age of eight, Josiah ascended his father's throne. While still young, he worked to abolish idolatry and purify the Temple service. During his reign the High Priest Hilkiah found "the book of the Law" in the Temple. The admonitions and curses in Deuteronomy shook the righteous king, who had no knowledge of the Torah because his father Amon had burnt all the Torah scrolls. Josiah read the scroll before the people; they too were moved by its contents and decided to cleanse themselves of idolatry.

In the thirty-first year of Josiah's reign he was mortally wounded in battle against Pharaoh-necoh, king of Egypt, near Megiddo, and he died on the way back to Jerusalem. Jeremiah eulogized him there, and all the people mourned their beloved and righteous ruler. According to the sages, Josiah foresaw the impending exile and therefore hid the Ark. "Josiah, king of Judah, arose and hid the Ark away, declaring: 'If it shall be exiled with you to Babylon, you will not restore it to its original place'" (Yoma 21b).

The rabbis taught that Josiah's birth had been foretold, as it is written: "A son shall be born unto the house of David, Josiah by name" (1 Kings 13.2). "Six persons were named before they were born . . . including Josiah" (Yalkut Shimoni).

The sages differed as to the meaning of the verse "And like unto him was there no king before him, that turned to the Lord with all his heart" (2 Kings 23.25). "Rabbi Samuel, son of Rabbi Nahmani, said: 'All who maintain that Josiah sinned are in error, for it is written: "And he did that which was right in the eyes of the Lord." ' . . . Rav disagreed, declaring: 'There was no greater penitent than Josiah in his generation'" (Yalkut Shimoni, 1 Kings 11.13).

17. JEHOAHAZ, SON OF JOSIAH

יהואחז
בן יאשיהו

2 Kings 23.30-34
2 Chronicles 36.1-5

Surrounded by idols, Jehoahaz is taken captive to Egypt by Pharaoh-necoh.

"And he did that which was evil in the sight of the Lord . . . And Pharaoh-necoh put him in bands at Riblah" (II. Kings 23.32-33).

The third son of Josiah, Jehoahaz ruled Judah after the death of his father. He was also known as Shalom in the books of Chronicles and Jeremiah. While he reigned for only three months, in that brief period he managed to do "that which was evil in the sight of the Lord." Pharaoh-necoh imprisoned him and took him first to Riblah, and then to Egypt, crowning Jehoiakim, his elder brother and the first-born son of Josiah, in his stead. Some interpreters of Ezekiel maintained that the prophet was referring to Jehoahaz when he spoke of the young man-eating lion who was brought down to Egypt with hooks (Ezekiel 19.1-9).

The sages tried to explain why Jehoahaz was anointed with the anointing oil (which was used for the consecration of the priests). "Why was Jehoahaz anointed? Because of Jehoiakim, who was two years older than he" (Horayoth 11b). Apparently, whenever there was a controversy over the succession, it was customary to anoint the man who was finally chosen king.

18. JEHOIAKIM, SON OF JOSIAH

יהויקים
בן יאשיהו

2 Kings 23.34-25.6
2 Chronicles 36.5-9

Jehoiakim rips the scroll containing Jeremiah's prophecies and hurls it into the fire.

"When Jehudi had read three or four columns . . . he cut it with the penknife, and cast it into the fire" (Jer. 36.23).

After Pharaoh-necoh captured Jehoahaz, he crowned the latter's brother Jehoiakim as king over Judah. The new monarch "did that which was evil in the sight of the Lord." Jeremiah's scroll was read before the king, warning him of the impending national calamity, but Jehoiakim burnt the scroll (Jeremiah 36); he also killed the prophet Uriah. After the fall of Pharaoh-necoh, Nebuchadnezzar attacked Jerusalem and Jehoiakim was forced to accept the suzerainty of Assyria. However, three years later he rebelled. Once more Nebuchadnezar attacked and defeated Jerusalem. The Judean monarch died or was killed and was given "the burial of an ass" (Jeremiah 22.19), after having reigned eleven years. His son Jehoiachin succeeded him.

The sages held Jehoiakim in contempt. "Rabbi Hiyya, son of Abuyah, said: 'On Jehoiakim's forehead this motto was inscribed: "This and more" ' " (Sanhedrin 82a). Rashi explained this to mean: "One revenge has already been carried out upon her; still another shall be executed" (*ibid.*).

The rabbis also accused Jehoiakim of having inscribed the name of heathen deities upon his body. "The sages maintain that tattoo marks were to be found upon his flesh" (Yalkut Shimoni, 2 Kings, § 24).

The verse: "He shall be buried with the burial of an ass" (Jeremiah 22.19), is explained by Rabbi Nehemiah as follows: "Nebuchadnezzar took him about, displayed him in all the cities of Israel, and killed him. He then cut slivers the size of olives from his flesh and threw them to his dogs. Hence the verse: 'He shall be buried with the burial of an ass.' Where is an ass buried, if not in the belly of a dog?" (Leviticus Rabbah 19).

Josephus relates (Antiquities X, 6.1) that Nebuchadnezzar killed Jehoiakim and took 3,000 of the aristocracy into captivity, including the prophet Ezekiel.

19. JEHOIACHIN (JECHANIAH, JECHANIYAHU, JOIACHIN, JOCHONIAH), SON OF JEHOIAKIM

יהויכין (יכניה, יכניהו, יויכין, יוכניה) בן יהויקים

2 Kings 24.6-17; 25.27-30
2 Chronicles 36.8-11

Jechoiachin, the queen-mother and the Temple vessels are taken into captivity by Nebuchadnezzar.

"And he carried away Jehoiachin to Babylon" (II. Kings 24.15).
"King Nebuchadnezzar sent, and brought him to Babylon" (II. Chron. 36.10).

According to the book of Kings, Jehoiachin ascended the throne at the age of eighteen, while according to Chronicles he was only eight years old at the time (2 Kings 24.8; 2 Chronicles 36.9). During the three months of his reign he "did that which was evil in the sight of the Lord." Nebuchadnezzar's army attacked and captured Jerusalem and took Jehoiachin, the leaders of the country, and a great deal of booty into captivity to Baby-

lon. Evil-merodach, king of Babylon, upon assuming the throne freed Jehoiachin from prison and had him eat at the royal table.

Josephus held that by surrendering, Jehoiachin saved Jerusalem (Wars of the Jews VI, 1.2). The Mishnah notes that the gate in the Temple through which the king passed into exile became known as "the Gate of Jehoiachin" (Middoth 2). Of the moment of his surrender to Nebuchadnezzar, the sages remarked: "'They came to Jehoiachin and said: 'Nebuchadnezzar seeks your life.' What did he do? He gathered together all the keys of the Temple, ascended to the roof and said: 'Master of the universe, inasmuch as we who were loyal trustees of Thy Temple are now unable to be its custodians—from this moment on the keys are Thine. A semblance of a fiery hand reached down and took the keys from him' (Leviticus Rabbah 19; Jerusalem Talmud, Shekalim, chapter 6).

20. ZEDEKIAH (MATTANIAH), SON OF JOSIAH

צדקיהו (מתניה) בן יאשיהו

2 Kings 24.17-25.7
2 Chronicles 36.10-20

Nebuchadnezzar kills Zedekiah's sons before his eyes, then blinds him and takes him captive to Babylon.

"And they slew the sons of Zedekiah before his eyes, and put out the eyes of Zedekiah . . . and carried him to Babylon" (II. Kings 25.7).

Mattaniah, the unfortunate last king of Judah, was crowned by Nebuchadnezzar, who changed his name from Mattaniah to Zedekiah. He ruled for eleven years, and like his predecessor refused to listen to Jeremiah. The Temple was filled with idols, and injustice prevailed throughout the land. At the outset of his reign, however, he did take the advice of Jeremiah; he submitted to the king of Babylon and even visited that country. Afterwards, though, he rebelled. Nebuchadnezzar attacked Jerusalem, besieged it, and finally broke into the famished city. Zedekiah fled, but was captured by Babylonian soldiers near Jericho. Nebuchadnezzar had Zedekiah's sons killed in full view of their father, who was then blinded. The Judean monarch was subsequently brought in chains to Babylon where he died in prison.

Some of the sages condemned the king for not having committed suicide. " 'For these things I weep' [Lamentations 1.16]. Rabbi Judah said: 'for the loss of understanding and the departure of the Divine Presence.' How was it that Zedekiah, who saw that his captors intended to gouge out his eyes, lacked the sense to beat his head against the wall until the breath departed from his body?" (Lamentations Rabbah 1).

Other sages dwelt upon the tragedy of the father who was forced to witness the execution of his children. "Zedekiah said (to Nebuzaradan): 'Kill me first, that I might not see the shedding of my children's blood.' His sons pleaded: 'Kill us first, that we might not see our father's blood spilled upon the earth.' "

Some sages explained Nebuchadnezzar's anger at Zedekiah was a result of the latter breaking his oath to him (Yalkut Shimoni, Kings, Zedekiah).

Yet, there were some rabbis who regarded Zedekiah as a righteous man. "The rabbis taught: 'Zedekiah and Shallum were one and the same person. And why was he called Shallum? Because he was perfect *(mushlam)* in his actions' " (*ibid.*).

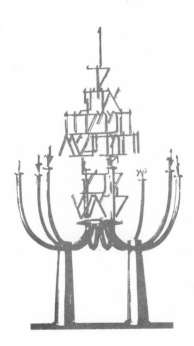

Royal Insignia of the Kings of Israel (Ephraim)

"Whereupon the king took counsel, and made two calves of gold; and he said unto them: 'Ye have gone up long enough to Jerusalem; behold thy gods, O Israel, which brought thee up out of the land of Egypt'" (I. Kings 12.28).

THE KINGS OF ISRAEL

THE KINGS OF ISRAEL
(EPHRAIM)

1. JEROBOAM, SON OF NEBAT

ירבעם
בן נבט

1 Kings 11.26-15.25
2 Chronicles 10.2-13.20

The prophet rebukes Jeroboam for offering sacrifices to the golden calf.

"And, behold, there came a man of God out of Judah by the word of the Lord unto Beth-el; and Jeroboam was standing by the altar to offer" *(I. Kings 13.1).*

Although he led the secession of the ten northern tribes from the united kingdom, and "sinned and caused others to sin," Jeroboam was nonetheless considered a great person by the sages.

Jeroboam, the son of Nebat, was a high official under King Solomon and had to flee to King Shishak of Egypt in the wake of an unsuccessful rebellion. Later, he led the delegation that asked Rehoboam to lower the people's taxes. The prophet Ahijah the Shilonite at first supported Jeroboam, in hopes that the latter would introduce necessary social and religious reforms in his government. However, when the new king set up the golden calves, the prophet cursed him. "I... will cut off from Jeroboam every man-child. . . . Him that dieth of Jeroboam in the city shall the dogs eat; and him that dieth in the field shall the fowls of the air eat" (1 Kings 14.10-11). This curse was fulfilled with the death of Nadab, son of Jeroboam.

In rabbinic literature Jeroboam is characterized both favorably and unfavorably. "Rabbi Abba said: 'The Holy One, blessed be He, took hold of Jeroboam by his cloak and said: "Repent, and you and I and the son of Jesse shall walk together in the Garden of Eden." Jeroboam said: "Who shall go first?" [God answered:] "The son of Jesse shall go first." Jeroboam replied: "Then I refuse." ' "

"Rabbi Johanan said: 'Why did Jeroboam merit kingship? Because he reproved Solomon. And why was he punished? Because he reproved him in public' " (Sanhedrin 22b).

Other sages saw only Jeroboam's failings. "Our rabbis taught that Jeroboam was so named because he stirred up controversy (*meribah*) among the people (*am*). Another explantion: he caused the rift (*meribah*) between Israel and their Father in heaven" (Sanhedrin 22b).

"He who causes the multitude to sin is not given the opportunity to repent . . . Jeroboam sinned and caused others to sin, hence the sin of the multitude is laid upon him; as it is said: 'Because of the sin of Jeroboam, who sinned and caused Israel to sin' " (Aboth 5).

2. NADAB, SON OF JEROBOAM

נדב
בן ירבעם

1 Kings 15.25-28

Nadab is killed by his commander-in-chief Baasa, while besieging a Philistine city.

"And Baasa . . . conspired against him . . . for Nadab and all Israel were laying siege to Gibbethon . . . Even . . . did Baasa slay him" *(I. Kings 15.27-28).*

Nadab walked in his father's footsteps, continuing the cult of the calves. When he besieged the city of Gibbethon, which was in Philistine hands, his general Baasa conspired against him, slew him and usurped the throne of Israel. Thus the prophecy of Ahijah the Shilonite concerning the destruction of the house of Jeroboam was realized.

Nadab reigned for less than two years.

3. BAASA, SON OF AHIJAH

בעשא
בן אחיה

1 Kings 15.27-16.8
2 Chronicles 16.1-6

Baasa seals the road to Jerusalem by building a fortress to the east of it.

"Baasa king of Israel went up against Judah, and built Ramah, that he might not suffer any to go out or come in to Asa king of Judah" (II. Chron. 16.1).

The third king of Israel, Baasa was chosen by the prophet Jehu, son of Hanani, to destroy the dynasty of the sinful Jeroboam. Baasa ascended the throne after murdering Nadab, son of Jeroboam. However, the hopes the prophet had entertained for Baasa were disappointed. The new king, who had been "exalted out of the dust" to become ruler over Israel, did not depart from the sinful ways of Jeroboam. Accordingly, the prophet declared that Baasa too would suffer the fate of the house of Jeroboam.

Taking note of the popularity and political successes of Asa, king of Judah, Baasa feared that the Ephraimites, who were already drawn to the Temple in Jerusalem, would ultimately forge ties with the Judean monarch. He therefore built a fortress in Ramah, blocking the road to Jerusalem and threatening the kingdom of Judah. Asa, king of Judah, then called upon Hadad, king of Aram, for aid. The latter attacked the cities of Ephraim, conquering many of them and enabling Asa to raze the fortress of Ramah.

Baasa ruled in Tirzah for 22 years.

4. ELAH, SON OF BAASA

אלה בן בעשא

1 Kings 16.8-14

Zimri slays Elah while the latter is in a drunken state.

"In the twenty and sixth year of Asa . . . began Elah the son of Baasa to reign over Israel . . . now he was in Tirzah, drinking . . . and Zimri went in . . . and killed him" (I. Kings 16.8-10).

Elah ruled over Israel in Tirzah for two years. Through him the prophecy uttered by Jehu, son of Hanani, to Baasa was fulfilled. "Thou hast walked in the way of Jeroboam...and I will make thy house like the house of Jeroboam the son of Nebat" (1 Kings 16.2-3). One of the royal servants, Zimri, killed Elah while the latter was drunk, wiped out the entire family of Baasa, and ascended the throne. Elah's death marked the end of the second dynasty of Ephraimite kings.

5. ZIMRI

זמרי

1 Kings 16.9-20

Zimri sets fire to his palace and perishes in the flames.

"When Zimri saw that the city was taken . . . he went into the castle . . . and burnt the king's house over him with fire, and died" (I. Kings 16. 18).

The captain of 500 of Elah's chariots, Zimri murdered his master in Tirzah and ruled in his stead. His name became a byword; Jezebel called Jehu: "Thou Zimri, thy master's murderer." Zimri reigned only seven days. When he saw that Omri was about to capture Tirzah, he set fire to the royal palace and perished in the flames.

6. OMRI

עמרי

1 Kings 16.16-28

Omri builds the hill-city of Samaria, capital of the kingdom of Israel.

"And he built on the hill, and called the name of the city which he built . . . Samaria" (I. Kings 16.24).

After Elah, son of Baasa, had been murdered by Zimri, the people crowned Omri king over Israel. He brought about the death of Zimri as well as that of Tibni, son of Ginath, with whom he had contended for the throne. Thereupon, he consolidated his rule over Israel. Among his outstanding achievements was the building of the city of Samaria, which he made the capital of Israel. The author of the book of Kings alludes to Omri's other accomplishments, but does not detail them. However, from the inscription of Mesha, king of

Moab, one gathers that Omri conquered Moab and made it a vassal state which rendered tribute to him. Also, according to the Mesha inscription, Omri ruled 25 years, and not twelve years, as is stated in the book of Kings.

It appears that Omri enacted statutes which were kept for many generations in the Northern Kingdom. The prophet Micah declared: "For the statutes of Omri are kept, and all the works of the house of Ahab" (Micah 6.16).

Despite the assertion that "Omri did that which was evil in the sight of the Lord, and dealt wickedly above all that were before him" (1 Kings 16.25), the sages found some virtues in him. "Why was Omri, captain of the hosts of Israel, considered more worthy than his predecessors, whose grandsons never reached the throne, while three generations of his own descendants succeeded to the throne? It is because he founded a great city in Israel [Samaria]" (Tanna d'bei Eliahu Rabbah).

7. AHAB, SON OF OMRI

אחאב
בן עמרי

1 Kings 16.28-22.40
2 Chronicles 18.1-34

Ahab and Jezebel worship the Baal.

"He took to wife Jezebel the daughter of Ethbaal king of the Zidonians and went and served Baal and worshipped him" (I. Kings 16.31).

Although Ahab "sinned and caused others to sin" he was nevertheless a brave warrior and a great statesman. Under the influence of his Zidonian wife, Jezebel, he dedicated himself to the worship of Baal and to Zidonian culture. He and Jezebel killed off all the prophets of God except Elijah. In retribution, Elijah prophesied to Ahab that there would be three years of famine in the land. At the end of that period, Elijah contended with the prophets of Baal and Asherah on Mount Carmel and killed them there. Jezebel sought Elijah's life, but he fled to safety. At the command of God, Elijah anointed Jehu, son of Nimshi, as king to replace Ahab. Ahab's wickedness reached its height in the killing of Naboth the

Jezreelite and the expropriation of his vineyard. Ahab was victorious in many wars, but was killed in a battle against Aram, and dogs lapped up his blood, as was foretold by Elijah.

The sages viewed Ahab as a man who was incapable of deciding on his ultimate loyalty. "The name Ahab means 'a brother [*ah*] to heaven and a father [*ab*] to idolatry'" (Sanhedrin 102b).

The rabbis blamed Jezebel for Ahab's transgressions. "'There was none like unto Ahab [who did give himself over to do that which was evil in the sight of the Lord]' (1 Kings 21.25). Rav interpreted this passage in a manner derogatory to Ahab. Ahab appeared before Rav in a dream and said: 'Wherein have I sinned? . . . You are regarding only the beginning of the verse and not its conclusion . . . "whom Jezebel his wife stirred up" (*Ibid.*)'" (Jerusalem Talmud, Sanhedrin, 10.32).

Some sages defended Ahab. "Rabbi Nahman said: 'Ahab was equally balanced (in good and evil deeds)' . . . Rabbi Joseph said: 'Ahab was very lavish with his money, and since he benefited students of the Torah through his wealth, half (of his sins) were forgiven'" (Sanhedrin 102b).

Nonetheless, the rabbis declared: "There are three kings . . . who have no share in the world to come: Jeroboam, Ahab and Manasseh" (Sanhedrin 90a).

Refering to Ahab's worldly success, Rab said: "The world was created solely for Ahab, son of Omri, and for Rabbi Hanina, son of Dosah: this world for Ahab, and the world to come for Rabbi Hanina, son of Dosah" (Berachoth 61b).

8. AHAZIAH, SON OF AHAB

אחזיה
בן אהאב

1 Kings 22.50
2 Kings 1.1-18

Ahaziah's ships sink on the way to Ophir. In the foreground, the noted Moabite Stone of King Mesha.

"For the ships were broken at Ezion-geber. Then said Ahaziah . . . 'Let my servants go with thy servants in the ships.'" (I. Kings 22.49-50).

Ahaziah ascended the throne after his father's death and ruled for two years. Together with

Jehoshaphat, king of Judah, he attempted to import gold from Ophir, but his ships were wrecked in a storm. When Mesha, king of Moab, rebelled against Israelite rule, Ahaziah took no steps to stop him. Even in his sickness the Ephraimite monarch did not pray to God, preferring to send messengers to supplicate on his behalf before Baal-zebub, the god of Ekron. Elijah sent the messengers back to tell the king that his death was imminent. Ahaziah left no heirs; after his death, his brother Jehoram succeeded him.

The particulars of the insurrection of Mesha, king of Moab, and the names of the cities which that king recovered from Israel are recorded on the Mesha inscription, which was discovered in the city of Sidon in 1868.

The sages included Ahaziah among the wicked kings: "Rabbi Simeon, son of Eleazar said in the name of Rabbi Meir: 'Ahaz and Ahaziah and all the other kings of Israel concerning whom Scripture says, "he did that which was evil in the sight of the Lord", will neither live nor be judged. [Rashi: They will neither live with the righteous in the world to come, nor be judged in Gehinom]'" (Sanhedrin 103b).

9. JEHORAM, SON OF AHAB   יהורם בן אחאב

2 Kings 1.17-9.28
2 Chronicles 22.5-6

Joram conquers Moab by means of Elisha's miracle of the "water turned to blood."

"The sun shone upon the water, and the Moabites saw the water some way off as red as blood" (II. Kings 3.22).

Jehoram reigned after the death of his brother Ahaziah. He rid the country of Baal worship, but allowed the calf cult instituted by Jeroboam to continue. He defeated Moab by means of the miracle of Elisha, whereby a valley was filled with water which took on the appearance of blood. Many of Elisha's outstanding miracles, such as the healing of Naaman's leprosy, occurred during the reign of Jehoram. Wounded in battle against Aram, Jehoram went to Jezreel to recover; but there, Jehu, son of Nimshi, the captain of the Ephraimite forces, conspired against him and killed him in the field of Naboth the Jezreelite, thus fulfilling Elijah's prophecy to Ahab (1 Kings 21.13).

The rabbis praised Jehoram for not standing on his dignity, but going directly to Elisha. "We find that Elijah went to Ahab . . . but Jehoram, son of Ahab, went to Elisha" (Berachoth 10a). Josephus describes Jehoram as a mighty and great king (Antiquities IX, 2.9).

10. JEHU (SON OF JEHOSHA-PHAT), SON OF NIMSHI   יהוא (בן יהושפט) בן נמשי

2 Kings 9.2-10.36
2 Chronicles 22.7-9

Jehu kills the priests of Baal. Elijah and Elisha are in the background.

"Thus Jehu destroyed Baal out of Israel" (II. Kings 10.28).

The founder of the fourth dynasty of the Northern Kingdom, Jehu, at the command of Elijah and Elisha, killed Jehoram, son of Ahab, as well as Ahaziah, king of Judah, the latter's nephew. He also had the 70 sons of Ahab put to death. Although these deeds were done at God's command, Jehu did not perform them for the sake of heaven. Hence the prophet Hosea declared: "I will visit the blood of Jezreel upon the house of Jehu" (Hosea 1.4).

Later, Jehu slaughtered the officers of Ahab and the 42 brothers of Ahaziah. He also killed the prophets of Baal, but did not remove the golden calves from the land and "did that which was evil in the sight of the Lord." Toward the end of his reign, Aram began to harass Israel; Shalmaneser, king of Assyria, recorded in his annals that Jehu paid him tribute to come to the aid of Israel against Aram.

According to the sages, Jehu was of the tribe of Manasseh (Genesis Rabbah 97).

Jehu reigned for 28 years and was succeeded by his son Jehoahaz.

11. JEHOAHAZ, SON OF JEHU

יהואחז
בן יהוא

2 Kings 13.1-9

Jehoahaz, horrified by the atrocities committed during the siege of Samaria, rends his garments.

"For there was not left to Jehoahaz . . . save fifty horsemen . . . for the king of Aram destroyed them . . . like the dust in threshing" (II. Kings 13.7).

Jehoahaz followed in the footsteps of his father, doing "that which was evil in the sight of the Lord"; he continued the calf cult which Jeroboam, son of Nebat, had instituted. As a punishment for this sin, the Arameans attacked Israel and captured city after city until Jehoahaz was left with but a small army. In his distress he cried to God, who sent Jehoahaz' heirs—his son Joash and his grandson Jeroboam II—to save Israel. They recaptured the cities that Aram had taken, possibly due to the aid of the king of Assyria. The latter attacked Aram, forcing that country to forego its offensive against Israel.

Josephus believed that the "saviour" sent by God to deliver Israel was Jehoahaz' son, Joash, who reigned after his father (Antiquities IX).

12. JOASH, SON OF JEHOAHAZ

יהואש
בן יהואחז

2 Kings 13.9-13,25; 14.16
2 Chronicles 25.17-25

Elisha gives Joash a sign of victory over Aram as the king shoots an arrow eastward.

"Then Elisha said: 'Shoot'; and he shot. And he said: 'The Lord's arrow of victory . . . for thou shalt smite the Arameans'" (II. Kings 13. 17).

Like his father before him, Joash persisted in the calf cult instituted by Jeroboam. Nevertheless, he was attached to Elisha and mourned when the prophet died. Elisha had given Joash a sign that he would be victorious over Aram. Defeating Aram three times, Joash recovered the cities that Hazael had taken. The military situation so improved during his reign that he was able to hire out 100,000 soldiers to Amaziah, king of Judah, as mercenaries. However, after Amaziah changed his mind and sent the Israelite soldiers back without using them, relations between the two kingdoms deteriorated rapidly, until war was declared. Joash was victorious and plundered Jerusalem, destroying its walls. He ruled over Israel for sixteen years and was succeeded by his son Jeroboam II.

The sages praised Joash for his sagacity, declaring him to be the wise man, and Amaziah the foolish man, referred to in the Biblical verse: "If a wise man contendeth with a foolish man, whether he be angry or laugh, there will be no rest" (Proverbs 29.9; Sanhedrin 103a).

13. JEROBOAM II, SON OF JOASH

ירבעם (השני)
בן יהואש.

2 Kings 13.13-14.29

The king points to his conquests right up to Damascus.

"The acts of Jeroboam, and all that he did . . . how he recovered Damascus, and Hamath, for Judah in Israel" (II. Kings 14.28).

During his long reign of 41 years, Jeroboam II raised the prestige of the Kingdom of Israel, which had previously been at a low ebb. He captured Damascus and Hamath, subdued Moab, and expanded the boundaries of Israel, all in accordance with the prophecy of Jonah, son of Amittai.

Amos, who prophesied during this era, painted a bleak portrait of the religious and ethical scene, and forecast the punishment of the people. Amaziah, the High Priest of Beth-el, informed Jeroboam of these prophecies, but the king took no steps against Amos. Hosea also prophesied at that time.

Although Jeroboam sinned, the sages found some virtue in him. "Rabbi Johanan said: 'Why was Jeroboam II, the son of Joash, king of Israel, considered worthy of being included with the kings of Judah? Because he paid no heed to the slanderous reports concerning Amos'" (Pesahim 87b).

The rabbis taught that God reversed an evil decree during Jeroboam's reign: "Rabbi Nahman, son of Isaac, said: 'It is written: "According to the word of God which He spoke by the hand of

His servant Jonah, the prophet." Just as Nineveh left off evil-doing and acted favorably in God's sight, so God, in the days of Jeroboam, abandoned the evil decree concerning Israel and looked upon them with favor' " (Yebamoth 98a).

After the death of Jeroboam, Zechariah ascended the throne of Israel.

14. ZECHARIAH, SON OF JEROBOAM II
זכריה בן ירבעם (השני)
2 Kings 14.29-15.11

Shallum kills Zechariah before the people's eyes.

"And Shallum the son of Jabesh conspired against him, and smote him before the people, and slew him" (II. Kings 15.10).

Zechariah ruled over Israel for six months. Like his forefathers, he "did that which was evil in the sight of the Lord." Shallum, son of Jabesh, conspired against Zechariah, killed him and reigned in his stead, thus fulfilling God's promise to Jehu: "Thy sons of the fourth generation shall sit on the throne of Israel" (2 Kings 10.30).

The commenatators Rashi, Kimhi and Abarbanel pointed out that for a period of eleven years —from Jeroboam II's death until the ascension of Zechariah, his son, to the throne—Israel had no king. Jeroboam died in the twenty-seventh year of Uzziah's reign, and Zechariah became king in the thirty-eighth year of the Judean king's reign. The commentators are of the opinion that during this interregnum there was a struggle between Zechariah and his officers, who refused him the crown; ultimately, however, he became king.

15. SHALLUM, SON OF JABESH
שלום בן יבש
2 Kings 15.10-15

Shallum on the throne surrounded by foreign guards.

"Shallum the son of Jabesh . . . reigned the space of a month in Samaria" (II. Kings 15.13).

Shallum murdered Zechariah, son of Jeroboam, during the thirty-ninth year of the reign of Uz-

ziah, king of Judah, but stayed on the throne for only one month. Menahem, son of Gadi, of Tirzah plotted against Shallum, murdered him in Samaria, and became king in his place. It is probable that the upheaval of the interregnum period carried over into Shallum's reign.

16. MENAHEM, SON OF GADI
מנחם בן גדי
2 Kings 15.14-22

The Assyrians support Menahem's reign.

"There came . . . Pul the king of Assyria; and Menahem gave Pul a thousand talents of silver, that his hand might be with him to confirm the kingdom in his hand" (II. Kings 15.19).

When news of the murder of Zechariah, son of Jeroboam II, by Shallum, son of Jabesh, reached Tirzah, Menahem went to Samaria, killed Shallum and ruled in his stead. When the city of Tirzah refused to open its gates to Menahem, he captured it and tortured its inhabitants.

Menahem's reign was not a stable one. When Tiglath-pileser invaded Israel, Menahem was forced to pay him a large tax, which was exacted from the richer citizens of the country. In an Assyrian inscription, Tiglath-pileser mentions Menahem as one who paid tribute to him.

Menahem, like his fathers before him, worshipped the golden calves which had been set up by Jeroboam.

Menahem reigned for ten years and was succeeded by his son Pekahiah.

17. PEKAHIAH, SON OF MENAHEM
פקחיה בן מנחם
2 Kings 15.22-26

Pekahiah is slain in the palace of Samaria by Pekah.

"And Pekah the son of Remaliah, his captain, conspired against him, and smote him in Samaria, in the castle of the king's house" (II. Kings 15.25).

After the death of his father, Pekahiah ascended the throne and ruled for two years. Like

Menahem, he continued in the worship of the golden calves set up by Jeroboam. He was killed in his palace at Samaria by Pekah, son of Remaliah, one of the captains of the Israelite army, who then succeeded him to the throne of Israel.

18. PEKAH, SON OF REMALIAH

פקח
בן רמליהו

2 Kings 15.25-31
2 Chronicles 28.6

Pekah kills one hundred and twenty thousand near Jerusalem.

"For Pekah the son of Remaliah slew in Judah a hundred and twenty thousand in one day" (II. Chron. 28.6).

After killing Pekahiah, Pekah reigned in his stead. He too committed evil and worshipped the calves. Towards the end of the reign of Jotham, king of Judah, Pekah conspired with Rezin, king of Aram, to remove Jotham from the throne. They invaded Judah and besieged Jerusalem. When Ahaz ascended the Judean throne, the prophet Isaiah urged him not to fear. Ahaz, however, turned to Tiglath-pileser, king of Assyria, for help; the latter invaded Galilee, and Pekah and Rezin were forced to return home to defend their countries. Some time thereafter Pekah was murdered by Hoshea, son of Elah, who reigned in his stead.

The sages attacked Pekah bitterly, labeling him an evil-doer, a glutton and a drunkard. " 'The curse of the Lord is in the house of the wicked' [(Proverbs 3.33)]. This refers to Pekah, son of Remaliah, who ate 40 s'ahs of young birds for dessert' (Sanhedrin 94b).

19. HOSHEA, SON OF ELAH

הושע
בן אלה

2 Kings 15.30; 17.1-18.13

Sargon captures Samaria and the Israelites are taken captive to Assyria.

"In the ninth year of Hoshea, the king of Assyria took Samaria, and carried Israel away unto Assyria" (II. Kings 17. 6).

In collusion with Tiglath-pileser, king of Assyria, Hoshea, son of Elah, plotted against Pekah, son of Remaliah, killed him and ruled in his stead. Hoshea "did that which was evil in the sight of the Lord," but he was not as wicked as the preceding kings of Israel. Relying on Egyptian support, he ceased to pay tribute to Assyria. Shalmaneser then attacked Israel and took Hoshea captive. Three years later, Sargon, king of Assyria, destroyed Samaria and exiled the ten tribes to Assyria. So it came about that the many sins of Israel led to the destruction of the Northern Kingdom.

The sages explained why Israel was destroyed during the days of Hoshea, although Scripture clearly states that he was less wicked than his predecessors. "Why had the decree of exile not been pronounced before [the time of Hoshea]? Because they relegated all responsibility to their kings" (Yalkut Shimoni 2). Thus, the people could not be held accountable for their sins. The sages went on to say: "Before that time idolatry was an individual matter, and it was unseemly for the Holy One, blessed be He, to exile the masses because of the sins of an individual. However, when Hoshea, son of Elah, destroyed the watch towers (which Jeroboam had erected to prevent pilgrimages to Jerusalem), saying: 'Whoever desires to go up to Jerusalem may do so,' and did not announce that all must go up to Jerusalem, Shalmaneser advanced against him; for by his declaration, Hoshea had transfered the onus of responsibility from himself to the masses" (Tanna d'bei Eliahu).

A prophet gazes heavenward and the heavens open.

"Hear O heavens, and give ear, O earth,
For the Lord hath spoken" (Isaiah 1.2).

THE PROPHETS

Prophecy, which is regarded as a singular Divine gift to Israel (Amos 3.7), is from its earliest beginnings bound up with the Torah revelation concerning the service of the true God. It is a call which is sent forth from God and then returns to Him and calls upon Him.

While the prophets were also miracle workers and seers, they felt that their main task was "to declare unto Jacob his transgression and to Israel his sin" (Micah 3.8) and to reform the people by virtue of "the spirit of the Lord" which they, as God's chosen messengers, possessed. Most of their utterances were addressed to their contemporaries; only those prophecies that were meant for all generations were written down. Every true prophecy has both an immediate and eternal relevancy. Consequently prophecy, perhaps more than any other factor, molded the faith and destiny of the Jewish people.

Although prophecy was a distinguishing characteristic of Israel, the servants of the one God, its origins predate Israel. The Torah, as well as the sages, recognized that the heathens, too, had prophets. Like his later Israelite counterpart, the heathen prophet believed that he had the power to see hidden things and foretell the future, and was quick to share such knowledge with kings and officials, warning them to abstain from certain undertakings. These prophets, however, were not concerned with ethical guidance, even though the heathens, according to the Torah, are required to observe a number of ethical injunctions; moreover, their faith in God was sullied with pagan practices and beliefs. Accordingly, with the revelation of the Torah at Mount Sinai, when prophecy reached a new and higher stage, heathen prophecy ceased. The sages for their part, felt that this came about because of Balaam's inciting the children of Israel "to break faith with the Lord" (Numbers 31.16). At any rate, it is clear that tradition was correct in maintaining that there were prophets among the heathens. In keeping with the tradition, the rabbis found the names of these prophets mentioned throughout the Bible.

In Scripture we are not told how many prophets there were or, in some instances, who delivered certain prophecies. However, the rabbis preserved some relevant information, most of which we find in Josephus as well. This would attest to the antiquity of the tradition and show that it was definitely known during the time of the Second Temple.

The sages stated that forty-eight prophets and seven prophetesses arose in Israel, but they did not list them by name. The question, therefore, is from which period one should begin to enumerate these prophets. Different schools of thought have come forward with different answers. Rashi, in agreement with Seder Olam, identifies Abraham as the first prophet; Rabbenu Hananel, and later, the Gaon of Vilna, on the other hand, begin with Moses. Furthermore, while Rashi lists forty-eight prophets and seven prophetesses, according to the Gaon of Vilna there are five lists in all, these being:

1. Seven Hebrew prophets prior to Israel's descent into Egypt.
2. Seven Hebrew prophets in Egypt.
3. Seven heathen prophets.
4. Forty-eight prophets who arose after the conquest of Canaan.
5. Seven prophetesses.

SOURCES

1. Rashi (Megillah 14a): "There are forty-eight prophets in all . . . In **Halakot Gedolot** they are given on the basis of the record in **Seder Olam**". (Joel Sirkes, a later commentator, explains this to mean that while the prophets are listed in **Halakot Gedolot**, most of their names were taken from **Seder Olam**.

Abraham, Isaac, Jacob, Moses and Aaron, Joshua and Phinehas, Elkanah, Eli, Samuel, Gad, Nathan, David, Solomon; during the reign of Jeroboam—**Iddo**; during the reign of Ahab—**Micaiah, son of Imlah**; during the reign of Asa—**Obadiah, Ahijah the Shilonite and Jehu, son of Hanani**; during the reign of Jehoshaphat (2 Chronicles 19)—**Azariah, son of Oded, Jahaziel the Levite of the sons of Mattaniah, and Eleazar, son of Dodo, from Mareshah**; during the reign of Jeroboam, son of Joash—**Hosea and Amos**; during the reign of Jotham—**Micah of Moresheth**; during the reign of Amaziah—**Amoz and Elijah, Elisha, Jonah, son of Amittai, and Isaiah**; during the reign of Manasseh—**Joel, Nahum, and Habakkuk**; during the reign of Josiah—**Zephaniah and Uriah of Kiriath-jearim**; during the exile—**Ezekiel and Daniel**; during the second year of Darius' reign—**Baruch, Neriah, Seraiah, Mahseiah, Haggai, Zechariah, Malachi and Mordecai-Bilshan.**

Seder Olam says: "Regarding Daniel, know that while the others were prophets, he was not a prophet. Delete Daniel and include Shemaiah, who said to Rehoboam, 'Ye shall not go up, nor fight against your brethren the children of Israel' (1 Kings 12.24). [Furthermore,] two [of these prophets] I do not know." The Gaon of Vilna comments at this point: "They are Hanani and Oded."

The Talmudic note reads as follows "Oded [is] the [first] prophet (2 Chronicles 15.1), according to David Kimhi, and the second [is] Hanani, who prophesied about Asa. We know that when a prophet is identified by his own name and his father's name that both father and son are prophets. Hence, Azariah, son of Oded, and Jehu, son of Hanani were prophets and sons of prophets. One ought also to include Zechariah, son of Jehoida the priest (2 Chronicles 24.20) and Oded, who prophesied in the time of Pekah, son of Remaliah" (2 Chronicles 28.9).

2. The list of Rabbenu Hananel (Megillah 14a-b, Romm edition): "**Moses, Aaron, Asir, Elkanah, Abiasaph and the sons of Korah, all of whom prophesied in the desert; Joshua; Phinehas, Elkanah; Gad the seer; Nathan the prophet; Asaph, Heman and Jeduthun; Samuel; David** [perhaps Solomon too should be added.—ed.]; **Ahijah; Shemaiah; Iddo; Azariah, son of Oded; Hanani the seer; Jehu, son of Hanani; Elijah; Micaiah; Obadiah; Elisha; (Ezekiel) Eleazar, son of Dodavahu; Jonah, son of Amittai; Zechariah, son of Jehoiada; Amoz; Habakkuk; Zephaniah, son of Kushi; Jeremiah; Isaiah; Ezekiel; Daniel; Baruch, son of Neriah; Azariah** (This is apparently an error and should be Seraiah), **son of Mahseiah; Zechariah; and Malachi.**

"**The seven prophetesses: Sarah, Miriam, Deborah, Huldah, Hannah Abigail and Esther.**"

1. ABRAHAM
אברהם

Father of the Jewish nation; the first to advance the concept of one God (monotheism). The land of Canaan was promised to Abraham and his descendants. He forsook Mesopotamia at the command of God, and settled in Canaan, where he made numerous converts. He demonstrated his faith by offering up his son Isaac for sacrifice. He fought with the local kings of Canaan to rescue his nephew Lot; pleaded with God to spare the wicked city of Sodom, for the sake of its few righteous inhabitants.

2. ISAAC
יצחק

Second of the patriarchs and only son of Abraham by his wife Sarah. Saved from the ordeal of child sacrifice, he symbolized man's devotion to his creator. Like Abraham, Isaac's faith was tested many times. Of his two sons Jacob received the birthright, and Esau, the elder, abandoned the patriarchal tradition to which Jacob was chosen the successor.

3. JACOB
יעקב

Third of the patriarchs and the father of the twelve tribes of Israel. He suffered greatly during his lifetime from his brother Esau's enmity; from the machinations of Laban, the Aramean; from the death of Rachel, his beloved wife; and from the sale of Joseph, his favored son, into slavery in Egypt. But Jacob wrestled with the angel of God and prevailed. With this victory he gained the name "Israel" and the double promise; eternity for his descendants, and their return to the Land of Israel.

4.
יע

Spiritual arch
with the appe
A descendant
up in the hous
When mature
erator of the
under Pharaoh
of Israel from
years in the de
for them at M
his failure in c
Meribah, Mose
the Promised I
in sight of the

8. ELKANAH
אלקנה

A descendant of the tribe of Levi, who dwelt in Mt. Ephraim. He was deemed worthy of fathering a great son by his pious wife Hannah—namely, Samuel. According to the sages, Elkanah was a prophet. He made the rounds of the cities of Israel calling his generation to worship God.

9. ELI
עלי

Priest and prophet, one of the sons of Ithamar, son of Aaron. He judged Israel for forty years, reared Samuel to be a prophet, and was "devoted to the word of God". He died when he heard of the capture of the Ark of the Covenant of God. Eli was the last High Priest to officiate in Shiloh.

10. SAMUEL, SON OF ELKANAH
שמואל בן אלקנה

Last of the judges in Israel. At infancy, he was consecrated to God by his mother Hannah. With the destruction of Shiloh he traveled about the cities of Israel and judged the people. Samuel reluctantly consented to popular demand and anointed Saul king. When Saul sinned, Samuel anointed David as king to replace him. He was the first of the prophets to enunciate the concept: "Obedience to God is more to be preferred than sacrifice".

14. SOLOMON
שלמה המלך

"Wisest of all men," builder of the Temple, he effected the golden age of the Israelite kingdom. God appeared to him in a dream at Gibeon, where, rather than wealth or power, he asked for an "understanding heart to judge the people." This was granted him. The sages considered Solomon a prophet.

15. AHIJAH
THE SHILONITE
אחיה השילוני

"Guardian of righteousness." When Solomon sinned, Ahijah prophesied the division of the kingdom and instigated Jeroboam to take the seceding ten tribes. When his hopes for Jeroboam were not realized, he prophesied the fall of Jeroboam's dynasty.

16. IDDO
THE SEER
עדו החוזה

According to the sages, Iddo is the Judean prophet who prophesied the destruction of Jeroboam's altar by Josiah (1 Kings 13.2). Mention is made in Chronicles of a "Midrash Iddo" that chronicled the reigns of Jeroboam and Rehoboam.

17. SHEMAIAH
שמעיה

Counsellor to Rehoboam who deterred him from engaging in warfare with Jeroboam. When Shishak invaded Judah, he reassured the nation of survival on its own soil. The "Words of Shemaiah" chronicle the history of Rehoboam.
(2 Chronicles 12.15-17)

18. MICAIAH
מיביהו

Prophesied in the reign of Ahab. He was the sole true prophet of God among the four hundred prophets in the king's court. According to the sages, he prophesied the fall of Ahab in battle. Imprisoned for this, though later freed and brought before Ahab and Jehoshaphat, he continued to prophesy the defeat of their armies.
(2 Chronicles 18.24-27)

19. ELIJAH
אליהו

Prophet who symbolizes the rebirth
redemption of the people of Israel, as
herald of Messianic times. His life was
of wondrous and miraculous deeds, end
in an ascent to heaven in a fiery char
He demonstrated the superiority of
God of Israel in the contest with Jezebe
priests of Baal at the foot of Mount Carm
He reprimanded Ahab for appropriating
vineyard of Naboth the Jezreelite. This
of boldness led to life-long persecution

MOSES
משה רב

...rect of the Jewish nation, ...tion "Master of Prophets." ...f the tribe of Levi, he grew ...e of Pharaoh, King of Egypt. ...e was chosen to be the lib- ...eople of Israel from slavery ... He delivered the children ...Egypt, led them for forty ...sert, and received the Torah ...unt Sinai. However, due to ...nnection with the waters of ...was not permitted to enter ...and, but died in the desert, ...hills of Judea.

5.

AARON
אהרן

Older brother of Moses, and his spokes-man before Pharaoh. He substituted for Moses when the latter ascended to receive the Ten Commandments. According to the Midrash, Aaron "loved peace and sought peace, loved all creatures and brought them nearer to the Torah." Thus, in the incident of the golden calf, he acquiesced to prevent bloodshed. When the Tabernacle was set up, Aaron and his descendants were chosen for the priesthood.

6.

JOSHUA, SON OF NUN
יהושע בן נון

Pupil of Moses. He was chosen to succeed Moses and to lead the new generation of the children of Israel into Canaan. He conquered the land and divided it among the twelve tribes. A fearless warrior, Joshua was also a man of spirit. According to the Ethics of the Fathers he received the Torah from Moses and transmitted it to the elders of Israel.

7.

PHINEHAS, SON OF ELEAZAR
פנחס בן אלעזר

As a reward for his zeal for God in the incident of Zimri, he was permitted to continue the dynasty of the high priest-hood of the house of Aaron. He was one of the national and spiritual leaders in the period of Joshua. According to the sages, he survived until the days of Jephthah and Gideon.
Phinehas is a symbol of wholehearted commitment to the Jewish tradition.

11.

DAVID, SON OF JESSE
דוד בן ישי

Warrior, "sweet singer of Israel," saintly man. The sages include David among the prophets on the basis of the psalms and prayers ascribed to him. David symbolizes the future redemption of Israel, both temporal and spiritual.

12.

GAD THE SEER
גד החוזה

Friend and mentor of David during his wanderings. He supported David after the King had numbered the people, and offered him the choice of one of three punishments that God was about to inflict on the Jews.
Gad is recognized as one of the redactors of Samuel's writings and an organizer of the Temple worship.
(Taanith 26b)

13.

NATHAN
נתן הנביא

Prophet who stood by David during the latter's struggles both with his foes and with problems of morality and conscience. He sanctioned the house of David as chosen for eternal royalty. Later, he supported the kingdom of Solomon, recognizing Solomon as worthy to build the Temple of God in Jerusalem.

20.

ELISHA, SON OF SHAPHAT
אלישע בן שפט

Disciple and successor of Elijah, particularly noted as a wonder-worker. Like Elijah, he demonstrated the Lord's superiority to Baal. Prophesying the fall of the house of Ahab he sent a prophet to crown Jehu and to command him to destroy the house of Ahab. He prophesied the death of Benhadad, King of Aram, and Hazael's succession.

21.

OBADIAH
עובדיה

He prophesied the fall of Edom and the salvation of Israel. According to the sages, he is to be identified as the "Obadiah of the palace," who during the reign of Ahab secreted and fed one hundred prophets of God in mortal danger from Jezebel. (1 Kings 18.3; Sanhedrin 39b)

22.

HANANI
חנני הרואה

He reproved Asa for not trusting in God, but relying on the strength of man. For this piece of effrontery Asa punished and imprisoned him.
(2 Chronicles 16.7-10)

23.

JEHU, SON OF HANANI
יהוא בן חנני

He prophesied that the ultimate end of Baasha, King of Israel would be like that of the House of Jeroboam. He opposed the treaty between Jehoshaphat and Ahab, and authored the chronicle of Jehoshaphat.
(2 Chronicles 20.34)

24.

AZARIAH, SON OF ODED
עזריהו בן עודד

He persuaded Asa to remove the idols, to renovate the Temple, and reform the government. Under his influence Asa renewed the covenant between the people and God.
(2 Chronicles 15.1-19)

25.

JAHAZIEL SON OF ZECHARIA
יחזיאל הלוי בן זכריה

He encouraged Jeho...shaphat in his war... against Ammon, Moa... and Seir.
(2 Chronicles 20.14-19...

26. ELIEZER, SON OF DODAVAHU

אֱלִיעֶזֶר
בֶּן דּוֹדָוָהוּ

A native of Mareshah in Judah, he opposed the pact between Jehoshaphat, King of Judah, and Ahaziah, King of Israel. Jehoshaphat paid no heed to his words, and sent ships to Eziongeber; these were smashed. (2 Chronicles 20.37)

27. AMOZ

אָמוֹץ

According to the sages, he was the brother of King Amaziah (Megillah 10) and the father of the prophet Isaiah. He reproved Amaziah for importuning the gods of Edom. He was opposed to the military alliance between the Kingdoms of Judah and Ephraim. (2 Chronicles 25.7-9)

28. ODED

עוֹדֵד

Prophesied in Samaria during the reign of Ahaz, king of Judah and Pekah, son of Remaliah. He reproved the Ephraimites for torturing and taking captive their brethren of the Kingdom of Judah. His words had an effect; the captives of Judah were returned home. (2 Chronicles 28.9-16)

29. JONAH, SON OF AMITTAI

יוֹנָה
בֶּן אֲמִתַּי

Prophesied to Jeroboam, son of Joash, urging the expansion of Israel's boundaries. He was sent by God to Nineveh, to persuade the people of that Gentile city to repent; Jonah fled this mission and was punished. The Book of Jonah is a lofty expression of the doctrine of universal repentance.

30. HOSEA, SON OF BEERI

הוֹשֵׁעַ
בֶּן בְּאֵרִי

Prophesied from the days of Uzziah until the beginning of the reign of Hezekiah.
He reproved the people for their depravity and their contentment with mere Temple ritual; what was needful was knowledge of God and the meaning of truth, loving-kindness, and the tradition. Hosea was pessimistic about the future of the people of Judah and opposed the institution of monarchy. The book of Hosea, nevertheless, contains some of the finest consolatory passages in the Bible.

31. ISAIAH, SON [OF]

[יְ]שַׁעְיָהוּ
בֶּן אָמוֹץ

Greatest of the prophets. [...] aristocratic family, he was [...] courts of the Kings of Jud[...] cated the spiritual and [...] pendence of his country, s[...] the purification of religiou[...] and the abolition of idola[...] ioned the end of days when [...] not lift up sword against na[...] shall they learn war any m[...]

36. HABAKKUK

חֲבַקּוּק

Some of the sages assign his prophecies to the reign of Manasseh; others, to Jeremiah's later period. Brilliantly the prophet poses the question of the suffering of the innocent contrasted with the prosperity of the wicked, symbolized by the Chaldeans. The answer God gives him is that the fall of the wicked is imminent.

37. ZEPHANIAH, SON OF CUSHI

צְפַנְיָה
בֶּן כּוּשִׁי

Contemporary of King Josiah, and a Judean aristocrat. He prophesied the punishment of the wicked, followed by the universal acceptance of God. At that time, the remnant of Judah will be redeemed.

38. JEREMIAH, SON OF HILKIAH

יִרְמְיָהוּ
בֶּן חִלְקִיָּהוּ

Most tragic of the Hebrew prophets, he both foretold and witnessed the destruction of the Kingdom of Judah. Personally gentle, it was his melancholy mission to admonish the people and to forecast their imminent exile. Inevitably, he had many and fierce enemies. He rebelled against his task, but could not escape it, for it was within his heart as a "burning fire." Influenced by Jeremiah's prophecies, Josiah renewed the covenant between the people and their God.

39.

44. SERAIAH, SON OF NERIAH

שְׂרָיָה
בֶּן נֵרִיָּה

Disciple of Jeremiah, to him the latter transmitted the book of prophecies which he cast into the midst of the Euphrates River (Jeremiah 51.63). According to the sages, he prophesied in the time of Haggai, Zechariah, and Malachi. (Megillah 14b)

45. HAGGAI

חַגַּי

He reprimanded the people for living securely in Exile while the Temple lay in ruins. His prophecies stimulated Zerubbabel, the governor of Judea, and Joshua, the High Priest, to complete the building of the Temple.

46. ZECHARIA[H]

[ז]כַרְיָה

Like Haggai, Zechariah prophes[...] ond year of Darius's reign. He [...] the building of the Temple, a[...] spirits of those who had beco[...] by hardship, with these pr[...] "There shall yet old men and [...] in the broad places of Jerusa[...] and girls playing in the broad p[...] (Zechariah 8.4).

7 PROPHETESSES

1. SARAH

שָׂרָה

The sages identified her with Iscah, "who perceived with the holy spirit," in keeping with the verse "in all that Sarah saith unto thee, hearken unto her voice" (Megillah 14a).

2. MIRIAM

מִרְיָם

Sister of Aaron and Moses, identified as a prophetess in the Book of Exodus: "and Miriam the prophetess, the sister of Aaron, took a timbrel in her hand." When the Egyptians were drowned in the Red Sea, she sang a song of praise to God.

3. DEBORAH

דְּבוֹרָה

Judge and prophetess who called the tribes to do battle with their oppressive neighbors. She sang a victory song over the defeated enemies of Israel.

4. HANNA[H]

חַנָּה

Mother of the prophe[t Sam]uel. The sages interp[...] the prayer of Hannah [...] prophecy of the do[...] of the wicked.

AMOZ

 per of an
se to the
He advo-
nal inde-
I justice,
servance,
He envis-
/ Neither

32. AMOS
עמוס

Contemporary of Hosea and Isaiah. A farmer from Tekoa in Judah, he was an innovator who markedly influenced succeeding prophets.
He preached the need for kindness and compassion between men and nations. Foreseeing the bitter end of the kingdom of Ephraim, Amos anticipated the happy return of the exiles to their homeland.

33. MICAH OF MORESHETH
מיכה
המורשתי

A younger contemporary of Isaiah. Inveighing against corrupt rulers and judges, he prophesied the destruction of Jerusalem. He taught that the Lord required only three things of men: "Only to do justly, and to love mercy, and to walk humbly with thy God."
Like Isaiah, his visions were apocalyptic.

34. JOEL, SON OF PETHUEL
יואל
בן פתואל

According to some of the sages, he lived during the reign of Manasseh, king of Judah, when the country was visited by a calamitous plague of locusts. Urging the people of Judah to repent, he reminds their enemies of the coming "day of the Lord" when they too will receive their just deserts. And then, Judah will dwell in security forever.

35. NAHUM THE ELKOSHITE
נחום
האלקשי

Prophesied in the reign of Manasseh. Of his utterances all that remains is the prophecy about Nineveh, the city of violence that the Lord was about to overturn.
Assyria in the Bible is the embodiment of an evil nation; the fall of its capital, Nineveh, symbolizes the victory of divine justice.

EZEKIEL, SON OF BUZI
יחזקאל
בן בוזי

of the greatest prophets. He prophe-
in Babylon, whither he had been
ed with the captivity of Jehoiachin.
thfully, he elaborates on the sins of
el both in their own land and in the
e. He prophesies God's revenge upon
wicked; but he also envisions the
v bones" rising again. A priest, he
cts an idealized Temple ritual in
wing colors.

40. URIAH, SON OF SHEMAIAH, OF KIRIATH-JEARIM
אוריה
בן שמעיה

Prophesied the destruction of Jerusalem in the days of Jehoiakim. He fled to Egypt from the anger of the king and his officers, only to be captured and killed there.

MAHSEIAH
מחסיה

Father of Neriah and the grandfather of Baruch, son of Neriah. According to the sages, he was a prophet.
(Megillah 14b)

42. NERIAH
נריה

Father of Baruch, pupil and secretary of Jeremiah. The sages regard him as a prophet.
(Megillah 14b)

43. BARUCH, SON OF NERIAH
ברוך
בן נריה

Disciple of Jeremiah, and his scribe. According to the sages, he prophesied in the time of Haggai.
(Megillah 14b)

H

47. MALACHI
מלאכי

Last of the prophets included in the Bible, admonished the people for neglecting both the ethical and the divine laws. He was particularly incensed at the priests. The Book of Malachi concludes with a vision of the Messianic era: "Behold I will send you Elijah the prophet. . . . and he shall turn the heart of the fathers to the children and the heart of the children to their fathers " (Malachi 3.24).

48. MORDECAI
מרדכי

Uncle and tutor of Queen Esther, who was instrumental in frustrating the anti-Semitic machinations of Haman, as reported in the Book of Esther, and celebrated in the holiday of Purim. The sages identified him with Mordecai Bilshan, one of the returnees from Babylon, whom they considered a prophet.

in the sec-
encouraged
revived the
discouraged
etic words:
I women sit
1 . . . boys
ces thereof "

ז הנביאר

5. ABIGAIL
אביגיל

Woman who dealt kindly with David when his life was in peril, and whose wife she became after the death of her husband Nabal. She prophesied David's ultimate rise to the throne.
(1 Samuel 25. 28-30)

6. HULDAH
חולדה

Prophesied in the reign of Josiah. When the "Book of the Law" was found, she was summoned to Josiah, who was shaken by the reproofs contained therein. She reassured the king: he himself would not behold the coming evil.
(2 Kings 22.14-20)

7. ESTHER
אסתר

As the Jewish consort of the Persian King Ahasuerus, she was able to avert the catastrophe threatened by the arch anti-Semite, Haman. According to the sages she was a prophetess.

am-
ed
s a
fall

THE FORTY EIGHT PROPHETS
ACCORDING TO RASHI

THE SEVENTY SIX PROPHETS
ACCORDING TO THE GAON OF VILNA

THE FORTY EIGHT PROPHETS AND SEVEN PROPHETESSES
According to Rashi   (Megillah 14, Halakot Gedolot and Seder Olam)

A. THE FORTY-EIGHT PROPHETS

1. **Abraham**
2. **Isaac**
3. **Jacob**
4. **Moses** our teacher
5. **Aaron**
6. **Joshua**
7. **Phinehas**
8. **Elkanah**
9. **Eli** the priest
10. **Samuel** of Ramah
11. **Gad** the seer
12. **Nathan** the prophet
13. **King David**
14. **Ahijah** the Shilonite
15. **King Solomon**
16. **Iddo** the seer
17. **Shemaiah**
18. **Elijah** the prophet
19. **Micaiah**, son of Imlah
20. **Obadiah**
21. **Hanani** the seer
22. **Jehu**, son of Hanani
23. **Azariah**, son of Oded
24. **Ezekiel** the Levite, of the sons of Mattaniah
25. **Eleazar**, son of Dodavahu of Mareshah
26. **Elisha**, son of Shaphat
27. **Jonah**, son of Amittai
28. **Hosea**, son of Beeri
29. **Amos**
30. **Amoz**
31. **Oded**
32. **Isaiah**, son of Amoz
33. **Micah** of Moresheth
34. **Joel**, son of Pethuel
35. **Nahum** the Elkoshite
36. **Uriah**, son of Shemaiah
37. **Habbakuk**
38. **Zephaniah**, son of Kushi
39. **Jeremiah**, son of Hilkiah
40. **Ezekiel**, son of Buzi the priest
41. **Neriah**
42. **Baruch**, son of Neriah
43. **Seraiah**
44. **Mahseiah**
45. **Haggai**
46. **Zechariah**
47. **Malachi**
48. **Mordecai**

B. THE SEVEN PROPHETESSES

1. **Sarah**
2. **Miriam**
3. **Deborah**
4. **Hannah**
5. **Abigail**
6. **Huldah**
7. **Esther**

THE SEVENTY SIX PROPHETS
ACCORDING TO THE GAON OF VILNA
(in his commentary on Seder Olam)

A. THE SEVEN PROPHETS PRIOR TO ISRAEL'S DESCENT INTO EGYPT

1. Adam
2. Noah
3. Japheth
4. Shem
5. Eber
6. Abraham
7. Isaac

B. THE SEVEN HEBREW PROPHETS IN EGYPT

1. Jacob
2. Moses
3. Zimri, son of Zerah
4. Ethan, son of Zerah
5. Heman, son of Zerah
6. Calcol, son of Zerah
7. Dara, son of Zerah

C. THE SEVEN HEATHEN PROPHETS

1. Be'or
2. Balaam
3. Job
4. Eliphaz the Temanite
5. Bildad the Shuhite
6. Zophar the Naamathite
7. Elihu, son of Barachel the Buzite

D. THE FORTY-EIGHT PROPHETS WHO AROSE AFTER THE CONQUEST OF CANAAN

1. Joshua, son of Nun
2. Phinehas, son of Eleazar
3. Elkanah
4. David
5. Samuel, son of Elkanah
6. Asir, son of Korah
7. Elkanah, son of Korah
8. Abiasaph, son of Korah
9. Gad the seer
10. Nathan the prophet
11. Asaph the Levite
12. Heman the Levite
13. Ethan the Levite
14. Jeduthun the Levite
15. Ahijah the Shilonite
16. Shemaiah
17. Iddo
18. Azariah, son of Oded
19. Hanani the seer
20. Jehu, son of Hanani
21. Micaiah, son of Imlah
22. Ezekiel, son of Zechariah
23. Eleazar, son of Dodavahu
24. Elijah the Tishbite
25. Elisha, son of Shaphat
26. Jonah, son of Amittai
27. Obadiah
28. Zechariah, son of Jehoiada
29. Amoz, brother of King Amaziah
30. Oded

31. Hosea, son of Beeri
32. Amos
33. Isaiah, son of Amoz
34. Micah the Morashtite
35. Joel, son of Pethuel
36. Nahum the Elkoshite
37. Habakkuk
38. Zephaniah, son of Kushi
39. Jeremiah, son of Hilkiah
40. Uriah, son of Shemaiah of Kiryath-jearim
41. Ezekiel, son of Buzi
42. Baruch, son of Neriah
43. Seraiah, son of Neriah, son of Mahseiah (Jeremiah 51.59)
44. Daniel
45. Mordecai, son of Jair
46. Haggai
47. Zechariah, son of Berechiah
48. Malachi

E. THE SEVEN PROPHETESSES

1. Sarah (Iscah)
2. Miriam
3. Deborah
4. Hannah
5. Abigail
6. Huldah
7. Esther

DIFFERENCES BETWEEN RASHI AND THE GAON OF VILNA IN THE ENUMERATION OF THE PROPHETS WHO AROSE AFTER THE CONQUEST OF CANAAN

The Gaon Adds

1. Assir, son of Korah
2. Elkanah, son of Korah
3. Abiasaph, son of Korah
4. Heman the Levite
5. Asaph the Levite
6. Ethan the Levite
7. Juduthun the Levite
8. Zechariah, son of Jehoiada
9. Daniel

The Gaon Deletes

1. Aaron
2. Eli the Priest
3. King Solomon
4. Mahseiah
5. Neriah

THE FORTY-EIGHT PROPHETS

1. ABRAHAM

אברהם

The covenant wherein God promises Abraham that his descendants will be as numerous as the stars.

"And He . . . said: '. . . count the stars . . . So shall thy seed be'" (Gen. 15.5).

The son of Terah and a descendant of Eber, Abraham is the father of the Jewish nation. His mother, according to tradition, was Amathlai, daughter of Karnebo (Baba Bathra 91a). At the age of 75 Abraham left his birthplace in Mesopotamia at God's command (according to Seder Olam he had departed once before at the age of 52) and journeyed to the land of Canaan. He traveled about the country with his flocks and wherever he stopped, as at Shechem, Bethel and Beersheba, he built an altar or planted a terebinth tree and "called upon the name of the Lord" (Genesis 12.7, 8: 13-4; 21.33). In order to rescue his captive nephew Lot, he pursued and defeated the four kings who had invaded Canaan; he then took from them all that they had plundered and restored it to its original owners. After that, God appeared to Abraham and made a covenant with him, vowing that all the land lying between the Nile and the Euphrates would belong to his descendants (Genesis 15.18).

Abraham twice suffered an ordeal because of his wife Sarah: once she was taken to Pharaoh's palace and once to the palace of Abimelech the Philistine.

Abraham felt compassion towards every living creature. When told that Sodom was about to be destroyed because of its sins, he pleaded with God to spare the city. "Wilt Thou indeed sweep away the righteous with the wicked? . . . shall not the Judge of all the earth do justly?" (Genesis 18.23,25). However, despite his compassion, when Abraham was commanded to sacrifice Isaac, his only son born of Sarah, he unhesitatingly prepared to do so, and only the intervention of God's angel stayed his hand. After the death of Sarah he obtained a bride for Isaac and willed his son all that he possessed. To the sons of Hagar and Keturah, his concubines, he gave gifts. Abraham was buried in the Cave of Machpelah in Hebron, in the grave he had purchased for Sarah (Genesis 25.9; 23.19).

According to one tradition, Abraham acknowledged God's existence when he was but three years old (Nedarim 32). When he grew up he shattered his father's idols (Genesis Rabbah 38; Tanna d'bei Eliahu 2.25).

At the age of 48 he set out to spread the knowledge of God amongst the multitude (Genesis Rabbah 64; Song of Songs Rabbah 31; Pirke d'Rabbi Eliezer 26) and converted many to monotheism (Genesis Rabbah 43). He suffered ten major ordeals during his lifetime and withstood all these trials successfully (Aboth 5.4; Aboth d'Rabbi Nathan 33; *ibid.* text B, 26; Pirke d'Rabbi Eliezer 26). He was a God-fearing man, the most merciful of the patriarchs (Shohar Tob 103.14) and a model of true humility (Aboth 5.22). The sages remarked: "He who does not show mercy unto all creatures is not a descendant of Abraham" (Bezah 32). He was very hospitable (Genesis 18.2-8) and waited on his guests himself (Kiddushin 32).

Abraham was the first to preach monotheism to the world; the first of the three patriarchs; the first Hebrew to settle in Canaan; and the first person to whom the land of Israel was promised for eternity.

2. ISAAC יצחק

Abraham binds Isaac upon the sacrificial altar on Mount Moriah.

"And Abraham built the altar there, and laid the wood in order, and bound Isaac his son" (Gen. 22. 9).

The only son of Abraham by his wife Sarah, Isaac was the second of the patriarchs. At the age of 40 he was bound and readied for sacrifice at God's command (Genesis 22.9). He married Rebekah, the granddaughter of his uncle, and after twenty years she gave birth to Jacob and Esau. Due to a famine in Canaan, Isaac went down to the land of the Philistines and there was tested in the same manner as was his father: his wife, too, was taken from him. After a while the servants of the local ruler Abimelech quarreled with Isaac over some wells which the former had dug. In the end, however, the king and his general came to Isaac and made a peace treaty with him. In his old age Isaac's eyesight dimmed; this came about, according to the sages, as a result of extreme grief over Esau's marriages with Hittite wives (Genesis 26.34,35; Genesis Rabbah 65).

Isaac is the symbol of complete self-sacrifice in Jewish tradition. The sages noted that when Abraham and Isaac went to the sacrificial binding, Abraham rejoiced as though he were preparing his son's wedding, and Isaac, too, looked as radiant as a man who had set up his own wedding canopy (Yalkut Shimoni, Vayera, §101). The sounding of the shofar on the New Year is considered to be a reminder of this sacrificial binding: "Sound the ram's horn, so that I may be reminded of the binding of Isaac, the son of Abraham" (Rosh Hashanah 16).

3. JACOB יעקב

Jacob wrestles with the angel before dawn.

"And Jacob was left alone; and there wrestled a man with him . . . And he said: 'Thy name shall be called no more Jacob, but Israel'" (Gen. 32.25-29).

The son of Isaac, Jacob was the third of the patriarchs and father of the twelve tribes of Israel. He struggled to preserve the spiritual heritage of Abraham although he was constantly plagued by the contention of his sons and neighbors.

Jacob, realizing that Esau had no respect for the birthright, which then entailed priestly duties (Genesis Rabbah 63), bought it from him. Considering himself to be the first-born from that moment on, he heeded his mother's advice and obtained from his father the blessing intended for Esau. This aroused his brother's anger and Jacob had to flee to the house of Laban, his maternal uncle.

After serving Laban for twenty years, during which time he was repeatedly cheated by his uncle, Jacob returned to his home a wealthy man, with four wives and eleven sons. In the course of the return journey, his beloved wife Rachel died giving birth to one more son, Benjamin. Jacob's only daughter was forcibly taken to the house of Shechem, as a result of which Simeon and Levi, sons of Jacob, killed all the men of that city. Some time afterwards Joseph, the first-born son of Jacob and Rachel, disappeared and only towards the end of his life was Jacob privileged to see his grandchildren and be given honor in the house of his beloved son, who had become the viceroy of Egypt.

Despite a life of adversity Jacob maintained the traditions passed down to him from Abraham. On three occasions—when he was about to depart to Haran (Genesis 28.13-16), when he returned from Paddan-Aram (35.10-12), and when he was about to descend into Egypt (46.3)—God assured him that He would fulfill, through him and his descendants, the promise made to Abraham: "The land whereon thou liest, to thee will I give it, and to thy seed. And thy seed shall be as the dust of the earth . . . and in thee and in thy seed shall all the families of the earth be blessed" (28.13,14). "A nation and a company of nations shall be of thee, and kings shall come out of thy loins; and the land which I gave unto Abraham and Isaac, to thee I will give it" (35.11,12).

Twice angels appeared to Jacob: once in a dream in Bethel on his way to Haran and once in Peniel, in Transjordan, when he was returning from Haran.

Jacob was the last of the patriarchs. With the acquisition of the name "Israel" upon his return to Canaan (Genesis 35.9,10), the history of the Jewish people commenced.

4. MOSES מֹשֶׁה רַבֵּנוּ

Moses receives the Law on Mount Sinai amidst thunder and lightning.

"*Moses came down from mount Sinai with the two tables of the testimony in Moses' hand*" (Exod. 34. 29).

The sages declared that Moses was equal to 600,000 Israelites (Song of Songs Rabbah 1). He was the greatest of the prophets. Of him Scripture says: "And there hath not arisen a prophet since in Israel like unto Moses, whom the Lord knew face to face" (Deuteronomy 34.10). Similarly, it is also written: "If there be a prophet among you, I the Lord do make Myself known unto him in a vision, I do speak with him in a dream. My servant Moses is not so . . . with him do I speak mouth to mouth, even manifestly, and not in dark speeches; and the similitude of the Lord doth he behold" (Numbers 12.6-8); "And the Lord spoke unto Moses face to face" (Exodus 33.11).*

Moses had a strong influence on all the prophets who followed him and is Israel's lawgiver for all time. "This Torah shall not be changed." Later prophets arose only to adjure the people to observe the laws of the Torah of Moses. "If Israel had not sinned," the sages observed, "they would have possessed only the Torah and the Book of Joshua" (Nedarim 25b).

5. AARON אַהֲרֹן

Aaron arrayed in the eight priestly garments.

"*And Moses brought Aaron . . . And he put upon him the tunic . . . the breast-plate . . . the Urim and the Thummim . . . the mitre . . . and . . . the golden plate, the holy crown*" (Lev. 8.6-9).

Aaron was born three years before Moses. Because of his eloquence he served as an intermediary between his brother and Pharaoh. He also helped Moses perform miracles before the

Egyptian ruler (Exodus 7.1,2,8,19). When the Torah was given, only Aaron ascended the mountain with Moses and when Moses went up to receive the Tablets of the Law, he and Hur became the judges of the people (Exodus 24.14); it was for this reason that the people turned to Aaron when they wished to make a golden calf (Exodus 32.1). After the Tabernacle was built, the priesthood was promised to Aaron and his descendants for eternity. God reaffirmed this promise after the revolt of Korah (Numbers 18.7). Aaron died at the age of 123 upon Mount Hor.

Aaron was second in rank to Moses during the wanderings of Israel in the desert (Psalm 99.6; 1 Samuel 12.8) and sometimes Scripture even gives him precedence over his brother (Mekhilta, Exodus 15, §71). At times God spoke to Aaron and Moses, and on four occasions the High Priest was addressed individually (Sifra, the beginning of Leviticus). The sages remarked that 80 years before Moses began to prophesy, Aaron already had prophesied in Egypt (Yalkut Shimoni, Exodus, §172). Also, in 1 Samuel, Eli the priest is admonished by a man of God, who says: "Did I [not] reveal Myself unto the house of thy father when they were in Egypt?" (see also Ezekiel 20.5). Aaron loved peace and pursued it, loved his fellow men and drew them near to the Torah (Aboth 1.12; Aboth d'Rabbi Nathan, Text A, 52; Pirke d'Rabbi Eliezer 17; see also Malachi 2.6; Psalms 133.2). According to the sages, Aaron bowed to the will of the people when they demanded a golden calf only because he sought to prevent bloodshed (Sanhedrin 7). The rabbis declared that "clouds of glory" accompanied the Israelites because of Aaron's presence and that when he died the clouds departed (Taanith 9).

6. JOSHUA יְהוֹשֻׁעַ

Joshua pays homage to God's angel who stands before him with drawn sword.

"*And the captain of the Lord's host said unto Joshua: 'Put off thy shoe from off thy foot; for the place . . . is holy'*" (Josh. 5.15).

The son of Nun, Joshua belonged to the tribe of Ephraim (Numbers 13.8; 1 Chronicles 7.20-

*However, see Megillah 19b where the sages tried to mitigate the force of the anthropomorphism.

29). His name was originally Hoshea, but Moses changed it to Joshua (Numbers 13.16). He was Moses' servant who "departed not out of the Tent," as well as one of the twelve scouts (Exodus 33.11; Numbers 13; 14). He led the Israelites in battle in the desert and defeated Amalek in Rephidim Exodus 17.8). During Moses' lifetime he was appointed to lead the people in the conquest of Canaan (Numbers 27.18). He succeeded in winning the area extending "from Baalgad in the valley of Lebanon even unto the bare mountain, that goeth up to Seir" (Joshua 12.7) and apportioned the land among the tribes of Israel by lot, while receiving his own portion from God (Yalkut Shimoni, Joshua, § 19).

The rabbis noted that Joshua judged the people for fourteen years (Seder Olam). Ten ordinances for civil welfare are attributed to him (Baba Kamma 80b) as well as the composition of some of the psalms of the Hallel (Pesahim 117).

According to the Aggadah, he married Rahab (Erubin 17.1), and eight prophets and priests were among their descendants (Megillah 14). Joshua is considered one of the principal transmitters of the Torah: he received the Torah from Moses and passed it on to the elders (Aboth 1.1).

7. PHINEHAS פנחס

Phinehas slays Zimri the Israelite and Cozbi the Midianitess who had retired to the tent.

"And . . . Phinehas . . . saw it . . . and took a spear in his hand. And he went . . . into the chamber, and thrust both of them through" (Num. 25.7-8).

According to Aggadic tradition, Phinehas, son of Eleazar, son of Aaron the priest, was descended from two Israelite tribes and from Jethro, Moses' father-in-law (Sotah 43; Baba Bathra 115). He slew Cozbi, the daughter of Zur, and consequently was granted "the covenant of an everlasting priesthood" for himself and his descendants (Numbers 25.13). The sages said that he was one of the two spies sent by Joshua to Jericho (Yalkut Shimoni, Joshua). Shortly before Joshua's death, Phinehas went up to Gilgal and prophesied there before the people (Yalkut

Shimoni, Judges, § 40.2). Scripture refers to Phinehas when it says: "The angel of the Lord came up from Gilgal" (Judges 2.1). He was alive when the incident of the concubine at Gibeah took place (Judges 19). The Aggadah declares that he lived into the period of Gideon and rebuked the people for worshipping Amorite gods (Judges 6.8 ff.), and that he was still alive when Jephthah saved the people (Genesis Rabbah 60.3; the end of Leviticus Rabbah). Only because he did not go to Jephthah to annul the latter's vow did the Divine Spirit depart from him (Leviticus Rabbah, based upon 1 Chronicles 9.20; and Yalkut Shimoni, Judges, § 88).

According to Maimonides, in his introduction to the Mishneh Torah, Phinehas received the Torah directly from Moses.

8. ELKANAH אלקנה

Elkanah and his wives Hannah and Peninah on their annual festival pilgrimage.

"And this man went up out of his city from year to year to worship and to sacrifice unto the Lord of hosts in Shiloh" (I. Sam. 1.3).

Elkanah was the son of Jeruhum, son of Elihu, son of Tohu, son of Zuf, a family of the tribe of Levi (1 Chronicles 6.19-24) that dwelt on Mount Ephraim (1 Samuel 1.1) in Ramathaim Zophim. According to tradition, he was one of the major prophets, "unparalleled in his generation" (Megillah 14; Numbers Rabbah 10.12). Every year he made four pilgrimages to Shiloh: three in accordance with the Torah, and a fourth of his own volition, with his family and relatives. He would pass through all the cities of Israel and bring the people to Shiloh. Therefore, tradition adds: "The Holy One, blessed be He, said to him: 'Elkanah, you have inclined the scale in Israel's favour; you have trained them in the observance of my commandments, and through you, many have become worthy in my sight. I will give you a son who will also incline the scale in their favour and teach them to fulfill my laws'" (Yalkut Shimoni, Ecclesiastes, §6). According to rabbinic lore, Elkanah is referred to in the verse which reads: "There came a man of God unto Eli" (1 Samuel 2.27), for he is one of ten persons known as "the man of God" (Yalkut Shimoni, 1 Samuel, § 93).

9. ELI THE PRIEST עלי הכהן

Eli collapses upon hearing of the capture of the Ark by the Philistines.

"When he made mention of the ark of God . . . he (Eli) fell . . . backward . . . and his neck broke, and he died" (I. Sam. 4.18).

Eli, the predecessor of Samuel, the last of the judges, was the last High Priest in the Tabernacle of Shiloh. He was a descendant of Ithamar, son of Aaron the priest (1 Chronicles 24.3,6; 2 Samuel 8.17; 1 Chronicles 18.16; 1 Samuel 14.3; 22.20). He judged Israel for 40 years (1 Samuel 4.18).

Eli was revered by all and his blessing was prized as one that came from the lips of a holy man of God (1.17). He stressed the importance of carrying out one's ethical responsibilities. "If one man sin against another, God shall judge him; but if a man sin against the Lord, who shall entreat for him?" (2.25). When informed by Samuel that God would punish his house for the sins of his two sons, he replied humbly, accepting the Divine Judgment: "It is the Lord; let Him do what seemeth Him good" (3.18).

Eli died at the age of 98 upon hearing that the ark of God had been captured by the Philistines. According to Maimonides, he received the tradition from the elders and from Phinehas.

10. SAMUEL שמואל הרמתי

Samuel anoints David as king in the presence of his seven brothers.

"Samuel took the horn of oil, and anointed him in the midst of his brethren; and the spirit of the Lord came mightily upon David" (I. Sam. 16.13).

Samuel was the son of Elkanah* and the last judge of Israel. As a child he served in the Temple at Shiloh, where he had been brought by his mother. There the prophetic spirit came upon him and he foresaw that the house of Eli would be destroyed because of the sins of the priest's sons (1 Samuel 3). When Samuel reached manhood he attained fame as a prophet throughout the land. Since Shiloh was destroyed and the nation lacked a religious center, he circuited the sanctuaries of Bethel, Gilgal and Mizpah, guiding the people in religion and uniting them politically.

The threat that the Philistines and the Ammonites presented to Israel led the heads of the people to ask Samuel to choose a king. The prophet felt that a monarchical system was tantamount to slavery and, moreover, he looked upon the request as an act of rebellion against God, who was the sole ruler of Israel and always provided leaders (judges) for the people when the need arose. Nevertheless, Samuel acquiesced and anointed Saul. However, when Saul twice failed to carry out God's commands (1 Samuel 15), Samuel despaired of him and secretly anointed David.

Samuel renewed prophecy in Israel. As a young man, seeing that visions were infrequent among the people (1 Samuel 3.1), he established schools for prophecy in Ramah (19.18-24).

Samuel expressed the view that ritual worship alone is not valued and that good actions are more important than ritual worship in the service of God. "Hath the Lord as great delight in burnt-offerings and sacrifices, as in hearkening to the voice of the Lord? Behold, to obey is better than sacrifice, and to hearken than the fat of rams" (15.22-23). His disdain for gifts and bribes is attested to by his challenge to the people: "Witness against me before the Lord . . . whose ox have I taken?" (12.3). The sages declared that in some respects Samuel was greater than Moses. While Moses told the children of Israel: "When they have a matter, it cometh unto me" (Exodus 18.16), Samuel exerted himself and 'went out to the people' (Yalkut Shimoni, Samuel, §111.12). The sages also pointed out that while Moses said: "I have not taken one ass from them," Samuel would not hire one, even if its owner was willing to rent it.

According to Maimonides, Samuel received the tradition from Eli.

*See above #8.

11. GAD THE SEER גד החוזה

Gad accompanies David in his wanderings.

"And the prophet Gad said unto David: 'Abide not in the stronghold; depart, and get thee into the land of Judah'" (I. Sam. 22.5).

Scripture refers to Gad as both prophet and seer (1 Chronicles 29.29). He accompanied and advised David during the latter's wanderings (1 Samuel 22.5). After the king took a census of the people, the prophet told him that God's punishment was imminent and bade him choose between famine, flight from his enemies, or plague. Later he advised David to build an altar to halt the plague's spread (2 Samuel 24.18). Gad was one of the authors of the chronicles of Samuel and also helped David organize the Levitical singers in the Temple (1 Chronicles 23.27; Taanith 15).

12. NATHAN THE PROPHET נתן הנביא

Citing the parable of the poor man's lamb, Nathan rebukes David for his conduct against Uriah the Hittite.

"And Nathan said to David: 'Thou art the man' . . . And David said unto Nathan: 'I have sinned against the Lord'" (II. Sam. 12.7,13).

Nathan was the most outstanding prophet in the generation that followed Samuel. He admonished David fearlessly for the latter's misconduct with Bathsheba (2 Samuel 12). On the other hand, he predicted that the house of David would have perpetual dominion over Israel and that Jerusalem would be a holy city (2 Samuel 7.16; 1 Chronicles 28.4). This prophecy had a great effect upon Jewish religious thought and on the teachings of other religions deriving from Judaism.

Nathan informed the king that his son and successor would build the Temple (2 Samuel 7.13 ff.). When Solomon was born the prophet named him *Jedidiah* ("beloved of God"). Nathan supported Solomon when the latter contended with

Adonijah for the kingship. The prophet was one of the authors of "the acts of David" and "the acts of Solomon" (1 Chronicles 29.29; 2 Chronicles 9.29), which might be portions of the Biblical books of Samuel and Kings. He was also one of the organizers of the Temple service (1 Chronicles 29.29, Taanith 26).

13. DAVID* דוד המלך

David in his palace intones a prayer of thanksgiving to God.

"And David spoke unto the Lord the words of this song in the day that the Lord delivered him . . . of all his enemies, and . . . of Saul" (II. Sam. 22.1).

The sages observed that David, too, was a prophet because Scripture says: ". . . whom David and Samuel the seer did ordain in their set office" (1 Chronicles 9.22). It is in reference to them, as well as to Nathan and Gad, that the sages said: "The first prophets established the 24 watches of priestly duty" (Taanith 26).

According to Maimonides, David received the tradition from Samuel and his court.

14. AHIJAH THE SHILONITE אחיה השילוני

Ahijah predicts the division of the kingdom by tearing the king's robe.

"And Ahijah laid hold of the new garment . . . and rent it in twelve pieces. And he said to Jeroboam: 'Take thee ten pieces . . . but he (Solomon) shall have one tribe'" (I. Kings 11.30-32).

Ahijah was active toward the end of Solomon's reign and prophesied the division of the kingdom "because that they have forsaken Me . . . and they have not walked in My ways, to do that which is right in Mine eyes, and to keep My statutes and Mine ordinances, as did David" (1 Kings 11.33). He also urged Jeroboam to accept the kingship over the ten tribes. However, it later became clear to him that Jeroboam would not fulfill the hopes he and the other true prophets entertained. Therefore, even though the king sent his wife to the

*See also section on kings.

prophet to learn what would become of their sick son, Ahijah continued to predict the utter destruction of the house of Jeroboam: "Forasmuch as I exalted thee from among the people . . . and rent the kingdom away from the house of David, and gave it thee; and yet thou hast not been as My servant David, who kept My commandments, and who followed Me with all his heart . . . but hast done evil . . . and hast gone and made thee other gods . . . therefore, behold, I will bring evil upon the house of Jeroboam . . . and will utterly sweep away the house of Jeroboam, as a man sweepeth away dung" (1 Kings 14.7-10). According to the sages, Ahijah prophesied to Solomon, too, at the beginning of that monarch's reign. "As for this house which thou art building, if thou wilt walk in My statutes, and execute Mine ordinances . . . then will I establish My word with thee, which I spoke unto David thy father; in that I will dwell therein among the children of Israel" (6.11-13). The prophet also brought to Solomon the bad tidings of the future division of the kingdom (11.11-13).

The Aggadah relates that Ahijah was a Levite who was born during the days of Amram, father of Moses, and died during the lifetime of Elijah, whose teacher he was (Baba Bathra 121; Maimonides, in his introduction to the Mishneh Torah). Rabbi Simeon, son of Yohai, praised the prophet in the following manner: "If Abraham will agree to suffer for the sins of all the generations up to my time, I shall suffer for all generations up to the Messianic era. If he will not agree to this, then let Ahijah the Shilonite join me and together we shall carry the burden of sin from Abraham's time to the days of King Messiah" (Genesis Rabbah 35).

According to Maimonides, Ahijah received the tradition from David and his court.

15. SOLOMON* שלמה המלך

In his dream Solomon chooses wisdom and justice above everything.

"*The Lord appeared to Solomon in a dream . . . and God said: 'Ask what I shall give thee' . . . 'Give Thy servant . . . an understanding heart to judge Thy people'*" (I. Kings 3.5,9).

The sages included Solomon among the prophets because of his dream at Gibeon wherein

*See also section on kings.

God appeared to him and said: "Ask what I shall give thee" and Solomon requested "an understanding heart" to judge the people (1 Kings 3.5,9).

16. IDDO THE SEER עדו החוזה

Jeroboam's hand is paralyzed as he extends it to arrest Iddo the prophet.

"*The altar was rent, and the ashes poured out . . . according to the sign which the man of God had given*" (I.Kings 13.5).

Iddo preached during the reign of Jeroboam, son of Nebat, according to the rabbis and Josephus (Antiquities VIII, 8.5; see also 2 Chronicles 12.15). It was he who came from Judah to Beth-el and prophesied the destruction of the altar which Jeroboam had built there and had sacrificed upon: "O altar . . . Behold, a son shall be born unto the house of David, Josiah by name; and upon thee shall he sacrifice the priests of the high places" (1 Kings 13.2). He performed signs before the king: the altar was rent, the ashes poured out upon the earth, and Jeroboam's hand, which he had stretched out to seize Iddo, dried up. Only after the prophet entreated God on the king's behalf was Jeroboam cured. After this incident, however, Iddo was enticed by a false prophet to eat at the latter's table, thus violating God's command, and shortly after leaving that prophet's house, he was killed by a lion.

The chronicles of Rehoboam, Abijah and Jeroboam were written in "the commentary of the prophet Iddo," apparently a synonym for "the histories of Shemaiah the prophet and Iddo the seer" (2 Chronicles 12.15; 13.22).

17. SHEMAIAH
THE MAN OF GOD שמעיה

Shemaiah exhorts Rehoboam not to engage in civil war with Jeroboam.

"*But the word of God came unto Shemaiah . . . 'Speak unto Rehoboam . . . Ye shall not go up, nor fight against your brethren'*" (I. Kings 12. 22-24).

A Judean, Shemaiah prophesied during the

reign of Rehoboam when the latter mustered his army in hopes of regaining his sovereignty over the Northern Kingdom. Shemaiah warned him not to wage war. "You shall not go up, nor fight against your brethren the children of Israel . . . for this thing is of Me." Rehoboam heeded the prophet's words and sent his forces home (1 Kings 12.22-24). When Shishak of Egypt attacked the land at a later date and terror was widespread, Shemaiah came to the people, who were gathered in Jerusalem, and reassured them. "They have humbled themselves; I will not destroy them; but I· will grant them some deliverance" (2 Chronicles 12.7,8).

The acts of Rehoboam were recorded in the histories of Shemaiah and Iddo (2 Chronicles 12.15).

18. ELIJAH   אליהו הנביא

Elijah's miraculous triumph over the prophets of Baal on Mount Carmel.

"Elijah the prophet . . . said: '. . . let it be known this day that Thou art God in Israel' . . . Then the fire of the Lord fell, and . . . all the people . . . said: 'The Lord, He is God'" (I. Kings 18. 36-39).

Elijah, a native of Gilead (Jabesh Gilead, according to Tosafoth Taanith 3), prophesied and wrought miracles in the kingdom of Ephraim during the reigns of Ahab and his son Ahaziah. He waged a ceaseless struggle against Jezebel and the Baal cult which she had brought to Israel from her birthplace, Tyre. Elijah prophesied a three-years' drought and then fled Jezebel's wrath. He first went into hiding near the brook of Cherith and later lived in the house of a widow in Zarephath. The dire famine forced Ahab to seek out Elijah and agree to a public contest between the worshippers of God and the worshippers of Baal (1 Kings 18). This resulted in the slaughter of the 400 priests of Baal and Asherah. The queen was incensed and Elijah fled to Mount Horeb in the desert of Sinai. There God appeared to him in "a still small voice," commanding him to return to Israel (19.12, 15, 16). Elijah did so and continued his relentless battle against evil of all sorts. When Naboth the Jezreelite was killed on the basis of false testimony, Elijah prophesied the utter annihilation of the house of Ahab, and

when, after the death of Ahab, Ahaziah sought to inquire of Baalzebub, the god of Ekron, Elijah prophesied the king's death (2 Kings 1).

The prophet's strange appearance suited his extraordinary deeds: his hair was long and flowing and his only garment was a hairy coat. He performed a great many miracles. At his word an unfailing supply of meal and oil was provided the widow at whose house he lived, and he later brought her son back to life (1 Kings 17); three years of famine came upon Israel as he predicted; a fire from heaven burnt up his offering to God on Mount Carmel; the officers of Ahaziah who were sent to capture him were consumed by Divine fire (2 Kings 1); and he ascended to heaven in a chariot of fire. Wondrous as these deeds were, however ,the victory of pure monotheism and its absolute standard of ethics, which he helped bring about by his unflagging vigor and zeal, was perhaps his greatest achievement.

Aside from the patriarchs, Elijah is the most outstanding of the prophets who left no written works. According to Malachi, who was the last of the prophets, he will usher in the Messianic era. "And he shall turn the hearts of the fathers to the children, and the hearts of the children to their fathers" (Malachi 3.24).

The rabbis noted that Elijah and Moses were similar in many respects (Yalkut Habakkuk § 209). According to the rabbis, Elijah withheld the rain because Ahab mocked Moses' curse against idol worshippers, boasting that although idolatry was widespread in the land, the rains still fell. Elijah immediately told him: "As god liveth, there will be no rain" (Sanhedrin 113a).

Elijah will resurrect the dead (Shekalim, end of chapter 2). It is also said that he will resolve all disputed issues. This is based upon the Biblical sentence: "How long halt ye between two opinions?" (1 Kings 18.21). Because he declared that the children of Israel had forsaken God's covenant, he came to be known as "the angel of the covenant".

The sages differed as to Elijah's origin. Some believed that he came from Gad; others traced him to the tribe of Benjamin. Some thought he was a priest and even identified him with Phinehas (Genesis Rabbah 71.4; Baba Mezia 114; and many other sources).

According to Maimonides, Elijah received the tradition from Ahijah the Shilonite and his court.

19. MICAIAH, SON OF IMLAH

מיכיהו בן ימלא

Micaiah, defying all the false prophets, warns Ahab and Jehoshaphat against war.

"Then the king of Israel . . . said: 'Fetch quickly Micaiah the son of Imlah' . . . And all the prophets prophesied . . . 'Go up to Ramoth-gilead'" (I. Kings 22.9-12).

In the days of Ahab, Micaiah was the only true prophet among 400 court prophets who told the king whatever he wished to hear (1 Kings 22.8; 2 Chronicles 18.14). According to the sages (Seder Olam) and Josephus (Antiquities VIII, 14.5) it was Micaiah who disguised himself with a headband and ashes and prophesied that Ahab would fall in battle. "Because thou hast let go out of thy hand the man whom I had devoted to destruction, therefore thy life shall go for his life" (1 Kings 20.35-43). Ahab commanded that Micaiah be put into prison, and only at the request of Jehoshaphat, king of Judah, was he released and brought before the two kings. He then prophesied: 'I saw all Israel scattered upon the mountains, as sheep that have no shepherd" (22.17). He is the first prophet known to us who actually envisioned God and the heavenly host. "I saw the Lord sitting on His throne, and all the host of heaven standing by Him on His right hand and on His left" (1 Kings 22.19; cf. Isaiah 6.5 and Job 1). His statement about "the spirit" going forth to "entice" Ahab to perish at Ramoth-gilead is explained by the sages as referring to the spirit of Naboth, whose death was brought about unjustly by Jezebel, Ahab's wife (1 Kings 22.20; Rabbi David Kimhi *ad loc.;* Rashi *ad loc.*).

20. OBADIAH

עובדיה

Obadiah rescues many prophets from slaughter by Jezebel.

"Obadiah . . . said: '. . . Was it not told my lord (Elijah) what I did when Jezebel slew the prophets . . . how I hid a hundred . . . of the Lord's prophets . . . and fed them'" (I. Kings 18.7-13).

Obadiah lived toward the end of the era of the First Temple and prophesied the downfall of Edom. "For the violence done to thy brother Jacob shame shall cover thee, and thou shalt be cut off for ever. In the day that thou didst stand aloof, in the day that strangers carried away his substance . . . even thou wast as one of them. . . . And the house of Jacob shall be a fire, and the house of Joseph a flame, and the house of Esau for stubble" (Obadiah 1.10, 11, 18). He also prophesied that the ruins of Israel would be rebuilt; that Israel would possess Mount Seir, the field of Ephraim and the field of Samaria; and that the territory of the tribe of Benjamin would extend to Gilead, at which time "saviours shall come up on Mount Zion to judge the mount of Esau; and the kingdom shall be the Lord's" (19, 21).

The sages identified the prophet with Obadiah the overseer of the royal household, who lived in the days of Ahab and hid and maintained 100 prophets sought after by the wrathful Jezebel (1 Kings 18.3; Sanhedrin 39b). The rabbis also considered him to be a proselyte descended from Eliphaz, son of Esau (Yalkut Shimoni, Obadiah). According to one opinion, his wife was the Shunamite woman.

21. HANANI THE SEER

חנני הרואה

Hanani reproves King Asa and is taken to prison.

"Hanani the seer . . . said unto him (Asa): 'Because thou . . . hast not relied on the Lord . . . the host of the king of Aram escaped'" (II. Chron. 16. 7).

Hanani rebuked Asa, king of Judah, for relying upon the king of Aram when in danger, and not upon God. "Were not the Ethiopians and the Lubim a huge host . . . yet, because thou didst rely on the Lord, He delivered them into thy hand. For the eyes of the Lord run to and fro throughout the whole earth, to show Himself strong in the behalf of them whose heart is whole toward Him" (2 Chronicles 16.8,9). Asa, angered, had the seer imprisoned (16.10).

22. JEHU, SON OF HANANI

יהוא בן חנני

Jehu denounces King Baasa for pursuing the calf-worship of Jeroboam.

"The Lord came to Jehu . . . against Baasa, saying: 'Forasmuch as . . . thou . . . hast made My people . . . to sin . . . I will make thy house like the house of Jeroboam'" (I. Kings 16.1-4).

Prophesying during the reign of Asa, Jehu declared that Baasa, ruler of the Northern Kingdom, would suffer Jeroboam's fate. "Forasmuch as I exalted thee out of the dust, and made thee prince over My people Israel; and thou hast walked in the way of Jeroboam, and hast made My people Israel to sin, to provoke Me with their sins; behold, I will utterly sweep away Baasa and his house; and I will make thy house like the house of Jeroboam the son of Nebat" (1 Kings 16.1-3).

Later, the prophet rebuked Jehoshaphat for becoming an ally of Ahab. "Shouldest thou help the wicked, and love them that hate the Lord? for this thing wrath is upon thee from before the Lord" (2 Chronicles 19.2).

Jehu wrote the chronicles of Jehoshaphat (2 Chronicles 20.34).

23. AZARIAH, SON OF ODED

עזריהו בן עודד

Azariah urges King Asa to remove the idols from Judah and Benjamin.

"Azariah . . . went out to meet Asa, and said: '. . . the Lord is with you, while ye are with Him' . . . when Asa heard . . . he . . . put away the detestable things" (II. Chron. 15.1-2,8).

During the reign of Asa, king of Judah, Azariah prophesied: "The Lord is with you, while ye are with Him; and if ye seek Him, He will be found of you; but if ye forsake Him, He will forsake you. . . . But be ye strong, and let not your hands be slack; for your work shall be rewarded" (2 Chronicles 15.1, 2, 7). The prophet's words had an effect on Asa and he removed the detestable idols from the land of Judah and Benjamin, and from the cities that he had conquered in the hill country of Ephraim. He also repaired the Temple altar and gathered together all of Judah and Benjamin and those "that sojourned with them out of Ephraim and Manasseh, and out of Simeon" into Jerusalem where they made a covenant "to seek the Lord, the God of their fathers, with all their heart" (2 Chronicles 15.8-17).

24. JAHAZIEL THE LEVITE, SON OF ZECHARIAH

יחזיאל הלוי בן זכריה מבני מתניה

Jahaziel encourages King Jehoshaphat in his battles against Moab and Ammon.

"Then upon Jahaziel . . . came the spirit of the Lord . . . and he said '. . . go out against them; for the Lord is with you'" (II. Chron. 20.14-17).

"Then upon Jahaziel the son of Zechariah, the son of Benaiah, the son of Jeiel, the son of Mattaniah, the Levite, of the sons of Asaph, came the spirit of the Lord" (II Chronicles 20.14). He encouraged Jehoshaphat prior to the battle against Ammon, Moab and Seir, saying: "Fear not, nor be dismayed; tomorrow go out against them; for the Lord is with you" (20.17).

25. ELIEZER, SON OF DODAVAHU OF MARESHAH

אליעזר בן דודוהו ממרישה

Eliezer prophesies the sinking of the fleet at Ezion-geber in the Gulf of Elath because the king had joined with Ahaziah.

"Eliezer . . . prophesied against Jehoshaphat . . . And the ships were broken" (II. Chron. 20. 37).

A Judean prophet, Eliezer told Jehoshaphat: "Because thou hast joined thyself with Ahaziah, the Lord hath made a breach in thy works." Jehoshaphat, refusing to heed the prophet's words, made an agreement with the king of Israel to have ships built in Ezion-geber. However, before the vessels were able to sail for Tarshish, their destination, they were destroyed (2 Chronicles 20.35-37).

26. ELISHA

אלישע בן שפט

Elijah mounts to heaven in a chariot of fire as his prophetic mantle falls on Elisha.

"And Elijah went up by a whirlwind . . . And Elisha saw it, and he cried: 'My father, my father' . . . And he took the mantle of Elijah" (II. Kings 2.11-14).

The son of Shaphat of Abel-meholah, Elisha was the disciple and successor of Elijah. According to the rabbis, he belonged to the tribe of Gad (Pesahim 68). Elijah came upon the young man while the latter was plowing and threw his mantle over him, signifying that Elisha would ultimately succeed him (1 Kings 19.16-21). When Elijah was taking final leave of him, Elisha asked his master: "I pray thee, let a double portion of thy spirit be upon me" (2 Kings 2.9). Unlike his predecessor, Elisha was on good terms with King Jehu, mainly as a result of his having told the latter, at Elijah's command, to found a new dynasty.

Elisha had an extraordinary career; he performed even more miracles than did Elijah. He spread out the mantle of his master and crossed the Jordan dry-shod (2 Kings 2.8); he purified the fountain in Jericho (2.19-22); he set bears upon children who mocked him (2.23,24); he correctly prophesied victory over Moab (3.14-27); he miraculously increased a widow's supply of oil (4.1-7); he foretold the birth of the Shunamite woman's son and when the boy died, brought him to life again (4.8-37); he made poisonous pottage edible (4.38-41) and by his word caused a sunken axehead to float to the surface of a well (6.1-7); he informed the king of Israel as to the location and activity of the king of Aram (6.8-23); with twenty loaves of bread and a few ears of corn he fed 100 persons (4.42-44); he cured Naaman the Syrian of leprosy (5.1-19) and laid a curse upon the house of Gehazi because of the latter's greed (5.20-27); he predicted the lowering of prices in Samaria and prophesied the death of the captain who refused to believe him (7.1-20); he foresaw the death of Ben-hadad and crowned Hazael in his place (8.7-15); he prophesied the annihilation of the house of Ahab (8.1-10) and the three victories of Joash (13.14-19). Even after Elisha's death miracles took place because of him: a dead man thrown into the prophet's grave was restored to life (13.20,21).

According to Seder Olam (see the Vilna Gaon on 2 Kings 13), the prophets mentioned in 2 Chronicles 24.19 are Elisha and Jonah: "Yet He sent prophets to them, to bring them back unto the Lord; and they admonished them, but they would not give ear."

According to Maimonides, Elisha received the tradition from Elijah.

27. JONAH, SON OF AMITTAI

יונה
בן אמתי

Jonah is thrown into the storm-tossed sea and is swallowed by a big fish.

"So they took up Jonah, and cast him forth into the sea" (Jonah 1.15). *"And the Lord prepared a great fish to swallow up Jonah"* (2.1).

A resident of Gath-hepher in the territory of the tribe of Zebulun (2 Kings 14.25; cf. Joshua 19.13), Jonah predicted that Jeroboam, son of Joash, would restore the boundaries of Israel "from the entrance of Hamath until the sea of the Arabah" (2 Kings 14.25). According to the book that bears his name, the prophet was sent to the people of Nineveh to make them repent of their evil-doing and so save themselves from disaster. Jonah refused to obey the Divine command, not wishing to help Israel's enemies repent and thereby make Israel the more culpable in God's sight (Mekhilta). Thinking that the Divine Presence was only to be found in the land of Israel, Jonah fled the country (Yalkut Shimoni, Exodus). However, in the end he was forced to come to Nineveh and rouse its inhabitants to repentance. Greatly vexed, he went outside the city to see what would become of it. There God caused a gourd to spring up and provide him with shade, but overnight made the plant wither. When the prophet, faint with heat, asked that he might die, God said to him: "Thou hast had pity on the gourd, for which thou hast not laboured, neither madest it grow . . . and should not I have pity on Nineveh, that great city, wherein are more than six score thousand persons that cannot discern between their right hand and their left hand, and also much cattle?" (Jonah 4.10,11). The book of Jonah is one of the most elevating works in world literature, proclaiming the value of repentance and the merciful nature of God.

The sages declared that Jonah was the son of the widow of Zarephath who was brought back to life by Elijah (1 Kings 17.17-24) and that he was the prophet who, at Elijah's command, anointed Jehu and ordered him to destroy the house of Ahab (2 Kings 9.1-13; Yalkut Shimoni, Jonah, § 550).

The rabbis differed as to his origin. Some believed that he came from the tribe of Zebulun and others thought he came from Asher. Still others maintained that his mother was of the tribe of Asher and his father was of the tribe of Zebulun (Genesis Rabbah, Vayehi, § 98). Jonah's wife is said to have made the pilgrimages to Jerusalem regularly (Erubin 96a).

28. HOSEA, SON OF BEERI

הושע
בן בארי

Hosea, the harlot and the three children.

"The Lord said unto Hosea: 'Go, take unto thee a wife of harlotry and children of harlotry; for the land doth commit great harlotry, departing from the Lord'" (Hosea 1.2).

According to the sages, Beeri is Beerah, prince of the Reubenites, whom Tillegath-pilneser, king of Assyria, carried away into captivity (1 Chronicles 5.6; Genesis Rabbah, Vayeshev, § 4). Hosea prophesied from the days of Uzziah and Jeroboam II until the beginning of the reign of Hezekiah (Hosea 1.1). He rebuked the people who carried out the Divine worship perfunctorily. The prophet argued that ritual service alone was valueless unless it was animated by a deep awareness of God; and that setting up many altars and crying out: "My God, we Israel know Thee" (8.2, 11-13) would accomplish nothing in the absence of deeds of truth and kindness, and fulfillment of the laws of the Torah (4.1,6).

Hosea was the first man to symbolize, through his personal life, Israel's relationship to God. At God's command the prophet married a harlot who gave birth to children not his own, and the names he gave the children further indicated God's rejection of His people: *Lo-ruhama* ("That has not obtained mercy") and *Lo-ammi* ("Not My people").

The prophet regarded the monarchy as an evil institution from its inception. "They have set up kings, but not from Me" (8.4). He taught that arrogance and reliance upon military power were evidence of lack of faith in God; accordingly, he opposed the making of covenants with idolatrous nations. He prophesied that Israel's corruption would lead to disastrous consequences. "Therefore am I unto Ephraim as a moth, and to the house of Judah as rottenness" (5.12). Worse than the famine, plague, sword and laying waste of the land would be the people's estrangement from God, the prophet declared. "With their flocks and with their herds they shall go to seek the Lord, but they shall not find Him; He hath withdrawn Himself from them" (5.6). Hosea maintained that only thorough repentance on the people's part, and a return to righteous living as in days of old, would restore the love which prevailed between God and Israel in the desert.

The sages said: "When God first told Hosea: 'Your children have sinned,' he should have answered: 'They are *your* children and the children of your chosen ones, Abraham, Isaac and Jacob. Have mercy upon them.' However, the prophet not only failed to give that answer, but even went so far as to say: 'O God, all the world is Thine; change them for another nation of your choice.' God then said: 'What shall I do with this old man? I shall order him to marry a harlot and let her bear him two children of harlotry. Afterwards I shall say to him, "Divorce her." If he divorces her, I shall divorce Israel.' Immediately God said to Hosea: 'Go, take unto thee a wife of harlotry' (Hosea 1.2). After she bore him two sons and one daughter, God said to him: 'Hosea, should you not have learned from your master (Moses)? As soon as I spoke to him he separated from his wife.' Hosea then said: 'Lord of the universe, I have had children by her. I cannot divorce her or separate from her.' God then said: 'Now your wife is a harlot, your children are of harlotry, and you do not even know whether they are yours or not; but I know that the children of Israel are the children of My chosen ones, Abraham, Isaac and Jacob, and that they are one of My four special possessions in this world—The Torah, Heaven,

The Temple and Israel; and yet you say, "Change them for another people!" ' Realizing that he had sinned, Hosea begged for forgiveness. God then said: 'You seek mercy for yourself; why do you not rise and plead for Israel, for I have decreed that they will suffer three punishments.' Immediately Hosea arose and pleaded for Israel and the decrees were nullified. The prophet then blessed the people: 'Yet the number of the children of Israel shall be as the sand of the sea'; and it is written: 'And I will sow her unto Me in the land; and I will have compassion upon her that had not obtained compassion' (Hosea 2.1,25)" (Pesahim 87).

According to Maimonides, Hosea obtained the tradition from Zechariah and his court.

29. AMOS   עמום

Amos the sycamore-dresser, prophesies the restoration of David's "Tabernacle".

"Amos . . . said . . . 'I was no prophet, neither was I a prophet's son; but I was a herdman, and a dresser of sycamore-trees'" (Amos 7. 14).

A native of Tekoa in Judah, Amos prophesied in the days of Uzziah, Jeroboam II, Jotham, Ahaz and Hezekiah (Amos 1.1). He was a herdsman and a dresser of sycamore trees (7.14) and the first prophet whose utterances have been transmitted to us in a separate book. He continued Elijah's war against ethical and religious degeneracy, but waged the battle on a larger scale. Unlike Elijah, his message was aimed not at the king alone, but rather at the entire ruling class. All the people, rather than select individuals, were on trial for their deeds. The prophet scorned ritual worship that was dissociated from pure thoughts and actions. "Take thou away from Me the noise of thy songs; and let Me not hear the melody of thy psalteries. But let justice well up as waters, and righteousness as a mighty stream" (5.23, 24). Amos protested vigorously against social injustice. "Therefore, because ye trample upon the poor, and take from him exactions of wheat; ye have built houses of hewn stone, but ye shall not dwell in them, ye have planted pleasant vineyards, but ye shall not drink the wine thereof" (5.11).

Only through repentance could there be salvation, the prophet taught, and he spoke of a time when all sinners in Israel would be destroyed and only the righteous would remain alive: "In that day I will raise up the tabernacle of David that is fallen . . . and I will build it as in the days of old. . . . And I will turn the captivity of My people Israel . . . And I will plant them upon their land, and they shall no more be plucked up" (9.8-11, 14, 15).

The sages declared (Makkoth 23b) that Amos reduced all the commandments of the Torah to one: "For thus saith the Lord unto the house of Israel: Seek ye Me, and live" (5.4).

According to Maimonides, Amos received the tradition from Hosea and his court.

30. AMOZ   אמוץ

Amoz rebukes King Amaziah for setting up the idols of Edom.

"The anger of the Lord was kindled against Amaziah, and He sent . . . a prophet" (II. Chron. 25. 15).

The sages held that Amoz was the brother of King Amaziah (Megillah 10) and that it was he who told that monarch: "Why hast thou sought after the gods of the people [Edom], which have not delivered their own people out of thy hand?" (2 Chronicles 25.15,16). He also opposed the importing of troops from the Northern Kingdom to aid Judah (25.7-9).

31. ODED   עודד

Oded orders the leaders of Ephraim to send back the captives of Judah.

"A prophet of the Lord . . . was Oded; and he went out to meet the host . . . to Samaria, and said . . . 'send back the captives . . . of your brethren'" (II. Chron. 28.9-11).

Oded prophesied in Samaria during the reign of Ahaz, king of Judah, and Pekah, son of Remaliah, king of Israel. When the children of Israel returned from Judah with numerous prisoners, the prophet went out and urged them in God's name to restore their captives to their native land. His words had a telling effect and the leaders of Ephraim did not bring any captives back to Samaria. "And the men . . . rose up, and took the captives, and with the spoil clothed all that were naked among them . . . and gave them to eat and to drink, and anointed them, and carried all the feeble of them upon asses, and brought them to Jericho . . . unto their brethren" (2 Chronicles 28.9-15).

32. ISAIAH, SON OF AMOZ ישעיהו בן אמוץ

Isaiah's vision of the Messianic era wherein all shall dwell together in amity.

"And the wolf shall dwell with the lamb, And the leopard shall lie down with the kid . . . And a little child shall lead them" (Isaiah 11.6).

Isaiah prophesied from the year of Uzziah's death (Isaiah 6.1) until the beginning of Manasseh's reign. According to one tradition (Yebamoth 49) he was killed by Manasseh. The sages declared that he was the nephew of King Amaziah (Megillah 10). He was close to the king and the ruling circles of Judah all his life, and was much involved in affairs of state. The Judean kings often sought his opinion and asked for "signs" from him. He gave his sons symbolic names to indicate what lay in store for the people: *Shear-jashub* ("A remnant shall return") and *Maher-shalal-hash-baz* ("The spoil speedeth, the prey hasteth").

Isaiah inveighed against luxuriance (Isaiah 3.18-23), social inequity and pride (2.17), and the levity (chapter 22) which led men to seek military aid from foreign nations (30, 31) rather than depend upon their Creator. Isaiah looked upon Egypt as a "broken reed" and viewed Assyria as God's rod of anger, the means of punishing His people (10.5). The prophet predicted that the arrogant king of Assyria would be punished after he had fulfilled the mission assigned to him (10.12).

Isaiah was the first prophet to declare that idolatry and evil would one day cease to exist (chapter 27) as a result of a reformation on the part of the people. "Zion shall be redeemed with justice, and they that return of her with righteousness" (1.27).

The very order of nature would be changed, the prophet taught. "And the wolf shall dwell with the lamb, and the leopard shall lie down with the kid; . . . They shall not hurt nor destroy in all My holy mountain; for the earth shall be full of the knowledge of the Lord, as the waters cover the sea" (11.6-9). The Temple Mount would become the spiritual center of the world, and a future king from the house of David would be "an ensign for the nations" (11.10). Wise, courageous and God-fearing, he would be sought out by the peoples of the earth and would usher in an era of eternal peace. "Nation shall not lift up sword against nation, neither shall they learn war any more" (2.4). Rabbi Simlai taught that Isaiah reduced all of the commandments of the Torah to six: "He that walketh righteously, and speaketh uprightly; he that despiseth the gain of oppressions, that shaketh his hands from holding of bribes, that stoppeth his ears from hearing of blood, and shutteth his eyes from looking upon evil; he shall dwell on high . . . his bread shall be given, his water shall be sure" (33.15,16). Later, he reduced the commandments to two: "Thus saith the Lord: Keep ye justice, and do righteousness" (56.1).

According to Scripture, Isaiah recorded "the acts of Uzziah" and "the acts of Hezekiah" (2 Chronicles 26.22; 32.32), but it is possible that both references are to chapters 37-39 of the book of Isaiah.

Ben Sira, in the apocryphal Ecclesiasticus, praised the prophet highly. "With strong spirit did he perceive the end of days, comforting the mourners of Zion, revealing the secrets of the coming events before their occurrence" (45.33, 34, according to the edition of M. H. Segal).

The sages declared that Isaiah was "the greatest of (the) prophets" (Yalkut Shimoni, Isaiah, § 385). Like Moses he lived 120 years. He did not intend to comfort only one generation by his prophecies, but all generations. "Israel said to Isaiah: 'Did you mean to comfort only that generation in which the Temple was destroyed?' He answered: 'I meant all generations' " (*ibid.* 445).

The son of Amoz undertook his prophetic role willingly. "Isaiah said: 'I was walking in my study and heard the voice of God saying: ". . . I sent Amos and they called him insulting names (a stammerer) . . . I sent Micah (Micaiah) and they struck him in the face . . . Now whom shall I send and who shall go for us?" Isaiah said: 'Here am I; send me.' God then said to him: 'Isaiah, my children are troublesome and stubborn; are you prepared to be beaten?' . . . Isaiah said: 'Even so I am willing, but I am not worthy to be an emissary to Thy children.' God then said to him: 'You love righteousness—you love to justify My children . . . and you hate to incriminate them . . . I swear that whereas all other prophets receive their messages one from another, as it is written: "The spirit of Elijah rested on Elisha," you alone shall prophesy directly from God' " (Yalkut Shimoni, Isaiah, § 443). According to another tradition, when Isaiah said: "I dwell in the midst of a people of unclean lips," an angel descended at once and struck him on the mouth. The prophet realized his error, accepted God's reproof and advocated Israel's cause.

According to Maimonides, Isaiah received the tradition from Amos and his court.

33. MICAH THE MORASHTITE

מיכה המורשתי

A Roman ploughs amidst the ruins of Jerusalem.

"Therefore shall Zion . . . be plowed as a field, And Jerusalem shall become heaps, And the mountain of the house as the high places of a forest" (Micah 3.12).

Prophesying in the days of Jotham, Ahaz and Hezekiah (Micah 1.1; Jeremiah 26.18,19), Micah spoke out against the social evils of his time, maintaining that they would bring about the nation's downfall. "[They] that build up Zion with blood, and Jerusalem with iniquity . . . yet will they lean upon the Lord, and say: 'Is not the Lord in the midst of us? No evil shall come upon us?' Therefore shall Zion for your sake be plowed as a field, and Jerusalem shall become heaps, and the mountain of the house as the high places of a forest" (Micah 3.10-12; cf. Jeremiah 26.18).

Micah reduced God's commandments to three (Makkoth 23b): "It hath been told thee, O man, what is good, and what the Lord doth require of thee: only to do justly, and to love mercy, and to walk humbly with thy God" (Micah 6.8). The prophet assured his countrymen that the Almighty, because of His oath with the patriarchs, would forgive His people's sins. "Who is a God like unto Thee, that pardoneth the iniquity, and passeth by the transgression of the remnant of His heritage? He retaineth not His anger forever, because He delighteth in mercy" (7.18). In a blessed future era Israel would "feed in Bashan and Gilead, as in the days of old. As in the days of thy coming forth out of the land of Egypt will I show unto him [Israel] marvelous things" (7.14,15).

According to Maimonides, Micah received the tradition from Isaiah and his court.

34. JOEL, SON OF PETHUEL

יואל בן פתואל

The plague of locusts. The Jews sound the shofar and pray.

"Blow the horn in Zion, Sanctify a fast" (Joel 2. 15).
"And I will restore to you the years that the locust hath eaten" (2. 25).

According to the sages, Joel was either the son or descendant of Samuel, and prophesied during the reign of Joram, king of Israel (Numbers Rabbah, Naso, § 10; Yalkut Shimoni, Joel, § 1). Another opinion holds that he lived in the time of Manasseh (Seder Olam Rabbah; Rashi, Megillah 14a).

The locust plague that took place during Joel's lifetime served the prophet as a symbol of the awesome events that would precede the coming of "the day of the Lord" when He would judge all the nations and be "a stronghold" to His people. These events would also cause the people to repent. "And it shall come to pass, that whosoever shall call on the name of the Lord shall be delivered" (Joel 3.5). The repentance God seeks, according to the prophet, lies in the performance of good deeds, and even more important, in the purification of the heart. "Turn ye unto Me with all your heart . . . And rend your heart, and not your garments, and turn unto the Lord your God"

(2.12, 13). From that time on Judah and Jerusalem would be inhabited forever (4.20) and the nations who harmed Israel would in turn be punished.

Those who maintained that Joel prophesied in the days of Manasseh claim that he was the person who admonished that king and the people (2 Chronicles 33.10).

According to Maimonides, Joel received the tradition from Micah.

35. NAHUM
THE ELKOSHITE
נחום
האלקשי

The siege of Nineveh by the Assyrians.

"The burden of Nineveh . . . the vision of Nahum the Elkoshite" (Nahum 1.1).
"Hark! the whip . . . And a multitude of slain . . . And there is no end of the corpses" (3.2-3).

Nahum lived during the reign of Manasseh, according to the sages, and prophesied the destruction of Nineveh. With great artistry and dramatic force he depicted the progress of the siege and capture of the city, and the joy of the Israelites at its destruction, which symbolized the downfall of wickedness. "Woe to the bloody city! It is all full of lies and rapine; the prey departeth not. . . . All that hear the report of thee clap the hands over thee; for upon whom hath not thy wickedness passed continually?" (Nahum 3.1,19).

The location of the prophet's city, Elkosh, is unknown. Some surmise that it is the Elkosh located near Nineveh.

According to Maimonides, Nahum received the tradition from Joel and his court.

36. URIAH,
SON OF SHEMAIAH
אוריהו
בן שמעיהו

Uriah escapes to Egypt pursued by Jewish soldiers.

"When Uriah heard it, he . . . fled . . . into Egypt; and Jehoiakim . . . sent men . . . and they . . . brought him unto . . . the king" (Jer. 26.21-22).

A native of Kiriath-jearim, Uriah prophesied during the reign of Jehoiakim. He foretold the destruction of the city and the country in much the same manner as did Jeremiah. "If ye will not hearken to Me, to walk in My law . . . then will I make this house like Shiloh, and will make this city a curse" (Jeremiah 26.4-6).

Because he aroused the anger of the king and his officers, Uriah fled to Egypt, but he was fetched from there and slain (Jeremiah 26.20-23).

37. HABAKKUK
חבקוק

Amidst the violence of the city a righteous man looks heavenward and survives unscathed.

"Why dost Thou show me iniquity? . . . So that there is strife, and contention ariseth" (Habakkuk 1.3).
"But the righteous shall live by his faith" (2.4).

According to the sages (Seder Olam Rabbah 10), Habakkuk, along with Joel and Nahum, prophesied during the reign of King Manasseh. Because the latter was not a devout monarch, his name was not mentioned together with those of the three prophets (Yalkut Shimoni, Habakkuk). He spoke of the Chaldeans and dealt with the problem of "the righteous who suffer" on a national level. How was it that a wicked kingdom could succeed in dominating the world, the prophet asked. "Wherefore lookest Thou, when they deal treacherously, and holdest Thy peace, when the wicked swalloweth up the man that is more righteous than he?" (Habakkuk 1.13). The answer which the prophet gave in the name of God is that while the wicked do enjoy temporary successes, they will ultimately be destroyed. "Though it tarry, wait for it" (2.3). "Because thou hast spoiled many nations, all the remnant of the peoples shall spoil thee; because of men's blood, and for the violence done to the land, to the city and to all that dwell therein" (2.8).

The prophet predicted that idolatry, along with its resulting wickedness, would ultimately disappear completely from the earth (2.18-20). Some rabbis held that Habakkuk, like Amos, reduced all the commandments of the Torah to one: "The righteous shall live by his faith" (2.4).

According to Maimonides, Habakkuk received the tradition from Joel and his court.

38. ZEPHANIAH

Zephaniah prophesies that the heathens will turn from their idols and seek the light of Zion.

"For then will I turn to the peoples A pure language, That they may all call upon the name of the Lord" (Zeph. 3.9).

Zephaniah was the son of Cushi, the son of Gedaliah, the son of Amariah, the son of Hezekiah (possibly the Hezekiah who was king of Judah, according to Ibn Ezra). Prophesying during the reign of Josiah, Zephaniah fought against the last vestiges of idolatry and against ethical and social depravity. "Her princes in the midst of her are roaring lions; her judges are wolves in the desert" (Zephaniah 3.3). He foresaw that a dreadful fate lay in store for the wicked nations on "the day of the Lord" and he prophesied an end to idolatry. "For then will I turn to the peoples a pure language, that they may all call upon the name of the Lord" (3.9). He saw in the upheavals among the nations the hand of God operating in history (2). The prophet taught that at the "end of days" foreign domination of Israel would cease, and he predicted the return of the remnant of Israel dispersed among the nations. "The remnant of Israel shall not do iniquity, nor speak lies, . . . for they shall feed and lie down, and none shall make them afraid. . . . At that time will I bring you in, and at that time will I gather you; for I will make you to be a name and a praise among all the peoples of the earth" (3.13,20).

The sages taught that Zephaniah was one of the three prominent prophets of his age, the other two being Jeremiah and Huldah. Huldah prophesied to the women, Jeremiah spoke in the market place and Zephaniah prophesied in the synagogues (Yalkut Shimoni, the beginning of Zephaniah).

According to Maimonides, Zephaniah received the tradition from Habakkuk and his court.

39. JEREMIAH

Jeremiah denounces the desecration of the Sabbath.

"Take heed . . . and bear no burden on the sabbath day . . . neither do ye any work; but hallow ye the sabbath day, as I commanded your fathers" (Jer. 17.21-22).

The son of Hilkiah, one of the priests of Anathoth, Jeremiah was apparently a descendant of Abiathar the priest (1 Kings 2.26; cf. Jeremiah (2.8; 11.21; 37.12; 29.27). He began to prophesy while still a child (1.6; 20.7-9) during the thirteenth year of Josiah's reign, and he continued to do so until some time after the exile of the inhabitants of Jerusalem to Egypt. He vigorously opposed the Judean pact with Egypt against Babylon and prophesied that as a result of it the city would be destroyed and the people sent into exile (chapter 21).

Jeremiah fought for the observance of the commandments of the Torah. He bitterly protested the desecration of the Sabbath (17.24 ff.); idolatry (2.7; 7.31 ff.; 15.11,20); false prophecy and venality (6.13; 8.10; 14.14-16); the shedding of innocent blood (22.17 ff.); the enslavement of the people; and Israel's placing its trust in men rather than in God (17.5). He spoke out strongly against all those who took Hebrew slaves and did not free them during the seventh year (34.8). The prophet inveighed against all ritual worship (including prayer) as being devoid of value unless accompanied by spiritual regeneration (14.11-12; 6.19-21). The plight of Israel depended upon its faith in God, Jeremiah maintained. "Cursed is the man that trusteth in man. . . . Blessed is the man that trusteth in the Lord" (17.5-7). He foretold a day when the knowledge of God would spread throughout the nation. "Behold, the days come . . . I will put My law in their inward parts, and in their heart will I write it . . . and they shall teach no more every man his neighbor, and every man his brother, saying: 'Know the Lord'; for they shall all know Me, from the least of them unto the greatest of them" (31.31-34). Jeremiah declared that the people of Israel would endure forever: "Thus saith the

Lord, who giveth the sun for a light by day, and the ordinances of the moon and of the stars for a light by night, who stirreth up the sea, that the waves thereof roar, the Lord of hosts is His name: If these ordinances depart from before Me, saith the Lord, then the seed of Israel also shall cease from being a nation before Me for ever" (31.35-37). Jeremiah foresaw an end to idolatry: "Unto Thee shall the nations come . . . and shall say: 'Our fathers have inherited nought but lies, vanity and things wherein there is no profit'" (16.19, 20). He also declared that Israel's neighbors would one day come to study "the ways of My people to swear by My name: 'As the Lord liveth' . . . then shall they be built up in the midst of My people" (12.16).

The sages declared that Jeremiah was a descendant of Rahab (Yalkut Shimoni, Jeremiah, §253,256) and pointed out many similarities between him and Moses. Like Moses he, too, prophesied to Israel for 40 years; and he, too, was set upon by members of his own tribe and was saved from their hands. His love for Israel was very great. When God said to him "Take this cup of wine of fury . . . and cause all the nations . . . to drink" (Jeremiah 25.15), he asked: "Who shall be first?" When he was told "Israel", the prophet began to curse the day of his birth, declaring that he was like a priest who, as he was about to give bitter waters to a woman suspected of adultery, looked up and saw his own mother. The sages also said that so long as Jeremiah was in Jerusalem it was not destroyed; only when he went to Anathoth to buy a field did an angel descend, breach the wall and allow the enemy to enter the city (Yalkut Shimoni, Jeremiah).

"When Jeremiah saw a group of young men in chains he joined them, but Nebuzaradan came and forced him to leave their company. When he returned he found their fingers and toes strewn about the road; these he gathered into his cloak, fondling and kissing them and weeping over them" (*ibid.*, §327.40).

Still another episode is told of Jeremiah. "When he came to Jerusalem he found a woman dressed in black, her hair disheveled, crying: 'Who will console me?' I approached her and said: 'If you are a woman, speak to me . . . If you are a spirit, depart.' She answered: 'Do you not recognize me? I am she who had seven sons. Their father

left for a distant land, and as I was weeping, someone came to me and said: "The house has fallen on your seven children and has killed them."' I said to her: 'You are no better than Mother Zion.' She replied: 'I am Mother Zion'" (*ibid.*, §293).

The sages taught that Jeremiah wrote not only his own book, but the books of Kings and Lamentations as well (Baba Bathra 15a). According to Maimonides, Jeremiah received the tradition from Zephaniah and his court.

40. EZEKIEL, SON OF BUZI THE PRIEST יחזקאל בן בוזי הכהן

Ezekiel sees a vision of the Temple rebuilt and of Zion restored.

"Like the vision that I saw by the river Chebar . . . a spirit took me up . . . into the inner court; and, behold, the glory of the Lord filled the house" (Ezek. 43.3,5).

Ezekiel went into exile to Babylon with the captivity of Jehoiachin (Ezekiel 33.21; 40.1) and dwelt in Tel-abib on the river Chebar (1.1,13; 3.15). He began to prophesy in the fifth year following the exile, or seven years before the destruction of the Temple, and continued to prophesy until the twenty-seventh year of Jehoiachin's captivity (1.1,2; 29.17). In more vehement terms than his predecessors used, he berated Israel for their transgressions of both the ethical and ritual commandments of the Torah. However, more than any other prophet he stressed the fact that all men are able to repent and that an individual is judged only for his own actions, and not those of his ancestors or descendants.

If Israel would not repent of their own accord, Ezekiel taught, the Almighty would redeem them and make them repent against their will for His name's sake, because they are known as His people. "That which cometh into your mind shall not be at all; in that ye say: We will be as the nations, as the families of the countries, to serve wood and stone. As I live, saith the Lord God, surely with a mighty hand, and with an outstretched arm, and with fury poured out, will I be king over you" (20.32,33; cf. 36.25-29,33; 37.23). God's redemption, however, would be preceded by the purging of transgressors from among the people (20.38). Ezekiel prophesied the reunion of Judah and the Northern Kingdom under a descendant of David in an era of peace and plenty. He also prophesied the rebuilding of the Temple, the restoration of the sacrificial service, and the permanent return of the Divine Presence to Israel (43.7,9). In those days miracles would occur in the vicinity of the Temple: a stream would come forth from the Temple and enter the Dead Sea to purify its waters (47.9-12). Nations from the north (Gog and Magog) would descend upon Israel in great multitudes but would fall on the mountains of Israel, thereby glorifying the name of God.

The sages differed as to whether the prophecy of the resurrection of the dry bones in chapter 37 of Ezekiel was to be interpreted literally or symbolically; and if literally, if it ever was fulfilled.

Some of the sages maintained that Ezekiel first began to prophesy in Israel (Moed Katan 25a).

41. NERIAH   נריה

Neriah witnesses the appointment of his son as scribe to Jeremiah.

"Then Jeremiah called Baruch the son of Neriah" (Jer. 36.4).

Neriah was the father of Baruch and one of the eight prophets descended from Rahab (Megillah 14b).

42. BARUCH, SON OF NERIAH   ברוך בן נריה

Baruch inscribes Jeremiah's words on a scroll.

"And Baruch wrote from the mouth of Jeremiah all the words of the Lord, which He had spoken unto him" (Jer. 36.4).

The scribe and pupil of Jeremiah, Baruch "wrote from the mouth of Jeremiah all the words of the Lord, which He had spoken unto him, upon a roll of a book" (Jeremiah 36.4). The

sages declared that together with Seraiah the son of Mahseiah, Daniel, Mordecai Bilshan, Haggai, Zechariah and Malachi, Baruch prophesied in the second year of Darius' reign (Megillah 15).

According to Maimonides, Baruch received the tradition from Jeremiah.

43. SERAIAH, SON OF NERIAH, SON OF MAHSEIAH   שריה בן מחסיה

The prophet throws a scroll, weighted with a stone, into the river.

"And Jeremiah said to Seraiah: 'When thou comest to Babylon . . . read . . . this book . . . and cast it into the midst of the Euphrates; and . . . say: Thus shall Babylon sink" (Jer. 51.61-64).

According to the sages, a prophet's disciple is also a prophet (Rashi, Megillah 15), and such was Seraiah, of whom Scripture says: "The word which Jeremiah the prophet commanded Seraiah the son of Neriah, the son of Mahseiah" (Jeremiah 51.59). The rabbis taught that Seraiah prophesied in the second year of Darius' reign, Megillah 15).

44. MAHSEIAH   מחסיה

Jeremiah, in prison during the siege of Jerusalem and confident of God's ultimate redemption of Israel, purchases a field.

"And I delivered the deed of the purchase unto Baruch the son of Neriah, the son of Mahseiah , . . before all the Jews" (Jer. 32.12).

Mahseiah was the father of Neriah and grandfather of Baruch, the scribe of Jeremiah (Jeremiah 32.12).

45. HAGGAI   חגי

Haggai reproves the people for living in costly houses while the Temple lies in runs.

"The word of the Lord by Haggai the prophet, saying: 'Is it a time for you yourselves to dwell in your ceiled houses, while this house lieth waste?'" (Haggai 1.3-4).

Haggai prophesied in the second year of the

reign of Darius (Haggai 1.1) and urged Zerubbabel, Joshua the son of Jehozadak and the rest of the people to rebuild the Temple, which lay in ruins. His words were effective, and the Temple was completed in the sixth year of Darius' reign (Ezra 5.1,2; 6.14). Haggai prophesied that "The glory of this latter house shall be greater than that of the former" (2.9), a prophecy which was fully realized at a later date.

According to Maimonides, Haggai received the tradition from Baruch the son of Neriah.

46. ZECHARIAH, SON OF BERECHIAH, SON OF IDDO

זכריה
בן ברכיהו
בן עדו

Ten heathens plead with a Jew to take them with him upon his return to Zion.

"In those days . . . ten men . . . of . . . the nations, shall even take hold of the skirt of . . . a Jew, saying: We will go with you" (Zech. 8.23).

Zechariah began to prophesy in the month of Kislev, during the second year of Darius' reign. Like Haggai, he too urged the Jews who had returned to Zion to complete the rebuilding of the Temple (Ezra 5.1; 6.14). He prophesied the ingathering of the exiles, Israel's liberation from foreign bondage (5.10-13) and the return of the Divine Presence. "Thus saith the Lord: I return unto Zion, and will dwell in the midst of Jerusalem; and Jerusalem shall be called The city of truth; and the mountain of the Lord of hosts The holy mountain" (Zechariah 8.3). He also declared that belief in God would spread throughout the nations and that idolatry would cease. "In those days it shall come to pass, that ten men shall . . . take hold of the skirt of him that is a Jew, saying: We will go with you, for we have heard that God is with you" (8.23). However, such happenings would have to be preceded by whole-hearted repentence on the people's part. "These are the things that ye shall do: Speak ye every man the truth with his neighbor; execute the judgment of truth and peace in your gates; and let none of you devise evil in your hearts

against his neighbor; and love no false oath" (8.16,17). Zechariah was unique among the prophets in that his visions were always interpreted to him by an angel.

According to Maimonides, Zechariah received the tradition from Baruch, son of Neriah, and his court.

47. MALACHI

מלאכי

Elijah will herald the advent of the day of the Lord and the dawn of the Messianic period.

"Behold, I will send you Elijah the prophet Before the coming Of the great and terrible day of the Lord" (Mal. 3.23).

The sages taught that Malachi was the last of the prophets and was none other than Ezra the scribe (Megillah 15a; Targum Jonathan, Malachi 1.1), the name *Malachi* ("My messenger") merely designating its bearer as a prophet of God.

Malachi dwelled mostly upon two points. First, he attacked the priests for desecrating the altar by not taking seriously both their responsibilities and the holiness of the work in which they were engaged. He pointed to Aaron as an example of the faithful priest. "The law of truth was in his mouth, and unrighteousness was not found in his lips; he walked with Me in peace and uprightness, and did turn many away from iniquity" (Malachi 2.6). Secondly, the prophet inveighed against intermarriage with foreign women and stressed the sanctity of marital bonds: "Because the Lord hath been witness between thee and the wife of thy youth . . . she is thy companion, and the wife of thy covenant. . . . Therefore take heed to your spirit, and let none deal treacherously against the wife of his youth" (2.14,15). The prophet is perhaps best known by the admonition with which he concludes his book: "Remember ye the law of Moses My servant, which I commanded unto him in Horeb for all Israel, even statutes and ordinances" (3.22).

Malachi also foretold the coming of Elijah. "Behold, I will send you Elijah the prophet before the coming of the great and terrible day of the

Lord. And he shall turn the heart of the fathers to the children, and the heart of the children to their fathers" (3.23,24).

According to Maimonides, Malachi received the tradition from Baruch, son of Neriah, and his court.

48. MORDECAI מרדכי

The Sanhedrin with Mordecai at its head.

"For Mordecai the Jew was next unto king Ahasuerus, and great among the Jews, and accepted of the multitude of his brethren" (Esther 10.3).

Mordecai was a descendant of Kish, a Benjaminite, who had been taken into exile along with Jeconiah, king of Judah (Esther 2.5). He lived in Shushan and reared Esther, his cousin, the daughter of Abihail. Because he frequented the courtyard of the royal palace, Mordecai overheard a plot to kill the king and by reporting it saved the latter's life. Haman, out of hatred for the obstinate Jew who would not kneel or bow down to him, obtained royal permission to destroy all the Jews. However, with Esther's help, Mordecai was able to thwart Haman's schemes and bring retribution upon the enemies of Israel. Mordecai was then appointed by Ahasuerus to be viceroy of the realm in Haman's stead (10.3).

The sages identified Mordecai with Mordecai Bilshan, who is mentioned in Scripture as one of the Jews who returned to Judah from Babylonia in the days of Zerubbabel (Ezra 2.2; Nehemiah 7.7), and held that he, together with Haggai, Zechariah and Malachi, prophesied in the second year of Darius' reign (Megillah 15a). Mordecai was a member of the Sanhedrin, knew 70 languages (Shekalim 5.2; Menahot 64b, 65a), and taught the Torah to many pupils.

According to Maimonides, Mordecai received the tradition from Baruch, son of Neriah, and his court.

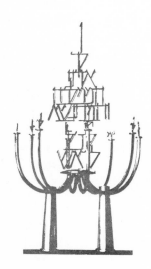

A woman with scroll in hand looks toward heaven and prophesies.

"And she said unto them: 'Thus saith the Lord, the God of Israel"
(II. Kings 22.15)

THE PROPHETESSES

The roster of prophetesses of Israel reveals that the Jewish woman had occupied a position of prominence even in the period of earliest Biblical antiquity. Distinguished indeed, was her contribution in the shaping of the national and ethical character of the Jew through her constant strengthening of his will to triumphant achievement in times of crisis. "Because of the merit of the righteous women who lived in that generation were the Israelites redeemed from Egypt". (Sotah 11b).

Imperishable ideas and values rooted in religion, statehood and the destiny of the Jewish people, rose to exalted expression in the songs of Deborah and Hannah.

It is appropriate to note, that in addition to the seven prophetesses who prophesied in Israel, we find too, the figures of other wise and discerning women who discoursed with prophets and who assumed significant roles in the social and political life of the people. To cite but a few, we name the daughters of Zelophehad; the wife of Manoah, who was the mother of Samson; the woman from Tekoa; the Shunammite woman and Elisha; the wife of Jeroboam, and Ahijah; Bath-sheba, the mother of Solomon; Jehoshabeath, the wife of Jehoiada the High Priest; and others.

In addition therefore, to the forty eight prophets enumerated above, there arose also the seven prophetesses in Israel whose activities and prophecies are described herein.

THE SEVEN PROPHETESSES

1. SARAH   שרה (יסכה)

Hagar and her son Ishmael leave Abraham's tent upon Sarah's demand.

"And God said unto Abraham: '. . . in all that Sarah saith unto thee, hearken unto her voice'" (Gen. 21.12).

In Scripture it is written: "Haran, the father of Milcah, and the father of Iscah" (Genesis 11.29). "Rabbi Isaac said: 'Iscah is Sarah. And why is she called Iscah? Because she perceived (*sakhtah*) by the Divine Spirit, as it is written: "And God said unto Abraham . . . all that Sarah saith unto thee, hearken unto her voice" (Genesis 21.12)'" (Megillah 14a).

2. MIRIAM   מרים

The prophetess leads the women in dance and song after the crossing of the Red Sea.

"And Miriam the prophetess, the sister of Aaron, took a timbrel in her hand; and all the women went out after her with timbrels and with dances" (Exod. 15.20).

Scripture explicitly refers to Miriam as a prophetess. "And Miriam the prophetess . . . took a timbrel" (Exodus 15.20). Another allusion to her prophetic role is found in the book of Numbers. Criticizing Moses for having married a Cushite woman, Miriam said: "Hath the Lord indeed spoken only with Moses? hath He not spoken also with us?" (Numbers 12.2). According to the sages, Miriam began to prophesy in Egypt, before the birth of Moses, when she said: "My mother shall give birth to a son who will save Israel." When Moses was born, the room was filled with light and her father kissed her forehead

and said: "My daughter, your prophecy has been fulfilled." However, when Moses was cast into the Nile, Amram struck Miriam and said: "Where is your prophecy now?" This is the meaning of the phrase "His sister stood at a distance to learn"—to learn what would become of her prophecy (Megillah 14a).

3. DEBORAH   דבורה

Deborah sings of the death of Sisera and the defeat of his army.

"As Barak pursued Sisera, Jael came out . . . and said . . . 'Come, and I will show thee the man whom thou seekest.' . . . and behold, Sisera lay dead" (Judg. 4.22). *"Then sang Deborah"* (5.1).

Scripture refers to Deborah as "a prophetess, the wife of Lapidoth." "What is the meaning of 'wife of Lapidoth'?—that she prepared wicks for the Temple, while sitting beneath a palm tree. What is the meaning of 'beneath a palm tree'?— just as the palm tree has no heart [no central core], so Israel at that time had a strange heart [turned away from God]" (Megillah 14a).

4. HANNAH   חנה

Hannah prays holding her son Samuel.

"For this child I (Hannah) prayed; and the Lord hath granted me my petition . . . therefore I also have lent him to the Lord" (I. Sam. 1.27-28).

"In Scripture it is written: 'And Hannah prayed, and said: My heart exulteth in the Lord, my horn is exalted in the Lord' (1 Samuel 2.1). 'My *horn* is exalted' and not 'my *pitcher* is exalted'. This means that the dynasties of David and Solomon, who were anointed with oil from a horn, would be prolonged, while the dynasties of Saul and Jehu, who were anointed with oil from a pitcher, would not be prolonged" (Megillah 14a).

Hannah's entire prayer is interpreted as a prophecy referring to Sennacherib, Nebuchadnezzar and Haman (Yalkut Shimoni, Samuel).

5. ABIGAIL אביגיל

Riding a donkey, Abigail brings abundant food to David and his troops.

"Then Abigail made haste, and took two hundred loaves . . . And . . . as she rode . . . by the covert of the mountain . . . David and his men came down towards her" (I. Sam. 25.18-20).

Scripture records that Abigail prophesied to David: "The Lord will certainly make my lord a sure house . . . and it shall come to pass, when the Lord shall have done to my lord according to all the good that He hath spoken concerning thee, and shall have appointed thee prince over Israel . . ." (1 Samuel 25.28-31).

6. HULDAH חולדה

Huldah tells the women of the Torah scroll found by Hilkiah and held by King Josiah.

"Huldah the prophetess, the wife of Shallum . . . said . . . 'Thus saith the Lord: Behold, I will bring evil upon this place'" (II. Kings 22.14-16).

The wife of Shallum, son of Tikvah, son of Harhas, keeper of the royal wardrobe, Huldah lived near the courts of learning in Jerusalem during the reign of Josiah (2 Kings 22.14). When "the book of the Law" was found and read before the king (according to the rabbis, the portion read was that of the admonitions and curses in Deuteronomy), he sent for Huldah to inquire about the book. She told the king that God had decreed to punish the people because of the sins of earlier generations, but because Josiah had repented, the punishment would not come upon him. "Neither shall thine eyes see all the evil which I will bring upon this place" (2 Kings 22.20).

The sages declared that Huldah was one of the three prophets of that generation, the other two being Zephaniah and Jeremiah, and that she prophesied to the women (Yalkut Shimoni, the beginning of Zephaniah). Also, according to the rabbis, she was one of nine prophets descended from Rahab and Joshua (Megillah 14b).

7. ESTHER אסתר

King Ahasuerus extends his golden scepter to Esther.

"When the king saw Esther the queen standing in the court . . . the king held out to Esther the golden sceptre that was in his hand" (Esther 5.2).

The rabbis regarded Esther as a prophetess because Scripture says of her: "Esther put on her royal apparel" (Esther 5.1). This is to be interpreted to mean that she was clothed with the Divine spirit, as it is written: "Then the spirit clothed Amasai" (1 Chronicles 12.19; Megillah 14b).

THE SEVENTY-SIX PROPHETS

ACCORDING TO ELIJAH THE GAON OF VILNA

A. THE SEVEN PROPHETS PRIOR TO ISRAEL'S DESCENT INTO EGYPT

1. ADAM (*See Genesis 3.8 ff.*)
2. NOAH (*See Genesis 6-9*)
3. JAPHETH
4. SHEM

That Shem was a prophet may be deduced from the verse: "Blessed be the Lord, the God of Shem. . . . God enlarge Japheth, and he shall dwell in the tents of Shem" (Genesis 9.26,27).

5. EBER
That Eber was a prophet may be deduced from the verse: "And unto Shem, the father of all the children of Eber . . . to him also were children born" (Genesis 10.21). Sforno, a commentator on the Pentateuch, explained this to mean that Shem had a child, namely Eber, who was endowed with the same prophetic powers as he was.

6. ABRAHAM (*See Rashi's list*)
7. ISAAC (*See Rashi's list*)

B. THE SEVEN PROPHETS IN EGYPT

1. JACOB (*See Rashi's list*)
2. MOSES (*See Rashi's list*)
3. ZIMRI, SON OF ZERAH
4. ETHAN, SON OF ZERAH
5. HEMAN, SON OF ZERAH
6. CALCOL, SON OF ZERAH
7. DARA, SON OF ZERAH

"For he [Solomon] was wiser than all men: than Ethan the Ezrahite, and Heman, and Calcol, and Darda, the sons of Mahol" (1 Kings 5.11). According to Seder Olam, all these men prophesied in Egypt.

C. THE SEVEN HEATHEN PROPHETS

"Rabbi Isaac said: 'Until the Tabernacle was erected there was prophecy among the heathen; when the Tabernacle was erected, phophecy ceased among them. Yet did not Balaam the son of Beor prophesy? Yes, but only because he prophesied good for Israel'" (Song of Songs Rabbah 2.13).

1. BEOR
The father of Balaam (Numbers 22.5), he was considered a prophet in accordance with the rabbinic rule that wherever the name of a prophet's father is mentioned, both father and son are prophets.

2. BALAAM
According to the sages, Balaam was superior to Moses in three respects: "Moses did not know who spoke to him, while Balaam did; Moses did not know beforehand when he would be spoken to while Balaam knew; and God did not speak to Moses unless he was standing, while Balaam was addressed even when he was lying down" (Sifre, Deuteronomy, §357).

However, Balaam had some bad traits: "An evil eye, a haughty spirit and excessive pride" (Aboth 5.9). He always sought ways to annihilate the people of Israel. At first, together with Jethro and Job he planned to destroy Israel with the aid of Pharaoh (Sanhedrin 106). Then he tried to dissuade the Israelites from listening to the Hebrew prophets, who admonished them for their transgressions. Balaam did his best to make Israel break faith with the Lord and sought to destroy the entire people by having them commit harlotry (Numbers 31.16). Because of Balaam's actions, the rabbis declared, God took the power of prophecy away from the heathens (Numbers Rabbah 2.1).

3. JOB
The sages maintained that Job lived either during Jacob's lifetime or at the time of the

exodus from Egypt (Baba Bathra 15; and other views are also recorded). According to one tradition his wife was Dinah the daughter of Jacob (Genesis Rabbah 57). The sages differed as to whether Job served God out of fear or out of love. The majority felt that he did serve out of love (Tosefta Sotah 7.1; Babylonian Talmud, Sotah 27b). Some even declared that Scripture speaks more highly of Job than of Abraham (Baba Bathra 15b), and that had he not spoken ill of God he would have been worthy of having his name recorded together with the patriarchs (Pesikta Rabbati 37). He was punished, some sages maintained, because he, together with Balaam, was a counselor of Pharaoh and when Balaam advised Pharaoh to cast the Hebrew children into the Nile, he did not demur (Sotah 11; Sanhedrin 106).

4. ELIPHAZ

Eliphaz was Job's friend from Teman (Job 2.11). In the fourth chapter of the book of Job, Eliphaz speaks of the prophetic vision which came upon him. "Now a word was secretly brought to me, and mine ear received a whisper thereof. In thoughts from the visions of the night, when deep sleep falleth on men, fear came upon me, and trembling, and all my bones were made to shake. Then a spirit passed before my face, that made the hair of my flesh to stand up. . . . A form was before mine eyes; I heard a still voice" (Job 4.12-16).

5. BILDAD THE SHUHITE

6. ZOPHAR THE NAAMATHITE

7. ELIHU

The son of Barachel the Buzite, Elihu was the youngest of Job's four friends (Job 32.2). He declared that a Divine revelation came upon him while he was sleeping. "For God speaketh in one way, yea in two, though man perceiveth it not. In a dream, in a vision of the night, when deep sleep falleth upon men, in slumberings upon the bed" (Job 33.14-15). The rabbis deduced from this verse, as well as from others (Genesis 31.24; Numbers 22.8, 20), that "the heathen prophets were spoken to only at night time" (Numbers Rabbah 20.9; Genesis Rabbah 52; Leviticus Rabbah 1).

D. THE FORTY-EIGHT PROPHETS WHO AROSE AFTER ISRAEL'S ENTRY INTO CANAAN

1. JOSHUA, SON OF NUN *(See Rashi's list)*
2. PHINEHAS, SON OF ELEAZAR *(See Rashi's list)*
3. ELKANAH *(See Rashi's list)*
4. DAVID *(See Rashi's list)*
5. SAMUEL, SON OF ELKANAH *(See Rashi's list)*

6.-8. THE SONS OF KORAH: ASSIR, ELKANAH, AND ABIASAPH

A number of psalms in Scripture bear the names of the sons of Korah, these being Psalms 42, 44-49, 84, 85, 87, and 88. The descendants of these three men included the prophet Samuel and Heman, the Temple singer.

Some of Korah's descendants kept the gates of the Temple (1 Chronicles 9.19; 26.19) or prepared the shew-bread (9.31,32). The sages, however, maintained that the term "the sons of Korah" (*bnei Korah*) always refers to Korah's own sons, Assir, Elkanah and Abiasaph (Exodus 6.24; Yalkut Shimoni, Psalms, § 44), who prophesied in the desert (Seder Olam). In the psalms which they wrote, however, they prophesied about the generations that came after the exodus from Egypt. Scripture says of them: "The sons of Korah died not" (Numbers 26.11; Yalkut Shimoni, Psalms, § 753).

9. GAD THE SEER *(See Rashi's list)*

10. NATHAN THE PROPHET *(See Rashi's list)*

11. ASAPH THE LEVITE

Asaph the seer (2 Chronicles 29.30), "who prophesied according to the direction of the king" (1 Chronicles 25.2), was the son of Berechiah of the family of Gershon of the tribe of Levi (1 Chronicles 6.47,56). When the ark was brought from the house of Obed-edom of Gath to Jerusalem, he, together with Ethan and Heman, sounded the brass cymbals (1 Chronicles 15.16-19). Later he was put in charge of all who played the cymbals during the Temple service (16.4, 5, 7). When David assigned various Levites certain functions in the Temple service, Asaph, Heman and Jeduthun were chosen to be permanent players in the Temple, and they retained their positions under Solomon (1 Chronicles 25.1-9; 2 Chronicles 5.12).

Twelve psalms in Scripture bear the name of Asaph (Psalms 73-83; and cf. 2 Chronicles 29.30).

The descendants of Asaph carried out the same duties in the Second Temple as they did in the First (Ezra 2.70; Nehemiah 7.73). They were also among the first exiles to return to Judah from Babylon in the days of Zerubbabel (Ezra 3.10).

12. HEMAN THE LEVITE

Heman the Levite was also known as "the king's [David's] seer" (1 Chronicles 25.5). The sons and grandsons of Heman, together with the male offspring of Asaph and Jeduthun, prophesied "with harps, with psalteries, and with cymbals" (25.1) in the Temple in Jerusalem. Heman was the son of Joel, son of Samuel the prophet, and so a descendant of Korah (15.17). Together with Asaph he sounded the cymbals before the ark (15.16-19). Later he was included among the singers of the tribe of Levi who were to minister daily before God (1 Chronicles 16.41, 42; 2 Chronicles 5.12).

13. ETHAN THE LEVITE

14. JEDUTHUN THE LEVITE

Jeduthun, like Heman, was also known as "the kings [David's] seer" (2 Chronicles 35.15). He, his sons and grandsons, together with Asaph and Heman and their progeny, ministered "before the ark continually" in the tent set up by David (1 Chronicles 16.37-42), and later prophesied "with harps, with psalteries, and with cymbals" during the service in the Temple (1 Chronicles 25.1-6). The descendants of these men continued in their fathers' roles in both the First and Second Temples (2 Chronicles 5.12; 35.16; Nehemiah 11.17).

Three psalms are attributed to Jeduthun: Psalms 39, 62, and 77.

Jeduthun was also known as Ethan, the son of Kushaiah (1 Chronicles 15.17, 19; cf. 16.38-41 and 25.1). The Gaon of Vilna, however, in his commentary to Seder Olam, regarded Ethan and Jeduthun as two distinct persons.

15. AHIJAH THE SHILONITE (*see Rashi's list*)

16. SHEMAIAH (*See Rashi's list*)

17. IDDO (*See Rashi's list*)

18. AZARIAH, SON OF ODED (*See Rashi's list*)

19. HANANI THE SEER (*See Rashi's list*)

20. JEHU, SON OF HANANI (*See Rashi's list*)

21. MICAIAH, SON OF IMLAH (*See Rashi's list*)

22. JAHAZIEL, SON OF ZECHARIAH (*See Rashi's list*)

23. ELIEZER, SON OF DODAVAHU (*See Rashi's list*)

24. ELIJAH THE TISHBITE (*See Rashi's list*)

25. ELISHA, SON OF SHAPHAT (*See Rashi's list*)

26. JONAH, SON OF AMITTAI (*See Rashi's list*)

27. OBADIAH (*See Rashi's list*)

28. ZECHARIAH, SON OF JEHOIADA

Zechariah admonished the people for breaking God's commandments. " '. . . because ye have forsaken the Lord, He hath also forsaken you.' And they conspired against him, and stoned him with stones at the commandment of the king [Joash] in the . . . house of the Lord" (2 Chronicles 24.20, 21). The author of Chronicles adds that Joash's own servants later murdered the king to revenge the killing of the prophet (2 Chronicles 24.25). The sages related that the blood of the dead prophet boiled with increasing vigor until the coming of Nebuzaradan, and was not quiet until Nebuzaradan had killed many school children and threatened to kill still more if the prophet's blood would not be still (Gittin 57a; Sanhedrin 96). It was in reference to that event that the author of Lamentations wrote: "Shall the priest and the prophet be slain in the sanctuary of the Lord?" (2.20).

According to Maimonides, Zechariah received the tradition from Jehoiada and his court.

29. AMOS, THE BROTHER OF KING AMAZIAH (*See Rashi's list*)

30. ODED (*See Rashi's list*)

31. HOSEA, SON OF BEERI (*See Rashi's list*)

32. AMOZ (*See Rashi's list*)

33. ISAIAH (*See Rashi's list*)

34. MICAH OF MORESHETH (*See Rashi's list*)

35. JOEL, SON OF PETHUEL (*See Rashi's list*)

36. NAHUM THE ELKOSHITE (*See Rashi's list*)
37. HABAKKUK (*See Rashi's list*)
38. ZEPHANIAH, SON OF CUSHI (*See Rashi's list*)
39. JEREMIAH, SON OF HILKIAH (*See Rashi's List*)
40. URIAH, SON OF SHEMAIAH OF KIR— YATH-JEARIM (*See Rashi's list*)
41. EZEKIEL, SON OF BUZI (*See Rashi's List*)
42. BARUCH, SON OF NERIAH (*See Rashi's list*)
43. SERAIAH SON OF MAHSEIAH (*See Rashi's list*)
44. DANIEL

Of royal lineage, Daniel was among those Judeans who went into exile with King Jehoiakim (Daniel 1.1; 3.7). In Babylon he and his three companions, Hananiah, Mishael, and Azariah, were chosen to serve Nebuchadnezzar. All four Hebrews took great care not to defile themselves by eating the king's food or drinking his wine (1.8).

The four youths excelled in their Chaldean studies. Daniel was brought before the king and interpreted the latter's dream, which had baffled all the wise men of the realm (chapter 2). As a reward he was made ruler of the entire province of Babylon and the "chief prefect over all the wise men of Babylon" (2.48). Later, he interpreted a second dream for Nebuchadnezzar and told the king that he would be transformed into a beast (chapter 4). In the days of Belshazzar, the last king of Babylon, Daniel read and interpreted the four words written on the palace wall: "Mene Mene, Tekel Upharsin" (5.25). At the instiga-tion of his courtiers, Darius cast the prophet into a lion's den, but the latter emerged unharmed (chapter 6). According to the book that bears his name, Daniel had many apocalyptic visions about Greece. According to many Jewish commentaries (written after the death of Isaac Abarbanel), they referred to Antiochus Epiphanes, the king who set up a graven image in the Temple. Unlike the prophets who preceded him, Daniel had visions of various beasts, and the meaning of each vision was explained to him by the angel Gabriel, who stood at his side. Later generations drew heavily upon the book of Daniel in attempting to determine precisely when the messiah would come. Daniel was also the first prophet to state explicitly that the dead would ultimately be resurrected (12.1-3).

According to Maimonides, Daniel was the disciple of Baruch, son of Neriah, and his court.

45. MORDECAI, SON OF JAIR (*See Rashi's list*)
46. HAGGAI (*See Rashi's list*)
47. ZECHARIAH, SON OF BERECHIAH (*See Rashi's list*)
48. MALACHI (*See Rashi's list*)

E. THE SEVEN PROPHETESSES

1. SARAH (*Iscah*) (*See Rashi's list*)
2. MIRIAM (*See Rashi's list*)
3. DEBORAH (*See Rashi's list*)
4. HANNAH (*See Rashi's list*)
5. ABIGAIL (*See Rashi's list*)
6. HULDAH (*See Rashi's list*)
7. ESTHER, DAUGHTER OF ABIHAIL (*See Rashi's list*)

THE PRIESTHOOD

While the children of Israel were charged to be "a kingdom of priests and a holy nation," it was the duty of the *Kohanim* ("priests"), the descendants of Aaron and his priestly sons to offer up all sacrifices and carry out various ritual tasks, first in the Tabernacle (in the desert and Canaan), and then in the Temple in Jerusalem. The priests were also obligated to instruct the people in God's commandments and concern themselves with the latter's health, physical welfare and moral well-being. The office of the High Priesthood entailed the observance of special rules concerning ritual purity and defilement, cleanliness, pedigree and prohibited marriages.

The priestly duties and the order of the service were outlined in the Pentateuch and then further organized in the *mishmaroth* ("watches") set up by David and Solomon for the service of the Temple.

Although the priests occupied a dignified and highly honored office, the rabbis looked upon them as emissaries of the people. During the First Temple period, when kings ruled the land, the priests' activities were limited mainly to the Temple service. However, during the era of the Second Temple, the priests were also the temporal rulers of the state, and exerted a very significant influence on the development of the Jewish people and its religion.

Today, in the absence of the Temple, and with the laws of the State of Israel being promulgated by a secular authority, the priesthood is almost purely a nominal office. However, the priests have retained some rights and duties in Jewish tradition. Thus, they are the first to be called to the Torah when it is read in the synagogue; they take part in the ceremony of the redemption of the first-born; they observe the laws of ritual purity by not coming near dead bodies and are enjoined from marrying divorced women. The *Kohanim* are also charged with pronouncing the priestly blessing; this is one of the impressive features of the synagogue service, expressing what is in our time, perhaps the primary function of the priest: to transmit the traditional divine benediction to the people of Israel.

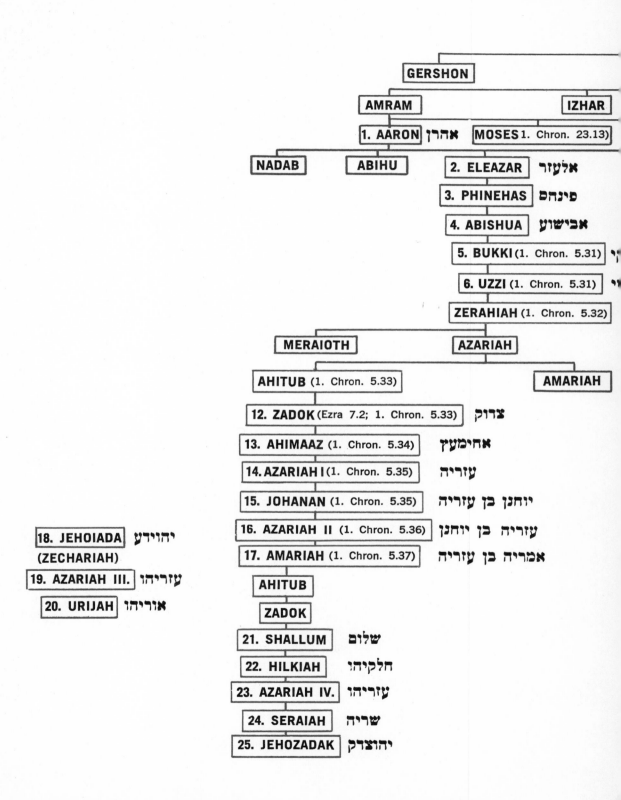

THE HIGH PRIESTS

FROM AARON UNTIL THE D

GERSHON

AMRAM — IZHAR

1. AARON אהרן — MOSES 1. Chron. 23.13)

NADAB — ABIHU — 2. ELEAZAR אלעזר

3. PHINEHAS פינחס

4. ABISHUA אבישוע

5. BUKKI (1. Chron. 5.31)

6. UZZI (1. Chron. 5.31)

ZERAHIAH (1. Chron. 5.32)

MERAIOTH — AZARIAH

AHITUB (1. Chron. 5.33) — AMARIAH

12. ZADOK (Ezra 7.2; 1. Chron. 5.33) צדוק

13. AHIMAAZ (1. Chron. 5.34) אחימעץ

14. AZARIAH I (1. Chron. 5.35) עזריה

15. JOHANAN (1. Chron. 5.35) יוחנן בן עזריה

16. AZARIAH II (1. Chron. 5.36) עזריה בן יוחנן

17. AMARIAH (1. Chron. 5.37) אמריה בן עזריה

18. JEHOIADA יהוידע
(ZECHARIAH)

19. AZARIAH III. עזריהו

20. URIJAH אוריהו

AHITUB

ZADOK

21. SHALLUM שלום

22. HILKIAH חלקיהו

23. AZARIAH IV. עזריהו

24. SERAIAH שריה

25. JEHOZADAK יהוצדק

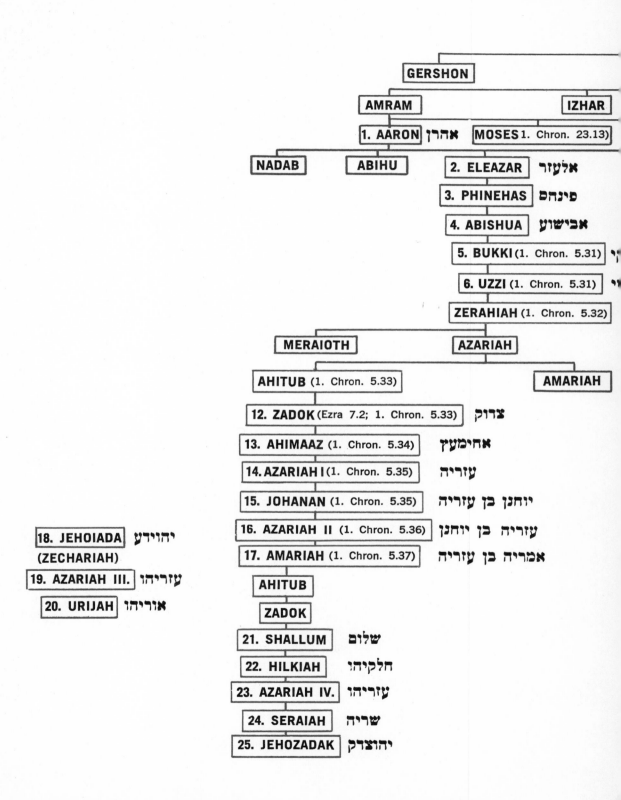

THE HIGH PRIESTS

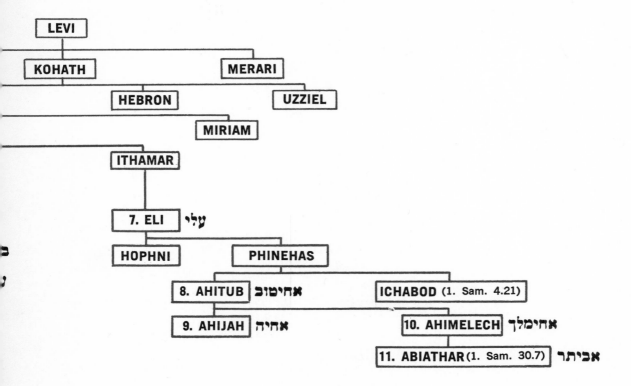

THE HIGH PRIESTS ARE IDENTIFIED BY A NUMBER

SEDER OLAM ZUTA RECORDS THE FOLLOWING HIGH PRIESTS OF THE FIRST TEMPLE ERA

Reigning King	High Priest
Solomon	12. Zadok
Rehoboam	13. Ahimaaz
Abihu	Abiathar
Jehoshaphat	Jehoahaz
Joram	Jehoiarib
Ahaziah	Jehoshaphat
Joash	18. Jehoiada and Pedaiah
Amaziah	Zedekiah
Uzziah	Joel
Ahaz	20. Urijah
Hezekiah	Neriah
Manasseh	Hoshea
Amon	21. Shallum
Josiah	22. Hilkiah
Jehoiakim	23. Azariah
Jehoiachin	24. Seraiah
Zedekiah	25. Jehozadak

In 2 Chronicles 26.17 there is mention of 19. Azariah

THE FOLLOWING IS AN HEREDITARY LIST OF THE HIGH PRIESTHOOD *(arranged by A. Shalit)*
According to Josephus

12. Zadok	Joel
13. Ahimaaz	Jotham
14. Azariah	Urijah
Joram	Neriah
15. Johanan (?)	Udiah
Axioramus	21. Shallum
Phideas	22. Hilkiah
(or Phiduis) (?)	23, (?) Hezir
Dodai	25. Jehozadak

THE HIGH PRIESTS

FROM AARON UNTIL THE DESTRUCTION OF THE FIRST TEMPLE

1. AARON אהרן

The elder brother of Moses, Aaron was the first High Priest. The Tabernacle was erected during his lifetime. Aaron died before the children of Israel crossed the Jordan and was buried upon Mount Hor.

2. ELEAZAR אלעזר

The third son of Aaron, Eleazar was anointed High Priest after the deaths of his brothers Nadab and Abihu. He served as High Priest under Moses and Joshua and participated in the conquest of Canaan. Eleazar was buried in Mount Ephraim in the hill of Phinehas, his son (Numbers 20.25 ff.: Joshua 24.33).

3. PHINEHAS פינחם

Phinehas turned away God's wrath from the children of Israel by his display of religious zeal in killing Zimri, son of Salu, and Cozbi, daughter of Zur, a Midianite woman (Numbers 25.7 ff.). Moses sent Phinehas and an armed force to battle the Midianites, taking with him "the holy vessels and the trumpets for alarm" (Numbers 31.6). Together with ten princes of the tribes of Israel, he went to Gilead to admonish the members of the tribes of Reuben, Gad and Manasseh for having erected an altar on the border (Joshua 22).

4. ABISHUA אבישוע

Abishua was the first High Priest to be anointed in the land of Canaan (1 Chronicles 5.30-31; 6.35; Ezra 7.5). He is known in Samaritan literature as Abisha, and to him is ascribed an abbreviated Torah preserved by the Samaritans in Shechem. He wrote the Torah scroll, according to their tradition, thirteen years after the Israelites had come to Canaan.

5. BUKKI בקי

The great-grandson of Aaron, Bukki was the second High Priest to be anointed in Canaan (Ezra 7.3; 1 Chronicles 5.31).

6. UZZI עזי

According to tradition, Uzzi was the last of the High Priests of the line of Phinehas to serve in the Tabernacle. The office was transferred to the family of Ithamar and was not restored to the family of Phinehas until the reign of King Solomon, when Zadok was anointed High Priest. Uzzi is mentioned in the books of Ezra (7.4) and 1 Chronicles (5.31-32).

7. ELI עלי

The first member of the family of Ithamar to serve as a High Priest, Eli officiated in the Tabernacle at Shiloh. Samuel the seer was born during his lifetime. In addition to being a High Priest, Eli also served as a judge. His sons, unfortunately, did not emulate their father. Eli judged Israel for 40 years (1 Samuel 4.18). When he heard that the ark of the Lord had been captured by the Philistines in the battle of Aphek, he fell from his chair and died (1 Samuel 4.18).

8. AHITUB אחיטוב

Son of Phinehas, grandson of Eli, brother of Ichabod and father of Ahimelech, who ministered during the reign of King Saul (1 Samuel 14.3; 22.9, 11-12, 20). Some scholars are of the opinion that he escaped from the destruction of Shiloh, settled in Nob and ministered there as a priest during the lifetime of Samuel the seer; and that it was he who established Nob as a city of priests.

165

9. AHIJAH אחיה

The son of Ahitub, Ahijah apparently was High Priest during the reign of Saul. He is mentioned as having taken part in the wars of Michmas, in which he wore the ephod in the camp of Saul (1 Samuel 14.3).

10. AHIMELECH אחימלך

According to tradition, Ahimelech was the son of Ahitub and the brother of Ahijah. He was the High Priest in the temple of Nob during the reign of King Saul (1 Samuel 21-22) and he supervised the 85 priests who wore linen ephods and were all members of the family of Eli (1 Samuel 22.15-18). When David fled from Saul, Ahimelech gave him some of the shewbread for provisions and gave him also the sword of Goliath. Saul killed all the members of the family of Ahimelech except Abiathar, who managed to escape to David, bringing with him the ephod.

11. ABIATHAR אביתר

The sole survivor of Saul's slaughter of the priests of Nob, Abiathar son of Ahimelech fled to David and served as the latter's priest throughout all of his wanderings (1 Kings 2.26). He inquired of the Urim and Thummim set in the ephod which he had brought with him from Nob (1 Samuel 23.6 ff.). After the death of King David, Abiathar supported the efforts of Adonijah, David's son to gain the throne. Consequently Solomon banished the priest to Anathoth (1 Kings 1.19; 2.26). With Abiathar, the line of High Priests of the family of Ithamar came to an end.

12. ZADOK * צדוק

According to tradition, with Zadok, the High Priesthood reverted back to the family of Phinehas. Zadok is mentioned in Scripture as a priest together with Abiathar (2 Samuel 8.17). Unlike Abiathar, however, Zadok supported Solomon and helped him become king over Israel (1 Kings 1.32 ff.). Zadok was the first High Priest to serve in the Temple which Solomon built in Jerusalem.

13. AHIMAAZ אחימעץ

Scripture relates that following the death of Absalom "Ahimaaz the son of Zadok said 'Let me now run and bear the king tidings, how that the Lord hath avenged him of his enemies.' And Joab said unto him: 'Thou shalt not be the bearer of tidings this day'" (2 Samuel 18.20).

Ahimaaz became High Priest after the death of his father Zadok. According to Seder Olam Zuta he ministered as High Priest during the reign of Rehoboam, son of Solomon (ca. 931-914 B.C.E.).

14. AZARIAH עזריה

Azariah was the son of Ahimaaz (1 Chronicles 5.35). In 1 Kings (4.1-2) it is written that "King Solomon was king over all Israel. And these were the princes whom he had: Azariah the son of Zadok . . ." According to Seder Olam Zuta, he was High Priest during the reign of Abihu, son of Rehoboam.

15. JOHANAN יוחנן בן עזריה

Johanan was the son of Azariah (1 Chronicles 5.35). His name was possibly corrupted in Seder Olam Zuta, which mentions one Jehoahaz or Jehoash, High Priest during the reign of King Jehoshaphat (871-846 B.C.E.).

---

* Concerning the list of High Priests from **Zadok** to Hilkiah, son of Shallum:

The Bible does not give us a detailed account of the High Priests during this period. The list given here is based upon the genealogical lists of the High Priests of the house of Zadok, especially the one recorded in 1 Chronicles 5.27-41. However, that list is not complete; many of the High Priests referred to in other Biblical sources are not included in it. For the sake of completeness, we have included the series of High Priests mentioned in Josephus' Antiquities of the Jews and the list recorded in Seder Olam Zuta, a work compiled in Babylon, probably during the Gaonic period. Most of the High Priests who are mentioned elsewhere in the Bible but do not appear in the Biblical tables of genealogy are to be found in one or the other of these two non-Biblical sources. Hence, the designation of the men that follow as High Priests is somewhat conjectural. The list given here is intended to serve as a useful guide. It does not lay claim to scholarly exactitude, nor does it conflict with traditional teachings.

16. AZARIAH II   עזריה (השני) בן יוחנן

The Biblical chronicler wrote of Azariah, son of Johanan: "He it is that executed the priest's office in the house that Solomon built in Jerusalem" (1 Chronicles 5.36). Since his son Amariah was High Priest during the reign of Jehoshaphat, it is probable that he lived during the reign of Asa (911-870 B.C.E.).

17. AMARIAH   אמריה בן עזריה

The son of Azariah (1 Chronicles 5.37), Amariah was High Priest during the reign of Jehoshaphat (872-852 B.C.E.). He was appointed to supervise the judges in Jerusalem in all that pertained to religious matters, while Zebadiah, son of Ishmael, was the official of the house of Judah in charge of all affairs of state (2 Chronicles 19.11).

18. JEHOIADA   יהוידע

Jehoiada ministered as High Priest during the reign of Athaliah. He saved Joash, an infant of the royal line, from Athaliah ,who murdered all the other members of the royal family. He succeeded in having Joash crowned king (2 Kings 11-12; 2 Chronicles 23-24). Joash reigned from about 836 to about 796 B.C.E.

19. AZARIAH III   עזריהו

Azariah was High Priest during the reign of King Uzziah. When that monarch sought to enter the Temple and offer up incense on the altar, Azariah and the priests turned to him saying: " 'It pertaineth not unto thee, Uzziah, to burn incense unto the Lord, but to the priests the sons of Aaron that are consecrated it pertaineth to burn incense; go out of the sanctuary; for thou hast trespassed; neither shall it be for thy honour from the Lord God.' Then Uzziah was wroth; and he had a censer in his hand to burn incense; and while he was wroth with the priests, the leprosy broke forth in his forehead" (2 Chronicles 26.18-19).

20. URIJAH   אוריהו

Urijah was High Priest during the reign of King Ahaz (c. 742-726 B.C.E.). When Ahaz went to Damascus and saw the altar there, he "sent to Urijah the priest the fashion of the altar, and the pattern of it, according to all the workmanship thereof. And Urijah the priest built an altar, according to all that King Ahaz had sent from Damascus" (2 Kings 16.10-11).

21. SHALLUM   שלום

The father of Hilkiah the High Priest, Shallum was also known as Meshullam. With him the High Priesthood reverted back to the line of the house of Zadok. According to Seder Olam Zuta, Shallum was High Priest during the reign of King Amon.

22. HILKIAH   חלקיהו

When the Temple was being repaired in the eighteenth year of the reign of King Josiah, Hilkiah the High Priest found there the book of the Law. Upon hearing the words of the book, Josiah rent his garments. He read the contents of the book to the people and then commanded Hilkiah, the priests of the second order, and the keepers of the door to remove from the Temple all the vessels that were made for Baal, Asherah and all the host of heaven. The king then burnt the vessels outside of Jerusalem in the field of Kidron and carried the ashes to Beth-el. Subsequently, he destroyed all the high places and abolished all remnants of idolatry in the land (2 Kings 22-23).

23. AZARIAH IV   עזריהו

Azariah, son of Hilkiah the High Priest, ministered during the reign of King Jehoiakim, according to Seder Olam Zutah.

24. SERAIAH   שריה

After the destruction of Jerusalem and the Temple by Nebuchadnezzar king of Babylon in the days of King Zedekiah, Nebuzaradan, the captain of the host, exiled and "took Seraiah the chief priest, and Zephaniah the second priest . . . and brought them to the king of Babylon at Riblah. And the king of Babylon smote them, and put them to death at Riblah" (2 Kings 25.18-21).

25. JEHOZADAK   יהוצדק

The son of Seraiah, Jehozadak was the last of the High Priests during the First Temple period. He was killed by the king .of Babylon. "And Jehozadak went into captivity, when the Lord carried away Judah and Jerusalem by the hand of Nebuchadnezzar" (1 Chronicles 5.41).

THE DUTIES AND PRIVILEGES OF THE PRIESTS *

A. THE CONSECRATION OF THE PRIESTS

Moses was commanded by God to consecrate Aaron and his sons to minister unto God (Exodus 28.41). The following are the details of the ceremony of sanctification.

First, Moses brought Aaron and his sons to the entrance of the Tabernacle of the tent of the meeting where the burnt-offerings were offered up (Exodus 29; 40.6) and he washed them with water (Exodus 29.4). Thereafter he dressed Aaron in the tunic and priestly garments (29.5). He then poured the anointing oil upon Aaron's head and anointed him priest.

Only Aaron was consecrated by having oil poured over his head. For the consecration of his sons, a mixture of anointing oil and blood from the altar was taken and sprinkled upon them and their garments, as well as upon Aaron and his garments (29.21). Aaron, then, was anointed twice.

The entire ceremony of inauguration lasted seven days, during which period sacrifices were offered up to God daily (Leviticus 8.33). God promised to consecrate Aaron and his sons and sanctify them before the eyes of the people and he did so. "And the glory of the Lord appeared unto all the people. And there came forth fire from before the Lord, and consumed upon the altar the burnt offering and the fat; and when all the people saw it, they shouted, and fell on their faces" (Leviticus 9.23-24).

In this manner, Aaron, his sons and his descendants were set apart to serve as priests amidst the congregation of Israel. Aaron's first-born son inherited the position of High Priest and was in turn succeeded by his own first-born son. This system was disrupted in the course of time, but was later reintroduced. The holy garments of Aaron were set aside for his descendants to wear during their anointing and consecration (Exodus 29.29). For seven days the garments were worn by the High Priest, who came into the tent of meeting to minister in the holy place (29.30). Wearing these garments, he made atonement for the most holy place, the tent of the meeting and the altar, and also atoned for the priests and for all the people (Leviticus 16.32-34).

B. DUTIES OF THE HIGH PRIESTS

The High Priest had to be the eldest son of the line of Aaron and like all other priests could have no blemish (Leviticus 21.16-23).

Only when all of the priestly qualifications had been fully met could he eat of the bread of his God, both of the holy and the most holy (21.22).

The High Priest was forbidden to marry a widow, a divorcee, a profaned woman, or a harlot; he could only wed a virgin of his own people (21.14).

The High Priest was not to exhibit any signs of mourning. He was not to allow his hair to grow overmuch, tear his clothes, leave the sanctuary during the Service, or defile himself for any dead body, including the bodies of his father and mother (21-10-12). Nevertheless, as an exception to this rule, we find that the High Priest Jehoiakim, in a period of dire national distress, wore a sackcloth and poured ashes upon his mitre along with the other priests (Judith 4.14-15; Joel 1.13).

Whenever he entered the tent of meeting he washed his hands and feet with water so that he would not die upon approaching the altar where he was to minister and cause an offering made by fire to smoke before the Lord (Exodus 30.19-21).

His Ministerial and Ritual Obligations

1. First, Aaron offered incense on the golden altar each morning when he prepared the lamps, and also each evening when he lit the lamps (Exodus 30.7-8).
2. It was his duty to carry out the prescribed ritual on the Day of Atonement (Leviticus 16).
3. He arranged the shewbread on the Sabbath and ate it in a holy place (24.9).
4. Whenever he was unclean he had to separate himself from the holy things of the children of Israel (22.1-3). If he were leprous or had any flow issuing from his body he could not eat of the holy things until he became clean (22.4-7).
5. If the High Priest sinned unintentionally and in so doing brought guilt upon the people, he was to sacrifice a bullock as a sin-offering (4.3-13). If the entire congregation of Israel sinned unintentionally, the congregation had to bring a sin-offering; the High Priest would then atone for them that they might be forgiven (Leviticus 4.13-21).
6. It was the duty of the High Priest and the common priests to eat the remains of the meal offerings of the children of Israel in a holy place (6.9).
7. The High Priest was to be present when a king was crowned or a leader chosen, and he was to inquire of God's will concerning their ventures for them,

*Refer to sources in the last page of Introduction.

by means of the Urim (Numbers 27.19-21).

8. He was to oversee the distribution of war booty. Eleazar, for example, along with other leaders of the Israelites, distributed the booty of the Midianites to the people (31.21-28).

The above are the special duties of the High Priest. What follows are duties shared by the High Priest and the common priests.

9. When the camp journeyed forward, Aaron and his sons had to dismantle and carry the Tabernacle and its implements; and take down the veil of the screen and use it to cover the ark of the testimony (Numbers 4.5-16).

10. The priests had to bless the people (6.23-27).

11. The priests were responsible for the sins in the Tabernacle (18.1) and were in charge of the holy things and the altar (18.5).

C. PRIVILEGES OF THE HIGH PRIESTS

Neither the High Priest nor any common priest received a portion of the land of Canaan when it was divided among the tribes of Israel (Numbers 18.20; Deuteronomy 18.1-2). The source of their livelihood was the heave-offerings and the tithes brought to them by the children of Israel. The priests also received a tithe from the tithe given the Levites (Numbers 18.28; Nehemiah 10.39). Josephus, too, noted that the heave-offerings and tithes constituted a communal fund in which all priests participated (Antiquities IV, 4.4).

D. GENERAL DUTIES OF THE PRIESTS

In addition to sharing the aforementioned duties with the High Priest, the common priests had the following obligations:

1. To be among the descendants of Aaron and physically unblemished (Leviticus 21.16-23).

2. Not to defile themselves for any corpse, except when the dead person was a mother, father, son, daughter, brother, wife or virgin sister (21.1-5).

3. Not to marry a profaned woman, a divorced woman or a harlot (21.7).

4. To keep charge of the holy things and guard the altar (Numbers 18.5).

5. To kindle the fire upon the altar, lay wood in order upon the fire and keep the fire burning (Leviticus 6.2).

6. To collect half of the blood of certain sacrifices in basins and sprinkle the remaining blood on the altar (Exodus 24.6).

7. To set the wood in order upon the fire of the altar and make the various sections of the offering smoke (Leviticus 1.5-10).

8. To pinch off the head of any bird offered as a sacrifice, drain its blood on the side of the altar, remove its crop and the feathers of the crop, and cast it by the east side of the altar among the ashes (Leviticus 1.15-17).

9. To make the daily offering of one lamb in the morning and one in the evening (Numbers 28.3), and offer up an additional sacrifice on Sabbaths, new moons and festivals (28.9-27).

10. To offer up the meal-offering and smoke a portion of it on the altar as a memorial (Leviticus 2.1-2).

11. To sprinkle the blood of the peace-offering about the altar (3.1-3).

12. To sacrifice the sin-offering of one who has committed an unintentional sin; take some of the blood of the offering upon the finger and place it upon the horns of the altar; and pour out the remaining blood at the base of the altar (4.30).

13. To eat of the guilt-offering in a holy place (7.6; 10.16-18).

14. To offer up the meal-offering (6.7-8) and sprinkle the blood of the guilt-offering about the altar (7.2).

15. To eat the shewbread in a holy place (24.9).

16. To make atonement for the woman who had given birth and who had already fulfilled the days of her purification (12.6-7).

17. To ascertain when the leprous spot(s) had departed from the leper (14.3-4); purify the leper (14.6-7); bring him before God and make atonement for him (14.10-32); determine if a house was afflicted with leprosy (14.33-47); and make atonement for the house and purify it (14.49-53).

18. To make atonement for any man suffering a flow and purify him (15.14-15), and purify any woman who was unclean (15.29-30).

19. To offer the sheaf of First Fruits (23.10-11).

20. To estimate the sum to be paid by a person who made a vow and could not afford the regular valuation (27.8); to set the value of an unfit animal brought as an offering to God (27.11-12); to set the value of a house consecrated to God (27.14); and to set the value of a field until it be redeemed in the jubilee year (27.23).

21. To prepare the water of bitterness used in testing a woman accused of adultery and to conduct the prescribed ritual (Numbers 5.12-31).

22. To make atonement for the Nazirite when the latter's period of abstinence had come to an end, or when he had suddenly become unclean (6.9-13).

23. To offer up the sin-offering and burnt-offering of the Nazirite when the period of the latter's consecration had been fulfilled (6.14-15).

24. To sound the silver trumpets on the required occasions (10.8).

25. To atone for the entire congregation or for an individual in the case of sins committed through error (Numbers 15.24-27).

26. To prepare the prescription of the spices (1 Chronicles 9.30).

27. To prepare the waters of sprinkling (Numbers 19.1-11).

28. To serve as judges when people sought them out to settle controversies (Deuteronomy 17.9; 19.17).

29. To encourage the soldiers who were going out to battle and address the people and their officers (this was to be done by the priest anointed for this purpose) (Deuteronomy 20.2-3).

30. To supervise the breaking of the neck of a heifer after a corpse was found in a field and the identity of the murderer could not be determined (Deuteronomy 21.1-9).

31. In later periods, on certain occasions, it was the task of the priests to flay the burnt-offerings (2 Chronicles 29.34) and slaughter the paschal lamb (Ezra 6.20).

32. The priest's daughter who committed harlotry was to be burnt, as profaning her father (Leviticus 21.9).

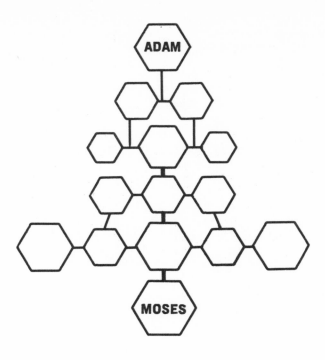

GENEALOGICAL TABLES

**The twenty-six generations from
Adam to Moses
as recounted in Genesis, Exodus and Numbers**

GENEALOGICAL TABLE 1.

From Adam to the "Scattered Generation"
comprising the 70 nations of the world
(10 generations)

GENEALOGICAL TABLE 2.

From the "Scattered Generation" to the Patriarchs
(10 generations)

GENEALOGICAL TABLE 3.

From Jacob till Moses (6 generations)
including the 70 descendants
who migrated with Jacob into Egypt.
(The 12 Tribes and their sons)

Direct Genealogy

———————————— father — son, daughter

· · · · · · · · · · · · · · · mother — son, daughter

Indirect Genealogy

· · · · · · · · · · · · · · · grandfather — grandchildren

<———————> brothers on maternal side

(2) refers to Table II

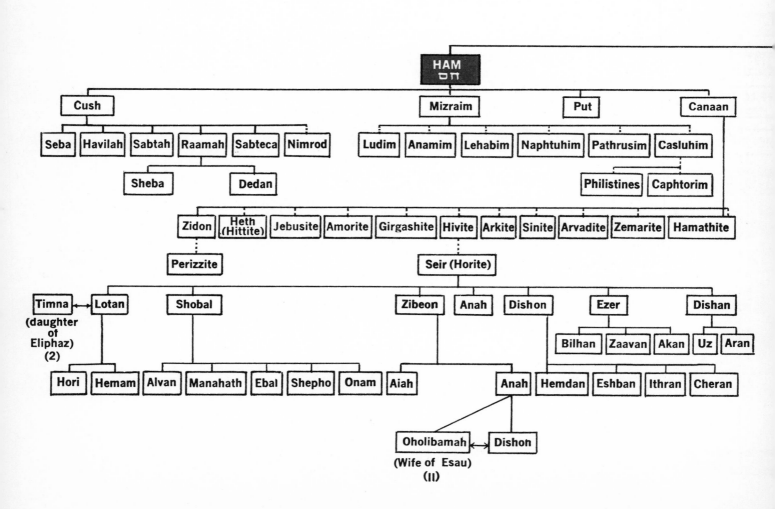

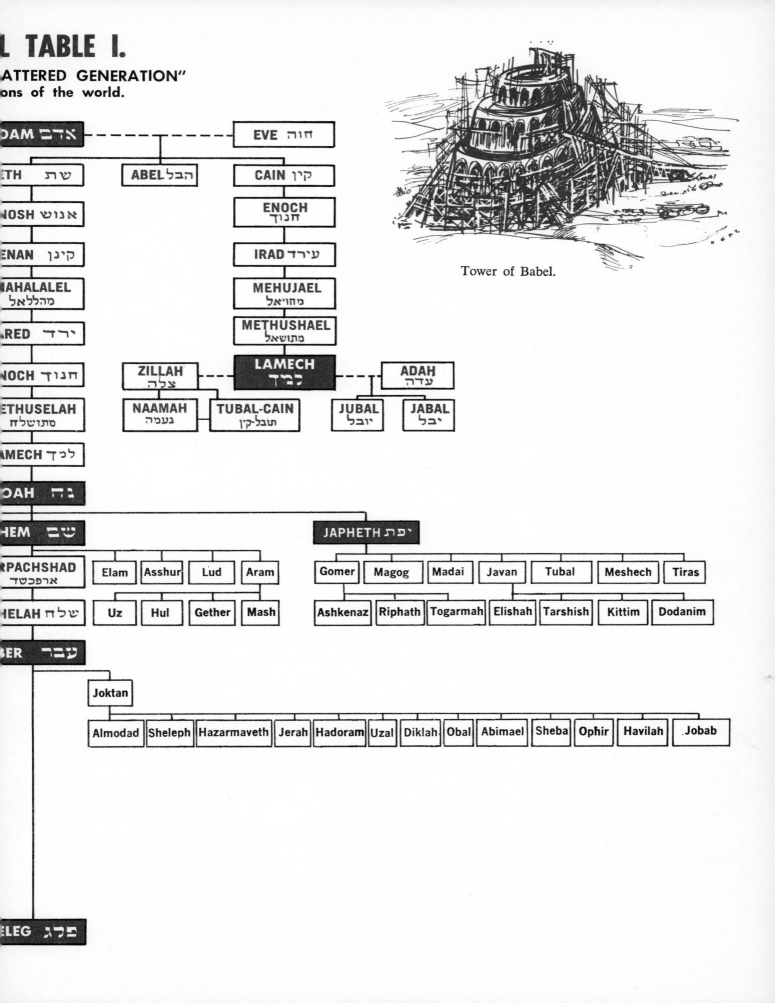

Tower of Babel.

| ADAM אדם | - - - - | EVE חוה |

| ETH שת | ABEL הבל | CAIN קין |

| NOSH אנוש | | ENOCH חנוך |

| ENAN קינן | | IRAD עירד |

| MAHALALEL מהללאל | | MEHUJAEL מחויאל |

| RED ירד | | METHUSHAEL מתושאל |

| NOCH חנוך | ZILLAH צלה | LAMECH למך | ADAH עדה |

| ETHUSELAH מתושלח | NAAMAH נעמה | TUBAL-CAIN תובל-קין | JUBAL יובל | JABAL יבל |

| AMECH למך |

| OAH נח |

| HEM שם | | JAPHETH יפת |

| RPACHSHAD ארפכשד | Elam | Asshur | Lud | Aram | Gomer | Magog | Madai | Javan | Tubal | Meshech | Tiras |

| HELAH שלח | Uz | Hul | Gether | Mash | Ashkenaz | Riphath | Togarmah | Elishah | Tarshish | Kittim | Dodanim |

| BER עבר |

| Joktan |

| Almodad | Sheleph | Hazarmaveth | Jerah | Hadoram | Uzal | Diklah | Obal | Abimael | Sheba | Ophir | Havilah | Jobab |

| ELEG פלג |

For references see Table I
I = Table I
III = Table III

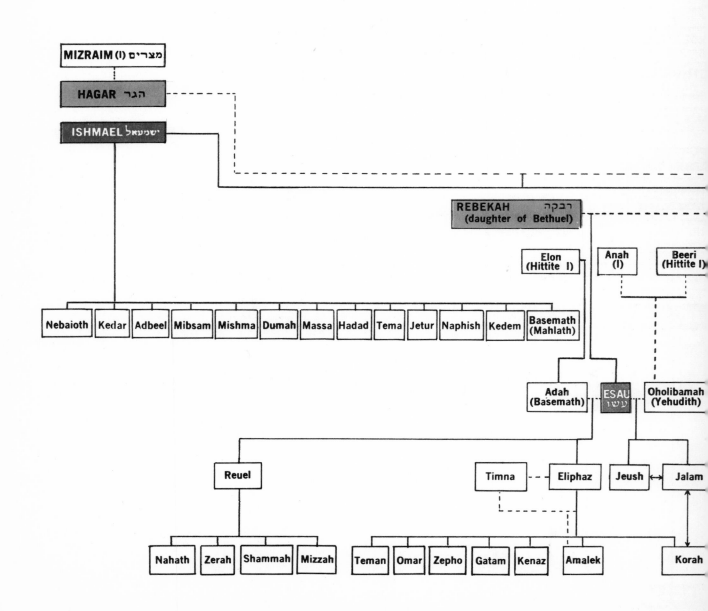

MIZRAIM (I) מצרים

HAGAR הגר

ISHMAEL ישמעאל

REBEKAH רבקה
(daughter of Bethuel)

Elon (Hittite I)

Anah (I)

Beeri (Hittite I)

Nebaioth | Kedar | Adbeel | Mibsam | Mishma | Dumah | Massa | Hadad | Tema | Jetur | Naphish | Kedem | Basemath (Mahlath)

Adah (Basemath)

ESAU עשו

Oholibamah (Yehudith)

Reuel

Timna

Eliphaz

Jeush

Jalam

Nahath | Zerah | Shammah | Mizzah

Teman | Omar | Zepho | Gatam | Kenaz | Amalek

Korah

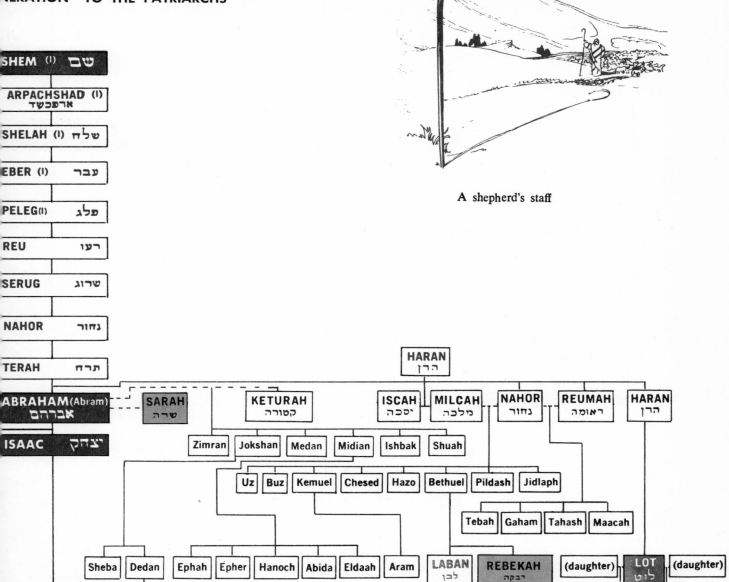

A shepherd's staff

SHEM (I) שם (I)

ARPACHSHAD (I) ארפכשד

SHELAH (I) שלח (I)

EBER (I) עבר (I)

PELEG (I) פלג (I)

REU רעו

SERUG שרוג

NAHOR נחור

TERAH תרח

ABRAHAM (Abram) אברהם

SARAH שרה

ISAAC יצחק

KETURAH קטורה

ISCAH יסכה

MILCAH מלכה

NAHOR נחור

REUMAH ראומה

HARAN הרן

HARAN הרן

Zimran | Jokshan | Medan | Midian | Ishbak | Shuah

Uz | Buz | Kemuel | Chesed | Hazo | Bethuel | Pildash | Jidlaph

Tebah | Gaham | Tahash | Maacah

Sheba | Dedan | Ephah | Epher | Hanoch | Abida | Eldaah | Aram

LABAN לבן

REBEKAH רבקה (Wife of Isaac)

(daughter)

LOT לוט

(daughter)

Asshurim | Letushim | Leummim

LEAH,(III) לאה

RACHEL,(III) רחל

ZILPAH,(III) זלפה

BILHAH (III) בלהה

Moab

Ben-Ami

JACOB יעקב (Israel)(III)

Moab

Ammon

* = found twice in this Table

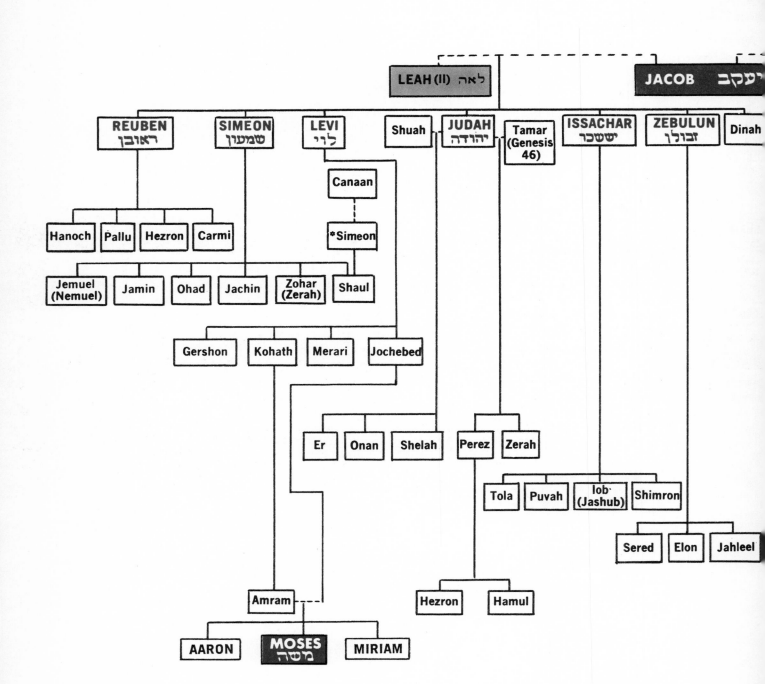

A pyramid.

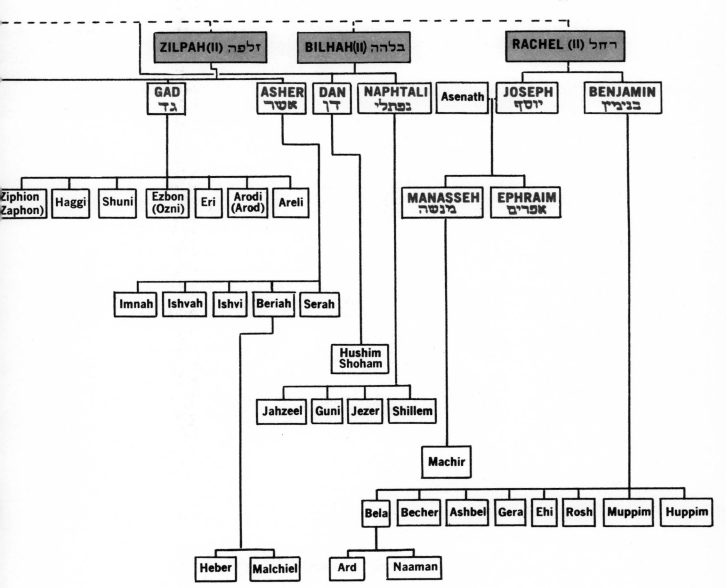

ZILPAH (II) זלפה   BILHAH (II) בלהה   RACHEL (II) רחל

GAD גד   ASHER אשר   DAN דן   NAPHTALI נפתלי   Asenath   JOSEPH יוסף   BENJAMIN בנימין

Ziphion (Zaphon)   Haggi   Shuni   Ezbon (Ozni)   Eri   Arodi (Arod)   Areli

MANASSEH מנשה   EPHRAIM אפרים

Imnah   Ishvah   Ishvi   Beriah   Serah

Hushim Shoham

Jahzeel   Guni   Jezer   Shillem

Machir

Bela   Becher   Ashbel   Gera   Ehi   Rosh   Muppim   Huppim

Heber   Malchiel   Ard   Naaman

For reference see Table I

CHRONOLOGICAL TABLES

"So all Israel were reckoned by genealogies; and, behold, they are written in the book of the kings of Israel." (I Chronicles 9.1).

The following tables present in juxtaposition various chronological versions. Though approximate, at times even inconsistent in themselves or irreconcilable with each other, they provide a broad and informative basis for further study and research in this field. Employing both the masoretic chronology and the modern framework of calendar calculation, it was deemed appropriate to equate the year One with 3760 B.C.E., (3760 B.C.E. plus 1963 equals 5723 A.M.) fixing the date of 5723 A.M.* as the current year acknowledged in the traditional Jewish calendar. Thus the year of Joshua's death which is set at 2516 A.M. corresponds with 1244 B.C.E.

Later calculations in the third and fourth Tables, p. 186 ff., depart from this previously established date of 1244. The Arrowsmith version, which adopts the initial year of this period as 1394 B.C.E., superseding the year of 1244 B.C.E. because of its more acceptable composite chronological plan, has been used for the period of the Judges and the first four Kings.

Recent studies relate to the general span of the entire period rather than to specific dates. Thus, there is an era of approximately two hundred years (1225 B.C.E. - 1020 B.C.E.) for the judges and one of approximately ninety years (1020 B.C.E. - 931 B.C.E.) for the first four kings before the division of the kingdom.*

See Notes, in Chart of Judges, pp. 92,93; and in Tables of Kings, pp. 101-103, for other data bearing on the various aspects of biblical chronology.

CHRONOLOGICAL TABLES

CHRONOLOGICAL TABLE 1.

    1 — From the Creation to the Deluge

    2 — From the Deluge till Abraham

    3 — From Abraham till the Descent into Egypt

CHRONOLOGICAL TABLE 2.

    4 — From the Descent into Egypt till the Exodus

    5 — The Forty Years of Wandering in the Desert

    6 — From the Entrance into Canaan till the Period of the Judges

CHRONOLOGICAL TABLE 3.

    7 — The Period of the Judges till the Beginning of the Monarchy

CHRONOLOGICAL TABLE 4.

    8 — Beginnings of the Monarchy till Solomon

    9 — From the birth of Solomon till the Division of the Kingdom

TABLE I

FROM THE CREATION
UNTIL THE DESCENT INTO EGYPT

1. From the Creation until the Deluge

Noah building the ark.

A.M. *	B.C.E. *	EVENT	SOURCE	
1	3760	The beginning of recorded time.	Genesis 1-2	
129	3631	Cain kills Abel.	"	4.8
130	3630	Seth, son of Adam, born; lives 912 years.	"	5.3
235	3525	Birth of Enosh, son of Seth; lives 905 years.	"	5.6
325	3435	Birth of Kenan, son of Enosh; lives 910 years.	"	5.9
395	3365	Birth of Mahalalel, son of Kenan; lives 895 years.	"	5.12
460	3300	Birth of Jared, son of Mahalalel; lives 962 years.	"	5.15
622	3138	Birth of Enoch, son of Jared; lives 365 years.	"	5.18
687	3073	Birth of Methuselah, son of Enoch lives 969 years.	"	5.21
874	2886	Birth of Lamech, son of Methuselah; lives 777 years.	"	5.25
930	2830	Adam dies at age of 930 years.	"	5.5
987	2773	Enoch is "taken" by God.	"	5.24
1056	2704	Birth of Noah, son of Lamech; lives 950 years.	"	5.28-29
1556-58	2204-02	Birth of Shem, Ham, and Japheth.	"	5.32; 6.10
1656	2104	The year of the Flood; death of Methuselah.	"	7.10

* See Introduction to Chronological Tables, page 178.

2. From the Deluge until Abraham

Abraham breaking an idol.

A.M.	B.C.E.	EVENT	SOURCE
1658	2102	Birth of Arpachshad, son of Shem; lives 438 years.	Gen. 10.22; 11.10
1693	2067	Birth of Shelah, son of Arpachshad; lives 433 years.	" 10.24; 11.12
1723	2037	Birth of Eber, son of Shelah; lives 464 years.	" 10.24; 11.14
1757	2003	Birth of Peleg, son of Eber; lives 239 years.	" 10.25; 11.16
1787	1973	Birth of Reu, son of Peleg; lives 239 years.	" 11.18
1819	1941	Birth of Serug, son of Reu; lives 230 years.	" 11.20
1849	1911	Birth of Nahor, son of Serug; lives 148 years.	" 11.22-25 I Chronicles 1.26
1878	1882	Birth of Terah, son of Nahor; lives 205 years.	Genesis 11.24
1948	1812	Birth of Abram, son of Terah, in Ur of the Chaldees; lives 175 years.	" 11.26; 25.7

3. From Abraham until the Descent into Egypt

Joseph supervising the storing of grain in Egypt.

A.M.	B.C.E.	EVENT	SOURCE
1948	1812	Birth of Abram.	Gen. 11.25
1958	1802	Birth of Sarai, wife of Abram.	" 11.29
2000	1760	* First departure of Abram from Haran to Canaan.	" 12.1
2018	1742	* God makes the Covenant with Abram, informing him of the bondage in Egypt and promising Canaan, "from the river of Egypt unto the great river, the river Euphrates", to his posterity.	" 15
2022	1738	Abram fights the five kings and frees Lot from captivity.	" 14.14
2023	1737	* The second departure of Abram from Haran to Canaan at the age of 75 years. He descends into Egypt.	" 12. 4-5
2033 2034	1727 1726	Sarai, the wife of Abram, who is barren gives Hagar the Egyptian as a concubine to Abram. Birth of Ishmael.	" 16. 1-4

* This chronology follows Abodah Zarah 9, and Elijah Gaon.

A.M.	B.C.E.	EVENT	SOURCE
2047	1713	God changes the name of Abram to Abraham and that of Sarai to Sarah. He promises Abraham that he will have a son by Sarah.	Gen.17. 1-22
2048	1712	The destruction of Sodom and Gomorrah; birth of Isaac.	" 19; 21. 1-3
2051	1709	The expulsion of Hagar and Ishmael. The covenant with Abimelech.	" 21. 9-34
2074 (2085)	1686 (1675)	Binding of Isaac.	" 22. 1-19
2085	1675	Birth of Rebekah.	" 22. 20-24
2085	1675	Sarah dies in Hebron.	" 23. 2
2088	1672	Isaac marries Rebekah, daughter of Bethuel.	" 24. 25
2108	1652	Rebekah gives birth to Jacob and Esau.	" 25. 19-26
2123	1637	Abraham dies, aged 175 years.	" 25. 5-11
2171	1589	Isaac blesses Jacob; Jacob flees in fear of Esau.	" 27
2185	1575	Jacob's dream and God's promise.	" 28
2185-2204	1575-1556	Jacob serves Laban for Leah and Rachel.	" 29
2192-2199	1568-1561	Birth of all of Jacob's sons except Benjamin.	" 29-30
2205 2207	1555 1553	Jacob flees Laban's house. His meeting with Esau. Simeon and Levi take revenge against the city of Shechem because of the attack on their sister Dinah. Death of Rachel.	" 31-33 " 34-35
2216	1544	Sale of Joseph.	" 37
2228-9	1532-31	Dream of Pharaoh and Joseph's interpretation; Pharaoh appoints Joseph viceroy over Egypt.	" 41
2236	1524	Jacob sends his sons to purchase corn in Egypt; Joseph accuses them of spying and imprisons Simeon.	" 42
2237	1523	Jacob is compelled once again to send his sons to Egypt for corn. Joseph imprisons Benjamin and reveals his identity to his brothers.	" 43-45
2238	1522	Jacob descends to Joseph in Egypt, with God's blessing.	" 46. 1-7

TABLE II

FROM THE DESCENT INTO EGYPT UNTIL THE PERIOD OF THE JUDGES

4. From the Descent into Egypt until the Exodus

The Israelites as slaves in Egypt.

A.M.	B.C.E.	EVENT	SOURCE
2255	1505	The Israelites remain in Egypt 210 years. Jacob dies at the age of 147 years. Before his death he blesses his sons. At his request, his sons take his body to Canaan to be buried in the Cave of Machpelah.	Genesis 47.28 ff " 48-49 50, 1-14
2309	1451	Joseph dies at the age of 110 years. He causes his brothers to swear that upon the Exodus from Egypt they will take his bones to Canaan for burial.	Genesis 50.25-26
2331 (2332)	1429 (1428)	A new King arises who does not know Joseph. He afflicts the children of Israel with hard labor and enslaves them to prevent them from becoming a great power.	Exodus 1.1-11
2365	1395	Pharaoh decrees that all newborn Israelite males are to be cast into the Nile.	" 1.15-22
2368	1392	Birth of Moses, son of Amram. Pharaoh's daughter removes him from the Nile and takes him to the palace, where he is reared.	" 2.2-9
2388 2406 2446	1372 1354 1314	Moses slays an Egyptian and flees to Midian. Birth of Joshua son of Nun; he lives 110 years. Moses saves the daughters of Jethro. He marries Zipporah.	" 2.12-15 Numbers 13. 8 Exodus 2.16-22
2447	1313	Revelation of God to Moses in the burning bush. God sends Moses to deliver the Israelites from Egypt. Moses and Aaron appear before Pharaoh.	" 3
2448	1312	God afflicts Egypt with ten plagues.	" 7-12
		The paschal sacrifice in Egypt on the 14th of Nissan at eventide. The slaying of the first-born in Egypt on the midnight of the 15th of Nissan. Pharaoh entreats Moses that the Israelites depart from Egypt.	" 12.21-28 Exodus 12.29-36
		The Israelites depart from Egypt on the 16th of Nissan.	" 13.17
		The waters of the Red Sea divide on the 21st of Nissan.	" 14. 21-31
		Moses and the Children of Israel sing the Song of Triumph at the Sea.	" 15

5. The Forty Years of Wandering in the Desert

The manna descending in the wilderness.

A.M.	B.C.E.	EVENT	SOURCE
2448	1312	16th of Iyar—God causes manna to descend for Israel in the desert.	Exodus 16
		23rd of Iyar—Moses strikes the rock, and water gushes forth.	" 17.1-8
		The war with Amalek.	" 17.8-16
		6th and 7th of Sivan—The Sinaitic Revelation.	" 19.8-25; 20
		17th of Tammuz—The incident of the golden calf. Moses breaks the first Tables of the Covenant.	" 32
2449	1311	10th of Tishri—Day of Atonement. Moses fetches the new set of the Tables of the Covenant down from Mount Sinai.	" 34.27-28
		1st of Nissan—The erection of the Tabernacle and its dedication.	" 35-40
		End of Iyar—The punishment at Kibroth-hattaavah (the graves of lust).	Numbers 11.4-34
2449	1311	29th of Sivan—8th of Ab—The spies explore Canaan.	" 13.1-32
		9th of Ab—The spies return with a false report.	" 13.1-32
		The decree of death for the desert generation.	" 14.28-36
		The premature attempt to enter the land.	" 14.42
		The rebellion of Korah and his followers.	" 16
2449-2487	1311-1273	The Israelites wander in the desert for 38 years, and finally cross the brook of Zared. During this period they halt at 20 stations in the desert, and the desert generation dies.	Deuteronomy 2.14
2487	1273	In Nissan Miriam dies in Kadesh in the desert of Zin.	Numbers 20.1
		The incident of the waters of Meribah ("strife").	" 20.2
		1st of Ab—death of Aaron at age of 123 years.	" 20.22 – 29
		The Caananite King of Arad battles with the Israelites.	
		Incident of the Copper serpent.	Numbers 21.1-9
		Elul—Israel's victory over Sihon, king of the Amorites.	Deuteronomy 21.21
2488	1272	Israel's victory over Og, king of Bashan.	Numbers 21.33-35
		Balak, son of Zippor, king of Moab calls Balaam, son of Beor, to curse Israel. Balaam blesses them instead.	Numbers 22-24
		The Zimri incident. The plague. The High Priest Phinehas avenges the honor of God.	" 25
		7th of Adar—Moses blesses Israel. He dies at the age of 120 years on Mount Nebo. "And no man knoweth of his sepulchre unto this day."	Deuteronomy 34
		6th of Nissan—Joshua sends spies to Jericho. The incident of Rahab the harlot.	Joshua 2

6. From the Entrance into Canaan until the Period of the Judges

The division of Palestine among the tribes.

A.M.	B.C.E.	EVENT	SOURCE
2488	1272	6th of Nissan—under Joshua's leadership the Israelites cross the Jordan and enter Canaan; the miracle of the division of the Jordan.	Joshua 3. 4.
		Joshua recites the blessings and curses before the people on Mounts Ebal and Gerizim. The people camp in Gilgal and set up the Tabernacle.	" 8.30-35
		Joshua circumcizes those born in the desert. The observance of Pass-over in the plains of Moab. The offering of the Omer.	" 5.2-3 " 5. 10
		22-27 of Nissan—the siege of Jericho; its walls fall down.	" 6
		The incident of Achan who takes from the banned spoils.	" 7
		The capture of Ai and its burning.	" 8. 1-29
		The Gibeonites save themselves by a ruse.	" 9
		The victory in Gibeon over the five Amorite kings. Miraculously, the sun stands still upon Gibeon.	" 10. 1-15
		The lengthy invasion and conquest of Canaan by Israel.	" 11.18
2488	1272	Joshua wars against Jabin, king of Hazor, and 30 other Canaanite kings. The capture of their cities.	" 11. 1-15
2495	1265	Joshua divides the portions of the tribes of Judah and the sons of Joseph by lot. Caleb, son of Jephunneh, receives Hebron as his inheritance.	" 13, 14, 15.13
		The apportioning of the land.	" 15-20
2503	1257	The Israelites erect the Tabernacle in Shiloh.	" 18.1
		Joshua completes the distribution of the land. He sanctifies the cities of refuge and sets aside 48 Levitical cities.	" 18.2-20 Judges 1.27 Joshua 21.13
		The tribes of Reuben and Gad and half of the tribe of Manasseh return to their land on the other side of the Jordan.	Joshua 22
2516	1244*	Joshua, "old and well-stricken in years," gathers the people before him, recites their history and makes a covenant between them and God.	" 23-24
		Joshua dies at the age of 110 years.	" 24 .29
		The tribes of Judah and Simeon battle the Canaanites and Perizzites, are victorious, and annihilate their foes. The capture of Adoni-bezek and his death in Jerusalem. The tribe of Judah captures Jerusalem and burns it.	Judges 1.1-9

* See Introduction to Chronological Tables, page 178.

TABLE III

THE PERIOD OF THE JUDGES TO THE MONARCHY

**7. The period of the Judges
until the
Beginning of the Monarchy**

The tribe of Dan sets up the idol of Micah near Lake Huleh.

JUDGES and RULERS	A.M.	B.C.E.	EVENT	SOURCE
1. OTHNIEL, son of Kenaz	2516- * 2524	1394*	For eight years Israel is subjected to Aram. The tribe of Dan, seeking land, captures Laish, (Dan), where they set up the idol of Micah.	Judges 3.8 " 17-18
			The incident of the concubine at Gibeah. The Israelites take vengeance on the tribe of Benjamin, in whose domain the atrocity was committed, and kill the men of Jabesh-gilead for not coming to the victim's aid.	" 19-20
			15th of Ab-The remnants of the tribe of Benjamin are permitted to take wives from the daughters of Jabesh-gilead whom they snatch in the vineyards.	" 21
			Othniel, son of Kenaz is judge for 40 years. "And his hand prevailed against Cushan-rishathaim, [King of Aram]. And the land had rest."	" 3.9-11
2. EHUD, son of Gera.	2556- 2636	1336	Eglon king of Moab holds Israel in vassalage for 18 years. Ehud delivers the Israelites by killing Eglon, and subduing Moab. The land is at rest for 80 years. Ehud judges Israel for eighty years.	" 3.12-30
3. SHAMGAR, son of Anath.		1296	Shamgar, son of Anath saves Israel from the Philistines. The events described in the Book of Ruth take place, according to the sages, during the days of Eglon, king of Moab. Shamgar judges for one year.	" 3.31 Book of Ruth
4. DEBORAH the prophetess, wife of Lapidoth; and BARAK son of Abinoam	2636	1296 ca. 1100**	For 20 years the children of Israel are in vassalage to Jabin, king of Canaan, and his general, Sisera. Deborah the prophetess encourages Barak, son of Abinoam, to wage war against Sisera. The forces of the enemy are defeated. Sisera is killed by Jael. The Song of Deborah. Deborah and Barak rule for 40 years.	Judges 4-5

* Dates recorded here refer to events; for the ruling years of each Judge, see Chart of Judges, page 92.

** All dates in italics reflect the modern calculation in the Chronological Tables. See Introduction, page 178.

JUDGES and RULERS	A.M.	B.C.E.	EVENT	SOURCE
5. GIDEON, son of Joash, saves Israel	2676-2683	1249	For seven years Israel is dominated by the Midianites who plunder their crops. God sends a prophet who chides the children of Israel for forsaking him. Gideon (Jerubbaal), son of Joash, is sent by God to deliver Israel from the Midianites. With 300 picked men whom he selects at En-harod he smites Oreb and Zeeb, the officers of Midian.	Judges 6,7
			The children of Ephraim upbraid Gideon for not asking them to fight with him against Midian. Gideon punishes the inhabitants of Succoth and Penuel for refusing his army bread. He slays Zebah and Zalmunna, kings of Midian, and the land is at rest for 40 years.	" 8
			Gideon refuses a crown. He returns to Ophrah and dies there.	" 8.22-29
6. ABIMELECH, son of Gideon	2723	1209	All Israel worships Baal. With the aid of the men of Shechem Abimelech, son of Gideon, slays all of his 70 brothers, except for the youngest, Jotham. The parable of Jotham.	" 9
	2726		After three years of internal warfare, Abimelech, son of Gideon, is killed besieging Thebez by a woman who cast an upper millstone on his head from the city tower.	" 9
7. TOLA, son of Puah		1206	Tola rules Israel for 23 years.	" 10.1-2
8. JAIR the Gileadite	2748	1183	Jair rules for 22 years.	" 10.3-5
	2770-2787		Israel worships strange gods for 18 years. The Israelites are vassals to the Philistines and the sons of Ammon.	" 10.6-18
	2774		Birth of Eli the priest, of the house of Ithamar. He lives 98 years. Jair dies.	
9. JEPHTHAH the Gileadite	2786	1143	Jephthah smites the Ammonites, who for 18 years had held the tribes of Judah, Benjamin and Ephraim in vassalage. Returning from battle victorious, Jephthah offers up his daughter as a sacrifice to God in fulfillment of a rash vow.	Judges 11
			The children of Ephraim dispute with Jephthah for not having enlisted them in his battles. The men of Gilead and Ephraim fight; thousands of the tribe of Ephraim are slain.	" 12.1-7
10. IBZAN	2788 -2795	1137	Jephthah dies and Ibzan of Bethlehem rules for seven years.	" 12.8-9
11. ELON	2795	1130	Elon the Zebulunite rules Israel for ten years.	Judges 12.11-12
12. ABDON	2805	1120	Abdon, son of Hillel, the Pirathonite rules Israel for eight years.	" 12.13-15

JUDGES and RULERS	A.M.	B.C.E.	EVENT	SOURCE
13. SAMSON	2812-2831	1120	The Philistines dominate Israel. Samson, son of Manoah of the tribe of Dan, and a powerful Nazirite, smites the Philistines and delivers Israel from their hands. Delilah tricks him and delivers him to the Philistines, who blind and imprison him. Later he pulls down the pillars of the Philistine Temple in Gaza, slaying more persons in his death than he had killed during his lifetime. Samson judges Israel for 20 years.	Judges 13, 14, 15, 16.

14. ELI the High Priest	2832 2837 2855 2872	1141 (ca. 1050)	Eli begins his 40 year rule in Shiloh.
			Birth of Samuel to Elkanah and Hannah, who consecrate him to God.
			God's first appearance to Samuel.
			Birth of David. He lives 70 years.
			Israel is defeated by the Philistines. The Ark of the Covenant is captured by the Philistines, and the two sons of Eli, Hophni and Phinehas are slain in the battle. Eli dies at the news at the age of 98 years.
				I Samuel 1.3-18
				    ,, 1·20
				    ,, 3
				    ,, 4

15. SAMUEL	2872 2881 2882	1095 -1060 (1020)	The Ark of the Covenant is carried through the cities of the Philistines for seven months, but leaves plagues in its wake. The Philistines return the Ark to the Israelites. The Israelites store it away for 20 years in Kiriath-jearim.
			Samuel the prophet is appointed Judge. He judges Israel for eleven years and travels about its cities.
			Samuel's sons, Joel and Abijah, are repugnant to the elders, who ask Samuel to anoint a king. Samuel at first refuses, but at the command of God, he sets out to find a suitable ruler.
			Samuel, last of the judges transfers the rule to Saul, son of Kish of the tribe of Benjamin. He anoints Saul, King of Israel.
			This concludes the period of the judges.
				I Samuel 5-7
				    ,, 7.3-17
				    ,, 8
				    ,, 9

TABLE IV

THE MONARCHY UNTIL THE DIVISION OF JUDAH AND ISRAEL

8. Beginnings of the Monarchy until Solomon

Joab captures Jerusalem by entering the city with his men through a water main.

JUDGES and RULERS	A.M.	B.C.E.	EVENT	SOURCE
SAUL, son of Kish	2883	1095* (1020)	The first year of the reign of King Saul. At first he rules in Gibeah, unrecognized by most of the tribes. After his victory over the Ammonites, he is recognized by all the tribes in a ceremony at Gilgal. Samuel reviews the history of Israel from the descent into Egypt up until the Monarchy.	I Samuel 10,11 " 13.1 " 12
	2884		Jonathan, son of Saul smites the Philistine garrison at Geba. Continuation of Saul's battles with the Philistines, Edomites, and Moabites, and with the army of Aram. Saul's uncle, Abner, son of Ner, serves as his general. Saul personally offers the burnt offering and the peace offering after his victory. For this act of presumption, Samuel prophesies the end of Saul's reign.	" 13.3 ff. " 14 " 14
		1065	War on Agag, king of the Amalekites. Samuel, angry at Saul for showing mercy on Agag and for permitting the people to use part of the war booty, prophesies Saul's end and abandons him.	" 15
		1063	God sends Samuel to choose one of the sons of Jesse the Bethlehemite to be king over Israel. Samuel secretly anoints David, son of Jesse, to replace Saul.	" 16
			Saul suffers from melancholia. He summons David to soothe his spirit with music. Saul appoints David as his arms-bearer.	" 16
			David slays Goliath the Philistine; afterwards, the Philistines are defeated. David forms a pact of friendship with Jonathan, and takes Saul's daughter Michal to wife.	" 17-18

* According to Arrowsmith, Saul was annointed by Samuel many years before the prophet's death. There is a margin of about 35 years (1095-1060 B.C.E.) for the initial year of Saul's reign. Modern scholars accept the year ca. 1020 as the date.

JUDGES and RULERS	A.M.	B.C.E.	EVENT	SOURCE
			Saul, jealous of David's popularity, attempts to kill him. David flees, when Jonathan reveals his father's plot.	1 Samuel 19
			At the command of Saul, Ahimelech son of Ahitub of the house of Eli and the inhabitants of the priestly city of Nob are killed for having given refuge to David. Ahimelech's son Abiathar flees to join David and his troop of 600 men.	" 22
			Saul pursues David. At one point, David has Saul at his mercy, but magnanimously does the king no harm. Saul and David make peace.	" 23 " 24
			Samuel dies at the age of 52 years and is buried in his residence at Ramah.	" 25.1
	2884		The churlishness of Nabal the Carmelite toward David. After Nabal's death David takes his widow Abigail to wife.	" 25
			David and his men go over to Achish, king of Gath, who gives him the city of Ziklag as a base. From there, David and his men raid and plunder the adjoining cities, occupied by the Geshurites, Gizrites, and Amalekites.	" 26
			The war with the Philistines. At En-dor Saul calls up the spirit of Samuel from the nether-world to learn the outcome of the next day's battle. Samuel prophesies Saul's imminent end. The children of Israel are defeated, Saul and Jonathan falling on the battlefield at Mt. Gilboa.	" 28-31
DAVID	2885	1055 (1004)	David laments the death of Saul and Jonathan. David, at the age of 30 goes to Hebron to be crowned by the Judeans. He reigns there over Judah for seven and a half years.	II Samuel 1 " 2.1-5 " 5.4-5 I Chronicles 3.4
ISH-BOSHETH	2890		Abner, son of Ner crowns Ish-bosheth, son of Saul as king. He is forty years old at this time and rules for two years.	II Samuel 2.8-10
	2891		The war between Abner, son of Ner, the general of Israel, and Joab, son of Zeruiah. Abner negotiates with David, to whom he offers the kingdom of all Israel. Joab kills Abner treacherously. David is angered at Joab and laments the death of Abner.	" 2.12-32 " 3
	2892	1048	Ish-bosheth is slain by two captains. David orders the death of the assassins.	II Samuel 4
DAVID (cont.)	2892	(998)	David crowned king in Hebron by all Israel. He rules for 33 years. David captures the fortress of Zion from the Jebusites and makes Jerusalem the capital of his kingdom.	" 5.3-10
		1047	David brings up the Ark of God from Kiriath-jearim to the house of Obed-edom and thence to Jerusalem.	" 6
	2893-2910		David wishes to build a House of God but the prophet Nathan informs him he cannot, because his hands are bloody. Nathan assures David that his son will build the Temple.	" 7

JUDGES and RULERS	A.M.	B.C.E.	EVENT	SOURCE
	2911-2912		King David defeats the Philistines, Arameans, Amalekites, Moabites and Edomites. He makes a treaty with the king of Hamath.	II Samuel 8
		1035	The incident of David and Bath-sheba. After insuring the death of Uriah, David marries Uriah's wife Bath-sheba. The prophet Nathan reproves David and prophesies his punishment. The first child that Bath-sheba bears David, dies.	II Samuel 11-12
			David captures Rabbat-ammon and expands the boundaries of the kingdom of Israel.	II Samuel 12.29

9. From the birth of Solomon until the Division of the Kingdom

Solomon judges his people.

JUDGES and RULERS	A.M.	B.C.E.	EVENT	SOURCE
	2913	1033	Solomon (also called Jedidiah) is born to David and Bath-sheba.	II Samuel 12.24-25
	2913		The incident of Amnon and Tamar. Absalom harbors hatred against Amnon.	II Samuel 13
	2915 2920	1030	Absalom kills Amnon and flees to Geshur. Absalom returns to Jerusalem and rebels against David. David flees to Transjordania. Absalom is killed by Joab's men. David mourns Absalom's death and returns to Jerusalem.	II Samuel 13 II Samuel 15-19
		1022	The unsuccessful rebellion against David led by Sheba, son of Bichri. Death of Sheba.	" 20
	2920-2922	1019	Years of famine interpreted as a punishment for Saul's killing of the Gibeonites. David delivers to the Gibeonites the descendants of the family of Saul; the famine ceases.	" 21 " 21
	2923	1017	David takes a census; there are 800,000 armed men in Israel and 500,000 in Judah.	I Chronicles 21.1-6
SOLOMON	2924	1015 (965)	The rebellion of Adonijah. David and Nathan anoint Solomon king. David's testament and will favoring Solomon. David dies at the age of 70 years. He has reigned 40 years, 7 in Hebron, and 33 in Jerusalem.	I Kings 1-2
	2925	1014	Solomon secures his rule, taking revenge on his adversaries and the enemies of David: Adonijah, Joab and Shimei son, of Gera.	I Kings 2

JUDGES and RULERS	A.M.	B.C.E.	EVENT	SOURCE
			Solomon's dream in Gibeon. He requests wisdom and knowledge from God; these are granted him, together with wealth and honor, which he did not ask for.	I Kings 3
	2927		Solomon's kingdom expands and he appoints commissioners over all Israel. Peace and prosperity throughout his realm.	" 4-5
	2928	1012	Solomon begins to build the Temple. 480 years have elapsed since the Exodus from Egypt. The construction of the Temple takes seven years. Solomon contracts a marriage with the idolatrous daughter of Pharaoh, and brings foreign rites into the land. As a punishment, God sends Hadad the Edomite against him.	" 6 II Chronicles 3 I Kings 3.1 " 11.14
	2935	1004	The dedication of the Temple and the observance of the Feast of Tabernacles. Solomon's prayer in the Temple.	II Chronicles 5
	2948-2964	992	Solomon's friendly relations with Hiram, king of Tyre. His merchant ships and trade. The Queen of Sheba visits Solomon to glean some of his wisdom.	I Kings 9 " 10 II Chronicles 9
		984	Solomon's foreign wives introduce idolatrous practices. Hence, God informs Solomon, his kingdom will be divided during the reign of his son.	I Kings 11.1-13
		980	Ahijah the Shilonite informs Jeroboam, son of Nebat, of the imminent division of the kingdom; he prophesies that Jeroboam will reign over the ten northern tribes of Israel.	I Kings 11.29-40
			Jeroboam rebels against Solomon; flees to Shishak, king of Egypt, for protection; and remains in Egypt until Solomon's death.	I Kings 11.27-40
	2964	975 (926)	Solomon rules over Judah and Israel for 40 years. He is succeeded by his son, Rehoboam.	" 11.41-43

SYNCHRONICAL TABLES
THE FIRST TEMPLE ERA

THE KINGS, THE PROPHETS AND THE HIGH PRIESTS OF JUDAH AND ISRAEL
(Events, Dates and Sources)

SYNCHRONICAL TABLE 1.

Rehoboam-Jeroboam till Jehoshaphat-Ahab

SYNCHRONICAL TABLE 2.

From Jehoshaphat-Ahaziah till Amaziah-Jehoash

SYNCHRONICAL TABLE 3.

From Amaziah-Jehoash till Manasseh and the Exile of Israel

SYNCHRONICAL TABLE 4.

From Manasseh till Ezra-Nehemiah

The Synchronical Tables which follow for the period of the Kings reflect a disparate margin of about forty five years between the version of S. Arrowsmith and those of recent research. This is evident only in the initial regnal years but subsequently converge to identical terminal dates for the Kingdom of Israel (722 B.C.E.) and of Judah (586 B.C.E.). The dates in the Synchronical Tables refer to events; numbers given in italics conform to modern dating of the Kings.

cf. Chart of Kings, pp. 101-103.

JUDAH

Source*	High Priest	Prophets**	Regnal Years	Kings of Judah	Main Events in Kingdom of Judah
					Solomon dies after reigning over all Israel for forty years.
1 Kings 12.1-18	AHIMAAZ	IDDO	17	1. REHOBOAM	The children of Israel gather in Shechem to crown Rehoboam, son of Solomon. They beseech him to reduce the tax burden, but he refuses. They murder Adoram, the official who is in charge of the levy. Rehoboam is forced to flee Jerusalem. He assembles an army to bring back the tribes of Israel into his kingdom. But the prophet Shemaiah prevents him. The priests, the Levites, and all those who are true unto the Lord gather and make the pilgrimage to Jerusalem.
		SHEMAIAH			Continuous warfare between Rehoboam and Jeroboam.
2 Chronicles 12					Rehoboam and all Judah forsake the Lord, offering sacrifices and incense to the idols upon the high places.
1 Kings 14.25					Thus Shishak, king of Egypt, invades Jerusalem and ransacks the Temple, in accordance with the word of God to the prophet Shemaiah. Jerusalem and the kingdom of Judah are looted, but Jerusalem is not destroyed.
1 Kings 15.1-2	AZARIAH*** (1 Chronicles 5.35)		3	2. ABIJAM (Abijah)	Abijam succeeds to the throne of his father Rehoboam. War continues between Judah and Israel.
2 Chronicles 13.1-2		IDDO			Abijam, in doing the right and the just, and trusting God, defeats Jeroboam.
					Abijam dies and is buried in the sepulchre of his fathers in the city of David.
1 Kings 15.9-10	AZARIAH		41	3. ASA	Asa succeeds to the throne of his father, Abijam.
		HANNANI, JEHU			
2 Chronicles 14.1					Continuous warfare between Asa and Baasa.
2 Chronicles 14.8-15.16					Asa destroys the idols. The land is tranquil; he devotes himself to reconstruction and fortification.
		ODED (or Azariah son of Oded)			Zerah the Ethiopian invades Judah with a large army, only to suffer defeat in the valley of Zephath at Mareshah.
					Asa, all Judah, and many of Israel pay heed to Azariah, son of Oded, and renew the covenant with the Lord. Asa deposes Maacah, the Queen Mother, because of her idolatry.

*Sources refer to the events.
**The exact dating of each prophet and the kings under whom the prophecies were spoken are subject to varying opinions of scholars.
***According to Seder Olam.

TABLE I

HIGH PRIESTS OF JUDAH AND ISRAEL

till Jehoshaphat — Ahab

Approx. Date	Main Events in Kingdom of Israel	Kings of Israel	Regnal Years	Prophets	Source
	Solomon dies after reigning over all Israel for forty years.				
975 *931*	The ten tribes rebel against the House of David and crown Jeroboam, son of Nebat. Jeroboam seizes the cities of Israel. He sets up calf idols for worship and sacrifice in Dan and Bethel, in competition with the Holy Temple in Jerusalem. He appoints new priests and Levites from among the people.	1. JEROBOAM	22	IDDO	1 Kings 12
975	A man of God comes from Judah to inveigh prophetically against the altar in Bethel. The hand Jeroboam puts forth against him withers. The prophet entreats God on Jeroboam's behalf, and he is healed. But the prophet fails to fulfill the terms of his mission and is killed by a lion.			A man of God who comes from Judah	
974	Jeroboam continues to appoint priests for calf worship.				
972					
971					
958					
958 *914*					
957					
956	Abijam, son of Jeroboam, falls sick. Jeroboam sends his wife to the prophet Ahijah in Shiloh to entreat the Lord for the child. The prophet informs her of the adverse judgment of God on the house of Jeroboam and the destruction of the kingdom of Israel. Ahijah foretells the child's death on her return to the city.			AHIJAH the Shilonite	
955					
911					
955	Jeroboam dies and is buried with his fathers in Tirzah.				
954 *909*	Nadab succeeds to the throne of his father Jeroboam.	2. NADAB	2		1 Kings 15.25
953	Nadab is murdered at Gibbethon by Baasa, son of Ahijah, of the tribe of Issachar, leader of a revolt.				
908	Baasa reigns. He destroys the entire house of Jeroboam.	3. BAASA	24	JEHU	1 Kings 15.28-33
951					
941					

Source	High Priest	Prophets	Regnal Years	Kings of Judah	Main Events in Kingdom of Judah
2 Chronicles 16-1-10					Asa removes all the gold and silver from the Temple and sends it to Ben-hadad, king of Aram, for aid in his campaign against Baasa. Baasa leaves off building Ramah out of the fear of Ben-hadad. The seer Hanani rebukes Asa for seeking aid from Aram; Asa puts him in prison.
					Asa sickens.
2 Chronicles 16.12					Though suffering from a foot disease, Asa does not pray for God's help, preferring to rely on physicians.
					Asa dies and is buried in the sepulchre of his fathers.
1 Kings 22.41-42	AMARIAH (2 Chronicles 19.11)	ELIEZER, son of Dodavahu — OBADIAH(?), ELIJAH — JAHAZIEL, son of Zechariah — JEHU, son of Hanani (also Hanani)	25	4. JEHOSHA-PHAT	Jehoshaphat succeeds his father Asa. He strengthens Judah.
2 Chronicles 17.6					Jehoshaphat destroys the high places in Judah. There is no king in Edom.
2 Chronicles 17.7-11	JOHANAN***				Jehoshaphat dispatches priests and Levites throughout the country to teach the people the law of God. Peace prevails; the Philistines and the Arabs pay tribute.
					Jehoshaphat makes a peace treaty with Ahab. He visits Ahab and joins him in battle against Aram. Jehoshaphat is miraculously saved and returns in peace to Jerusalem.
1 Kings 22					Jehoshaphat cooperates with Ahaziah in building a fleet of ships of Tarshish to transport gold from Ophir. He refuses however to send his servants to sea together with those of Ahaziah.

Approx. Date	Main Events in Kingdom of Israel	Kings of Israel	Regnal Years	Prophets	Source
940	Baasa attacks Judah. He builds a fortification at Ramah to prevent Israel from making the pilgrimage to Jerusalem. On hearing of Ben-hadad's attack on Israel, he ceases the construction and returns home to defend his country.				
930	Jehu, son of Hanani, prophesies the destruction of the house of Baasa. Baasa dies.				
885	Elah succeeds his father Baasa to the throne.	4. ELAH	2		1 Kings 16. 6-15
929	Elah is murdered by Zimri, a captain of chariots.				
884	Zimri reigns in place of Elah. He destroys all of the house of Baasa. When this becomes public, the Israelites crown Omri, the captain of Zimri's guard. Omri defeats Zimri, who sets fire to his palace and dies there, when escape proves impossible.	5. ZIMRI	7 days		1 Kings 16. 15-16
925 / 884	Omri reigns for 4 years. A faction turns from Omri to Tibni, son of Ginath; but Omri is the victor and Tibni dies. Omri builds Samaria as his capital and reigns there another 6 years. Omri dies and is buried in Samaria.	6. OMRI	12		1 Kings 16.21-22
918 / 875	Ahab succeeds his father Omri. He marries Jezebel, the daughter of Ethbaal of Sidon, and builds an altar to the worship of Baal.	7. AHAB	22	JAHAZIEL, ELIEZER	
917					
914					
871					
914				MICAIAH OBADIAH*	
912					
910	Elijah prophesies to Ahab coming years of famine. He flees to the brook Cherith, where he is fed by ravens. Then he goes to Zarephath and resuscitates the son of a widow.				1 Kings 17.1
906	During the worst of the famine years Elijah is sent by God to Ahab. He meets Obadiah, who takes him to Ahab. On mount Carmel, Elijah proves to Ahab and all Israel that the Lord is God. His sacrifice is consumed by heavenly fire; the sacrifice of the priests of Baal is not. He kills all of the priests of Baal, and flees to Beer-sheba fearing the vengeance of Jezebel. In Horeb, God appears to Elijah and orders him to anoint Hazael, Jehu, and Elisha, Elijah's aide.				1 Kings 18-19
901	Ben-hadad, king of Aram, conquers Samaria; but the forces of Aram are defeated, with the aid of the prophet.			A man of God who prophesies for Ahab	1 Kings 20
900	Ahab defeats Aram twice in Aphik according to the word of God through the prophet. But he releases Ben-hadad, the king of Aram for which the prophet rebukes him.				
899	Ahab steals the vineyard of Naboth the Jezreelite. Elijah informs Ahab of God's judgment against him for this act. Ahab is remorseful, and the punishment is postponed.				
898 / 853	Ahaziah joins his father in ruling the country, perhaps in preparation for a campaign against Aram.	AHAB and AHAZIAH jointly		ELISHA, son of Shaphat ELIJAH the Tishbite	
897	After three years of peace between Aram and Israel, Ahab, encouraged by the false prophet Zedekiah, attacks Aram; on the hills of Gilead he is joined by Jehoshaphat. Ahab falls in battle, is buried in Samaria, and the dogs lick his blood—all in fulfillment of God's word.				

*See biographies of the Prophets.

JUDAH

Source	High Priest	Prophets	Regnal Years	Kings of Judah	Main Events in Kingdom of Judah
2 Chronicles 19-20	AMARIAH	JAHAZIEL son of Zechariah — ELIEZER son of Dodavahu — JEHU son of Hanani			Returning from Ramoth-gilead, Jehoshaphat meets Jehu, son of Hanani, the seer, who reproves him. He proclaims a fast throughout Judah because of the attacks upon the country by Moab, Ammon, and Aram.
					The prophet Jahaziel prophesies the defeat of the enemies of Judah, which takes place near the valley of Berachah. Jehoshaphat joins with Ahaziah, king of Israel, in building ships of Tarshish, to transport gold from Ophir. The prophet Eliezer, son of Dodavahu, rebukes him for this. The ships are broken in Ezion-geber.
					Jehoshaphat joins with Joram in battle against the king of Moab; they are joined by the king of Edom. Confronted with a lack of water, at the advice of Jehoshaphat the three kings appeal to Elisha. He promises them water as well as success in battle. Moab is defeated, and the eldest son of King Mesha is sacrificed.
				JEHOSHAPHAT and JEHORAM rule jointly	Jehoram reigns as co-regent with his father Jehoshaphat for four years; then he rules alone for four years.
					Jehoshaphat dies and is buried with his fathers in the city of David.
1 Kings 22.51			8	5. JEHORAM	Jehoram succeeds his father Jehoshaphat. He marries the daughter of Ahab and kills all of his brothers, to whom his father had bequeathed different cities. The Edomites rebel, choosing a king of their own, but are defeated; later, however, they are victorious. Libnah revolts at the same time.
					Elijah sends Jehoram letters of admonition for sacrificing on the high places.
2 Chronicles 21.17 21.19 21.20					The Lord stirs up the Philistines and the Arabians against Jehoram. They capture Jerusalem and carry away all the king's substance, his wives and all his sons but Jehoahaz, the youngest. The Lord punishes Jehoram with a fatal disease of the bowels for sacrificing on the high places.

TABLE II

THE HIGH PRIESTS OF JUDAH AND ISRAEL

till Amaziah—Jehoash

ISRAEL

Approx. Date	Main Events in Kingdom of Israel	Kings of Israel	Regnal Years	Prophets	Source
	Ahaziah rules over Israel. He joins with Jehoshaphat in building ships of Tarshish to transport gold from Ophir. He tries unsuccessfully to persuade Jehoshaphat to help man the ships. The ships built jointly by Ahaziah and Jehoshaphat are broken at Ezion-geber.	8. AHAZIAH	2	ELIJAH A man of God who speaks to AHAB / ELISHA	1 Kings 22.49-52
896	Moab rebels against Israel. Ahaziah sickens and sends to inquire of Baalzebub, god of Ekron, whether he shall recover. Elijah prophesies his death. Ahaziah twice sends messengers to capture Elijah, but they are consumed by fire from heaven. The third time, the messengers return to Ahaziah with the word of Elijah, who foretells the king's death. Ahaziah dies.				2 Kings 1
852	Jehoram, the second son of Ahab, succeeds Ahaziah, who has died childless. He takes a census of Israel. Elijah is taken to heaven in a chariot of fire. Elisha divides the Jordan with the mantle of Elijah and succeeds him as prophet. He sweetens the bitter waters at Jericho. Bears devour the children who mock him. Moab rebels against Israel.	9. JEHORAM	12	JOEL* / JONAH ELISHA	2 Kings 1.17 2.1-25 3.1 3.4-5
895	Jehoram joins forces with Jehoshaphat and the king of Edom against Moab. Confronted with a lack of water, on the advice of Jehoshaphat the three kings appeal to Elisha. He promises them water as well as success in battle. Moab is defeated. Elisha performs a number of miracles through prayer: replenishing a cruse of oil, causing a woman to conceive, resurrecting the dead.				2 Kings 3 2 Kings 4.38-45
894	Naaman the Aramean visits Elisha in Samaria to be cured of his leprosy. Elisha bids him dip himself in the Jordan; Naaman is cured. Gehazi, Elisha's servant, is punished with Naaman's leprosy for his greed.				2 Kings 5
893	Elisha performs other miracles: e.g., the ax floating in water. He thwarts the plan of the King of Aram to capture him: he causes the forces of Aram to be smitten with blindness and taken to Samaria; they are returned peaceably to their own land.				2 Kings 6.1-23
892	Ben-hadad besieges the famished city of Samaria. Jehoram blames Elisha, and tries to have him killed. Four lepers report the flight of the Aramean army. The Israelites despoil the deserted camp of the enemy.				2 Kings 6.24
891	Elisha prophesies seven years of famine. The miracle of the prophets and the pottage.				2 Kings 8.1
889					
889 851					
887					
885	Elisha goes to Damascus. Sick, Ben-hadad sends Hazael to Elisha to inquire whether he will recover. Elisha prophesies that Hazael will succeed Ben-hadad; Hazael kills Ben-hadad and succeeds to the throne.				2 Kings 8.7-15

See biographies of the Prophets (beginning p. 134).

Source	High Priest	Prophets	Regnal Years	Kings of Judah	Main Events in Kingdom of Judah
2 Chronicles 21.19-20					After two years Jehoram dies and is not cremated in the royal fashion. He is buried in the city of David but not in the sepulchres of the kings.
2 Kings 8.25 2 Chronicles 22.1-9			1	6. AHAZIAH	Ahaziah succeeds to the throne.
					On the advice of his wicked mother, Athaliah, Ahaziah joins the king of Israel in battle against Hazael, king of Aram. In Ramoth-gilead Jehoram is wounded; he returns to Jezreel to recover. Ahaziah visits Jehoram, but is caught by Jehu, who kills him hiding in Samaria. Jehu also slays the sons and brethren of Ahaziah, who are attending him.
2 Chronicles 22.10-12 2 Chronicles 23 2 Kings 11 12.1	**JEHOIADA** (2 Kings 11.4-8) (2 Chronicles 22.11)		6	7. ATHALIAH	Athaliah rules after the death of her son Ahaziah. She destroys the entire royal family of the House of David, except for Joash the son of Ahaziah, who is saved by his aunt Jehoshabeath and hidden in the Temple for six years.
					Jehoiada the priest, husband of Jehoshabeath, crowns Joash at the age of 7. Athaliah is murdered.
2 Chronicles 24.1	ZECHARIAH son of Jehoiada	ZECHARIAH, son of Jehoiada	40	8. JEHOASH (JOASH)	Jehoiada the priest makes a covenant between God and the people of Judah. He restores the service of God in the Temple. The temple of the Baal is demolished, and Mattan, the priest of Baal slain. But the people continue to sacrifice and make offerings in the high places.
2 Kings 12.5-17 2 Chronicles 24.5-14					Jehoash orders the repair of the Temple. After some time the Temple is repaired. Sacrifices are offered daily in the Temple throughout Jehoiada's reign.
2 Chronicles 24.15					Jehoiada the priest dies at the age of 130 years and is buried in the city of David near the sepulchres of the kings.
2 Chronicles 24.18-25					Joash and the people worship idols. God sends them prophets; but no one will pay them heed. Zechariah, the son of Jehoiada, is stoned in the house of God. Aram attacks Judah, captures Jerusalem, kills all the princes of the country, and sends the spoil to Damascus.
					The servants of Joash rebel and murder him. He is buried in the city of David, but not in the sepulchres of the kings.
2 Chronicles 24.27-25.5		A man of God who speaks to Amaziah / AMOZ	29	9. AMAZIAH	Amaziah succeeds to the throne of his father Jehoash. He kills the murderers of his father, and takes a census of the men of Judah for his army.

Approx. Date	Main Events in Kingdom of Israel	Kings of Israel	Regnal Years	Prophets	Source
885 *843* **884**	Jehoram joins Ahaziah in battle against Hazael at Ramoth-gilead. There wounded, he returns to Jezreel to recover. Elisha sends a prophet to Ramoth-gilead to anoint Jehu king of Israel. Jehu declares himself king, rides to Jezreel and kills Jehoram in the field of Naboth. He also slays Jezebel and casts her body to the dogs.				2 Kings 9.1-37
884 *842-41*	Jehu succeeds to the throne. He destroys the survivors of the house of Ahab, its priests and officials, as well as 40 of the brethren of Ahaziah and all who worship Baal. Nevertheless, he himself practices idolatry.	**10. JEHU**	28	ELISHA JONAH	2 Kings 10.1-31
878 *836*					
862 **860**	The prophet Jonah is sent to Nineveh to prophesy its destruction. The inhabitants of Nineveh repent and God forgives them. "In those days the Lord began to cut Israel short; and Hazael smote them in all the borders of Israel."				2 Kings 10.32-33
856	Jehu dies and is buried in Samaria.				2 Kings 10.35
814	Jehoahaz succeeds his father Jehu.	**11. JEHOAHAZ**	17		2 Kings 10.35
850					
849 **842**	God delivers Israel into the hands of Aram. Jehoahaz prays to God; He sends a savior.			ELISHA JONAH	2 Kings 13.3-5
841	Joash shares the reign with his father Jehoahaz.				
840					
839	Jehoahaz dies and is buried in Samaria. Elisha becomes deathly sick. Hazael, king of Aram, dies, and is succeeded by his son Ben-hadad.				2 Kings 13.9-13.24
839 *796; 798*	Jehoash (Joash) succeeds his father Jehoahaz. Elisha, on his death bed, prophesies to Jehoash three victories over Aram.	**12. JOASH** **(JEHOASH)**	16	ELISHA JONAH	2 Kings 13.10
838	Elisha dies. The Moabites invade the land. The bones of Elisha cause the revival of one being buried.				2 Kings 13.20
837 **836**	Jehoash recovers the cities of Israel captured by the Arameans, fulfilling Elisha's prophecy.	JEHOASH and JEROBOAM II rule jointly			2 Kings 13.25

JUDAH

Source	High Priest	Prophets	Regnal Years	Kings of Judah	Main Events in Kingdom of Judah
2 Chronicles 25.6-16 2 Kings 13.12		A man of God who speaks to AMAZIAH		AMAZIAH	Amaziah hires Israelite mercenaries to do battle against the Edomites. But he follows the advice of a prophet and sends them back home. He smites the children of Seir in the Valley of Salt. His victory transforms him and he worships the gods of Edom, refusing to accept the admonition of the prophet.
2 Chronicles 25.17-21 2 Kings 14.8-15					Amaziah fights with Joash, king of Israel at Beth-shemesh. Joash is victorious and brings Amaziah captive to Jerusalem, destroying the city. His forces plunder the city and the Temple.
2 Kings 14.19-20 2 Chronicles 25.27-28					When Amaziah turns away from the Lord, his servants conspire and kill him in Lachish. He is brought to Jerusalem and buried with his fathers in the city of Judah.
2 Kings 15.3 2 Chronicles 26	AZARIAH II (III) (2 Chronicles 26.17)	JOEL	52	10. UZZIAH (AZARIAH)	Uzziah (or Azariah) succeeds his father Amaziah. He builds Elath and restores it to Judah. Under the influence of the prophet Zechariah he seeks God's help; but he does not remove the high places.
					Joel prophesies. Uzziah prospers, subduing the Philistines and the Arabs. The Edomites and other nations seek his aid and protection. He strengthens the walls of Jerusalem and of other cities.
		HOSEA, AMOS MICAH ISAIAH			
2 Kings 15.5-6					Isaiah begins to prophesy. Uzziah, in his vainglory seeking to be compared to David, enters the Temple to burn incense. He is punished with leprosy till the day of his death. His son Jotham reigns in his stead and judges the people.
2 Chronicles 26.23					Uzziah dies and is buried in the royal field of burial (and not in the sepulchre of his fathers), because he is a leper.

TABLE III
HIGH PRIESTS OF JUDAH AND ISRAEL
and the Exile of Israel

Approx. Date	Main Events in Kingdom of Israel	Kings of Israel	Regnal Years	Prophets	Source
836	Jehoash is thrice victorious over Aram, as foretold by Elisha.	JEHOASH			
827	Jehoash permits 100,000 Israelite soldiers to hire out as mercenaries to Amaziah in his war against the Edomites. In accordance with the prophetic word they are sent home. In their anger they plunder the cities of Judah, killing many of the inhabitants.			ELISHA JONAH	
826	Taunted by Amaziah, Jehoash goes forth to battle. He is victorious and takes Amaziah captive; he destroys the walls of Jerusalem. His forces plunder the city and Temple. After that he returns to Samaria.				
	Jehoash dies and is buried in Samaria in the sepulchre of the kings of Israel.				
825 786	Jeroboam II succeeds his father Jehoash as king in Samaria.	13. JEROBOAM II	41	HOSEA JONAH AMOS	
822	Jeroboam II expands the boundaries of Israel in accordance with the words of God to the prophet Jonah.				
810	He regains Hamath and Damascus, originally part of Judah.				
810 791					
800					
787	Amos prophesies.				
785	Hosea begins his prophecies.				
784	Jeroboam dies and is buried in the sepulchre of the kings of Israel.				2 Kings 14.29
784-773	An interregnum of 11 years without a king in Israel.		11	HOSEA AMOS	
746	Zechariah, son of Jeroboam II, begins to rule.	14. ZECHARIAH	6 months	HOSEA AMOS	
772	Zechariah is murdered by Shallum, son of Jabesh.				
745	Shallum, son of Jabesh, takes the throne.	15. SHALLUM	1 month	HOSEA AMOS	2 Kings 15.10
772 745	Shallum is murdered in Samaria by Menahem, son of Gadi, who ascends the throne.				
772	Menahem, son of Gadi, devastates Tiphsah and its environs.	16. MENAHEM	10	HOSEA AMOS	2 Kings 15.14
771 765	Pul, king of Assyria, attacks Israel. Menahem bribes Pul to confirm his reign.				2 Kings 15.16
761	Menahem dies.				
761	Pekahiah succeeds his father Menahem to the throne.	17. PEKAHIAH	2	HOSEA AMOS	2 Kings 15.22-26
736 759	Pekahiah is murdered in Samaria by one of his officers, Pekah, son of Remaliah.				
751(736)*	Pekah reigns.	18. PEKAH	20	HOSEA ODED*	2 Kings 15.25-28
758					

*Because of the disturbing interregnum there is a variance in reckoning. Tradition (II Kings 16.27) records 20 years inclusive for Pekah. The modern reckoning limits the reign to approximately 2 years.

*See biographies of the Prophets.

Source	High Priest	Prophets	Regnal Years	Kings of Judah	Main Events in Kingdom of Judah
2 Chronicles 27.1-9 2 Kings 15.32-36 2 Kings 15.34-37		MICAH HOSEA, AMOS ISAIAH	16	11. JOTHAM	Jotham succeeds his father Uzziah. He does not enter the Temple of the Lord, and he allows the high places to stand. Jotham fortifies Jerusalem and the cities of the land. He is victorious over the Ammonites; Judah is strong and prosperous during Jotham's reign.
					Micah begins to prophesy.
2 Kings 15.37-38 2 Chronicles 27.9					The Lord sends Rezin, king of Aram, and Pekah, son of Remaliah, against Judah. Jotham dies and is buried with his fathers in the city of David.
2 Kings 15.38 16.1-4 2 Chronicles 28.1	URIAH (2 Kings 16.10)	HOSEA, ODED, AMOS ISAIAH	16	12. AHAZ	Ahaz succeeds his father Jotham. He makes molten images for the Baalim and burns his children in the fire after the heathen fashion. He sacrifices and offers on the high places and under every leafy tree. Though he succeeds in repelling the attack of Pekah, son of Remaliah, and Rezin, king of Aram, Aram annexes Elath.
2 Chronicles 28.5-8 17-19					Ahaz is defeated by the kings of Aram and Israel, who take many captives to Samaria and Damascus. Maaseiah, the king's son, is killed. The Philistines and Edomites invade Judah; all this because of Ahaz' idolatry.
2 Kings 16.7-19 2 Chronicles 28.20-27 2 Kings 16.10-20		MICAH			Ahaz takes the silver and gold of the Temple and pays Tiglath-pileser, king of Assyria, to help him against Aram and Israel. Tiglath-pileser is victorious. Ahaz goes to Damascus with precious gifts from the House of God.
2 Chronicles 28.27					Ahaz dies and is buried in the city of David, but not in the royal sepulchre.
2 Kings 16.20 2 Kings 18.1-4 2 Chronicles 29.1-16	AZARIAH III (2 Chronicles 31.10-13)	HOSEA, AMOS ISAIAH	29	13. HEZEKIAH	Hezekiah succeeds his father Ahaz. He removes the high places, breaks the pillars, cuts down the Asherah, and breaks in pieces the brazen serpent that Moses had made. Hezekiah repairs the Temple and restores the traditional service.
2 Chronicles 30,31 2 Kings 18.7-8					Hezekiah proclaims the observance of the Passover in Judah and Israel; he reorganizes the administration in the Temple, and the service of the priests and Levites. Hezekiah rebels against the king of Assyria, and subjugates the Philistines "unto Gaza and the borders thereof". God is with him in all his endeavors.
2 Chronicles 32.1-20 32.24 2 Kings 20.1-11 Isaiah 38-39 2 Kings 20.12-19 2 Chronicles 32.25-26		MICAH NAHUM			Sennacherib, king of Assyria, invades Judah; but on obtaining a huge tribute, he leaves. Hezekiah sickens and Isaiah informs him that he will not recover. But God listens to Hezekiah's prayer and lengthens his life 15 years. Nahum prophesies the destruction of Nineveh.
					Merodach-baladan, king of Babylon, sends emissaries to Hezekiah to bless him upon his recovery. Hezekiah shows them all his treasures. Isaiah rebukes him for this, prophesying the beginning of the Babylonian domination over Judah.
2 Chronicles 32.9-23 2 Kings 18-19 Isaiah 36-37					Sennacherib, king of Assyria, dispatches letters and messengers to Judah taunting the Lord as well as king Hezekiah. Hezekiah and Isaiah pray to God. The Lord sends an angel, who destroys the Assyrian army. Shortly afterward, Sennacherib is killed by his sons.
2 Chronicles 32.27-33					Hezekiah dies and is buried in the sepulchre of the Davidic kings.
2 Kings 20.21 21.1-17		ISAIAH NAHUM JOEL HABAKKUK	55	14. MANASSEH	Manasseh succeeds his father Hezekiah. He builds high places to Baal, prostrates himself before the hosts of heaven, and makes his sons pass through fire in the valley of Hinom. God sends prophets to Manasseh and all the people, but they refuse to hearken. Manasseh sheds much blood.

Approx. Date	Main Events in Kingdom of Israel	Kings of Israel	Regnal Years	Prophets	Source
758 *751* *736** 750				HOSEA	
742	Pekah invades Judah.				
742 *742*	Pekah and Rezin, king of Aram, lay siege to Jerusalem. They vanquish Ahaz, but cannot capture the city. Rezin drives the Judeans from Elath and annexes it to Aram.				
741	Pekah and Rezin defeat Ahaz, plunder his country, and lead large numbers of Judeans captive to Israel and Damascus. On the advice of the prophet Oded, the captives are returned from Samaria to Jericho.				2 Kings 15.29
740	Tiglath-pileser, king of Assyria, hired by Ahaz, attacks Pekah. He marches through Gilead, Galilee, and Naphtali and exiles the inhabitants to Assyria. Defeating Rezin, king of Aram, he captures Damascus and transfers its inhabitants to Kir.				
739 – 730	A state of anarchy continues for 9 years.				
730	Hoshea, son of Elah, conspires against Pekah and murders him.	19. HOSHEA (the last Israelite king)	9		2 Kings 15.30-31
730 *731*	Hoshea, son of Elah, takes the throne of the kingdom of Israel. Shalmaneser, king of Assyria, defeats Hoshea, who is forced to pay tribute.				2 Kings 17.3
726				HOSEA	
726 *726*	Hoshea makes a treaty with the king of Egypt and stops paying taxes and tribute to the king of Assyria. The king of Assyria imprisons Hoshea.				2 Kings 17.4
725					
723	The king of Assyria conquers Samaria after three years of war.				2 Kings 17.6
721 *722*	The Israelites are exiled by the Assyrian army to Halah, Habor on the River of Gozan, and the cities of the Medes.	Israel in Exile			
713					
712					
710					
698					
698					
678 *697*	The various nations settled in Samaria by the king of Assyria are attacked by lions. They convert to Judaism, yet continue to worship the pagan gods.				2 Kings 17.24-25

JUDAH

Source	High Priest	Prophets	Regnal Years	Kings of Judah	Basic Events in Kingdom of Judah
2 Chronicles 33.10-16		ISAIAH, JOEL HABAKKUK NAHUM		MANASSEH	Manasseh is taken captive by the forces of the king of Assyria and brought to Babylon. He repents and prays to God. On his release he forsakes the pagan gods.
2 Kings 21.18					Manasseh dies and is buried in the garden of his own house.
2 Kings 21.18-26 2 Chronicles 33.20-25	SHALLUM		2	15. AMON	Amon rules. He forsakes the God of his fathers.
					The servants of Amon conspire against him and put the king to death in his own house. He is buried in his sepulchre in the garden of Uzza.
2 Chronicles 34.1 2 Kings 22.1; 2 Chronicles 34.2-7	HILKIAH (2 Chronicles 34.8-9)	HULDAH the prophetess HABAKKUK ZEPHANIAH JEREMIAH	31	16. JOSIAH	Josiah succeeds to the throne of his father Amon. The people of the land slay all those that have conspired against Amon.
					Josiah removes all the pagan objects in Judah and Israel.
					Zephaniah prophesies.
					Jeremiah begins to prophesy.
					Habakkuk prophesies.
2 Kings 22.3-20 23.1-20					Josiah begins to repair the Temple. A scroll of the law is discovered and he sends to Huldah the prophetess to inquire of God. She foretells the impending destruction of Jerusalem. Josiah has the Book of Law read to the people and purifies them.
2 Kings 23.21-24					Josiah celebrates Passover, as it had not been celebrated since the days of the judges.
					Nineveh is destroyed, according to the word of God as delivered by Nahum.
2 Kings 23.29-30 2 Chronicles 35.20-27					Pharaoh-nechoh, king of Egypt, goes out to battle against the king of Assyria. Josiah marches against the Egyptian army crossing his territory; he is killed in Megiddo, brought to Jerusalem, and buried in the sepulchre of his fathers. Jeremiah and the people mourn him.
2 Chronicles 36.1-4 2 Kings 23.30-35		JEREMIAH	3 months	17. JEHOAHAZ	Jehoahaz (Shallum), son of Josiah, rules in Judah. Pharaoh-nechoh puts him in chains in Riblah. Later he takes Jehoahaz to Egypt, where he dies.
2 Kings 23.34-36	AZARIAH (1 Chronicles 5.39)	JEREMIAH URIAH DANIEL	11	18. JEHOIAKIM	Jehoiakim (Eliakim) is crowned by Pharaoh-nechoh in place of his father Josiah. Jehoiakim pays a heavy tribute to the king of Egypt.
2 Chronicles 36.5-7 2 Kings 24.1-7					Nebuchadnezzar, king of Babylon, subjugates Jehoiakim. Nebuchadnezzar plunders Jerusalem and the Temple and carries the booty to Babylon. Daniel is taken to Babylon, where he begins to prophesy.
2 Kings 24.1-7					Jehoiakim rebels against Nebuchadnezzar. Daniel interprets the dream of Nebuchadnezzar.
					Jehoiakim dies and is buried in the gates of Jerusalem.
2 Kings 24.6 2 Kings 24.8-17		JEREMIAH DANIEL	3 months	19. JEHOIACHIN	Jehoiachin succeeds his father Jehoiakim. Jerusalem is captured by the Babylonian army; Jehoiachin and many of the people are taken captive to Babylon.
2 Chronicles 36.10 2 Kings 24.17-20 Jeremiah 52.3	SERAIAH (1 Chronicles 5.40) JEHOZADAK	OBADIAH JEREMIAH DANIEL EZEKIEL	11	20. ZEDEKIAH	Nebuchadnezzar names Zedekiah, uncle of Jehoiachin, king of Judah. Zedekiah refuses to hearken to the word of God as transmitted through Jeremiah.
					Ezekiel begins to prophesy in the exile by the river Chebar.
					Zedekiah rebels against the king of Babylon.
					The people and officials of the country forsake God, rebelling against the words of the prophets. Nebuchadnezzar begins the siege of Jerusalem.

TABLE IV

HIGH PRIESTS OF JUDAH AND ISRAEL

Ezra-Nehemiah

ISRAEL

Approx. Date	Israel and Neighboring Countries (after the Exile of the Ten Tribes)	King		
678	Ashurbanipal, king of Assyria, invades Egypt.	ASHURBANIPAL		
652	Ashurbanipal captures Babylon and dethrones his brother Shamash-shum-ukin, for having led a revolt by the Eastern provinces against the domination of Babylon. Ashurbanipal receives tribute from Manasseh, king of Judah.			
643				
642				
641*				
641 / 640				
634				
630 / 629	Nabupolassar, king of Babylon, reigns over Judea (630-609). The Chaldeans are freed from the domination of Assyria.	NABUPOLASSAR		
626				
624			ISRAEL IN EXILE	
623	Pharaoh-nechoh reigns in Egypt.	PHARAOH-NECHOH		
612				
610				
610 / 609				
610 / 608				
606	Nebuchadnezzar reigns in Babylon (605-562).	NEBUCHADNEZZAR		
603				
599				
599 / 597				
599 / 597				
595				
593	Psamtik II reigns in Egypt (593-588).	PSAMTIK II		
590				

Source	High Priest	Prophets	Regnal Years	Kings of Judah	Basic Events in Kingdom of Judah
2 Kings 25 Jeremiah 52.1-11	JEHOZADAK (1 Chronicles 5.40-41) SERAIAH	DANIEL EZEKIEL JEREMIAH OBADIAH*		ZEDEKIAH	Famine shatters the defense of the besieged city of Jerusalem. Zedekiah is captured. His sons are killed before his very eyes; the king of Babylon puts out Zedekiah's eyes and takes him to Babylon. The Temple and Jerusalem are consumed by fire; the city's walls are leveled; the princes are murdered, and many of the Judeans taken captive. Only the poorest Judeans remain, to be vine-dressers and husbandmen.
					The Temple is destroyed on the 9th of Ab.
	Fifty year interval with no priesthood	OBADIAH	2 months	GEDALIAH	Gedaliah is appointed by the king of Babylon governor over the survivors, and is killed by Ishmael. Some of the people flee to Egypt, out of fear of the Babylonian king.
		DANIEL EZEKIEL JEREMIAH ZECHARIAH			Obadiah prophesies.
					Nebuzaradan exiles some of the inhabitants of Judah and Israel.
2 Kings 25.27-30					Evil-merodach, king of Babylon, releases Jehoiachin from prison and gives him special status.
					The last banquet of Belshazzar, and his murder. Darius the Mede captures Babylon and raises Daniel to a high position of responsibility.
					Daniel is saved from the lion's den.
Ezra 3. Josephus, Contra Apionem 1.21	JESHUA, son of Jozadak (Ezra 3.2)	DANIEL SERAIAH, BARUCH HAGGAI ZECHARIAH MORDECAI		ZERUBBABEL (Judah under Persian dominion)	After 70 years of exile Cyrus proclaims the return to Zion. Many Judeans return to Jerusalem and begin to build its walls. Zerubbabel is appointed governor of Judea.
					The returnees to Zion lay the foundation for the Temple, refusing the aid of the Samaritans.
					The Samaritans hinder the Judeans in building the Temple; they continuously malign the Judeans throughout the reign of Cyrus.
Ezra 4.7					At the beginning of the reign of Artaxerxes (Cambyses), the Samaritans send a defamatory letter against the Jews who have returned to Zion.
Ezra 4.24					The work of building the Temple ceases.
Ezra 5.1					The prophets Haggai and Zechariah urge the people to resume rebuilding the Temple. The ritual of service is revived.
Ezra 6.1-12	JEHOIAKIM (Nehemiah 12.10)				The Samaritans again seek to disturb the builders. Darius finds Cyrus' decree permitting the rebuilding.
Esther 2.15-17	ELIASHIB (Nehemiah 12.10)				The building of the Second Temple is finished. The dedication of the Temple. The observance of Passover. Esther replaces Vashti as queen of Persia.
Esther 5-9					Haman receives permission from King Ahasuerus to annihilate the Jews. Esther prevents the calamity. Haman is hanged on the gallows, and the Jews take revenge on their enemies.
Esther 9.14					The Jews of Shushan, the capital, hang the ten sons of Haman. The observance of Purim.
					Ahasuerus imposes a tax on all the provinces of his land.
Ezra 7-10				EZRA	Ezra is sent by Artaxerxes to head the returnees to Zion. He forces the Judeans to give up their heathen wives.
Nehemiah		MALACHI		NEHEMIAH	Nehemiah is chosen governor of Judea. He fortifies the walls of Jerusalem, despite the antagonism of Sanballat. He settles Jerusalem, reorganizes the religious administration, and purifies the worship of God.
					Nehemiah leaves Jerusalem to appear before the king of Persia. He soon returns and continues his reforms.
					Malachi prophesies.

See biographies of the Prophets.

Approx. Date	Israel and Neighboring Countries (after the Exile of the Ten Tribes)	King		
588	Hophra-Apries reigns in Egypt.	HOPHRA-APRIES		
	The 18th or 19th year of Nebuchadnezzar's reign. Zedekiah is caught and brought to Riblah. Nebuchadnezzar puts out his eyes and sends Zedekiah to Babylon, fulfilling the prophesy of Ezekiel (12.13).			
588				
588				
587				
585				
	In the 23rd year of his reign, Nebuchadnezzar invades Egypt and captures Tyre.			
562	Evil-merodoch (Amel Marduk) reigns in Babylon.	EVIL-MERODOCH		
538	Cyrus, king of Persia, conquers Babylon.	CYRUS		
537				
536	Judea falls under the domination of Cyrus, king of Persia.			
535				
534				
529	Cambyses reigns in Persia (529-522).	CAMBYSES		
522				
	Darius Hystaspis reigns in Persia (521-486).	DARIUS		
520				
519				
	The Persians are defeated by the Greeks at Marathon.			
515	Xerxes I—Ahasuerus reigns in Persia (486-465).	XERXES I		
510	The Persians vanquish the Greeks at Thermopylae, but they are defeated near Salamis.			
509	The Persians are defeated by the Greeks near Platae.			
495				
457	Artaxerxes I Longimanus reigns in Persia (465-424).	ARTAXERXES I		
445				
434				
397				

APPENDICES *

PROPHETIC MESSAGES RECORDED
IN THE BIBLE

PROPHET	SENT TO	SOURCE
1. Aaron	Pharaoh	Exodus 7.1
2. Anonymous	Israel	Judges 6.8-10
3. A man of God	Eli	1 Samuel 2.27-36
4. Samuel	Israel	1 Samuel 7.3
5. Samuel	Saul, in Gilgal	1 Samuel 13.11-14
6. Samuel	Saul, after the battle with the Amalekites	1 Samuel 15
7. Nathan	David, to inform him that his son will build the Temple	2 Samuel 7
8. Nathan	David, after the latter's sin with Bath-sheba	2 Samuel 12
9. Gad	David, after he had taken a census of Israel	2 Samuel 24.12
10. Ahijah the Shilonite	Jeroboam	2 Kings 11.29-39
11. Shemaiah	Rehoboam	1 Kings 12.21-24; 2 Chronicles 11.2-4
12. A man of God	The altar of Jeroboam	1 Kings 13.1-2
13. Ahijah the Shilonite	The wife of Jeroboam	1 Kings 14.5-16
14. Jehu, son of Hanani	Baasa	1 Kings 16.1-4
15. Anonymous	Ahab	1 Kings 20.13-28
16. One of the disciples of the prophets	Ahab	1 Kings 20.35 ff.
17. Elijah	Ahab	1 Kings 21.17-26
18. Micaiah, son of Imlah	Ahab and Jehoshaphat	1 Kings 22.8-14
19. Elisha	Jehoram and Jehoshaphat	2 Kings 3.11
20. A young prophet sent by Elisha	Jehu	2 Kings 9.1-10
21. Jonah	Jeroboam II	2 Kings 14.25
22. Isaiah	Hezekiah	2 Kings 19-20
23. Huldah	Josiah	2 Kings 22.14
24. Shemaiah	Rehoboam	2 Chronicles 12.5-8
25. Azariah, son of Oded	Asa	2 Chronicles 15.1-7
26. Hanani	Asa	2 Chronicles 16.7-9
27. Eliezer, son of Dodavahu	Jehoshaphat	2 Chronicles 20.37
28. Elijah (via a scroll)	Jehoram	2 Chronicles 21.12-15
29. Zechariah, son of Jehoiada	Israel, in the days of Joash	2 Chronicles 24.20
30. A man of God	Amaziah	2 Chronicles 25.7-9
31. Anonymous	Amaziah	2 Chronicles 25.15-16
32. Oded	Pekah and his army	2 Chronicles 28.9-11

*Refer to sources in the last page of Introduction.

PRAYERS IN THE BIBLE

#	UTTERED BY	OBJECT OF PRAYER	OUTCOME OF PRAYER	SOURCE
1.	Abraham	That God forgive the sin of Sodom.	God agrees to forgive Sodom if ten righteous persons can be found in the city.	Genesis 18.23-33
2.	Abraham	That Abimelech's wives no longer be barren.	The house of Abimelech is healed.	Genesis 20.17-18
3.	Abraham's Servant	That he succeed in his mission.	He meets Rebekah.	Genesis 24.12-14
4.	Isaac	That Rebekah bear children.	Jacob and Esau are born.	Genesis 25.21
5.	Jacob	That he be protected from Esau.	The brothers make peace with each other.	Genesis 32.9-12
6.	Moses	That Israel be forgiven for the sin of the golden calf.	God forgives the people.	Exodus 32.31-35
7.	Moses	That God continue to show grace to His people.	God continues to be gracious to Israel.	Exodus 33.12-18
8.	Moses	That Miriam be cured of her leprosy.	Miriam is cured after seven days.	Numbers 12.18
9.	Moses	That the people be forgiven for having believed the spies sent into Canaan.	God forgives the people.	Numbers 14.13-19
10.	Moses	That he be permitted to enter the Promised Land.	God shows Moses the Promised Land before his death.	Deuteronomy 3.23-25
11.	Samson	That he be avenged upon his enemies.	With his death he avenges himself.	Judges 16.28
12.	Hannah	That she be given a son.	Samuel is born.	1 Samuel 1.11
13.	David	That God make good His promise concerning David.	The Davidic line continues as the reigning dynasty	2 Samuel 7.18-29
14.	Solomon	That God cause His Presence to dwell in the Temple.	God causes His Presence to dwell in the Temple.	1 Kings 8.23-62
15.	Elijah	That the Lord vanquish Baal.	Fire descends from heaven and consumes Elijah's offering.	1 Kings 18.36-37
16.	Hezekiah	That Israel be saved from Sennacherib.	An angel smites the Assyrian camp.	2 Kings 19.15-20
17.	Asa	That God help his army defeat the Ethiopians.	God smites the Ethiopians.	2 Chronicles 14.11
18.	Jehoshaphat	That God defend His people against the armies of Moab and Ammon.	God grants Jehoshaphat the victory.	2 Chronicles 20.6-12
19.	Hezekiah	That God forgive the people for not having sanctified themselves before eating the paschal lamb.	God forgives the people.	2 Chronicles 30.18-19
20.	Nehemiah	That God aid His captive people.	God promises that He will rebuild the walls of Jerusalem.	Nehemiah 1.5-11
21.	Daniel	That God rebuild Jerusalem.	Jerusalem will be rebuilt in 70 weeks.	Daniel 9.4-19
22.	Jonah	That he be taken out of the whale.	The whale casts Jonah out upon dry land.	Jonah 2.2-9

THE MIRACLES OF ELIJAH

	MIRACLE	SOURCE
1.	The withholding of dew and rain.	1 Kings 17.1
2.	The feeding of Elijah by ravens at the brook of Cherith.	1 Kings 17.6
3.	God's blessing of the jar of meal and the cruse of oil in Zarephath.	1 Kings 17.14
4.	The revival of the son of the widow of Zarephath.	1 Kings 17.21
5.	The descent of fire upon the altar on Mount Carmel.	1 Kings 18.38
6.	Elijah's causing the rain to fall.	1 Kings 18.45
7.	The cake baked on hot stones and the cruse of water.	1 Kings 19.6
8.	Elijah's journey in the desert for 40 days and 40 nights without food.	1 Kings 19.8
9.	The vision of God on Mount Horeb.	1 Kings 19.9
10.	The consumption of the messengers of Ahaziah by fire from heaven.	2 Kings 1.10
11.	The splitting of the waters of the Jordan.	2 Kings 2.8
12.	His ascent to heaven in a whirlwind.	2 Kings 2.11

THE MIRACLES OF ELISHA

	MIRACLE	SOURCE
1.	The splitting of the waters of the Jordan.	2 Kings 2.14
2.	The healing of the waters of Jericho.	2 Kings 2.21
3.	The killing of the youths by the bears.	2 Kings 2.24
4.	The filling of the trenches with water, without wind or rain.	2 Kings 3.20
5.	God's blessing of increase from the pot of oil of Obadiah's widow.	2 Kings 4.6
6.	The birth of the son of the Shunammite woman.	2 Kings 4.17
7.	The resuscitation of the son of the Shunammite woman.	2 Kings 4.35
8.	The curing of the bitter pottage of the sons of the prophets by means of some meal.	2 Kings 4.41
9.	God's blessing of increase of the bread of the sons of the prophets.	2 Kings 4.42-44
10.	The healing of Naaman's leprosy.	2 Kings 5.14
11.	The cleaving of Naaman's leprosy to Gehazi.	2 Kings 5.27
12.	The floating of the axehead upon the water.	2 Kings 6.6
13.	The opening of the young man's eyes so that he saw the mountains full of horses and chariots of fire.	2 Kings 6.17
14.	The smiting of the army of Samaria with blindness.	2 Kings 6.18
15.	The confusion caused by God in the Aramean camp.	2 Kings 7.6
16.	The lowering of prices in the markets of Samaria and the death of the captain who had jeered at Elisha.	2 Kings 7.16
17.	The resurrection of the man who came in contact with Elisha's bones.	2 Kings 13.21

THE QUEEN MOTHER
(Gebirah)

THE MEANING OF THE TERM

Gebirah means both the wife of the king and the mother of the king. The Hebrew word is of the feminine gender and derives from the masculine *gebir*, which denotes mastery or ascendancy, as in Isaac's blessing of Jacob: "Be lord (*gebir*) over thy brethren" (Genesis 27.29).

THE ROLE AND STATUS OF THE QUEEN MOTHER

The mother of the king occupied a unique and powerful position, often having more influence upon affairs of state than the queen. This is especially evident in the case of Bath-sheba. Working in conjunction with Nathan the prophet, Bath-sheba managed to thwart the plans of Adonijah, who aspired to the throne, and obtained the assurance of her dying husband David that Solomon would reign over Israel after his (David's) death. Later, when Adonijah sought to obtain Abishag, the widow of David, as his wife, he turned to Bath-sheba, the queen mother, declaring that "Solomon . . . will not say thee nay" (1 Kings 2.17). The young King Solomon honored his mother publicly; when she entered he arose from his throne, bowed down before her and seated her at his right hand (1 Kings 1-2).

Jezebel was a very influential figure even while her husband Ahab was alive, but only after his death was she called *gebirah* (2 Kings 10.13).

Athaliah, daughter of Jezebel and mother of Ahaziah, was the only queen mother to place the crown upon her own head after the death of her son the king, and rule the country (2 Chronicles 23).

THE KINGS OF JUDAH AND THEIR MOTHERS

NAME OF KING	NAME OF QUEEN MOTHER
Solomon	Bath-sheba
Rehoboam	Naamah
Abijam	
Asa	Maachah (*or* Maacah)
Jehoshaphat	Azubah
Joram	
Ahaziah	Athaliah
Jehoash	Zibiah
Amaziah	Jehoaddan
Uzziah	Jecholiah
Jotham	Jerusha
Ahaz	
Hezekiah	Abijah
Manasseh	Hephzi-bah
Amon	Meshullemeth
Josiah	Jedidiah
Jehoahaz	Hamutal
Jehoiakim	Zebudah
Jehoiachin	Nehushta
Zedekiah	Hamutal

THE DAVIDIC DYNASTY

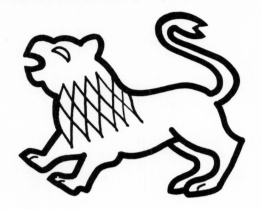

Ancestry of David
(according to Ruth 4. 18-22 and 1 Chron. 2.9-16)

1. Judah
2. Perez
3. Hezron
4. Ram
5. Amminadab
6. Nahshon
7. Salma
8. Boaz
9. Obed
10. Jesse

Genealogy of the Davidic Kings
(according to Kings & Chronicles)

1. David
2. Solomon
3. Rehoboam
4. Abijam (Abijah)
5. Asa
6. Jehoshaphat
7. Jehoram (Joram)
8. Ahaziah
9. Jehoash (Joash)
10. Amaziah
11. Azariah (Uzziah)
12. Jotham
13. Ahaz
14. Hezekiah
15. Manasseh
16. Amon
17. Josiah
18. Jehoahaz (Johaaz, Johanan, Shallum)
19. Jehoiakim (son of Josiah)
20. Jehoiachin (Mattaniah)
21. Zedekiah (son of Josiah)

The Davidic Line after the Destruction
(according to 1 Chron. 3. 17-24)

Assir-Shealtiel, son of Jehoiachin, Pedaiah
Zerubbabel, son of Pedaiah
Meshullam and Hananiah
Pelatiah and Jeshaiah (sons of Hananiah)
Rephaiah, son of Jeshaiah
Arnan, son of Rephaiah
Obadiah, son of Arnan
Shecaniah, son of Obadiah
Shemaiah, son of Shecaniah
Hattush, etc., Neariah, etc., Igal and Bariah
Elioenai, Hizkiah and Azrikam (sons of Neariah)
Hodaviah (the first of the seven sons of Elioenai)

SOURCES QUOTED

Listed below are the post-Biblical authors and texts used in the preparation of this volume. The 39 Books of the Bible are individually summarized in the text itself.

BABYLONIAN TALMUD

Berakoth	Nedarim
Baba Kamma	Pesahim
Baba Mezia	Rosh Hashanah
Baba Bathra	Sanhedrin
Abodah Zarah	Shabbath
Bezah	Shekalim
Erubin	Sotah
Gittin	Sukkah
Horayoth	Taanith
Kiddushin	Temurah
Makkoth	Yebamoth
Megillah	Yodayim
Menahoth	Yoma
Middoth	Zebahim
Moed Katan	

JERUSALEM TALMUD

Sanhedrin
Shekalim

TOSEFTA

Berakoth	Sanhedrin
Abodah Zarah	Sotah

BARAITOTH

Aboth d'Rabbi Nathan
Pirke d'Rabbi Eliezer

CIRCLES OF AUTHORS

(Books of the Bible)
Hezekiah and his Circle
The Men of the Great Assembly

MESHA INSCRIPTIONS discovered 1868 in Sidon

Mesha, King of Moab (2 Kings 3.4)

TRANSLATIONS

Jonathan ben Uzziel
The Vulgate (Latin translation of the Bible
in the 4th century)

MIDRASHIM

AGGADIC and HALLAKHIC MIDRASHIM

COMMENTARIES, COLLECTANEA & GENEALOGIES

Bereshith Rabbah
Shemoth Rabbah
Leviticus Rabbah
Numbers Rabbah
Song of Songs Rabbah
Ruth Rabbah
Lamentations Rabbah
Ekhah Rabbathi
Midrash Esther
Midrash Tanhuma
Sifra
Sifre
Mekhilta (of R. Simeon b. Yochai)
Pesikta Rabbathi
Tanna d'be Elijah
Midrash Shohar Tov
Seder Olam Rabbah
Seder Olam Zuta
Midrash Yelamdenu
Yalkut Shimeoni

APOCRYPHAL LITERATURE

Ezra III.
Ecclesiasticus — Joshua ben Sirach
The Book of Judith
Josephus Flavius
  Wars of the Jews
  Antiquities
  Contra Apionem

LATER AUTHORS & COMMENTATORS

Halakhot Gedolot (Jehudai Gaon)
Rabbenu Hananel
Rambam (Moses Maimonides)
  Mishneh Torah
Ramban (Moses Nachmanides)
Rashi (R. Solomon Yitzhaki)
Radak (R. David Kimchi)
Nahalath Aboth (Don Isaac Abarbanel)
Habah (R. Joel Sirkis)
  Bayit Hadash
Hagrah (R. Elijah Gaon of Vilna)
Annotations to the Talmud
Samuel Arrowsmith
Dr. Leopold Zunz
Interpreters Bible
The Popular Bible and Encyclopaedia
  and Scriptural Dictionary
Barnes' Biblical Dictionary
Ayre's Treasury of Bible Knowledge

INDEX